D1549073

ALLE·ZEIT·WACH
1842

Meaning and the Growth of Understanding

Wittgenstein's Significance for Developmental Psychology

Edited by
Michael Chapman and
Roger A. Dixon

Springer-Verlag
Berlin Heidelberg New York
London Paris Tokyo

Dr. Michael Chapman

Max-Planck-Institute for Human Development and Education,
Center for Psychology and Human Development,
Lentzeallee 94, D-1000 Berlin 33

Dr. Roger A. Dixon

Department of Psychology, University of Victoria,
Victoria, British Columbia V8W 2Y2, Canada

With 4 Figures and 3 Tables

ISBN 3-540-17516-4 Springer-Verlag Berlin Heidelberg New York
ISBN 0-387-17516-4 Springer-Verlag New York Berlin Heidelberg

Media conversion and bookbinding: Appl, Wemding; printing: aprinta, Wemding
2126/3130-543210

Preface

In the beginning it seemed to us that someone was missing and that something was amiss. He was often mentioned, occasionally discussed, but seldom cited or credited explicitly. And when he was acknowledged, it was sometimes for reasons that seemed anachronistic and misleading. His influence could be felt in a number of areas of our discipline, but few scholars seemed to know just how, just where, and to what extent. We discovered, almost accidentally, that we shared an interest in his legacy, in unravelling at least some portion of this riddle. Shortly thereafter, we began discussing ways in which, by pooling our resources with those of interested others, we could move closer to a resolution.

Put simply, the protagonist of this riddle is Ludwig Wittgenstein (1889-1951), the son of a wealthy Viennese industrialist, the influential Cantabrigian philosopher, the rural Austrian schoolteacher. And the subject of our study is his largely unexplored legacy for developmental psychology. Although Wittgenstein's thought seemed to hold special promise for the study of human development, the philosopher and his work could walk virtually unrecognized through the landscape of contemporary developmental issues.

How is it that Wittgenstein, whose intellectual presence in the 20th Century is formidable and unrelenting, could be overlooked in developmental psychology, a discipline that has struggled as much as any in recent years to understand its roots, its nature, and its mission? The editors and contributers to this book share a conviction that, if properly illuminated, the figure of Wittgenstein will cast a shadow across the landscape of developmental theory, method, and substantive research. Our hope is that, through this small book introducing Wittgenstein to developmental psychologists and scientists in allied disciplines, his presence will come to be recognized. More importantly, we hope this book helps the psychologist to take the measure of Wittgenstein's shadow: How wide-ranging, how specific, how timely, and how pertinent are the lessons of Wittgenstein to the vast and variegated field of developmental psychology?

A number of people have provided us with invaluable intellectual stimulation, as well as personal and professional encouragement during the development of this project. We are especially indebted to Paul B. Baltes, Harry Beilin, Nancy L. Galambos, Richard M. Lerner, and

Victoria Watters. The Max Planck Institute for Human Development and Education, Berlin, has provided a generous context in which to pursue this enterprise. We are deeply grateful to our colleagues there who have contributed, at one point or another, to the preparation and editing of the chapters of this book: Katrin Götz, Karen Hill, Peter Jaschner, Angelika Katterfeld, Manuela Menzer, and Amy Michèle. We also appreciate the expert professional guidance of our editor at Springer-Verlag, Thomas Thiekötter. One further note: As the first draft of the full book manuscript was nearing completion in Berlin the second editor moved to the University of Victoria, Victoria, British Columbia, Canada. For help in preparing the indexes, we thank Lori Moore and Sherri Oman in Victoria. Finally, the indirect contribution of several teachers and friends, through whom we came to know Wittgenstein better, are appreciated more than words can say.

MICHAEL CHAPMAN
ROGER A. DIXON

Acknowledgments

The authors and publisher would like to thank the following copyright holders for permission to quote from the sources indicated:

Academic Press for material from "On the internal structure of perceptual and semantic categories," by E. Rosch, in T. E. Moore (Ed.), *Cognitive development and the acquisition of language* (1973).

Basil Blackwell for material from the following: From *Culture and value,* by L. Wittgenstein (University of Chicago Press, 1980). From *Language, sense and nonsense,* by G. P. Baker & P. M. S. Hacker (1984). From *On certainty,* by L. Wittgenstein (Harper & Row, 1967). From *Philosophical investigations,* by L. Wittgenstein (Macmillan, 1968). From *Remarks on the philosophy of psychology* (in two volumes), by L. Wittgenstein (University of Chicago Press, 1980). From *The blue and brown books,* by L. Wittgenstein (Harper & Row, 1965). From *Wittgenstein and the Vienna circle,* by F. Waismann (1979). From *Wittgenstein on rules and private language,* by S. Kripke (1982). From *Zettel,* by L. Wittgenstein (1981).

Cambridge Center for Behavioral Studies for material from "in defence of memory viewed as stored mental representation," by S. S. Rakover, *Behaviorism* (1983, Vol. 11, No. 1).

Cambridge University Press for material from *Two treatises of government,* by J. Locke (Mentor, 1965) and from *Mental models,* by P. N. Johnson-Laird (1983).

Columbia University Press for material from *Wittgenstein: A social theory of knowledge,* by D. Bloor (1983).

Cornell University Press for material from *Memory and mind,* by N. Malcolm (1977) and from *Thought and knowledge,* by N. Malcolm (1977).

J. M. Dent & Sons for material from *Critique of pure reason,* by I. Kant (1969).

Encounter, Ltd., for material from "Ludwig Wittgenstein," by S. Toulmin, *Encounter* (1969, Vol. 32).

Foundation for International Philosophical Exchange for material from "Wittgenstein's last word: Ordinary certainty," by H. L. R. Finch, *International Philosophical Quarterly* (1975, Vol. 15).

W. H. Freeman & Co. for material from *Vision: A computational investigation and processing of visual information,* by D. Marr (1982).

Harper & Row for material from "The psychological ideas of L.S.Vygotsky," by A.N.Leontiev & A.R.Luria, in B.B.Wolman (ed.), *Historical roots of contemporary psychology* (1968) and from *The Language of thought,* by J.A.Fodor (1975).

Harvard University Press for material from *Mind in society,* by L.S.Vygotsky (1978) and from *Personal being,* by R.Harré (1984).

Harvester Press and Cornell University Press, for material from *Wittgenstein's Lectures on the foundations of mathematics, Cambridge, 1939,* edited by C.Diamond (1976).

Helen Dwight Reid Educational foundation for material from "The problem of the cultural development of the child," by L.S.Vygotsky, *Journal of Genetic Psychology* (1929, Vol.36).

Humanities Press International for material from *Wittgenstein - the later philosophy,* by J.L.Finch (1977).

Macmillan Publishers for material from "Philosophy and computer simulation," by K.Gunderson, in G.Pitcher (ed.), *Ryle* (1971).

Mrs. D.L.Miller for material from *George Herbert Mead: Self, language, and the world,* by D.L.Miller (University of Texas Press, 1973).

M.I.T. Press for material from *Language, thought, and other biological categories,* by R.G.Millikan (1984).

Oxford University Press for material from the following: From *Human growth and development,* by J.S.Bruner & A.Garton (Clarendon Press, 1978). From *Recollections of Wittgenstein,* by R.Rhees (1984). From *Spreading the word: Groundings in the philosophy of language,* by S.Blackburn (Clarendon Press, 1984). From *The claim of reason: Wittgenstein, skepticism, morality, and tragedy,* by S.Cavell (1979).

Charles S.Peirce Society for material from "Josiah Royce and George H.Mead on the nature of the self," by D.L.Miller, *Transactions of the Charles S.Peirce Society* (1975, Vol.11) and from "Peirce on man as a language: A textual interpretation," by M.J.Fairbanks, *Transactions of the Charles S. Peirce Society* (1976, Vol.12).

Pergamon Press for material from "The grammar of psychology: Wittgenstein's *Bemerkungen über die Philosophie der Psychologie,"* by G.P.Baker & P.M.S.Hacker, *Language and Communication* (1982, Vol.2, No.3).

Prentice-Hall Media for material from *Men and movements in American philosophy,* by J.L.Blau (1952) and from *A history of experimental psychology* (2nd ed.), by E.G.Boring (1957).

Princeton University Press for material from *The descent of man and selection in relation to sex,* by C.Darwin (1981).

Psychonomic Society for material from "Memory metaphors in cognitive psychology," by H.Roedinger, *Memory and Cognition* (1980, Vol.8).

D.Reidel Publishing Co. for material from "Wittgenstein on following a rule," by J.McDowell, *Synthese* (1984, Vol.58).

Routledge & Kegan Paul for material from *Dreaming,* by N. Malcolm (1959).

Springer-Verlag for material from *The self and its brain,* by J. C. Eccles & K. R. Popper (1977) and from "Apprenticeship in word-use: Social convergence processes in learning categorically related nouns," by A. K. Adams & D. Bullock, in S. A. Kuczaj & M. D. Barrett (eds.), *The development of word meaning* (1986).

S. Toulmin for material from *Human understanding,* by S. Toulmin (Princeton University Press, 1972) and from *Wittgenstein's Vienna,* by A. Janik & S. Toulmin (Simon and Schuster, 1973).

University of Chicago Press for material from *Mind, self and society,* by G. H. Mead (1962).

Yale University Press for material from *Formal philosophy: Selected papers,* by R. Montague (1974).

Contents

Contributors

Jochen Brandtstädter, Department of Psychology, University of Trier, D-5500 Trier, West Germany

Karl Brose, Department of Education, University of Münster, D-4400 Münster, West Germany

Daniel Bullock, Center for Adaptive Systems, Boston University, Boston, MA 02215, USA

Michael Chapman, Max Planck Institute for Human Development and Education, D-1000 Berlin 33, West Germany

Jeff Coulter, Department of Sociology, Boston University, Boston, MA 02215, USA

Roger A. Dixon, Department of Psychology, University of Victoria, Victoria, British Columbia V8W 2Y9, Canada

Rom Harré, Linacre College, Oxford University, Oxford OX1 4JJ, England

Joseph Margolis, Department of Philosophy, Temple University, Philadelphia, PA 19122, USA

Charlotte J. Patterson, Department of Psychology, University of Virginia, Charlottesville, VA 22903, USA

Eleanor Rosch, Department of Psychology, University of California, Berkeley, CA 94720, USA

James Russell, Department of Psychology, University of Liverpool, Liverpool L69 3BX, England

Abbreviations Used in Citing Wittgenstein's Works

Throughout this book, references to Wittgenstein's published works are indicated with the following abbreviations, plus the respective paragraph numbers. In cases in which paragraphs are not numbered, page numbers are given instead.

BB	*The blue and brown books*. New York: Harper & Row, 1965
CV	*Culture and value*. Chicago: University of Chicago Press, 1980
LFM	*Lectures on the foundations of mathematics*. Hassocks, Sussex: Harvester Press, 1976
LW	*Last writings on the philosophy of psychology*. Chicago: University of Chicago Press, 1982
OC	*On certainty*. New York: Harper & Row, 1969
PI	*Philosophical investigations* (3rd ed.). New York: Macmillan, 1968
RPP1 & *RPP2*	*Remarks on the philosophy of psychology* (Vols. 1 & 2). Chicago: University of Chicago Press, 1980
T	*Tractatus logico-philosophicus*. London: Routledge & Kegan Paul, 1961
Z	*Zettel* (2nd ed.). Oxford: Blackwell, 1981

Chapter 1 Introduction: Wittgenstein and Developmental Psychology

Michael Chapman and Roger A. Dixon

Why Wittgenstein and developmental psychology? What does the renowned philosopher of language have to do with psychological development? At first glance, this juxtaposition might appear to be far-fetched, but a closer look reveals at least three types of connections. First, there are certain aspects of Wittgenstein's life and thought that are directly related to the subject matter of developmental psychology. Second, Wittgestein's philosophy has specific implications for the conceptual and metatheoretical foundations of psychology in general and of developmental psychology in particular. Third, certain aspects of his philosophy may also have specific implications for both theoretical and empirical research in developmental psychology. Although the chapters contained in this book do not all fall neatly into one and only one of these categories, they can generally be classified as emphasizing one of these connections more than the others. Thus, Chapters 2 through 4 (by Karl Brose, James Russell, and Roger Dixon) deal mainly with thematic relations between Wittgenstein's philosophy and aspects of developmental psychology, Chapters 5 through 8 (by Jochen Brandtstädter, Jeff Coulter, Michael Chapman, and Joseph Margolis) address conceptual and metatheoretical issues, and Chapters 9 through 12 (by Eleanor Rosch, Charlotte Patterson, Daniel Bullock, and Rom Harré) describe some implications of a Wittgensteinian perspective for developmental theory and research.

The Developmental Dimension in Wittgenstein's Life and Thought

After completing the *Tractatus logico-philosophicus* (published in 1922), Wittgenstein gave up philosophy for a time and became an elementary schoolteacher in Lower Austria. His second book, and the only other book published during his lifetime, was a vocabulary workbook for elementary school children (Wittgenstein, 1926). Recent scholarship has recognized the importance of this period of Wittgenstein's life for the subsequent development of his thought (Bartley, 1973; Wünsche, 1985), and some commentators have claimed to discern specific connections between his experience as a teacher and certain aspects of his later work (Bartley, 1973, 1974; for a contrasting view, see Hargrove, 1980).

Whether such connections are direct or indirect, distinct *pedagogical* themes run through much of his later work. For example, in the *Philosophical investigations* Wittgenstein's method consists in focusing attention on the concrete ways in which words are used rather than on abstract conceptions of meaning. For any given word or expression, there exist certain conventional *criteria* that serve to determine whether that word or expression is used correctly. One way of identifying these criteria is to answer the question, "How would one go about teaching a child this word"? The criteria for justifying the use of a particular word are those things one might point to in trying to teach a child what we mean when we use that word (*Z,* 412 ff.). To use another of Wittgenstein's comparisons, teaching children the use of language is something like teaching them how to play a game. In learning language, they learn the rules of various language-games, including the use of certain words and their criteria. The initial language-games which are first learned by children in learning language are "primitive" in the sense of basic or fundamental (*PI,* p. 200 e). Later, children will learn more complex conceptual connections among linguistic expressions, but these connections can only be acquired once the "primitive" language-games have been mastered. In this respect, the process of language acquisition resembles that of learning to play increasingly complex games; learning a game with codified rules (e.g., a competitive ball game) presupposes the mastery of more rudimentary games (e.g., throwing a ball back and forth). The idea that certain language-games must be learned before others become possible is another example of an implicit developmental dimension in Wittgenstein's work (see Brose, this volume; Dixon, this volume).

There may be a point in the development of language-games, however, where words and concepts may become disconnected from their original context of use. This is typically the point at which language begins to "idle" (*PI,* 132, 291). In Wittgenstein's colorful phrase, "Language *goes on holiday*" (*PI,* 38). In everyday life, the words and phrases of ordinary language are *usefully employed.* In this functional context, their meanings are relatively unproblematic. In relieving them of their practical functions, we are in danger of losing sight of the context which gave them meaning in the first place. At this point, philosophical problems arise (*PI,* 38). But these problems are not confined to philosophy as a discipline. As we shall have occasion to see in this volume, Wittgenstein believed that psychology was especially prone to "philosophical" problems of this kind (*PI,* p. 232 e). Wittgenstein's remedy for such problems was to return words to their "original homes" in ordinary language (*PI,* 116). In practice, Wittgenstein often accomplished this "return" to ordinary language by considering how a given word or concept would be taught to someone encountering it for the first time. Thus, a more or less explicit dialogue between teacher and pupil can be found throughout his later works.

This dialogue, as it occurs in Wittgenstein's last book *On certainty,* is explored in depth by *Karl Brose* in Chapter 2 of the present volume. Brose begins by considering the role of the child or pupil in this colloquy. As portrayed by Wittgenstein, the child learns language by "believing" the teacher. This is not to say that the child suspends its doubts, but rather that the child at this initial stage cannot have any doubts in the usual sense. Doubting can occur only after certain learning has already occurred. The child cannot question its teachers' knowledge of the rules of language until it has already learned what those rules are. In effect, the teacher's message takes the form, "This is the way we play the game" (cf. *PI*, 659, 656; *OC*, 56, 212). The pupil's task is to master the rules of the game. This mastery is above all a practice. Brose briefly notes the implications of this approach for pedagogical practice (see also Marshall, 1985). The unilateral relation between teacher and pupil in *On certainty* might appear to reflect an "authoritarian" philosophy of education. But this is deceptive. Wittgenstein's pedagogy does not exclude critical thinking on the part of the learner; it simply emphasizes the understanding *presupposed* by all criticism.

Another important developmental aspect of Wittgenstein's thinking, rule-following, is taken up by *James Russell* in Chapter 3. In teaching a child the rules of language-games, how does the teacher (or anyone else) know when the child has understood? In particular, how does one know that the child has learned what it means to follow the rules of the game? Russell's discussion of these questions is connected with several important themes in Wittgenstein's later works, including rule-following and the meaning of the concepts of "meaning" and "understanding." In the famous part of the *Philosophical investigations* dealing with the possibility of a "private language," for example, Wittgenstein argues in effect that "understanding" and "meaning" cannot be identified with private mental processes. They are intelligible only in the context of public practice. According to Russell, the point is not that there is no relation whatsoever between mental states and rule-following (as some interpreters have maintained), but that the former are not *sufficient* for the latter. Russell goes on to describe the relevance of this line of thinking to psychological theory and research. In the psychological investigation of logical competence, for example, psychologists must decide when their subjects have understood a particular concept or when they have followed a particular rule in drawing an inference. Wittgenstein provides a method for determining when such attributions are meaningful. According to Russell, providing an account of the psychological processes which may accompany the logical inferences in the sense of "mental models" may be a meaningful theoretical enterprise (and is by no means prohibited by a Wittgensteinian view of rule-following), but such an account would not constitute a complete explanation of logical competence.

Roger A. Dixon begins the fourth chapter by describing the conceptual context of contemporary developmental psychology, with special attention to the substantive topics of memory development and language acquisition. A contextual approach is identified as one of the leading models of contemporary developmental theory and research. In its emphasis on the consideration of, for example, (1) multidirectionality of change patterns, (2) multidimensionality of constructs, (3) relatively "active" organisms and environments, and (4) ecologically or practically relevant materials, procedures, tasks, and performances, the contextual approach is seen to be a natural ally of the later Wittgenstein. This alliance is explored for conceptual, methodological, and empirical repercussions. For example, it is found that, somewhat independently, contextualists (from pragmatic philosophers to early functional psychologists to some modern developmental psychologists), dialectical psychologists (such as Vygotsky), and Wittgenstein proposed some similar views regarding (1) the nature of (developmental) psychological inquiry, (2) the functioning of remembering, and (3) the functioning of language. Having identified Wittgenstein as an intellectual "colleague" of the pursuers of current or "new" approaches to developmental study is tantamount to identifying both a fertile source of ideas and critiques for use in further conceptual refinement and a resource for addressing viable (and salient) theoretical issues and empirical research questions. Thus, this chapter serves as a bridge from the first section (describing some ways in which Wittgenstein's thought is related to the subject matter of contemporary developmental psychology) and the second section (describing some implications for the conceptual foundations of developmental psychology).

Conceptual and Metatheoretical Issues

In the final paragraphs of the *Philosophical investigations,* Wittgenstein characterizes psychology as consisting of empirical methods and "conceptual confusion." The methods of psychology appear to provide it with a rigorous means for answering questions about the nature of psychological processes, but problem and methods "pass one another by" (*PI,* p. 232 e). This situation, and not the fact that psychology is a young science, explains the "barrenness" of psychology. Wittgenstein foresaw that such conceptual confusion could be clarified through an investigation into the character of psychological concepts as such. The beginning of such an investigation was carried out in his remarks published together in the volume entitled *Zettel* and in the two-volume collection entitled *Remarks on the philosophy of psychology*.

One can certainly dispute the description of psychology as "barren," if only by objecting that psychology has come a long way since Wittgenstein wrote. But that would be to miss the point. In order to evaluate these remarks, it is necessary to consider the nature of the "conceptual confusion" diagnosed by Wittgenstein and then to investigate the extent to which it does or does not characterize contemporary psychology.

Wittgenstein's point would appear to be that questions regarding the nature or causes of a given psychological phenomenon X are not *purely* matters of fact. They also depend in part upon what we *mean* by X. It seems clear that if different investigators mean something different by X (even if they use the same terms), then they are also likely to differ with regard to the facts of the matter (the nature or causes of X). Their differences in this case may not be primarily empirical; that is, conceptual differences may obtain even when the facts are not in dispute. The answers to our questions will be conditional both upon "the facts" and upon our understanding of the concepts used in framing the questions the facts are supposed to answer. The meanings of scientific concepts may also change with time, as discussed in the writings of Feyerabend (1975), Kuhn (1970), Shapere (1984), and Toulmin (1972) – a discussion directly influenced by Wittgenstein's philosophy. According to the present view, "conceptual confusion" results when we are unclear about or do not agree upon the meanings of our concepts, even if we are not always aware of such differences in meaning. The first step in clearing up such conceptual confusion is becoming aware of the conceptual unclarity or lack of agreement. And if we are not aware of this unclarity or lack of agreement, we are likely to mistake conceptual differences for theoretical or empirical differences.

This distinction between the conceptual and empirical aspects of psychological investigations is discussed in Chapter 5 by *Jochen Brandtstädter* in terms of the Kantian distinction between analytical and empirical propositions. Some propositions are clearly analytical: Their truth or falsehood follows from a consideration of the meanings of the terms involved. Other propositions are clearly empirical: Their truth or falsehood can be established only with reference to experience. Still other propositions may not be obviously classifiable as one or the other: Certain propositions which appear at first glance to be empirical may, following closer structural analysis, prove to be analytic in character. Still other propositions may be read *either way,* depending on how one construes the terms involved. Brandtstädter suggests that propositions of this latter kind are frequent in psychology and cites a number of examples. "Conceptual confusion" typically results when propositions which are properly analytical are treated as if they were empirical, or when different interpreters treat the same proposition in different ways. A number of examples from developmental psychology are discussed. The point is by no means to replace empirical investigation by a priori analyses, but simply to make clear what is (and is not) decidable by empirical means. In this way, Brandstädter puts earlier discussions in developmental psychology of related matters on firm philosophical grounds (see, e.g., Overton & Reese, 1973; Reese & Overton, 1970).

Another kind of conceptual confusion is diagnosed by *Jeff Coulter* in Chapter 6 with regard to "recognition." This is the kind of confusion that Wittgenstein described as occurring when we mistake a particular instance or a particularly compelling "picture" (or model) of something for the thing itself (*PI,* 115, 352, 426, p. 184e). Recognition, for example, is often thought of as a process by which we match a perceived object with a memory image. According to Coulter, this may indeed be the case for *some* instances of recognizing, but other instances may be thought of in which we recognize something immediately, as it were, without any explicit matching of the thing perceived with the image of the thing remembered. A psychologist might argue at this point that, even if we are not aware of matching the "stimulus" with a "memory trace," this matching process might occur implicitly without awareness. Indeed, some theories of perceptual recognition attempt to explain recognition precisely in these terms. The problem with this type of explanation, according to Coulter, is that it is not clear how "recognition" understood in terms of the unconscious matching of "stimulus input" with "memory traces" is related to the conscious recognition actually experienced by the person involved. Nor can psychology simply dispense with this conscious, everyday-type recognition so long as the latter is what one seeks to explain. What usually happens, Coulter argues, is that two language-games involving two different levels of description are simply conflated. The description of unconscious causal mechanisms frequently modelled on physical or neurophysiological processes is conflated with an ordinary-language description of the reasons that a person might give for a judgment of recognition based on personal experience.

This confusion or conflation of ordinary-language usages with those of a technical vocabulary is further discussed by *Michael Chapman* in Chapter 7. Following a brief review of the relevance for psychology of Wittgenstein's ideas on the role of psychological concepts in ordinary language, his method is applied to a concrete problem in developmental psychology: The problem of "response criteria" in assessing children's understanding. Children are found to grasp a concept at different ages by investigators who have adopted different "response criteria" for understanding the concept in question. Such differences in empirical results are frequently discussed in theoretical or methodological terms, but Chapman argues that they may also reflect differences in meaning: Having adopted different operational definitions of the "same" ordinary-language concept, different investigators may no longer be talking about the same thing. This difference in meaning is obscured by the fact that both operational definitions in question refer back to the same ordinary-language concepts, - as if two players became dissatisfied with the ordinary rules of a game, each invented slightly different variations on those rules, and they played against each other using the regular board and pieces, but following their own respective sets of rules! The main point is that conceptual confusion results when the (potentially distorting) effects of language are overlooked. It is not so much a question of "defining our terms" as of reflecting upon how we may be misled by the grammar of those terms.

In Chapter 8, *Joseph Margolis* carries this reflection on language in psychology one step further in attempting to explicate Wittgenstein's difficult and enigmatic concept, "forms of life." According to Margolis, "forms of life designate the entire complex of the behavior and activity of viable human societies and of whatever regarding thinking, desire, intention and the like is involved in such behavior and activity." As such, forms of life constitute the basis of linguistic practice. The conventions of language themselves presuppose the sharing of common forms of life in this sense. This is why the understanding of other cultures or other species which do not share our own forms of life (or even the understanding of young children who do not *yet* share our forms of life) is inherently problematic. We cannot step outside of our own forms of life in order to understand them, since our language as the medium of understanding is based upon these very forms of life. As described by Margolis, Wittgenstein's concept of forms of life not only calls our attention to the cultural context in which all scientific investigation takes place, but also provides a "cultural template" for theories of human development. By recognizing that even social conventions presuppose certain shared possibilities of experience, the Wittgensteinian template holds out the promise of reconciling the human and natural sciences without thereby reducing the one to the other.

Implications for Theory and Research

In the last four chapters of this book, the "Wittgensteinian template" is applied to research and theory in developmental psychology. In Chapter 9, *Eleanor Rosch* describes one of the few existing concrete research programs in psychology directly inspired by Wittgenstein's writings: research on natural categorization. As opposed to classical categorization theory, in which categories are understood as classes defined by common attributes, Wittgenstein's concept of family resemblance implies that natural categories can be based on individual members that share different but overlapping properties, none of which is necessarily shared by all members. Consequently, all members of the category need not be equally good members of that category, and the boundaries of the category can be more or less ill-defined. Rosch reviews empirical research on family resemblance and prototypes which supports this "non-classical" view of natural categorization. At the same time, she offers a critique of a tendency in prototype theory to reify the concept of a prototype. The prototype has come to be thought of as the "entity" to which class names refer and which provides them with their meaning. But Wittgenstein's larger point was that word meaning does not depend on having objects of reference. Rosch concludes her chapter with some suggestions for further research based on a Wittgensteinian perspective.

Another central theme in Wittgenstein's work, the social character of human existence, is raised in Chapter 10 by *Charlotte Patterson* in a discussion of human individuality. From the epistemological tradition of the British empiricists, Anglo-American psychology has inherited an atomistic view of individual persons. As opposed to collectivists (who view the social group as the primary reality) and relationists (who view the relations between persons as primary), individualism views the person in isolation from others as fundamental. Patterson shows how this "self-contained individualism" (Sampson, 1977) leads to a skepticism regarding our knowledge of other persons and their experience. Wittgenstein, however, calls our attention to the fact that knowing is only possible in the larger context of shared conventions and common forms of life. These reflections suggest that one of the central problems for psychology is not how we overcome our isolation in coming to know about other persons, but how we ever develop the idea of an autonomous self when we are so fundamentally embedded in social reality to begin with. In developing this topic, Patterson touches upon a central, but generally neglected dimension in Wittgenstein's thinking: viz., his passionate concern for questions of meaning and value in human life (Wittgenstein, *CV*; see also Engelmann, 1968; Toulmin, 1969).

The social nature of human beings is also a central topic in *Daniel Bullock's* discussion of Wittgenstein and the theory of intellectual development in Chapter 11. Another consequence of the individualist perspective is the view that intelligence is something that can be localized within the individual (and especially within the brain). Against this, Bullock proposes the radical thesis that intelligence be considered a socially distributed phenomenon. This follows from a consideration of inter-specific variation in intelligence in terms of differences in adaptation rates following changes in the environment. Since constructive imitation, purposive instruction, and symbolic communication of various kinds among the individual members of a given species can contribute to the adaptation rate of that species, intelligence cannot be considered as a property of individual members only. Instead, adaptive knowledge, skills, and attitudes are the collective property of the group as a whole. This social theory of intelligence does not obviate a concern for individual differences, because individuals may well differ in their competence to engage in different modes of interaction. But this view of individual differences differs greatly from that reflected by what Bullock identifies as individual-centered views of intelligence.

Another example of the irreducibly social character of human psychology is provided by *Rom Harré* in the final chapter. Arguing that a form of life involves a moral order which includes public criteria for holding persons in respect or contempt, as well as procedures for judging in accordance with those criteria, Harré suggests that human development is likely to reflect changes in capacities of various kinds and/or changes in socially recognized rights to display those capacities. The developmental sequences observed by psychologists may not directly reflect only sequences in the development of underlying capacities; they may also reflect some combination of age-related changes in the target capacity and in the understanding of public performance rules governing the rights of display. Certain psychological capacities themselves may arise from the demands of growing up within a moral order. Even the consciousness of self, which from the individualist perspective appears to be the most intimately private of psychological experiences, is seen to result from the moral requirement that each person be considered as a unity. According to this view, language-games involving self-ascription and self-exhortation are learned through a process of "psychological symbiosis" in which the attributes of selfhood are first ascribed to children by others in their environment. Selfhood is acquired when children *imitate* these ascriptions of selfhood by appropriating the conventions by which the self is constituted. Thus, individuality itself arises as a product of social practice (and in reaching this conclusion, Harré supplies one answer to Charlotte Patterson's question on the origins of individuality).

In Place of a Conclusion

Having summarized some of the main themes treated in the individual chapters, one can then attempt a summary of the "message" of the book as a whole. Such an attempt does not imply that common themes run through all the chapters, nor even that the authors would necessarily agree with each other on all their interpretations. Instead of a necklace linked by common threads, this book would be better compared to a mosaic pattern formed by multiple connections between the individual chapters. Some of the more important of these connections are the following:

1. Certain developmental dimensions may be discerned in Wittgenstein's thinking. These include the connection between meaning and teaching (*Z*, 412) as well as the idea that certain things must be learned before others are even intelligible. Thus, belief precedes doubt (*OC*, 115, 263, 450, 480), mastery of language-games precedes "knowing" (*OC*, 534ff.), and understanding the meanings of words precedes the distinction between appearance and reality (*Z*, 413ff., esp. 422).

2. Certain uses of language can lead to conceptual confusion. Numerous examples of such confusion can be found in (developmental) psychology. Because of the character of psychological concepts in ordinary language, psychology may even be especially prone to such confusions. These confusions can be overcome by a radical reflection on the grammar of psychological terms.

3. Psychological states and processes come to be recognized and understood only in the context of social practice. This is true even for the most private of subjective experiences, such as that of self-consciousness. Human individuality may itself be socially constructed. This suggests potential new directions for psychological research and theory.

To be sure, the implications of Wittgenstein's philosophy for scientific psychology are not exhausted by these themes. This book makes no claims of completeness. It is easy to identify relevant topics not dealt with in any detail in this volume: for example, the implications of Wittgenstein's philosophy of language for studies of language development (e.g., Bruner, 1975, 1983) or comparisons between Wittgenstein and major psychological theorists (Toulmin, 1969, 1981).

Far from wishing to present our readers with a finished sketch of the relations between Wittgenstein's philosophy and developmental psychology, the editors of this book would rather emulate Wittgenstein's own intentions as expressed in the Preface to the *Philosophical investigations*. Our purposes will be fulfilled if we succeed in stimulating others to have thoughts of their own on these subjects.

References

Bartley, W. W., III. (1973). *Wittgenstein.* London: Quartet Books.

Bartley, W. W., III. (1974). Theory of language and philosophy of science as instruments of educational reform: Wittgenstein and Popper as Austrian schoolteachers. In R. S. Cohen & M. W. Wartofsky (Eds.), *Methodological and historical essays in the natural and social sciences.* Dordrecht, Holland: Reidel.

Bruner, J. S. (1975). The ontogenesis of speech acts. *Journal of Child Language, 2,* 1-19.

Bruner, J. S. (1983). *Child's talk.* New York: Norton.

Engelmann, P. (1968). *Letters from Ludwig Wittgenstein with a memoir.* New York: Horizon Press.

Feyerabend, P. (1975). *Against method.* London: NLB.

Hargrove, E. C. (1980). Wittgenstein, Bartley, and the Glöckel school reform. *Journal of the History of Philosophy, 18,* 453-461.

Kuhn, T. (1970). *The structure of scientific revolutions* (2nd ed.). Chicago: University of Chicago Press.

Marshall, J. D. (1985). Wittgenstein on rules: Implications for authority and discipline in education. *Journal of Philosophy of Education, 19,* 3-11.

Overton, W. F., & Reese, H. W. (1973). Models of development: Methodological implications. In J. R. Nesselroade & H. W. Reese (Eds.), *Life-span developmental psychology: Methodological issues.* New York: Academic Press.

Reese, H. W., & Overton, W. F. (1970). Models of development and theories of development. In L. R. Goulet & P. B. Baltes (Eds.), *Life-span developmental psychology: Research and theory.* New York: Academic Press.

Sampson, E. E. (1977). Psychology and the American ideal. *Journal of Personality and Social Psychology, 35,* 767-782.

Shapere, D. (1984). *Reason and the search for knowledge.* Dordrecht, Holland: Reidel.

Toulmin, S. (1969). Ludwig Wittgenstein. *Encounter, 32,* 58-71.

Toulmin, S. (1972). *Human understanding.* Princeton, NJ: Princeton University Press.

Toulmin, S. (1981). Epistemology and developmental psychology. In E. S. Gollin (Ed.), *Developmental plasticity.* New York: Academic Press.

Wittgenstein, L. (1926). *Wörterbuch für Volksschulen.* Vienna: Hölder-Pichler-Tempsky.

Wünsche, K. (1985). *Der Volksschullehrer Ludwig Wittgenstein.* Frankfurt a. M.: Suhrkamp.

Chapter 2 Pedagogical Elements in Wittgenstein's Late Work, *On Certainty*[1]

Karl Brose

Through the entire work of the later Wittgenstein, pedagogical remarks on child language, thought, and action as well as didactic statements regarding the relation between teacher and pupil are to be found. This is also true for Wittgenstein's last book, *On certainty*. The pedagogical elements in these notes are based on philosophical insights regarding "doubt," "certainty," "believing," and "learning." But the central concept of Wittgenstein's later work, the *language-game* (together with the related concept of "forms of life"), will also be a major theme of this chapter. The concept of the language-game together with the thoughts expressed in *On certainty* will be extended through a pedagogical (and especially a linguistic-pedagogical) element, which has been insufficiently appreciated in previous accounts of these last remarks and of the later work in general (cf. Morawetz, 1978; Svensson, 1981). The following exposition is intended to make up for this deficiency.

The Role of the Child in On Certainty

Wittgenstein's examples in *On certainty* have a compelling facticity and persuasive power, even when they only remain "preparatory" (*PI*, 26 ff.). His thoughts and "conclusions" are both topical and problematic. In analogy to the language-game, that complex product of contextual language, thought, and action as found in the *Philosophical investigations*, there is a game of "facts" in *On certainty* that is important in connection with the role of the child: "Suppose some adult had told a child that he had been on the moon. . . . – But a child will not ordinarily stick to such a belief and will soon be convinced by what we tell him seriously" (*OC*, 106). In order to learn and to be taught, the child must proceed from the assumption that the teacher's position is "indubitable" and "beyond doubt" (*OC*, 470). "Isn't this altogether like the way one can instruct a child to believe in God, or that none exists, and it will accordingly be able to produce apparently telling grounds for the one or the other?" (*OC*, 107).

The teacher must eliminate the initial "doubts" of the child so as not to hinder the process of learning. Can this be accomplished through "reasons?" Where are the boundaries between indubitable certainty and pedagogical practice?

1 Acknowledgement: This chapter was translated by Michael Chapman.

What answers do religion, metaphysics, philosophy, or the educational tradition give to these questions? Already in the *Notebooks 1914–16,* Wittgenstein is aware that ethics and religion are not imparted through reasons, certainly not through "common sense" as Moore, Wittgenstein's opposite in *On certainty,* would have it. For the later Wittgenstein, the "way out of the fly-bottle" (*PI,* 309) constituted by this philosophical-pedagogical dilemma is the *language-game.* This "describes" the practical use of ordinary language in "countless" situations (*PI,* 23), through the most varied "bearers" (*PI,* 40 ff.) and in the most varied circumstances (*PI,* 35 ff.). For the sake of the language-game and the related concept of "forms of life" (*PI,* 19 ff.), the later (and last) Wittgenstein pushes the indubitable certainty of the "facts" to be learned to the very boundaries of "believing" (*OC,* 72 ff.) and "training" (*PI,* 5 ff.): "A child learns there are reliable and unreliable informants much later than it learns facts which are told it. . . . It swallows this consequence down, so to speak, together with *what* it learns" (*OC,* 143).

Children are not yet able to check the facts that are imparted to them with respect to their "certainty" and "reliability." As yet, they receive them through "learning (training)" (*PI,* 189). They are "taught" (*OC,* 140). The younger child that Wittgenstein had in mind in the above citation (*OC,* 144) must still "believe" the facts imparted to him, unhampered by doubt and error on the side of both the teacher and the taught. Criticism and doubt come only later and belong to the extended language-game and more complex forms of life: "As children we learn facts; e.g., that every human being has a brain, and we take them on trust. ... The child learns by believing the adult. Doubt comes *after* belief (*OC,* 159–160).

The pedagogical consequences of this sentence are clear: the prevention of *precocious* doubt and criticism in children. "Scepticism" is no educational goal for the later Wittgenstein. Children are neither willing nor able to "doubt" and to "criticize." They have neither reached "majority," nor are they sufficiently "enlightened" – to use Adorno's (1976) terms, whose conception of education is diametrically opposed to that of Wittgenstein (see also Weischedel, 1980). Wittgenstein places children in a pedagogical "nursery" free of doubts and criticism. From this a broader pedagogical consequence follows: Teachers must restrain their own doubts, criticism, "proofs," and "justifications" (*OC,* 175 ff.) with respect to the children who are still learning, in particular with respect to their practice in "mastering the technique" (*PI,* 31 ff., 150) of a language-game belonging to the future world of adults. He leaves children in a doubt-free educational space in order to prepare them for the later questions and problems, language-games and forms of life of the more complex and more complicated daily world of adults with its *"customs,* (uses, institutions)" (*PI,* 199).

The Problem of the "World Picture" in On Certainty

In *On certainty,* the later Wittgenstein places children in a doubt-free environment, such that they will obtain from it an "immediately sure" knowledge (*OC,* 510f.).[2] This knowledge has nothing to do with the "logic" of the adult nor with the latter's problems, doubts, or certainties. These must still develop in children through pedagogical language-games. Then they can exchange what they have learned, a first step to the complex language-game: "One child might say to another: 'I know that the earth is already hundreds of years old' and that would mean: I have learnt it" (*OC,* 165). Such a complex language-game develops through the pupil's learning until the "world-picture" of the adult emerges: "He has got hold of a definite world-picture – not of course one that he invented: he learned it as a child" (*OC,* 167). And Wittgenstein continues: "I say world-picture and not hypothesis, because it is the matter-of-course foundation . . . and as such goes unmentioned" (*OC,* 167).

The "world-picture" *[Weltbild]* is quite simply a "picture of the world," just as earth or mountains might be pictured, and it is here that the concept of education or development *[Bildung]* has its origin. These "world-pictures" are not "world-views" *[Weltanschauungen]*.[3] They are not conceived intuitively, but are language-games or "networks" (*PI,* 66) and "systems" (*OC,* 411) of language-games that are acquired, learned, and practiced without doubt. To these "world-pictures" doubt has yet to be added; it "only works in a language-game" (*OC,* 24). With this language-game and the "game of doubting" (*OC,* 115), Wittgenstein demonstrates the flexibility and openness, the possibilities for teaching and learning, of language-games and the "practice of language" (*PI,* 51ff.; *OC,* 501ff.) that overlaps with "doubting" and thereby with any "dogmatism and scepticism" (cf. Lorenz, 1971). This overlap occurs prior to "world-views" which might follow from the problems of "absolute certainty," "sureness," or "believing" raised in Wittgenstein's *On certainty.*

The flexibility of the language-games of "world-pictures" stands behind the "world-views" of adults and thereby also behind the "upbringing" of children. As the foundation of education, such world-pictures require learning and teaching, as will become clear from the examples which follow. The contact that adults have with existing world-pictures is linguistically uncritical, that is, limited to their "surface grammar" (*PI,* 664) and without a concern for their "depth grammar" (*PI,* 664). This means that possible dogmas of their world-views are never unlocked with the key of language and turned into language-games. It is otherwise for children who begin to question that which is beyond doubt. They have as yet no world-views, and their doubts develop only in the course of the educational process: "If a child asked me whether the earth was already there

---

[2] Or more precisely: "This direct taking-hold corresponds to a *sureness,* not to a knowing" (*OC,* 511). On the "Platonic" interpretation of this "knowledge," see Prange (1972).

[3] In the *Philosophical investigations,* Wittgenstein still asks sceptically: "Is this a 'world-view'?" (*PI,* 122)

before my birth, I should answer him that the earth did not begin only with my birth, but that it existed long, long before. And I should have the feeling of saying something funny. ... I should have to be imparting a picture of the world to the person who asked it. If I do answer the question with certainty, what gives me this certainty?" (*OC*, 233).

The sureness and indubitability of the answer follows from the "practice of language" and practicability of the language-game that underlies the "world-picture." With their openness, complexity, and flexibility, these world pictures broaden the scope of conventional upbringing and education. Their traditional basis (in terms of "world-views," etc.) remain "surface grammatical," because they have not yet penetrated to the "evidence" of the *"acting,* which lies at the bottom of the language-game" (*OC*, 204) and which is obligatory for linguistic practice. Only from out of this ("depth grammatical") evidence of language-games and of the acting involved in linguistic practice, with this sureness and *"certainty"* (*OC*, 56), can an upbringing free of doubt ensue: "Doubt gradually loses its sense. This language-game just *is* like that. And everything descriptive of a language-game is part of logic" (*OC*, 56). (Cf. the similarly apodictic remarks: "This is how I act." "*This* is how we calculate." "This is how we acquire conviction" - *OC*, 148, 212, 294.)

Teachers and Pupils in On Certainty

Without attempting to treat the problematics of the "language-game" (and "forms of life") in detail, especially as they occur in the *Philosophical investigations, On certainty* focuses on their pedagogical application to "belief," "doubt," and "certainty" (not yet envisioned in the earlier book). In his last remarks in *On certainty,* Wittgenstein sharpens his language-game thinking, not only in regard to "traditional" problems (in metaphysics, the humanities, etc.), but also in regard to the linguistic education of children, or pupils. From the certainty and indubitability ("evidence") of the language-game, there follows a specific "authority" of teachers and their lessons: "The schoolboy *believes* his teachers and his schoolbooks" (*OC*, 263); "For how can a child immediately doubt what it is taught? That could mean only that he was incapable of learning certain language-games" (*OC*, 283). The whole structure of "science and education" rests on the *"customs* (uses, institutions)" (*PI*, 199) which make up the rules and conventions of language-games and (social) "forms of life." (For a social interpretation of this concept, see Habermas, 1975.) "'We are quite sure of it' does not mean just that every single person is certain of it, but that we belong to a community which is bound together by science and education" (*OC*, 298).

Whereas children must still be introduced to this language-game structure, adult teachers are already "certain" of it, "assert" themselves within it, and can make indicative "assertions": "I myself wrote in my book that children learn to understand a word in such and such a way. Do I know that, or do I believe it?

Why in such a case do I write not 'I believe, etc.' but simply the indicative sentence" (*OC*, 290). The "expunging" (*OC*, 31) of doubt and the compulsion to "give grounds" (*OC*, 110ff.) and to "justify" (*OC*, 175ff.) every action leads to that "certainty" of adults and educators and to their self-"assertion" within the framework of their training and "mastery of the technique" (*PI*, 150) of language-games, and even of a "system of our language-games" (*OC*, 411). Children (or pupils) must still be introduced into these language-games; they must become practiced in the functions of everyday thinking, speaking, and acting through the pedagogical certainty of "successful" or "skilled" (*PI*, 66) games of teaching and learning, of instruction and education.

This sureness and certainty of pedagogical action on the basis of language-games carries over into the relationship between teacher and pupil: "A pupil and a teacher. The pupil will not let anything be explained to him, for he continually interrupts with doubts, for instance as to the existence of things, the meaning of words, etc. The teacher says 'Stop interrupting me and do as I tell you. So far your doubts don't make any sense at all'" (*OC*, 310). In the relationship between teachers and pupils, Wittgenstein is concerned with the justification of "doubts" with which the "certainty," "sureness," and practicability of linguistic action and language-games are confronted. His goal is the smoothest possible conveying of such a language-game to children, as long as the latter "cannot as yet *ask*" (*PI*, 6). The question whether the truly *pedagogical* element in this kind of "functional" instruction gets short shrift may be clarified by the concepts of "growing out of," "holding up," and "getting stuck" in the following examples which continue the problems of "doubting" (*OC*, 310ff.): "Perhaps the teacher will get a bit impatient, but think that the boy will grow out of asking such questions. That is to say, the teacher will feel that this is not really a legitimate question at all. ... The teacher would feel that this was only holding them up, that this way the pupil would only get stuck and make no progress. – And he would be right. ... He has not yet learned to look for things. And in the same way this pupil has not learned how to ask questions. He has not learned *the* game that we are trying to teach him" (*OC*, 314–315). "This doubt isn't one of the doubts in our game. (But not as if we *chose* this game!)" (*OC*, 317). This is just the way the game is played; *this* is just the way we act: A multitude (or "multiplicity" – *PI*, 23) of (language-game) phrases in Wittgenstein's later work sound similarly practical, even pragmatic: *"This language-game is played."* "Look on the language-game as the *primary* thing" (*PI*, 654, 656). And with respect to the more broadly framed concept of "forms of life": "What has to be accepted, the given is – so one could say – *forms of life*" (*PI*, p. 226e). (Cf. *PI*, p. 200e: "What we have rather to do is to *accept* the everyday language-game, and to note *false* accounts of the matter *as* false. The primitive language-game which children are taught needs no justification; attempts at justification need to be rejected.")

In this connection, Wittgenstein gives no "explanations," "hypotheses," or "theories," even with respect to pedagogical matters; the "practice of language," the "acting" as the basis of the language-game remains "what happens as a 'proto-phenomenon'" (*PI*, 654). From the standpoint of a critical pedagogy, one naturally wants to ask: Are not the questions and doubts of the pupils much too rigorously rejected? Are they not the first steps to their own thinking and "game of judgment?" (*OC,* 131) (Cf. *OC,* 480: "And doubting means thinking.") Is it not true that this questioning and doubting has been *the* pedagogical method of learning and teaching since the beginning of education? Wittgenstein's last notes frankly provoke the recollection of traditional forms of teaching and learning. To be sure, these are always contained as philosophical-pedagogical impulses in the comprehensive "language-game" as well; only that they must be proved or "made sure" (*OC,* 147) on the "rough ground" (*PI,* 107) of the language-game and of "ordinary language" and "forms of life." (On this concept of "proving" in *OC,* 9ff., 147, 170, 474, and 603, see Zimmermann, 1976).

Language and Convention

In *On certainty,* Wittgenstein allows doubt, mistrust, and inquisitiveness - possible steps in the development of children - only if they do not hinder learning in the context of the language-game. From this point of departure, Wittgenstein views "believing" as a barrier against doubt and mistrust: "What if the pupil refused to believe that this mountain had been there beyond human memory? We should say he had no *grounds* for this suspicion" (*OC,* 322). Without this pedagogical "belief," the pupil would not be able to learn the language-game at all. The lesson must not get stuck in sceptical questions. It is a question whether Wittgenstein sees only the first half of the educational process, which must be completed by doubting and questioning. A more certain teaching and learning process is guaranteed by the later Wittgenstein through intuitive "pictures" and "descriptions" (*PI,* 6ff., 24ff.). "I want to say: our learning has the form 'that is a violet', 'that is a table.' Admittedly, the child might hear the word 'violet' for the first time in the sentence 'perhaps that is a violet', but then he could ask 'what is a violet?' Now this might of course be answered by showing him a picture. But how would it be if one said 'that is a ...' only when showing him a picture, but otherwise said nothing but 'perhaps that is a ...' - What practical consequences is that supposed to have? A doubt that doubted everything would not be a doubt" (*OC,* 450). Further: "If you tried to doubt everything you would not get as far as doubting anything. The game of doubting itself presupposes certainty" (*OC,* 115).

In *On certainty,* Wittgenstein wants to eliminate total, destructive, and nihilistic doubt, while he allows a constructive and "practical doubt" (*OC,* 19) in the framework of the language-, teaching-, and learning-game throughout (cf. "the fact that a doubt about existence works only in a language-game" - *OC,* 24; further: "the feeling of being sure, admittedly with a slight breath of doubt" - *OC,* 524). These practical doubts are allowed only insofar as they do not hinder the function of the language-game: "When a child learns language it learns at the same time what is to be investigated and what not. When it learns that there is a cupboard in the room, it isn't taught to doubt whether what it sees later on is still a cupboard or only a kind of stage set" (*OC*, 472). The teachers must also avoid their own doubts in conveying to the children a posture of "certainty" and "sureness," even with recourse to "believing" if this removes the doubts about the language-game. As mentioned, Wittgenstein sharpens this (pedagogical) posture toward the end of his remarks in *On certainty*. Increasingly, he speaks of "mastering" and "being able to do things" - his "translation" for "knowing" (*PI*, 150; *OC*, 534) - and thereby takes up the matter of "mastering the technique" (*PI*, 31 ff., 150) of a language-game, as described in the following passage: "We say: if a child has mastered language - and hence its application - it must know the meaning of words. It must, for example, be able to attach the name of its colour to a white, black, red or blue object without the occurrence of any doubt" (*OC*, 522).

This certainty of the language- or learning-game is not only connected to the indubitable designation and naming of a "thing," but also to the "mastery" of one's "mother tongue" (*OC*, 630; *PI*, 156), the essence of a complete "normal language-game" (*PI*, 142, 288) and of "normal linguistic exchange" (*OC*, 260). With it, children learn a "convention," a "network," and a "system" of language-games and forms of life. For example, the English language: "An Englishman who calls this colour 'red' is not: 'sure it is called "red" in English.' A child who has mastered the use of the word is not 'sure that in his language this colour is called ...'. Nor can one say of him that when he is learning to speak he learns that the colour is called that in English; nor yet: he *knows* this when he has learnt the use of the word. And in spite of this: if someone asked me what the colour was called in German and I tell him, and now he asks me 'are you sure?' - then I shall reply 'I *know* it is; German is my mother tongue" (*OC*, 527-528). For the later Wittgenstein, "language" is thus not detached from "praxis" nor from the conventions, "*customs* (uses, institutions)" (*PI*, 199) of contemporary society and its forms of life. This "fact" of the "certainty" and "sureness" of language- games as anchored in conventions lies at the basis of all knowledge: "I shall give up other things but not this" (*OC*, 380). That is, "the fact that I use the word 'hand' and all the other words in my sentence without a second thought, indeed that I should stand before the abyss if I wanted so much as to try doubting their meanings - shews that absence of doubt belongs to the essence of the language-game, that the question 'How do I know ...' drags out the language-game, or else does away with it" (*OC*, 370).

Mastery of the Language-Game

The language-game's context of employment and use, the "ability to do" and "mastery" (*PI*, 150) of the *"practice of language"* (*PI*, 51 ff.; *OC*, 501 ff.), comes *before* "knowing" and "doubting." According to Finch (1975): "Our action is .... embedded in a matrix of surety, which is prior to knowledge, being the matrix of knowing-and-doubting and knowing-and-being-mistaken" (p. 390). This mastery of the language-game inhibits that doubt and scepticism that hinders the teaching and learning of children: "But is it wrong to say: 'A child that has mastered a language-game must *know* certain things'? If instead of that one said 'must be *able to do* certain things', that would be a pleonasm, yet this is just what I want to counter the first sentence with .... The child knows what something is called if he can reply correctly to the question 'what is that called?'" (*OC*, 534–535) "The child, I should like to say, learns to react in such-and-such a way; and in so reacting it doesn't so far know anything. Knowing only begins at a later level. Does it go for knowing as it does for collecting?" (*OC*, 538–539)

The latter question must naturally be answered in the negative, for since the *Tractatus* one knows that the world is no "collection of objects": "Language" and the "world of facts" (*T*, 1 ff.) cohere through the "logical form" of "elementary propositions" ("picture" theory).[4] Then in the *Philosophical investigations,* an object is said to occur – despite Wittgenstein's talk of "sleekness of landscapes" in an "album" (*PI*, preface) – only in the *context* of certain "surroundings" and "circumstances," in a certain "situation" and "bearing," in "forms of life" and in the context of use belonging to the "practice of language": in other words, in the "language-game." This constitutes the context prior to the mere "collection" of facts. In the context the language-game is employed, linguistic "signs" begin to "live": "Every sign *by itself* seems dead. *What* gives it life? – In use it is *alive.* Is life breathed into it there? – Or is the *use* its life?" (*PI*, 432). In regard to the language-game: "It is there – like our life" (*OC*, 559). The *"use"* is the "breath" of linguistic "signs," as it is of the "meaning of a word" and the "learning" of this word in "our language": "A meaning of a word is a kind of employment of it. For it is what we learn when the word is incorporated into our language" (*OC*, 61).

It belongs to the acquisition of language, that children learn to "use" ("employ") and "master" personal and proper names, in order to enter into the language-games of adults. The functionality of this acquisition of language-games and names and thereby of "using" *before* "knowing" is further accentuated in the following passages: "A child can use the names of people long before he can say in any form whatever: 'I know this one's name; I don't know that one's yet'" (*OC*, 543). "One can't yet say to a child who is just beginning to speak and can use the words 'red' and 'blue': 'Come on, you know what this colour is called!' A child must learn the use of colour words before it can ask for the name of a colour" (*OC*, 547–548). From these passages, practical consequences for instruction can be drawn. In order to promote children's readiness for language-games, no "direct" questions would be posed (cf. Engelmann, 1968). Rather, the "living" flow of everyday, "normal," and "natural" ordinary language is to be taken in. On this point, Wittgenstein himself offers "multiple" games: "puzzle-picture" (*PI*, p. 196 e), drawings (*PI*, 177), or colored squares (*PI*, 48).

[4] See Engelmann (1968) on the "collection of objects."

One could have many children make such a drawing. As an example of language-games, Wittgenstein suggests "constructing an object from a description (a drawing)" (*PI,* 23). One could have many children make such a drawing in order to observe the genesis of "child language" and the invention of language-games, or in order to promote, guide, or even "breaking off" (*PI,* 133, 143 f.) this process. In doing this, children show their original languages and their abilities or possibilities in using them until they achieve the "'mastery' of a technique" (*PI,* 150). Or actual games could be played with children (such as ball games, card games, board games, etc. – *PI,* 66 ff.) in order to test the language-game behavior of children, their forms of life and "rules" of conduct: "rules as we go along" (*PI,* 83). In this way it often becomes clear *how* children employ names, the meanings of which they cannot (yet) explain. But it is just such things which matter to the later Wittgenstein: All "explanations," "hypotheses," "proofs," "justifications," or "theories" must disappear and *language-games* must take their place.

Evidence of the Language-Game

Toward the end of *On certainty,* Wittgenstein apparently comes to "doubt" the evidence of the language-game. He calls for a "higher authority" to "dissolve" (*T,* foreword; *PI,* 91 ff.) the problems of "doubt" and "certainty": "But mightn't a higher authority assure me that I don't know the truth? So that I had to say 'Teach me!'? But then my eyes would have to be opened" (*OC,* 578). Against this apparent doubt in "biblical tone" – for which there are numerous examples in *On certainty* (e.g., "The proposition 'It is written'" – OC, 216 ff.) – Wittgenstein brings forward arguments for his kind of certainty and sureness. In doing so, he returns to a *pedagogical* paradigm: "But ask yourself: how did the child learn the expression? 'I know that' may mean: I am quite familiar with it – or again: it is certainly so. 'I know that the name of this in ... is "..."' – How do you know? – 'I have learnt ... '." (*OC,* 581–583). Wittgenstein's apparent doubts about the "evidence," "sureness," and "certainty" of the language-game could lie in a subjectivistic moment that he tries to "expunge" (*OC,* 33) in his whole work, whether in the "solipsism" of the *Tractatus* or in the so-called "private language" and "meaning" of the *Philosophical investigations* (see also *OC,* 393). It is necessary to eliminate Cartesian doubt, or at least to switch to the reliability of the language-game, its "evidence," and finally to the "fact" of the contextuality of "ordinary language." The well-ordered functioning of the latter brings the doubts and "confusions" (the "bewitchment" – *PI,* 109) of language which "torments" (*PI,* 133) the later Wittgenstein under control – from the beginnings of "child language" onwards (Brose, 1985). Such a "therapy" (*PI,* 133) and regulation of language is not to be confused with the apparent assurance of "knowledge" and Moore's "common sense." For Moore "is really enumerating a lot of empirical propositions which we affirm without special testing" (*OC,* 136). For

Wittgenstein, however, it is not a matter of "empirical" propositions (*PI*, 85 ff.), but of "conceptual" or "logical" (*PI*, 187 ff.; *OC*, 447) investigations, however "vague" (*PI*, 98 ff.) these might be, even in the analyses of "use" in the later work (cf. the linguistic analyses of Austin, 1975, and Searle, 1970).

The entire later work as well as the last remarks in *On certainty* indicate that Wittgenstein took the problem of subjective doubt as the origin of metaphysical confusion and "one-sidedness" very seriously: "A personal experience simply has no interest for us here" (*OC*, 389); "'I know ...' states what *I* know, and that is not of logical interest" (*OC*, 401); "But isn't 'know' *just* as subjective? ... True, but one isn't trying to express the greatest subjective certainty, but rather that certain propositions seem to underlie all questions and all thinking" (*OC*, 415). In doing so, he uses the concept of "evidence," which is somewhat loaded in traditional philosophy (e.g., in Husserl), as a constituting factor of "absolute" certainty: "If I don't trust *this* evidence why should I trust any evidence?" (*OC*, 672). However, Wittgenstein views this final certainty of "evidence" in connection with the "bearer" of the *language-game*, the *speaking* "subject". Thus, he speaks about Moore as follows: "To say of man, in Moore's sense, that he *knows* something; that what he says is therefore unconditionally the truth, seems wrong to me. – It is the truth only inasmuch as it is an unmoving foundation of his language-games" (*OC*, 403).

Truth, logic (*OC*, 401 ff.), and "knowledge" are always "described" from the "rough ground" (*PI*, 107) of the language-game, the "practice of language," and linguistic "*acting*, which lies at the bottom of the language-game" (*OC*, 204). This is the final "evidence" that needs no "justification" (*OC*, 204), in a pedagogical connection, from the language-game of "child language" to the teaching- and learning-games of education and individual "objects" of instruction. Here Wittgenstein uses above all the paradigm of mathematics: "I have a right to say 'I can't be making a mistake about this' even if I am in error. It makes a difference: whether one is learning in school what is right and wrong in mathematics, or whether I myself say that I cannot be making a mistake in a proposition" (*OC*, 663–664). To the generally binding and "regulated" language-game, each individual bearer adds "new (spontaneous, 'specific')" (*PI*, p. 224 e) language-game elements, connects new "threads" (or removes old ones) in the "network" (*PI*, 66) and "nest" of "countless" and "multiple" language-games: "New types of language, new language-games ... come into existence, and others become obsolete and get forgotten" (*PI*, 23); "What I hold fast to is not *one* proposition but a nest of propositions" (*OC*, 225).

Against the background of language-games, which becomes ever more certain, evident, and indubitable for the later Wittgenstein, subjectivistic ("private" or "solipsistic") "doubts" prove to be "errors" or "lies" (*PI*, 249 ff.) as "exceptions to the rule," that is, from the generally obligatory rules, conventions and "customs" of ordinary language. In sum, Wittgenstein's bearers of the language-game persist in their "certainty" even when an "error" occurs. Or more exactly, the "correctness" of the language-game – Wittgenstein's functional concept of linguistic truth – is *always* "given;" even error, mistakes, and lies are played out only within the framework of a language-game. (In this case, the problem of morality is linguistically or pragmatically "dissolved.") "Ethics" as the foundation of traditional philosophy or pedagogical practice is deposited at the level of general ("common") obligation and function ("institution" - *PI,* 199) of the language-game, much as the early Wittgenstein exiled "ethics" to the sphere of the "transcendental," the "mystical," and the "unutterable" (*T,* 6.42ff.). However, these are "borderline" considerations, about which one should perhaps "remain silent," if one "cannot speak" about them (*T,* 7). They would exceed the boundaries of this exposition.

Conclusion

As "pragmatic" as the later Wittgenstein acknowledges himself to be (in paragraphs 601 and 669 of *On certainty,* he still speaks of such "praxis," in which a sentence is used), so complex, complicated, and involved ("entangled") is he when it comes to *pedagogical* applications ("praxis" and "use"). Even if Wittgenstein's notes do not add up to any single ("one-sided") theory, the traditional problem of "theory and praxis" nevertheless arises and the "practice of language" and language-games often succeeds in dissolving this problem only in a "theoretical" manner, and not merely "therapeutically" (*PI,* 133, 255) as Wittgenstein would have it. The following practical-pedagogical consequences can, still be drawn: (1) In his exposition of the "language-game" and especially of "children's language," the later Wittgenstein provides a "systematic" approach to instruction and education with respect to the linguistic aspects of everyday life. Thus: "(My) doubts form a system (*OC,* 126); "our whole system of evidence" (*OC,* 185); "the entire system of our language-games" (*OC,* 411). (2) He provides an approach for practical-*empirical* research on children's, teacher's, and adults language, and the teaching- and learning-games of the latter, in the framework of ordinary language (see Rest, Brose, Heitkämper, & Neumann, 1977, pp. 68-135).

Wittgenstein also said of his most complicated propositions that they are "truth-functional propositions" (Engelmann, 1968). Although he followed other conventions and presuppositions (e.g., his encounters with the "Vienna Circle," Frege, and Russell - see Waismann, 1967/1979; Janik & Toulmin, 1973), an application to the language-games of the present is possible with due consideration of the contemporary usages of everyday language, from "jargon" to "all sorts of slogans" (*OC,* 610) found in advertising, the media, and politics (the "ideologizing" of language). In this connection, the philosophy of "linguistic analysis" which followed Wittgenstein especially in the anglo-american world, has it's critical and continuing value (see Tugendhat, 1976; Savigny, 1974). By this standard, the "usefulness" of Wittgenstein's linguistic philosophy (and pedagogy), upon which he placed so much value, must also be measured. The present trial run of his language-game thinking could be calmly "accepted" (*PI,* pp. 200e, 226e) by Wittgenstein. Today there are serious deficiencies when it comes to a difficult and subtle attitude toward language. Nevertheless, the "*practice* of language" (*OC,* 524) and the language-games in the work of the later Wittgenstein must be easily accessible to the "pragmatism" of the contemporary (younger) generation. They must be shown the "games" of their everyday language and its "surroundings" by teachers schooled in linguistic philosophy and pedagogy. The thinking, speaking, and acting of a future (younger) generation will be prepared from the foundation of an ordered and regulated ("grammatical") language and everyday language-games in the framework of binding communication and the "*customs* (uses, institutions)" (*PI,* 198 ff.) of a linguistically-conscious adult world.

References

Adorno, T. W. (1976). *Erziehung zur Mündigkeit: Vorträge und Gespräche (1959-69)* (6th ed.). Frankfurt a. M.: Suhrkamp.

Austin, J. L. (1975). *How to do things with words* (2nd ed.). Cambridge, Mass.: Harvard University Press.

Brose, K. (1985). *Sprachspiel und Kindersprache: Studien zu Wittgensteins "Philosophischen Untersuchungen".* Frankfurt a. M.: Campus.

Engelmann, P. (1968). *Letters from Ludwig Wittgenstein with a memoir.* New York: Horizon Press.

Finch, H. L. R. (1975). Wittgenstein's last word: Ordinary certainty. *International Philosophical Quarterly, 15,* 383-395.

Habermas, J. (1975). Sprachspiel, Intention und Bedeutung: Zu Motiven bei Sellars und Wittgenstein. In R. Wiggershaus (Ed.), *Sprachanalyse und Soziologie.* Frankfurt a. M.: Suhrkamp.

Janik, A., & Toulmin, S. (1973). *Wittgenstein's Vienna.* New York: Touchstone.

Lorenz, K. (1971). *Elemente der Sprachkritik: Eine Alternative zum Dogmatismus und Skeptizismus in der Analytischen Philosophie.* Frankfurt a. M.: Suhrkamp.

Morawetz, T. (1978). *Wittgenstein and Knowledge: The importance of 'On Certainty'.* Amherst, Mass: University of Massachusetts Press.

Prange, K. (1972). Können - Üben - Wissen: Zur Problematik des Lernens in der Sprachphilosophie Ludwig Wittgensteins. *Pädagogische Rundschau, 26,* 707-734.

Rest, W., Brose, K., Heitkämper, P., & Neumann, S. (1977). *Wortschatzuntersuchung: Das normale Kind.* Opladen: Westdeutscher Verlag.

Searle, J. R. (1970). *Speech acts.* Cambridge: Cambridge University Press.

Svensson, G. (1981). *On doubting the reality: Moore and Wittgenstein on sceptical doubts.* Stockholm: Almqvist & Wiksell International.

Tugendhat, E. (1976). *Vorlesungen zur Einführung in die sprachanalytische Philosophie.* Frankfurt a. M.: Suhrkamp.

von Savigny, E. (1974). *Die Philosophie der normalen Sprache: Eine kritische Einführung in die "ordinary language philosophy".* Frankfurt a. M.: Suhrkamp.

Waismann, F. (1979). *Wittgenstein and the Vienna Circle.* New York: Barnes & Noble. (Originally published, 1967).

Weischedel, W. (1980). *Skeptische Ethik.* Frankfurt a. M.: Suhrkamp.

Zimmermann, J. (1976). Zu Wittgensteins "Über Gewißheit": Versuch eines Überblicks (1974/75). *Studia Philosophica, 36,* 226-239.

Chapter 3 Rule-Following, Mental Models, and the Developmental View

James Russell

It would be nice to believe that the "conceptual confusion" which Wittgenstein noted in the state of scientific psychology some years ago has given way to conceptual order and consensus. But of course it has not; and it never will so long as there remins the possibility for serious disagreement in the philosophy of mind. "Is psychology possible?" asks Johnson-Laird (1983) in the first sentence of the book that I shall later be discussing. Indeed the guiding question in this chapter will be: "May it not turn out that cognitive psychologists often produce general theories in areas where general theories are not appropriate?" More precisely: "Can there be general theories of *what goes on in the mind* when we understand something or make an inference?" My answer will be the somewhat chauvinistic one that general theories of cognition must have a developmental aspect.

My approach to this problem will be through a study of the tension that exists between Wittgenstein's skepticism about theories of the mental processes (principally as expressed in *PI,* 122–242) and Johnson-Laird's recently presented thesis that general theories of cognition can be expressed in terms of the 'mental models' which people construct for themselves and internally manipulate. A not entirely misleading description of this tension is that it exists between antirepresentational and representational theories of mind. I will discuss Wittgenstein (at some length), then Johnson-Laird, finally suggesting some lessons for cognitive-developmental theory.

Wittgenstein's Target

Kripke (1982) was the first student of the *Philosophical investigations* to point up the intimacy of the connection between the anti-private language argument (roughly paragraph 243 onwards) and the 100 or so paragraphs which precede it concerned with rule-following. He says that the basic argument *precedes* paragraph 243. Whether or not his interpretation of Wittgenstein is correct (see below) he is surely correct about the relation between the two sections. In both, the target is the view that *introspection* can reveal to us the nature of mental processes (e.g., understanding a formula) or mental states (e.g., being in pain). Our language puts us in the grip, he argues, of the following theory of mind: for any mental expression (intending, pain, being guided by . . ., grasping the meaning of . . . etc.) there is a particular mental essence of which we gain knowledge through reflection. In paragraphs 123 to 242 he tries to cure us of this belief through examples, such as that of "knowing how to continue" a series like "2, 4, 6, 8. . . ." Then in the famous anti-private language argument he deals with an important corollary of the denial that mental processes have phenomenal essences: that it is impossible to learn the meaning of mental words (pain being his primary example) from the examination and labeling of our own experiences *alone*. The main strand of argument between the two sections is the proposal that mental processes of the kind he is considering have no meaning outside of systems of public practice.

In the section between paragraphs 146 and 154 Wittgenstein's clear target is the conception of the process or act of "understanding" as if it were the "source" of correctness in rule application, as if understanding were an introspectible process – like a formula or table coming into the mind's eye telling us how to go on. Two kinds of view are denied: (1) that understanding how to follow a rule can be construed in terms of the consultation of a conscious mental representation of some kind, and (2) that understanding is a "mental state" in the sense that (say) depression or euphoria are mental states. The arguments against (1) are well known. Any kind of representation, be it iconic or propositional, is open to an infinity of interpretations. Could it be, for example (*PI*, 139), that we understand the meaning of the word "cube" because a representation of a cube comes into our minds? The question *then* is: What makes the picture fit the word? And how do we know that it does? We must have some back-up knowledge so as to disallow, for example, a "triangular prism" should that, perchance, pop into our consciousness instead. So, because pictures are open to an infinity of interpretations[1] we might think that we need "a method of projection" (*PI*, 141) – perhaps in the form of a "schema." But then what does it mean to have grasped this schema of projection? How can *the* method of projection that the teacher intends come into the pupil's mind? When has the pupil grasped the principle?

"Now clearly," writes Wittgenstein, "we accept two different kinds of criteria for this: on the one hand the picture (of whatever kind) that at some time or other comes before the mind; on the other, the application which – in the course of time – he makes of what he imagines. (And can't it be clearly seen here that it is absolutely inessential for the picture to exist in his imagination rather than as a drawing or model in front of him; or again as something that he himself constructs as a model?)" (*PI*, 141). The construction of pictures or models, either mentally or concretely (I am of course deliberately anticipating the section on Johnson-Laird), always leaves open the possibility of a "collision between picture and application" (*PI*, 141). So introducing schemas of projection into the mind does not get us any further.

Wittgenstein then extends this line of argument to the understanding of arithmetical rules of the "2, 4, 6, 8 ..." variety. Predictably, he argues against the

[1] "I see a picture; it represents an old man walking up a steep path leaning on a stick. How? Might it not have looked just the same if he had been sliding downhill in that position? Perhaps a Martian would describe the picture so. I do not need to explain why *we* do not describe it so" (*PI*, 139-(b)).

assumption that "knowing how to go on" (i.e., 10, 12 ...) could consist in the appearance of a formula (e.g., "n + 2 every time") in our mind's eye. This line of thought fails for the same kind of reasons that the mental-picture-as-the-meaning-of-a-word suggestion fails: We can certainly conceive of having the correct formula before our minds's eye and yet *fail to understand it or fail to go on to apply it appropriately,* and we can also imagine following the rule correctly when *no* such phenomenal event has taken place (*PI,* 152). In the next passage, in which Wittgenstein *appears* (but see below) to adopt the garb of a behaviorist or Turing-tester, he lampoons the assumption that "understanding" is the mental event by virtue of which we follow rules. The assumption that all kinds of understanding must have something in common is wrong – even if we found such a phenomenal something, why would *this* be "understanding"? (And how would we find it?) In any case, the phenomenal facts of the case are that in looking for such a something it just melts away: Is it like a "that's easy!" sensation, maybe accompanied by a sharp intake of breath (*PI,* 151)? We are led into such absurdities through the grammatically-induced error of assimilating mental performances like understanding to mental states such as being depressed or being happy or being in pain or hearing a tune (see (2) above). One criterion for being a genuine mental state for Wittgenstein is that it should have a *duration.* In *that* sense (not because he is a "behaviorist") Wittgenstein meant "understanding is not a mental process" (*PI,* 154) – the stress should be on "process" not on "mental."

Wittgenstein was not arguing against the possibility that mental performances may have ineluctable, phenomenal features. His view was that mental process words have a number of facets, that we can take a number of perspectives on them, and that they are not constituted by phenomenal essences. He goes on to illustrate the point with reference to *reading.* He does not mean here reading-plus-understanding; but reading as "the activity of rendering out loud what is written or printed" (*PI,* 156). The obvious remark here is to say that there *surely* is a difference between reading a passage for the first time and seeming to read it but in fact reciting it from memory – or (in the case of an unknown foreign language) reading it via a phonetic translation. Wittgenstein does not deny that there is a difference, what he does deny is that it is our *belief* that we are really reading that makes the difference. For example (*PI,* 160), what would we say to the case of somebody who was *in fact* reading a passage for the first time but under the influence of a drug believed that he was really reciting it? We would surely say that he was wrong about the fact that he was reading, the question of reading versus reciting being decided by reference to the context and the history of the performance. The "feel" of the mental performance, Wittgenstein was denying (and thereby foreshadowing the anti-private language argument), is not the arbiter of the nature of the performance. But in arguing this way, Wittgenstein does not need to deny that we can regard reading as a particular kind of experience: "If on the other hand we use 'reading' to stand for a certain experience of transition from marks to spoken sounds, then it certainly makes sense to speak of the *first* word that he really read" (*PI,* 157). That is, reading is assimilable to the category of mental states, if that is what we want to do for our purpose. This kind of reading will have a duration.

Similar remarks are made about other performance verbs such as "being guided": We expect there to be some kind of mental commonality between the various cases (e.g., following a field track, being lead by the hand). "Being guided is surely a particular experience" says Wittgenstein's alter ego (*PI*, 173), in answer to which Wittgenstein says, in effect, you *think* of a particular experience of being guided. That's different. There is, in fact, no such "ethereal, intangible influence" (*PI*, 175).

In all this the pressing question for the contemporary cognitive psychologist (although it is not in fact our question) is whether this skeptical argument can also be applied to the *nonconscious* mental performances – or processings of information – that support mental procedures like understanding, reading and so on. It is not easy to judge what Wittgenstein would have said here. He did, however, suggest that the argument about mental performances lacking a real-time essence applied equally well to brain processes as to phenomenal processes. In paragraph 158 he imagines that we know enough about "the brain and nervous system" to be able to tell the difference between someone's true reading and the other kinds by "look[ing] into his brain: 'Now he has *read* this word, now the reading connexion has been set up'." The next question is whether, this being logically possible, we should *assume* that there must be "a priori" some brain process that is present in all genuine cases of reading. "But if it is a priori, that means that it is a form of account which is very convincing to us." (This final remark is not exactly perspicuous.) I would not, however, be inclined to regard this as a piece of prescient skepticism about information-processing psychology, for two reasons. First, information-processing psychologists certainly do not have to assume that the processes inside their "black boxes" are inevitably reducible to determinate neural processes. Second, what Wittgenstein was really leading up to here was an assault on the idea that rule-following can be given an entirely mechanistic explanation – this we turn to next.

If pictures or formulae coming into the mind's eye cannot constitute the process of understanding, why should we not attempt a wholly mechanistic account of such mental processes as "knowing how to go on?" Can we not say that the performances are "determined by the algebraic formula" (*PI*, 189). The determination that the objector has in mind is one of strict causality, in the sense that, given the laws of physics, the future behavior of a machine can be firmly predicted on the basis of its present state. The answer to this (*PI*, 193) is that such a conception elevates the determination of a machine's behavior to one of *necessity*, rather than high probability. Real machines, as opposed to the idealized machines that inhabit our metaphors, can go wrong because there is always the possibility of parts "bending, breaking off, melting, and so on." Real machines lack the kind of inevitability that the objector wants to give to the sequence "formula → behavior." Appeals to "machine-as-symbol" (*PI*, 193) do not help; it is like a metaphor seeking a foothold in the world to make it a metaphor.

Rather than discuss the rest of the argument up to paragraph 243 and the anti-private language argument proper, it would be well to now try to get clear about the object of Wittgenstein's skepticism. Kripke (1982) proposed that Wittgenstein was denying the existence of any psychological fact of the matter about whether an individual is following a rule in one way or another, focussing on the following kind of case. Wittgenstein (*PI*, 185) imagines that the pupil appears to us to have understood the rule "n + 2 every time," but then after 1,000 continues the series 1,004, 1,008, 1,012... and so on. But perhaps by his own lights the pupil *is* correct. If a formula such as "n + 2" is *interpretable,* as all formulae must be, why should the pupil not interpret it as holding in this form only for numbers up to 1,000, after which time "n + 4" comes in to operation (and then after 2,000 "n + 8")?[2] For nothing can fix one interpretation of the formula rather than another.

Now, as I have presented Wittgenstein's case, what is being denied is the idea that *all there is* to following a rule is the possession of some introspectable mental essence which contains every case to infinity. It is the denial that the possession of a bit of phenomenology is sufficient for us to be following a rule in one way or in another. Wittgenstein points out that there can be rule-following without such a mental essence and we can be (introspectively) wrong about which rule we are following: The case has to be decided in terms of the context, a history of performances and, presumably, further facts about the individual. Kripke, however, interprets Wittgenstein's denial as being more radical than this: There can be *no* mental fact of the matter about whether a rule is being followed in one way or another. This means, so far as I can see, that the beliefs a person has about which rule he is following cannot only be wrong, but that they are not even in the running for truth. Kripke takes this as following from Wittgenstein's insistance that all rules are up for interpretation: If this is so then one interpretation is as good as another, and if *this* is so there can be no mental fact about whether a rule is being followed in one way or another. Kripke compares this kind of skepticism with Humean skepticism. In Hume there is the denial that any individual cause-effect sequence has any "necessity" outside of a history of prior connections; in Kripke's Wittgenstein there is the denial that an individual episode of rule-following has *any* meaning outside of a set of past rule-following behaviors (Kripke, 1982, pp. 62–68).

This view has very drastic consequences for language. What is true for rule-following in the above case will be true for word meaning because word meaning is a form of rule-following. *There will be no mental fact as to whether I mean a word in one way or in another way.* And given this, meaning cannot be decided by the states of affairs in the world that make a sentence true or false (the "truth conditions") because the mental representations that underlie the act of meaning

---

[2] Kripke's own example is of somebody who gives "5" as the answer to the sum "68 + 57" because his use of "plus" is only the same as ours for numbers up to 57. Beyond 57 all addition sums are given the answer 5. Kripke calls this "quus" as opposed to "plus." He interprets Wittgenstein as denying that there is anything in our past arithmetical intentions which fixes "plus" as opposed to "quus." "First, ['the skeptic', i. e. Wittgenstein] questions whether there is any *fact* that I meant plus not quus, that will answer his skeptical challenge. Second, he questions whether I have any reason to be so confident that I should answer '125' rather than '5'" (Kripke, 1982, p. 11).

a word or a sentence (whatever they are) cannot be true *of* anything. This position is known as "anti-realism"[3] because it is based on the thesis that there are no mind-independent facts to determine the truth of an utterance. What then *does* determine meaning? Must we draw, as Kripke puts it, "the incredible and self-defeating conclusion that all language is meaningless" (Kripke, 1982, p. 71)? Meaning is constituted – on the anti-realist thesis – by the assertability conditions under which utterances are justified through given social practices: The behavior of the speech community determines truth, not what is in the world.

Is this Wittgenstein's thesis? If it is, then the attempts by cognitive psychologists to develop theories of semantic representation are doomed from the start.

McDowell (1984) and others (e.g., Blackburn, 1984a, 1984b and see below) have suggested that Kripke's reading is in error. Kripke interprets Wittgenstein as aiming, like Hume, to provide a "solution" to "a skeptical paradox" – the paradox that "no course of action could be determined by a rule because every course of action can be made out to accord with the rule. The answer was: if everything can be made out to accord with the rule, then it can also be made to conflict with it. And so there would be neither accord nor conflict here" (*PI*, 201). The "solution," for Kripke, is that rule-following consists in a social practice, and that only. But, McDowell says, in the same paragraph Wittgenstein goes on to write:

> *It can be seen that there is a misunderstanding here* [my italics] from the mere fact that in the course of our argument we give one interpretation after another; as if each one contented us at least for the moment, until we thought of yet another standing behind it. What this shews is that there is a way of grasping a rule which is *not* an *interpretation,* but which is exhibited in what we call "obeying the rule" and "going against it" in actual cases. (*PI,* 201)

So it is precisely Kripke's interpretation of Wittgenstein that Wittgenstein is attacking! It is a *misunderstanding* to say that no course of action could be determined by a rule because rules are open to multiple interpretations. This would indeed mean denying (in McDowell's words) "that there is anything that constitutes my understanding an expression in some determinate way" (McDowell, 1984, p. 331). Indeed, Wittgenstein makes much the same point earlier in paragraph 198 where he says that the fact that the range of rule interpretations is infinite means only that rule-following is not constituted by an interpretation (i.e., not that rule-following episodes have no determinate mental content). The alter ego speaks, but it could equally well be Kripke: "But how can a rule shew me what I have to do at *this* point? Whatever I do is, on some interpretation, in accord with the rule." Wittgenstein says in answer, "This is not what we ought to say, but rather: any interpretation still hangs in the air along with what it interprets, and cannot give it any support. Interpretations by themselves do not determine meaning." What this tells us is that reference to interpretations in this con-

---

[3] As Scruton (1984) has pointed out, Wittgenstein's position should be regarded as a kind of *nominalism* not anti-realism. Nominalism is the view that we cannot step outside of language to give an account of how it is attached to the world. Anti-realism is stronger: the view that there are no mind-independent facts.

text is misleading. We should suppress the inclination to say that "every action according to a rule is an interpretation.... we ought to restrict the term 'interpretation' to the substitution of one expression of the rule for another" (*PI,* 201). So Wittgenstein's statement that "to *think* one is obeying a rule is not to obey a rule. Hence it is not possible to obey a rule 'privately': otherwise thinking one was obeying a rule would be the same thing as obeying it" (*PI,* 202) should not (*pace* Kripke) be taken as meaning that following a rule in one way or another has no determinate mental content. It means that there has to be more to rule-following than the belief.

For McDowell's Wittgenstein, "rule-following as interpretation" is one horn of a dilemma. The other horn is the machine analogy that we have already discussed: It is tempting to say that if rule-following is not open to interpretation then our behavior with regard to a rule must be rigidly determined, rather as the future states of a perfect machine are determined by its past states. But, says Wittgenstein, are we then imagining that rule-following *never* goes wrong, *can* never go wrong, just as 2+2 can "never" make 5?[4]

If we accept McDowell's reading, as I believe we should, then Wittgenstein is telling us that this dilemma is not compulsory and that we require a view of rule-following such that it is *"not* an *interpretation."* But what is Wittgenstein's *positive* thesis? Although Wittgenstein denied that there could be "theses" in philosophy, we surely have a right to expect something. In paragraph 198, when pressed by the alter ego to say what is the connection between a rule (e.g., a signpost) and the behavior of following the sign he says that it is a connection set up because "I have been trained to react to this sign in a certain way, and now I do so react to it." Now to a psychologist a passage like this might too easily suggest something akin to a conditioning process. This is not all wrong but it is wrong insofar as it suggests that Wittgenstein was saying something about how the process of training works, and it is wrong in that "conditioning" suggests simple S-R or S-S processes. From what else Wittgenstein had written (e.g., *PI,* 241) the interpretation of "training" as meaning "initiation into a form of life" (see also Hamlyn, 1978) would be far more accurate. It is correct, though, insofar as conditioning is an *unthinking* process.

Why is "unthinking" an appropriate way of describing how Wittgenstein wanted rule-following to be regarded? Rule-following is not unthinking through being mechanically caused (*pace* the "rigid machine" analogy), but because it is the point at which thinking (*qua* deliberation or cognitive assessment) *stops.* Wittgenstein's analogy is between rule-following and a *bedrock* – something beneath which cogitation cannot dig. One cannot *justify* following a rule (e.g., calling a yellow thing "yellow"): "If I have exhausted the justifications I have reached bedrock, and my spade has turned" (*PI,* 217). And a little later: "When I obey a rule I do not chose. I obey the rule blindly" (*PI,* 219).

---

[4] Wittgenstein wrote elsewhere: "How queer: It looks as if a physical (mechanical) form of guidance could misfire and let in something unforeseen, but not a rule! As if a rule were, so to speak, the only reliable form of guidance" (*Z,* 296). This passage is quoted in McDowell (1984).

In all this it is very important to recognise that this "bedrock" is not produced by the rule-follower's reverence for social consensus. Rule-following is a social practice, right enough, but this does not mean that our confidence in the consensual usage of words or in consensus about what is or is not a good inference lies at the heart of rule-following. To believe this is to fall right back again into the original trap – taking states of consciousness as constituting the essence of rule-following performances. McDowell makes the point clearly through considering a famous passage in which Wittgenstein lampoons the notion that rule-following is a kind of inelectable mental essence.

> Could the justification of an action as fulfilment of an order run like this: "You said 'Bring me a yellow flower,' upon which this one gave me a feeling of satisfaction; that is why I have brought it"? Wouldn't one have to reply: "But I didn't set you to bring me the flower which should give you that sort of feeling after what I said!"? (*PI*, 460)

But this does not, argues McDowell [and *pace* commentators such as C. Wright (1980)] imply a social consensus alternative. He modifies the passage to present what Wittgenstein's argument against *this* might have looked like:

> Could the justification of an action as fulfilment of an order run like this: "You said 'Bring me a yellow flower,' upon which this one received the approval from all the bystanders; that is why I have brought it?" Wouldn't one have to reply: "But I didn't set you to bring the flower which should receive approval from everyone else after what I said!"? (p. 335)

To summarise, Wittgenstein's remarks on rule-following were directed against the view that the essence of rule-following is to be found in the "private" mental episode – in particular, a state of consciousness – undergone by the subject at the time of the performance. This does not mean that he denied that there is a fact of the matter about whether a subject is understanding a rule in one way or in another. Neither does it mean denying the reality (*qua* the determinate character) of individual mental episodes. It is to deny that the mental episode – viewed ahistorically and aculturally – *is* the rule-following. Rule-following cannot be understood without consideration of its public face. But might Wittgenstein have over-emphasised the public nature of the "training" on which the ability to follow rules depends? In the next section I briefly consider some contemporary arguments against the "anti-private language argument."

How Public Must Rule-Following be?

If rule-following is not constituted by a private mental episode then it cannot be the case that we could develop our own private language for our own sensations, given that language is a system of rules. But is it really the case that "to *think* one is obeying a rule is not to obey a rule. Hence it is not possible to obey a rule 'privately'" (*PI*, 202)? I will briefly mention, and try to answer, two kinds of objection to Wittgenstein's anti-private language argument. If these objections work then they must do so by removing some of the force from Wittgenstein's case that rule-following performances are not solely constituted by mental episodes.

Dummett[5] imagines a Crusoe who has never had any contact with other human beings finding a Rubik's Cube washed up on the shore one day. He sets about trying to solve the puzzle (or stated neutrally, to get a plain colour on each face). After much trial and error he discovers a method of doing this, a method that he can follow at will, and in doing so he follows rules that he himself constituted. Is this private rule-following? It is, but not in any sense that cuts against the Wittgensteinian argument. The rules followed in order to solve the puzzle are means to an end, not different in kind from rules (*qua* procedures) that Crusoe might use to catch fish. Verbal reference, however, is a different matter. Although verbal reference may well have extralinguistic purposes, it is an end in itself. The mental act of meaning flower by "flowers" or "Blumen" or "little red thingies" is not characterizible as a simple intention to create an extralinguistic effect. Of course this point has been made by Grice (1957) – a second-order intention is involved which is linguistically *sui generis* (to get the listener to believe *p* by means of his recognition of my intention to mean *p* by *s*). A similar point has also been made by Bennett (1964, pp. 15–21) through his distinction between "rule-guided" and "regulated" behavior. And within psychology the *sui generis* nature of referring has been eloquently described by Sugarman (1983) in her commentary on a study of ape language teaching (Savage-Rumbaugh, et al., 1983). The apes had been trained to use language, but not in the Wittengsteinian sense of training – which, as I said, could be paraphrased as "initiation into a form of life." They had been rewarded with food for producing certain symbolic associations.[6] The target of the anti-private language is then, the mental act of reference, not the adoption of rule-bound procedures.

We must spend much more time on the second objection to the anti-private language argument. It is essentially: Why must the argument be directed only to individuals; why not to rule-following *groups* as well? Blackburn (1984a, 1984b) has recently argued that Wittgenstein's skepticism about the role of "internal" or private experience in reference is too strong because just the same kind of skepticism can be directed against *public* rule-following. The bare bones of the argument are as follows. Imagine, first of all, three cases of incorrect application of a word. In the first case the person normally uses the word *circle* correctly, but then happens to call what is clearly a square a "circle" one day. In this case we just say that there was a simple mistake – a "performance slip" maybe. In the second case somebody's understanding of the intension of the word "circle" changes so that it becomes radically different from ours. He is following a "bent rule" (Goodman, 1955, chapter 4), so that in some circumstances he claims that the intension of "circle" includes squares. In the final case the individual has *nothing* determinate in mind at all when he uses the word "circle." It just so happens

[5] This argument has not been published (to my knowledge), but is ascribed to Dummett in the literature. Dummett is, in fact, only suggesting it as a *possible* argument. His case in support of Wittgenstein can be found in Dummett (1978).

[6] For example, the animals were trained to associate symbols on a keyboard with specific kinds of food. They could request these foods by pressing keys. The tests were administered when the animals were hungry.

that, through good luck, he has always got the reference right in the past; but now his application has been shown up as hollow. Blackburn calls these, respectively, (1) the right-rule, (2) the bent-rule, and (3) no-rule cases.

The question now asked is: What kinds of facts can determine whether a mistake has an (1), (2) or (3) character? On what Blackburn calls "semantic externalism" the correctness or incorrectness *is only relative to a public practice*. In opposition to this Blackburn places "semantic internalism" – the view that the existence of three different, determinate semantic intentions on the part of the three people is what makes the difference. The Wittgensteinian argument against this is, of course, that if somebody is a wholly private language user, no criteria for discrimination can be applied, because whatever *feels* right will *be* right. The distinction between the three kinds of error can only be drawn in the context of a system of public practice.

Now, Blackburn argues, this challenge "threatens to destroy public language as well" (1984a, p. 98). Imagine (this is not Blackburn's way of putting it) that we encountered a community of Crusoes who seemed to have developed a language something like our own. If we are semantic externalists, why should we be charitable and assume that *the community as a whole* is a right-rule follower? What facts tell us that it is a right rule-follower and not a bent-rule or no-rule follower? If we interviewed each Crusoe all he could do would be to tell us that he knows what he is up to, that he is following a public rule. But how do we know that this is not simply a case of only *thinking* that he is following such a rule and indeed *thinking* he is correcting others.

Blackburn says that the fact that we can derive this kind of skepticism from the anti-private language argument weakens the Wittgensteinian position. These requests for verification, from which this skepticism is indissociable, mean that Wittgenstein's argument is entirely dependent on a verificationist theory of meaning. Whether or not this is the case,[7] something has clearly gone wrong. The skepticism seems to be too strong. A representative of the Crusoes could say, in effect, that this demand for facts which show whether their rule application is (1), (2) or (3) is just one of the many meaningless kinds of skeptical challenge that can be made (e.g., how do we *really* know that the world is not a dream?) which we cannot answer but which, as Blackburn puts it, "does not disturb the genuineness of the distinction" (i.e., between the three). Well ... if the rebuttal works for the groups of Crusoes why cannot it work for a solitary, private-language-using Crusoe as an answer to semantic externalism? The skeptical challenger will then reply to the effect that we must be told what the differences *consist in*. "But why," Blackburn says, "should this request be legitimate? A distinction made with one kind of vocabulary often cannot be captured except by using that vocabulary: The distinction between red and green is essentially a distinction of colors, and

---

[7] For the view that Wittgenstein does *not* need to rely on verification principles see, for example, Kenny (1971). Kenny's argument is persuasive because in the case of a private language follower there is nothing to be right or wrong *about*. (There are mind-independent facts, but a private language cannot capture them by rule-bound reference.) Wittgenstein asks what the conception of verification consists in.

cannot be shown to 'consist in' some difference that does not refer to colors.... Notice too that by urging the negative point, Wittgenstein has already led us to think of intention as irreducible, in the sense that the issue of the intentions with which a person uses a term is never just the issue of which display he has before his mind" (Blackburn, 1984a, pp. 98-99).

Blackburn goes on to argue that if we view the private linguist as someone trying to "bring order into his life... by correlating the recurrence of one experience with the recurrence of others (warmth-pain! visual experience *x*, tactile experience *y* etc.)," because "an ordered subjective life is a nice thing to have," then it is this for which the solitary Crusoe strives. Within this plot things may "go well or go badly" (*ibid.*, p. 100).

So what Blackburn has done here is "following Kripke [to] put Wittgenstein's challenge in the garb of skepticism." But should we? On the present analysis (after McDowell) the object of Wittgenstein's skepticism is the view that *all* there is to rule-following is a particular phenomenal essence. He is not denying that there cannot be a determinate mental differences between (1), (2) and (3) so long as there is a framework of rule-following outside of the individual (and thus the possibility of there having been a history of "training").

Once the Wittgenstein skepticism is appropriately weakened in this way there is no sense in which the anti-private language argument can be applied to groups as well as to individuals. The question of whether an individual is following a rule in way (1), (2) or (3) is a question about mental contents which can be asked *so long as the individual is located within a group*. Similarly, given "external" rules about arithmetic, an individual can be said to be following *either* rule "n+2" *or* "n+2 up to 1,000 and then n+4," because he can have a determinate intention to do one or the other despite the fact that his behavior before encountering numbers above 1,000 is consistent with both. The Wittgensteinian denial is that such contents can exist in individuals outside of groups, given that rule-following is not constituted by a private phenomenal essence. Groups, however, do not have mental states – they are abstractions away from individuals – so there is no fact of the matter as to whether the group is following a rule in one way or another. The group creates a practice of correction; it does not itself follow anything. The only challenge one can address to a group as a whole is in regard to the nature and consistency of its practices over time *relative to our own*. From our perspective its practices of correction may seem unpredictable and strange; but this fact cannot destroy the reality of the practice. In short, the individual-group relation is *not* analogous to the group-metagroup relation because groups lack mental states. I am suggesting, therefore, that a Wittgensteinian can and should say that the possession of mental states is a necessary condition for being a rule follower. Wittgenstein's skepticism was directed against the *sufficiency* of mental states – the belief that all that is required to be following a rule of a given kind is a mental state of a given kind, irrespective of the subject's relation to other subjects.

But even if Wittgensteinian skepticism *could* be extended to public usage, Blackburn still has the task of drawing a realistic picture of what it means to be a solitary rule-follower. Blackburn's picture is of somebody sufficiently socialized within our conceptual system that he can understand and answer the skeptical challenges addressed to him. But imagining such a request as part of an argument involves violating the rules of the fantasy on which the argument depends; that is, we have to ascribe our notions of consistency and justification to such a creature. If we can write, "suppose the private linguist defends himself by saying: 'We already know ...'" (Blackburn, 1984a, p. 98), and so on, then any skeptical challenge about solitary rule-following can be made to look absurd. In fact, one of the reasons why it is inappropriate to cast Wittgenstein in the role of the questioning skeptic is because of his insistence here that there is nothing to be skeptical about in the mental life of a truly solitary "rule-follower." There are no successes and no failures on our terms (see note 7).

What can we say about Blackburn's suggestion that the private linguist could have become such through a desire to bring order into his mental life? He might have used language to correlate one kind of experience with another, says Blackburn. Presumably the symbols are used as mnemonics - as means of fixing the character of each experience. Is this a serious challenge to the anti-private language argument? In this case the symbols may be viewed as analogous to twists of the Rubik's Cube in Dummett's example - as a means to a determinate end. In this case the end is a more ordered subjective life rather than six faces of solid colour. On the surface the analogy looks quite a good one: A completed Rubik's Cube gives a "more ordered" visual input than a Rubik's Cube before completion. To say this would be tantamount to *denying* the previous claim that there is something *sui generis* about the act of linguistic reference.

The difficulty with Blackburn's suggestion lies in the assumption that a private language *is capable* of clarifying experiences in such a way as to bring order into the subjective life, without which "we can have no understanding of ourselves as conscious of an objective or spatially extended world" (Blackburn, 1984a, p. 100). I will leave aside the somewhat obvious worry that the would-be private linguist must already have a pretty advanced state of self-consciousness before he could ever attempt such an ordering operation. (Such an objection could possibly be met through reference to "Just So Stories" of the kind which Dennett (1984, p. 41) has used to suggest how the notion of self-consciousness might have arisen in language users.)

The more serious objection springs from considering the fact that language is infinitely extensible and ambiguous (see Russell, in press, for discussion). The idea that there is some phenomenal essence in a word's meaning that could *prevent* its infinite over-extension is, of course, Wittgenstein's primary target in the anti-private language argument. Why, therefore, should we expect that coupling, say, the vocalization *blah* with a pain and the vocalization *glub* with a red glow should create order and help us to understand our relationship with fire and its harmful properties? Moreover, would the private linguist, experiencing a pain on Wednesday and wondering if it is the same kind of experience that he had on Monday, be *helped* by trying to recall whether he vocalised *blah* at the time of Monday's pain. This is merely a duplication of the question. And because words are infinitely extensible and ambiguous, if the solitary linguist recalls saying *blah* on Monday the bearing that this recall should have on his present behavior is not determinable. How is he to decide if this pain is sufficiently like Monday's to merit the label or whether some other label (e.g., *blop* meaning a sharp twinge) is more appropriate? By its very elasticity a private language would seem to be the agent of disorder rather than order here. And, paradoxically, suggestions of the kind that Blackburn makes seem to err on the side of linguacentrism: For could not an entirely non-linguistic human be both self-conscious and the possessor of an ordered subjective life?

One response to this objection might be that the Wittgensteinian view fails to acknowledge the possibility that some kinds of linguistic capacity could be innate. Let us imagine, then, that the concept of a "conceptual error" or of "misnaming" is innate - that humans are, by some means, capable of dividing themselves into "practitioner" and "assessor." Perhaps there are two distinct cognitive "modules" (in the modern jargon) which communicate with each other? The problem with this suggestion, however, is that although it is entirely possible that such a capacity should be innate, in the case of the solitary linguist it would *never come to be exercised* because the assessor is still a solitary assessor whose (innate) notion of an error is entirely *unconstrained.*

I will illustrate this point about constraint through a comparison between claims about the innateness of conceptual rules and claims about the innateness of object knowledge. As regards object knowledge, some evidence suggests that human infants come into the world with a set of perceptual "expectations" about which visual inputs define the continuing unseen existence of objects and which inputs define object disappearance (e.g., Bower, 1967); indeed we even be innately primed to pick up the visual input that defines self-movement forwards versus backwards (Butterworth & Hicks, 1977). But how could such a capacity be *exercised* in a world in which the behavior of objects was not fundamentally *refractory* (Baldwin, 1906), in a world in which there was no possibility of a perception being non-veridical, in which the behavior of objects was *entirely* predictable, and in which objects were infinitely controllable by the will? I would suggest (merely citing Piaget's Kantian arguments about the necessity for *accommodation* as well as assimilation)[8] that the result would be that these innate capacities would never be exercised in the development of objective knowledge and self-world dualism.

The situation for the solitary linguist (or assessor-module in the linguist's brain) would be very similar. He may understand, on some level, what a misapplication of a term would be but never get into the position to make an error. (Compare the case of a solitary chess-player - the fact of understanding what winning the game would consist in is not sufficient to make play against oneself a case of "winning.") So in this case there would be no self-language dualism, no division between the self and the self's linguistic performances. It is not a big assumption to make that such a language would lack rules; although an observer

[8] For discussion, see Russell (1984, pp. 128-132).

of the linguist's behavior may want to assess his behavior in terms of what the observer calls "consistency."

In concluding this section, I want to elaborate on the analogy between the refractoriness of objects in the world and the refractoriness of linguistic rules as expressed by the linguistic community. I think this analogy helps to illuminate the developmental relevance of the anti-private language argument. The behavior of objects *vis-à-vis* ourselves is unpredictable within a rule bound system, whilst also being uncontrollable with a system of possible control. To explain: we can predict what objects will do but only within certain limits. This predictability is well described through Piaget's (1953) application of Group Theory to sensorimotor object knowledge. "Unpredictability" means the fact that we never quite know what is going to happen next or what we will meet round the next corner. Similarly, in acting on objects we control them, and we control ourselves as objects, but only some kinds of control are effective in some kinds of circumstance. Our reach necessarily exceeds our grasp. Within the Piagetian school of thought the predictability and controllability are seen as the main agents in the constitution of mental structure in development. Within Baldwin's (1906) genetic epistemology it is the unpredictability and "control" (Baldwin's term in fact) *of thought by objects* that is emphasized, because these are seen as being partly responsible for forgeing the division between the striving agent and the refractory datum.

The analogy with the linguistic system is a close one. There is both unpredictability and ruleboundness within the linguistic system, both the possibility of strict control over another's linguistic output and the lack of control necessary for the other to be autonomous. Language is tightly rule-bound, and yet the linguistic output from others has an inevitable degree of unpredictability. For example, after hearing the word "the," we can be very confident indeed that the next word is not going to be a main verb or an indefinite article, a predictability which becomes greater as we move towards the end of the sentence. But the actual words that we hear are always, more or less, *news*. Similarly, we can control an interlocutor's output to some degree (ask her if she has the time, or tell her that you have set fire to her handbag), but only so far (she may misinterpret the request, or disbelieve the information). As in the case of objects, one can suppose that failure to predict and control is one of the agents through which language comes to be regarded as mind-independent by the subject. And as for objects, the ruleboundness is not imposed, nor is it exactly discovered (because our own mental constitution contributes to the "discovery") but encountered – bumped up against. My suggestion is, in short, that the solitary would-be linguist is in a similar situation to an organism confronted by a non-refractory world of pseudo-objects: In both cases, no matter how elaborated the innate structure, the native capacities will not be exercised so as to produce knowledge. There will be no knowledge of an objective world and no knowledge of language. Such a radical lack of linguistic knowledge entails lack of "language" in any significant sense.

But is it surely not possible for the solitary individual to be a rule-user whilst lacking any significant idea of what he is up to? Could it not *turn out* that his usage has been perfectly consistent without his realizing it (c.f. Fodor, 1975, p.70)? I would suggest – not having the space to elaborate the point – that a language which cannot be assessed by its user is a language which must fail to be regarded by its user as independent of his own mental states and that *such* a language could never be a medium of thought. In such a case, what would such a private language be *for?* The bare logical possibility that a born Crusoe might start talking about things (and that when we rescue him we might be able to translate the outputs into our own language) *without* any ability to represent and manipulate these outputs mentally is not a very interesting one.

Before discussing mental models I shall summarise this section. Wittgenstein's target was the view that there must be a phenomenal essence to rule-following episodes such that this essence *is* the rule-following. The anti-private language argument was a means of showing that word use (as a case of rule-following) is not fixed by a phenomenal essence. These arguments leave intact, however, the view that there can be a mental fact of the case as to whether a piece of rule-following behavior is due to the following of one rule or another (e.g., "n+2" or "n+2 up to 1,000 and then n+4"). But whatever account we give of rule-following it cannot be regarded as a species of interpretation of a mental content, and neither can it be regarded as a kind of mechanical determination. The case against the phenomenal essence view of rule-following collapses without the anti-private language argument, so the latter had to be defended. The anti-private language argument cannot be applied to groups because only individuals within groups can be said to follow rules, given that only individuals have mental states. Arguments *for* the coherence of the notion of a private language of the kind launched by Blackburn have the following flaws: (1) they treat the solitary language-user too much on the model of the social language user (imagining him answering skeptical points etc.), (2) they underplay the order and coherence that a *non*-linguistic mental life might possess, and (3) they assume that an invented private language could possess a kind of *sui generis* structure sufficient to order mental life, when language without an refractory mode of exercise (i.e., other language users) is infinitely extensible and ambiguous. Finally, I suggested that, however rich the human cognitive endowment, the endowment must remain unused without a refractory field for its exercise – be it a world of objects or of language users (at least one language-user?). What remains intact through all this is Wittgenstein's case against the view that the rulebound features of human understanding consist in sets of determinate and introspectable mental essences, abstracted from human social existence.

Realism and Mental Models

This interpretation of Wittgenstein's remarks on rule-following leaves no room for the claim that Wittgenstein was an anti-realist (see above and note 3), that is, somebody holding the view that there are no language-independent facts. His conclusion is rather that words cannot carry along with them their rules of application to the world – if they could, then a wholly private language would be possible. [Indeed, I suspect that Wittgenstein would have appreciated McDowell's pastiche of the social consensus view (a form of anti-realism), modelled on his own rebuttal of the phenomenal essence view (see above).]

I am saying this now because a superficial inspection of the Wittgensteinian and the mental models views of cognition might lead one to conclude that Wittgenstein's view was essentially anti-realist and Johnson-Laird's realist. This is not so. Not only was Wittgenstein not an anti-realist but mental models theory turns out, as we shall see, to be far less realist than was intended. Now to explain the point about realism within mental models.

The best way to appreciate the attempt at realism within mental models theory is within the context of semantic theory. Semantic theories fall naturally into two categories. There are, on the one hand, *translational* theories (e.g., Katz & Fodor, 1963) which propose that in understanding the meaning of a word or a sentence we translate it into some form of mentalese – expressed by semantic markers, formal logic or some special computational language. Fodor has held more (Fodor, 1975, 1980) or less (Fodor, 1978) to such a view since the work with Katz. On this view the representational aspects of language are prized above its "aboutness" – so the connection which the translated-into language has with the world need not be spelt out. Given this lack of world-representation connection, the conceptual system which language expresses must be innate in this view (Fodor, 1975). This is a form of anti-realism, although Fodor in fact borrows Putnam's phrase *methodological solipsism* (Fodor, 1980) to describe his position. It is, in fact, a version of translational theory that Wittgenstein was attacking: the view that what is represented "in the head" *is* the meaning of a word. (Contrast this with the position that to understand a meaning we require representations of *some* kind. Wittgenstein was not – the point I have been labouring – attacking the view that mental representations are *necessary* for grasping a meaning.)

In contrast, there are the *realist* or *truth-conditional* accounts of meaning (see Evans & McDowell, 1976, for a defence of this approach versus the translational approach). In these theories meaning is specified in terms of truth conditions, that is, the necessary and sufficient conditions in the world for the truth of the sentence or application of the word. These rely on a correspondence theory of truth. Now what Johnson-Laird is espousing in his book *Mental Models* (1983) is a form of truth-conditional semantics. He is quite clear that he is not intending some form of "representational theory of the mind" in the translational or Fodorian sense because he denies (pp. 146 ff.) that a theory of mind in terms of syntactic representations alone is possible.

One route that Johnson-Laird takes towards the notion of a mental model is by way of the late Montague's (1974) realist semantics. Employing the resources of set theory and the predicate calculus Montague aimed to formalize the way in which the intension of an expression can be explained in terms of its extension. For example Montague said that the semantic value (symbolized by ⟦...⟧) of a term (e.g. a verb) can be given by citing the truth values (in the Boolean sense: 1 = "true," 0 = "false") of functions from individuals. Thus:

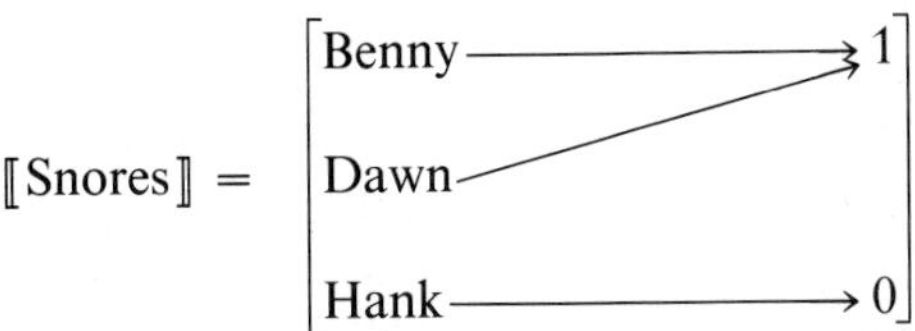

All semantic values grow from individuals plus truth values via the combinatorial apparatus of set theory. So for Montague the meaning of a predicate was the function from an argument to a truth value.[9] The hope was that the notion of an intension as a representation with ineluctably mental properties could be mathematized away: that, as Montague put it, in producing a semantics for English "we have been able to do with denotation alone" (Montague, 1974, p. 217).

But how does Montague semantics deal with the fact that truth varies with the field of reference or "context" of utterance? (It comes to the same thing to say that utterances *must* be potentially *ambiguous.*) The fact must be formalized within the semantic theory. For instance, whether "Hilda is strident" is true or not and thus what the sentence means, depends on whom "Hilda" picks out. So the meaning of a sentence, for Montague, is relative to, what he calls "the model." In a model in which "Hilda" picks out Mrs. Margaret Thatcher the Prime Minister of Great Britain it is true; in a model in which it picks out the sweet old lady who serves in our local greengrocers it is false. So: a model is an ordered pair $<A, F>$ where A is a set (of individuals or objects) and F is a function assigning semantic values of the appropriate sort. Thus when ⟦Hilda⟧ = Margaret Thatcher and ⟦is strident⟧ has a function from individuals to truth values which maps Margaret Thatcher onto "1" then "Hilda is strident" is *true in the model.* (Note the parallel with set intersection.)

But Johnson-Laird's concern is with general cognition rather than semantic theory. What he attempts is the construal of the representational processes in understanding in "model theoretic terms." His "models," like Montague's are *selections* from reality. Thus a mental model is a kind of inner, selective, concrete, re-construction (an "internal tableau" is the term frequently used by Johnson-Laird, see also Johnson-Laird, 1984) of a bit of reality. It is not a representation in the sense that a mental image (this is a *view* of a mental model) or a verbal

---

[9] The expressions "argument" and "function" are being used in their mathematical senses here. For example, in mathematics, squaring a number is one kind of *function*. The number to be squared is the *argument*. The result is the *value* (c.f. "semantic value"). In language, we may have "capital of" as the function, "France" as the argument, and "Paris" as the value.

proposition (this can be a stage prior to the construction of a mental model) are representations. Their construction is a means of understanding something by mental acquaintance with a concrete, selective re-construction of the situation: "Mental models of discourse are used in order to experience vicariously the events that are described" (Johnson-Laird, 1983, p. 443).

Perhaps the best way of understanding Johnson-Laird's claims is through the case of syllogistic reasoning. For example, how do we understand the following?

All artists are beekeepers.
All beekeepers are chemists.

First, Johnson-Laird very convincingly demonstrates that the theories of syllogistic reasoning currently on offer are implausibly complicated and unable to deal convincingly with both rational and erroneous inferences at the same time. They are, in fact, logico-mathematical *descriptions* of mental processes (in terms, for example, of Venn diagrams or truth tables), when what we require is a characterization of the mental models which people actually employ in real-time reasoning. Mental models are not descriptions or formal accounts of mental representations, but "effective procedures" (in the computational sense) constructed and manipulated *by subjects*. The reliance upon abstract logico-mathematical characterizations of rationality (competence theories, broadly understood) he calls the "doctrine of mental logic." I do not think it does any great violence to Johnson-Laird's intentions to call his approach a performance theory of reasoning.[10]

Johnson-Laird gives the following illustration. One way ("effective procedure") of understanding the syllogism given above would be by getting a troupe of actors to form a tableau of the premises. Three actors (the exact number is not important) might play the joint roles of artist and beekeeper, whilst (say) two actors would play beekeepers alone in order to leave open the possibility that some beekeepers might not be actors. Then, in order to add the second premise, the three actors/beekeepers could also take the role of chemists (the reader's "mental model" of their performance may be getting a little fuzzy at this point!), while a new actor could take on the role of chemists who are not beekeepers, as the exclusively beekeeper actors could double up as chemists to cover that possibility. We therefore have (see Johnson-Laird, 1983, p. 95):

artist = beekeeper = chemist
artist = beekeeper = chemist
artist = beekeeper = chemist
(beekeeper) = (chemist)
(beekeeper) = (chemist)
(chemist)

(The parentheses are a directorial device to mean "optional" or "unspecified.")

[10] Johnson-Laird has long been a critic of Chomsky's notion of deep structure and, by implication, his way of drawing the competence-performance distinction (see Johnson-Laird, 1970).

"At this point," writes Johnson-Laird, "if you were asked whether it followed that *All artists are chemists,* you could readily inspect the tableau and determine that this conclusion is indeed true" (p. 95). Passing over the many complications, Johnson-Laird's claim is that in syllogistic reasoning we carry out an internal version of this tableau construction. We construct a tableau of something that "*corresponds directly* to the structure of the state of affairs that the discourse describes" (Johnson-Laird, 1983, p. 125, my italics). (Note the dependence upon a correspondence theory of truth that I signposted earlier.)

Now – staying with syllogistic reasoning – what I do *not* want to do is to criticize the theory of mental models, an effective procedure theory, as a performance theory. It seems to be more capable than its rivals of accounting for the common types of error and the relative difficulty of different kinds of syllogism. It is even introspectively plausible that we attempt something like this. But, as I said before, mental models theory is not intended to *cover the performance aspects* of reasoning: It is a theory that is meant to *replace* competence or "mental logic" theories.

Bearing this in mind let us turn to Johnson-Laird's arguments against the doctrine of mental logic. Piaget is the principal target here. Piaget's theory of logical development is essentially that sensorimotor experience with objects in infancy leads the child to "construct" a logical framework which later, on the level of verbal-conceptual thought, produces the understanding of abstract scientific concepts (amount, space, time, number) in middle childhood and the understanding of abstract logical principles (e.g., necessity, systematized relations between logical possibilities) in adolescence. In this view, any *failures* of understanding of scientific concepts (e.g., the demonstration that undergraduates can be tricked into affirming nonconservation (Hall & Kingsley, 1968) or failures of logical reasoning in normal adults (e.g., Wason & Johnson-Laird, 1972) are performance failures. In the present context (and this is what Piaget *could* say rather than what he may or may not have actually said), a logical performance error is such that the subject is capable of seeing where he has gone wrong. He need not see the error of his ways *in every case* (indeed we may sometimes want to regard failure to see the error as a performance error itself);[11] but there must at least be the notion of accepting correction, of trying to do the right kind of thing and failing, of gaining "insight" from the exposure to one's error. So Piaget's "groupings" and INRC groups should not be regarded as "mental representations" that the adult thinker uses when he reasons, but are idealizations of the system of thought to which the "normal adult" has access. Sometimes the access is good, sometimes poor.

Johnson-Laird's main objection to the doctrine of mental logic is simple and

[11] I am suggesting that for there to be such a thing as a performance error there must be the *possibility* of seeing one's mistakes as failing to do the right kind of thing well enough. (In my experience subjects do indeed sometimes refuse to accept their errors in the AK47 task from Wason & Johnson-Laird, 1972.) It is, of course, an empirical question – albeit one that is enormously difficult to answer – as to whether somebody is incapable of appreciating a logical point or refusing/failing to make the mental effort to appreciate it.

inevitable: "The most glaring problem is that people make mistakes. They draw invalid conclusions, which should not occur if deduction is guided by mental logic" (Johnson-Laird, 1983, p.25). But this can only be a telling objection if we *do* regard Piaget's competence model as a piece of computational psychology, as a performance theory, as the claim that determinate mental operations (computations on the 16 binary propositions?) inevitably (cf. Wittgenstein's super rigid machine analogy) produce the correct answer. The fact that adults make mistakes in reasoning (e.g., failing to aim at falsifying the rule to test it in Wason & Johnson-Laird's, 1972, "four card trick") is no more evidence against Piaget's competence theory of logical development than is the occurrence of grammatical errors in everyday speech evidence against Chomsky's competence theory of grammar.

Now it is certainly the case that Piaget (though not "neo-Piagetians", e.g., Case, 1984) seriously underestimated performance factors in reasoning; but it is quite another matter to insist, as Johnson-Laird is insisting, that a performance theory can give a sufficient account of logical understanding. I will illustrate this point with a contemporary example. As Bryant and Trabasso (1971) argued, Piaget neglected the role of memory weaknesses in children's failures to make the transitive inference (e.g., $A > B$; $B > C$; therefore $A > C$): when memory for the premises is insured performance improves dramatically. Since Bryant & Trabasso's classic demonstration of transitive performance in 3- and 4-year-olds, researchers have been trying to elucidate the kinds of "mental representation" that the child utilizes in correct and incorrect transitive performances. Perhaps the child forms, for example, a mental image of a color sequence with larger to the left; or perhaps he or she codes the premises verbally (see Perner & Aebi, 1985, for recent data on these questions). Now: there is *no* Wittgensteinian "anti-representation" argument that can be levelled against this kind of research strategy. As we have seen, in denying that rule-following must have a phenomenal essence one does not have to deny that there is some fact of the matter about what kinds of mental operations take place in following particular rules. On the whole, trying to tease out the nature of the encodings and retrievals in transitive performance has been a fruitful enterprise.

But what the Wittgensteinian argument does cut against is the position that the mental representation-cum-phenomenology (we can afford to run the two together for present purposes) is all there is to be explained. Consider one paradox that this belief leads us into. Brainerd and Kingma (1984) have recently demonstrated that premise memory and inferential performance can vary independently. That is to say, not only can a child recall the premises whilst failing to make the inference (see Russell, 1981), but he or she may fail to recall the premises and yet make the inference! Brainerd's explanation of this phenomenon is that the mental representation is in the form of a "fuzzy trace" which does not allow the subject to retrieve information about all adjacent terms. This is transitive *performance* right enough, but it is not following the rule of transitive deduction. It is not acting in accordance with knowledge of the relation between premises and the inference to which they give rise. What it *means* to understand transitivity (and you cannot, in the present terms, follow a rule that you do not understand) is to understand a relation between premises and inference: If you do not know what the premises are, then it has to be true that you are not making any kind of inference. What is the alternative? If we render the question of premise knowledge irrelevant then *any* behavior can count as rule-following: We simply describe the behavior as falling under certain rules (see Toulmin, 1977). Of course, in understanding this relation we employ mental representations, but this is not all that understanding the nature of the inference consists in. This was Wittgenstein's argument and it is the reason why he drew our attention to the history of the performance and the social context.

I am sure that some Wittgensteinian scholars would say that I have got things the wrong way round here, particularly those who adopt the Kripkean interpretation. They could, for example, cite Wittgenstein's remarks about mental performances such as reading (see above) in which he seemed to be saying that the important thing was the subject's successful performance (e.g., in reading aloud what is written down), *whatever* the subject happens to believe about the nature of his or her performance. But the case is quite different here: Although the child's beliefs about what he is doing are just as irrelevant as they were in the reading case, in the case of logic the possession of factual knowledge is all important given that logical knowledge, *unlike* reading which can be regarded solely as performance, can only be evinced through the possession of certain criterial items of information. It is not that the children in Brainerd and Kingma's experiments lacked some ineluctable mental presence called "understanding."

Returning now to Johnson-Laird, although he is not proposing a representational theory of thinking of the Fodorian kind, and although the use of the Montaguesque notion "model" suggests a committment to realist (versus syntactic/solipsistic/translational) theories of thought and to a correspondence theory of truth,[12] the mental model concept as used by Johnson-Laird inevitably produces a representational theory of mind not qualitatively different from the other varieties. The differences between, for example, imagist theories and the mental model theory are significant, but mental models are no more than the "concrete" end of abstract-concrete continuum of representational theories (we could put truth-table accounts of syllogistic reasoning at the abstract end). What is more, it is fair to say that there is a sense in which mental models are supposed to have a phenomenology. For what is supposed to constrain the construction of mental models is, at least in part, that which also constrains the construction of images before the mind's eye. Johnson-Laird says, for example, that we cannot construct a mental model of the sentence, "Two hundred men driving cars." How then is it understood? It can be understood *propositionally,* without the need for a mental model ... "A propositional representation that is set up but never actually used

[12] Note Johnson-Laird's "principle of structural identity" which states that "the structures of mental models are identical to the structures of states of affairs, whether perceived or conceived, that the models represent" (Johnson-Laird, 1983, p.419).

in a procedure to construct a mental model. It is a cheque that is not presented for payment, but which if presented would be honoured" (Johnson-Laird, 1983, p.443). But what if we wanted to use the representation to make an inference? Then we would produce "a scaled-down mental model in which a *manipulable number* of tokens is taken to represent the set of two hundred individuals ... this model would be used to produce a conclusion that could be scaled back to the appropriate numerical quantity" (my italics). Or we could have a compromise, part mental model and part propositional representation, in which we have a "fragment" of the model with "part of the procedure representing the number 200 functioning as a proposition-like label attached to the model" (ibid.).

This passage is variously illuminating about the mental model theory. First it illustrates, as I said, the fact that what constrains mental model construction is that which also constrains a significant aspect of our phenomenology - imagibility. So far as I can see, this is what the reference to "manipulability" amounts to. Second, it obviously raises questions about the *utility* of mental models: We seem to be able to get an awfully long way into verbal comprehension without them. And third - crucially - the passage very starkly highlights the fact that, for Johnson-Laird, the mental model is something for which we not only supply an interpretation but which is constructed on the basis of an interpretation. A mental model is stylized, convention-bound and profoundly opaque ... as the original dramaturgical metaphor suggested. Perhaps another kind of analogy suggests itself: with the idiosyncratic symbols, boxes, arrows and semi-cartoons that we often draw in rough to help us think through difficult abstract problems, making the field of consciousness the scratch-pad and the scratches the mental model. The production and utilization of mental models, therefore, is not comprehension or logical understanding *itself,* but rather, a way of conceptualizing the real-time mental life of a rule-follower.

Where does Wittgenstein come in here? The point that I have labored is that Wittgensteinian skepticism does not deny that the mental life of a rule-follower can have a particular phenomenal quality, that, in the current jargon, "there is something that it is like" (see Nagel, 1974) to be a follower of a particular rule. But this "something" is a product of a system of knowledge which can only be made intelligible through considering what lies outside the rule-follower in the social world. So we should not seek a complete explanation for logicality in the mental events that take place when we do things such as draw inferences. On the other hand, of course, no theory of logical capacity is going to be complete without processing models of real-time performance - theoretical neuropsychology - but this is no more rule-following *itself* (see above) than is the phenomenal essence the rule-following itself.

The Wittgensteinian argument is, of course, very thin on positive claims. Certainly reference to "training" in the thoroughly Wittgensteinian sense of meaning "initiation into a form of life" must surely point us towards some important developmental questions about how a child's experience with rule-bound systems realises a capacity for rule-following. And here I return to the analogy between the existence of objects and the existence of verbal rules: It is sufficient that the rules should be *there* and that being there they should have that particular combination of the refractory and the predictable which also characterises objects' relations to ourselves. It may also be necessary that adults should, in Hamlyn's phrase, put children in the way of things (Hamlyn, 1978) and should treat children as persons (Hamlyn, 1974). But all we *need* to say is that the rules should be there in a form that enables the child to recognise their refractory and prediction-generating nature.

The picture which I hope has gradually emerged is of a kind of Piagetianized Wittgensteinianism (or Wittgensteinianized Piagetianism!): of there being an intimate relation between (1) the claim that the child must interact with socially-realized rules which have an object-like status in order to be a rule-follower and (2) the claim that rule-following does not consist of having (interpreting? being causally determined by?) a particular kind of "mental representation." We do indeed need a kind of realism about rule-following (unless, that is, we want to embrace Fodorian solipsism about the relationship of the rule-follower to the world); but Johnson-Laird's realism is essentially a realism of the desire to evade the consequences of a syntactic-representational theory, and of the intellectual ancestry of the term "mental models." Mental models theory inherits the deep problems with all representational theories of thought: How can the use of the mental model not be an interpretation, and yet how can the model rigidly determine future behavior? More precisely: "How does the rule-follower know what to do when she constructs her mental model?" And "How does the thinker know that the mental model is the right one?".

So if we require a realist theory of logical understanding it seems that we are going to have to look beyond this kind of representational theory toward developmental processes. Piagetian theory, in fact, expresses a *kind* of realism about logical understanding, insofar as it grounds knowledge of abstract principles in the child's early interaction with objects. This is not, of course, the kind of empirical realism which Piaget (1953) explicitly rejected in which the mind's function is to reflect the nature of reality. The logical principles are "constructed" via interaction with a refractory physical reality. And then we should add - I am suggesting - "a refractory social reality."

And what might be the cash value of this latter suggestion in terms of specific research programs? We should, I think, look for the determinants of logical understanding in the children's developing appreciation of the language system *as a system* ("metalinguistic awareness" in the current jargon). Specifically, we should pay more attention to the developing sense of (in Baldwin's terminology) the *limitation* that such a system places on what cannot be said and on what cannot be denied. We are certainly not going to run out of research topics: nominal realism (Piaget, 1929), co-reference across hierarchies (Piaget & Inhelder, 1964, on "class inclusion"), the interpretation of mental verbs (see Johnson, 1982, for a review), understanding the relation between communicative intention and the words used (e.g., Robinson, Goelman & Olson, 1984), how beliefs are expressed in language (e.g., Wimmer & Perner, 1983), intensionality (Russell, 1987), the autonomy of linguistic meaning from world states (Osherson & Markman, 1975;

Russell & Haworth, 1986). The problem, of course, is that this kind of research is essentially descriptive: There is a lamentable lack of interventional and causal studies aimed at pin-pointing the kind of socio-linguistic experiences that facilitate this development (see Robinson & Robinson, 1982, for one, at least).

I shall conclude with some brief remarks on the competence-performance distinction – because my skeptical points about mental models theory have depended very heavily on it. For present purposes this is the distinction between knowing the right kind of thing to do and the question of whether we can do it well enough, between mental logic, on the one hand, and questions about the mental strategies and processing capacities of the reasoner on the other. Now, when Chomsky (1965) originally presented his version of the competence-performance distinction he suggested that a criterion for grammatical competence was the deployment of "intuitions" about grammaticality versus ungrammaticality. I believe we should make exactly parallel assumptions regarding intuitions as a criterion for the possession of logical competence. We may say, for example, that what lies at the heart of the concept of logical necessity is the ability to assess the *status* of different kinds of sentence (e.g., "1 + 1 = 2" has a radically different status from "Paris is the capital city of France"). Indeed Wittgenstein's remarks about rule-following being a "bedrock" (see above) which requires no justification have some bearing on this: A rule-follower must know what *kinds* of judgment require justifications and which kinds do not (see Russell, 1978, pp. 153–157).

But does this not fly in the face of Wittgenstein's original denial that rule-following consists in the possession of a particular kind of "inner" experience? "So it must have been," he writes, "intuition that removed this doubt? [i.e., that I chose one interpretation rather than another.] If intuition is an inner voice, how do I know *how* I am to obey it? And how do I know that it doesn't mislead me? For if it can guide me right, it can also guide me wrong. (("Intuition is an unnecessary shuffle.))" (*PI*, 213). But this is only true if our understanding of the term "intuition" is as a kind of inner voice – a cognitive superego. Intuition is a success, not a mental essence.

Intuitions are indeed paradoxical: They do not have a determinate mental content (voices, tables, images etc.), and yet there is certainly something that it is "like" to have them. We feel differently about – have different "mental orientations" to – logical principles and geographical facts, for example. The possession of such mental orientations is part of what it means to be a human rule-follower and rule-assessor. Given this, as I have argued elsewhere (Russell, 1982), one current in cognitive development may be the developing ability to have the right kinds of mental orientations to classes of judgment – necessary versus contingent, for example. In this sense, then, intuition may not be an "unnecessary shuffle."

References

Baldwin, J. M. (1906). *Thought and things* (Vol. 1). London: Swann & Sonnenshein.

Bennett, J. (1964). *Rationality*. London: Routledge & Kegan Paul.

Blackburn, S. (1984a). *Spreading the word: Groundings in the philosophy of language*. Oxford: Clarendon Press.

Blackburn, S. (1984b). The individual strikes back. *Synthese, 58*, 281-380.

Bower, T. G. R. (1967). The development of object permanence: Some studies of existence constancy. *Perception and Psychophysics, 2*, 411-418.

Brainerd, C. J., & Kingma, J. (1984). Do children have to remember to reason? A fuzzy-trace theory of transitivity development. *Developmental Review, 4*, 311-377.

Bryant, P. E., & Trabasso, T. (1971). Transitive inferences in very young children. *Nature, 260*, 773-778.

Butterworth, G. E., & Hicks, L. (1977). Visual proprioception in infancy: a developmental study. *Perception, 6*, 255-262.

Case, R. (1984). The process of stage transition: A neo-Piagetian view. In R. Sternberg (Ed.), *Mechanisms of cognitive development*. San Francisco: Freeman.

Chomsky, A. N. (1965). *Aspects of the theory of syntax*. Cambridge, MA: M. I. T. Press.

Dennett, D. C. (1984). *Elbow room*. Oxford: Clarendon Press.

Dummett, M. (1978). The social character of meaning. In M. Dummett, *Truth and other enigmas*. London: Duckworth.

Evans, G., & McDowell, J. (1976). Introduction. In G. Evans & J. McDowell (Eds.), *Truth and meaning*. Oxford: Oxford University Press.

Fodor, J. A. (1975). *The language of thought*. New York: Thomas Crowell.

Fodor, J. A. (1978). Tom Swift and his procedural grandmother. *Cognition, 6*, 229-247.

Fodor, J. A. (1980). Methodological solipsism considered as a research strategy in cognitive psychology. *The Behavioural and Brain Sciences, 3*, 63-109.

Goodman, N. (1955). *Fact, fiction and forecast*. London: University of London Press.

Grice, H. P. (1957). Meaning. *Philosophical Review, 66*, 377-388.

Hall, V. C., & Kingsley, R. (1968). Conservation and equilibration theory. *Journal of Genetic Psychology, 113*, 195-212.

Hamlyn, D. W. (1974). Person-perception and our understanding of others. In T. Mischel (Ed.), *Understanding other persons*. Oxford: Blackwell.

Hamlyn, D. W. (1978). *Experience and the growth of understanding*. London: Routledge & Kegan Paul.

Johnson, C. N. (1982). Acquisition of mental verbs and the concept of mind. In S. Kuczaj (Ed.), *Language development* (Vol. 1). Hillsdale, NJ: Erlbaum.

Johnson-Laird, P. N. (1970). The perception and memory of sentences. In J. Lyons (Ed.), *New horizons in linguistics*. Harmondsworth: Penguin.

Johnson-Laird, P. N. (1983). *Mental models*. Cambridge: Cambridge University Press.

Johnson-Laird, P. N. (1984). Deductive reasoning ability. In R. J. Sternberg (Ed.), *Human abilities: An information-processing approach*. San Francisco: Freeman.

Katz, J. J., & Fodor, J. A. (1963). The structure of semantic theory. *Language, 39*, 170-210.

Kenny, A. (1971). The verification principle and the private language argument. In O. R. Jones (Ed.), *The private language argument*. London: Macmillan.

Kripke, S. (1982). *Wittgenstein on rules and private language*. Oxford: Blackwell.

McDowell, T. (1984). Wittgenstein on following a rule. *Synthese, 58*, 325-363.

Montague, R. (1974). *Formal philosophy: Selected papers*. New Haven: Yale University Press.

Nagel, T. (1974). What is it like to be a bat? *Philosophical Review, 83*, 435-451.

Osherson, D. N., & Markman, E. M. (1975). Language and the ability to evaluate contradictions and tautologies. *Cognition, 3*, 213-226.

Perner, J., & Aebi, J. (1985). Feedback-dependent encoding of length series. *British Journal of Developmental Psychology, 3*, 133-141.

Piaget, J. (1929). *The child's conception of the world*. London: Routledge & Kegan Paul.

Piaget, J. (1953). *The origin of intelligence in the child.* London: Routledge & Kegan Paul.

Piaget, J., & Inhelder, B. (1964). *The early growth of logic in the child.* London: Routledge & Kegan Paul.

Robinson, E. J., & Robinson, W. P. (1982). The advancement of children's referential communication skills: The role of metacognitive guidance. *International Journal of Behavioural Development, 5,* 329-355.

Robinson, E. J., Goelman, H., & Olson, D. R. (1983). Children's understanding of the relation between expression (what is said) and intention (what is meant). *British Journal of Developmental Psychology, 1,* 78-87.

Russell, J. (1978). *The acquisition of knowledge.* London: Macmillan.

Russell, J. (1981). Children's memory for the premises in a transitive measurement task assessed by elicited and spontaneous justifications. *Journal of Experimental Child Psychology, 31,* 300-309.

Russell, J. (1982). Propositional attitudes. In M. Beveridge (Ed.), *Children thinking through language.* London: Edward Arnold.

Russell, J. (1984). *Explaining mental life: Some philosophical issues in psychology.* London: Macmillan.

Russell, J. (1987). *Can we say ...? Children's understanding of intensionality. Cognition, 25,* 205-225.

Russell, J. (in press). Cognizance and intelligence. In M. Khalfa (Ed.), *Can intelligence be explained? The Oxford Symposium.* Oxford: Oxford University Press.

Russell, J., & Haworth, H. M. (1986). *Children's understanding of tautology and contradiction.* Manuscript submitted for publication.

Savage-Rumbaugh, E. S., Pate, J. L., Lawson, J., Smith, S. T., & Rosenbaum, S. (1983). Can a chimpanzee make a statement? *Journal of Experimental Psychology: General, 112,* 457-492.

Scruton, R. (1984). Critical notice: "Wittgenstein on rules and private language" by Saul Kripke. *Mind, 43,* 592-603.

Sugarman, S. (1983). Why talk? Comment on Savage-Rumbaugh et al., *Journal of Experimental Psychology: General, 112,* 493-497.

Toulmin, S. (1977). Rules and their relevance for understanding human behaviour. In T. Mischel (Ed.), *The self.* Oxford: Blackwell.

Wason, P., & Johnson-Laird, P. N. (1972). *The psychology of reasoning: Structure and content.* London: Batsford.

Wimmer, H., & Perner, J. (1983). Beliefs about beliefs: Representation and constraining function of wrong beliefs in young children's understanding of deception. *Cognition, 13,* 103-128.

Wright, C. (1980). *Wittgenstein on the foundations of mathematics.* London: Duckworth.

Chapter 4 Wittgenstein, Contextualism, and Developmental Psychology[1]

Roger A. Dixon

The list-like title of this chapter conveys that there are some connections (whether conjunctive or disjunctive) among Wittgenstein, contextualism, and developmental psychology. This signification is indeed what I intend. The title does not suggest, however, that Wittgenstein was in fact either a contextualist or a developmental psychologist, and I do not contrive to make it appear so. Instead, my goal is to identify some parallels, coincidences, and shared meanings among Wittgenstein's later work, that of some contextualists, and the current endeavors and tendencies of some (contemporary) developmental psychologists.

Two purposes are served by identifying these intellectual similarities. First, developmental psychology - a discipline that has, as much as any other in the social sciences, searched for its intellectual roots - may be introduced to a thinker who, although not an ancestor per se, is, at least, an intellectual coeval and anticipator of one of the recent movements in the field. Second, the description of this connection may lend some further legitimacy to the recent movements and, more importantly, open further avenues of historical, conceptual, and empirical scholarship. To foreshadow the ramifications of Wittgenstein's thought for developmental psychology, and to illustrate a given conceptual and methodological connection, two substantive examples are invoked throughout the chapter. These examples of commonality are the contextual nature of remembering and the pragmatic view of language (language-in-use).

The paper is organized into three parts. In the first section, a brief introduction to contextualism and contemporary developmental psychology is given. Some examples of early contextual thinking regarding language and remembering are provided. In the second section some global and specific features of Wittgenstein's "contextualism" are furnished. In the final section, a conclusion, with emphasis on the conceptual overlap between Wittgenstein and some contextual psychologists, is proposed.

[1] The first draft of this chapter was written while the author was at the Max Planck Institute for Human Development and Education, Berlin. The author appreciates the helpful comments of Michael Chapman and Richard Lerner on this draft. Subsequent drafts were written while the author was at his current address: Department of Psychology, University of Victoria, Canada.

Contextualism and Contemporary Developmental Psychology

In recent years, developmental psychology has, as much as any other area of psychology, examined its assumptive roots and participated in metatheoretical parlance. In the early 1970s, Pepper's (1942/1970) book, *World hypotheses*, was discovered, read, and cited frequently by developmental theorists and methodologists. Given the coincidental currency (in the social sciences) of Kuhn's (1970) work on scientific revolutions, world hypotheses were soon identified with paradigms, and several paradigms were located in the developmental landscape. Furthermore, of course, far from coexisting peacefully, their periodic relations were described metaphorically as "paradigm clashes." Specifically, mechanism (represented in behavioral psychology) and organicism (represented in cognitive structuralism, especially Piagetian psychology) were set off against, not only each other, but the "new" world view of contextualism (represented by pragmatic, ecological, and functional psychologies).

A number of deliberations and debates occurred from general metatheoretical, conceptual, and methodological forums (e.g., Bronfenbrenner, 1977; Lerner, Hultsch, & Dixon, 1983; Manicas & Secord, 1983; Reese & Overton, 1970), to forums of such specific subdisciplines as personality and temperament development (e.g., Blank, 1986; Lerner & Lerner, 1986; Sarbin, 1977), intelligence (e.g., Dittmann-Kohli & Baltes, in press; Sternberg, 1983), cognition (e.g., Dixon & Hertzog, in press; Jenkins, 1974; Hultsch & Pentz, 1980) and language (e.g., Bates, 1976). Indeed, contextualism has been allied with one of the major recent movements in developmental psychology, namely, the life-span perspective.

As a confederate of the life-span movement, it has acquired its most general range of application to developmental psychology. Most of the discussants of the specific developmental forums cited above would adhere to the admixture of the life-span perspective and contextual psychology. For example, from the former perspective, psychological development is viewed as a lifelong phenomenon, influenced by multiple historical, cultural, and personological factors (Baltes & Reese, 1984; Baltes, Reese, & Lipsitt, 1980). From this perspective, many psychological constructs are viewed as *multidimensional*, with *multiple directions* of change patterns associated with given dimensions or components. Furthermore, empirical and theoretical emphasis is given to both *interindividual variability*, a conception reflecting the large differences in the life-course change patterns of individuals, and *intraindividual plasticity*, which indicates that, in principle, throughout the life course individual behavioral patterns are modifiable (Baltes et al., 1980; Baltes & Willis, 1979; Lerner, 1984; Willis & Baltes, 1980). Indeed, these four conceptions form the core of this perspective on psychological development. One ramification of this broad orientation is that the study of psychological development across the life span is an inherently interdisciplinary enterprise (Baltes et al., 1980; Featherman, 1983; Riley, 1979). The alliance of contextualism and the life-span perspective has been explored elsewhere (e.g., Dixon, 1986). As shall be seen later, this alliance - and in particular the features alluded to above - implicates Wittgenstein.

Contextualism derives in part from contextual pragmatists such as Charles S. Peirce, William James, John Dewey, George Herbert Mead, and from functional psychologists such as James Rowland Angell, Harvey Carr, and James Mark Baldwin. A number of reviews of its emphases and ramifications have appeared in recent years (e.g., Georgoudi & Rosnow, 1985; Lerner et al., 1983; Rosnow & Georgoudi, 1986; Sarbin, 1977). These reviews indicate that, overall, contextualism emphasizes multi-level change and novelty as well as the functional interrelationship of these constantly changing multiple levels. Insofar as contextualism has been a tangible sponsor of an approach to psychology, that approach (most notably the life-span perspective) has portrayed psychological development as an active, continuing, adaptive lifelong process, related to other "internal" or mental processes, and interacting with biological processes, external activities, and sociohistorical processes. In this way, a contextual psychology is related to (and occasionally identified with) psychologies derived from pragmatism, functionalism, and dialecticism.

As a metatheory, contextualism is relatively amorphous, and, given its own tenets, it is appropriately so. It provides little explicit logic of explanation (or guidelines for understanding) and precious few rules of empirical inquiry. Therefore, in much developmental research it has been adopted selectively. That is, it has been employed to inform (but not determine) the selection of the problem, the nature of the variables, the choice of methods, and the framework of interpretation. Given this situation, it is not surprising that psychological research conducted under the banner of contextualism is multifarious, if not multidimensional. This observation applies as much to research in the domain of human cognition (e.g., Dixon & Hertzog, in press; Sternberg, 1983), as it does to research in other psychological domains. That is, although very often broad in conception (even in a given domain, such as cognition), specific research projects are selective in their contextual focus. For example, research has focused on: (1) intergenerational or advice-giving relationships (such as mentoring), (2) purposive intelligent action, (3) adaptive or practical cognition, (4) the impact of social change (such as maternal employment) on interpersonal and intrafamilial interactions, and (5) age, cultural, historical and other context differences.

Some workaday features of the model are presented in Table 1. Of course, this collection of emphases (organized as anchors of continua) is not designed to distinguish this model completely from other models. Although contextual emphases are on the left-hand side of the table, few actual research projects may be located entirely at this end of each continuum. That is, specific research projects (to their credit) are selective in their contextual focus. Furthermore, because there are two anchors to these continua and because they cover an exhaustive conceptual space, all research could of course be said to cut across them. But contextual research seems either (1) to be generally located in practice at one end of each continuum or (2) to construct a logic of research and interpretation that at least considers these continua. That is, it appears that contextual developmen-

Table 1. Some emphases of contextualism relevant to developmental psychology

Multidirectionality of change	————	Unidirectionality of change
Multidimensionality of constructs	————	Unidimensionality of constructs
Relatively active organism	————	Relatively passive organism
Relatively active environment	————	Relatively passive environment
More emphasis on ecological representativeness	————	Less emphasis on ecological representativeness
More consideration of practical cognition	————	Less consideration of practical cognition
Developmental plasticity	————	Developmental fixedness

tal research is constituted neither by any particular research question posed or variable selected nor by a particular position taken on a set of dimensions. Rather, it is constituted by a pattern (or family) of positions or tendencies – one of a number of possible patterns – that informs the posing of research questions, selections of procedures and materials, and the contemplation and forwarding of interpretations. Two themes of the contextual approach – the concepts of function and temporality – are addressed in more detail in the following subsections.

The Concept of Function

It has been noted often that contextualism is a post-Darwinian world view and that it has sponsored a functional psychology in which the influence of evolutionary thinking is unmistakable (Bawden 1910; Ghiselin, 1969; Morris, 1970; Wiener, 1949). Clearly, the concept of *function* was one way in which Darwin's theory of evolution was incorporated into turn-of-the-century American psychology (Dallenbach, 1915). The biological version of this concept suggested that anatomical structures, shaped as they were by natural selection, functioned so as to further the survival of the organism (Ghiselin, 1969). According to Boring (1957, pp. 551–552) functional psychology is concerned with: "success in living, with the adaptation of the organism to its environment, and with the organism's adaptation of its environment to itself...."

Early contextualists such as James (1890, 1907) applied these principles to psychology in a rather straightforward manner. Consciousness, although having no mechanical function, is useful in securing the survival needs of the organism because of its presumed causal efficaciousness. Put simply: the mind is an organ selected for its utility in benefiting the adaptation of the complex human organism to a complex environment. Consciousness is not, however, simply passively useful; rather, it is actively so, for one of its most salient characteristics is its selectivity (James, 1890). In contemporary terms, James viewed consciousness as a changing, adaptive, selective system of knowledge. Indeed, if cognition is a principal function of mind (James, 1890, 1907), then knowledge is a principal commodity of cognition.

One implication is that dynamic portrayals of adaptive activity were favored by many contextualists. The emphasis was on developing a practical, dynamic psychology (Bawden, 1910; Dewey, 1908), with attention directed not so much to mental contents (see structuralists such as Titchener, 1898, 1899), but to processes and operations, as well as their utilities and what they accomplish, that occur (and merit study) under actual living conditions (Angell, 1907, 1908; Dewey, 1910; Heidbreder, 1933). Several authors (e.g., Dewey, 1896) argued that these processes cannot be reduced atomistically or isolated from other external and internal activities. Dewey's (1896) argument against elementism emphasized the *coordination* of the stimulus and the response. By extension, it is the coordination of the internal and the external, of one mental process with another, of the "cognitive" with the "affective," of the stimulus and the response, of the organism's past and present, of the single activity to the complex of activities, that form the proper units of analysis for the psychologist (Dewey, 1896).

Even from a contemporary perspective such a view is as laudable as it is difficult to operationalize (Brunswik, 1952; Petrinovich, 1979). A concern with the ecology of behavior, as well as implicated issues such as organism-environment relationships, adaptive significance of behavior, ecological validity, and representativeness of situations sampled as part of the measurement of behavior, is evident (e.g., Bronfenbrenner, 1977; Brunswik, 1952; Petrinovich, 1979).

Temporality

Another important feature of contextualism and early functional psychology was the concern with the temporality of mental and behavioral phenomena and, by implication, the relationship to early developmental approaches to psychology. It is well known that the intellectual climate surrounding (and in part inspired by) Darwinism propagated a temporal approach to the study of human social and psychological phenomena (Dixon & Lerner, 1985; Toulmin & Goodfield, 1965; White, 1968). In brief, this temporization of psychological phenomena led to more vigorous study of mental development. Indeed, many of the major contemporary models of human development can be traced to the intellectual climate of evolutionary thinking (Dixon & Lerner, 1984). Many contextualists (e.g., Angell, 1907, 1908; Baldwin, 1895; and Dewey, 1910) were explicit in their linkage of Darwinism and the study of psychological development.

The seemingly evanescent and fleeting nature of mental contents was discussed by some contextualists. Most importantly, the obvious empirical problems this perspective engendered were not left unattended. Angell (1907) argued that, as in the physical realm, in mental life it is the functions that endure. Mental contents may be evanescent but successive contents may have the same meaning, i.e., they may function in the same practical way. As with biological phenomena, the functions may persist even though different structures may, under special conditions, be called upon to perform them. The transitory, state-like nature of mental phenomena is an important aspect of this approach, for it is one way in which affective elements and cognitive processes are interrelated. That is, a given mental event is portrayed as dependent upon such features of the internal conditions as moods and goals as well as on its functional relationship with selected external circumstances (Angell, 1907, 1908). Both senses of temporality – the developmental and the state-like – are of considerable interest to contemporary contextual developmental psychology.

Summary

Although contextualism did not propagate a school of psychology, many of the major contributions have, by now, a certain common-sense ring to them (Heidbreder, 1933). That is, few behavioral scientists would deny the relevance of such concepts as contexts, history, temporality, functional or adaptive activity, and internal and external interactions. Nevertheless, some explicit formulations of contextualism and the functional approach have been proffered in recent years (see, e.g., Beilin, 1983; Brunswik, 1952; Dixon, 1986; Georgoudi & Rosnow, 1985; Lerner et al., 1983; Nilsson, 1984; Petrinovich, 1979). In the following subsections, I describe briefly some features of the contextual approach to, first, memory development and, second, language acquisition and use.

Overview of Contextualism and Cognition

Memory Development

James' (1890, p. 648) view of memory, as shall be seen later, was in some respects, similar to that of Wittgenstein (e.g., Malcolm, 1977a). For both men, no mental activity is intrinsically an act of remembering. Because expressions of memory occur in circumstances and contexts of life (Malcolm, 1977a), without the setting of the thought, it is indistinguishable from "a mere creation of fancy" (James, 1890, p. 658). Since James (1890) and Baldwin (1893), contextualists have argued that memory is a process and not a thing or entity (e.g., Dixon & Hertzog, in press; Hoffman, in press; Hultsch & Pentz, 1980; Jenkins, 1974, 1979). In addition, remembering (and selective forgetting) is functional, that is, it serves as an instrument of survival, adaptation, and effective living (Angell, 1908; Bruce, 1985; James, 1890). That this skill is active and functional implies that it is developed for its usefulness within particular ecologies (Bruce, 1985; Neisser, 1976, 1978).

Two implications, relevant to Wittgenstein's thinking on the matter, should be noted. First, some nomothetic portrayals of memory development are, in principle, falsifiable, especially when methods sensitive to intraindividual differences across both time and contexts are employed (Bruce 1985; Dixon & Hertzog, in press; Hoffman, in press; Neisser, 1978). Second (and implied in the first), temporally sensitive research designs (e.g., longitudinal or, at least, cross-sectional) are encouraged (and have been since Angell), as is the use of ecologically relevant tasks and testing conditions. These recommendations have been echoed and pursued by memory researchers identified with a contextual or functional approach (e.g., Bartlett, 1932; Dixon & Hertzog, in press; Hoffman, in press; Jenkins, 1974; Nilsson, 1979), an ecological approach (e.g., Bruce, 1985; Neisser, 1976, 1978, 1982), an evolutionary or comparative approach (e.g., Bruce, 1985; Wagner & Paris, 1981), a cross-cultural approach (e.g., Cole, Gay, Glick, & Sharp, 1971), and a sociohistorical or dialectical approach (e.g., Smirnov & Zinchenko, 1969). In addition, as shall be seen later, Wittgenstein and associated philosophers and social theorists (e.g., Coulter, 1983, this volume; Malcolm, 1977a) share some of these tendencies.

However, a cautionary note may be in order. The present treatment necessarily glosses over some points of contrast and focuses instead on points of correspondence. Whether an amalgamation of these approaches is appropriate - i.e., whether several fundamental differences among them may be overlooked or underestimated in the production of this common-sense model - is perhaps less important at this juncture than that the major themes of confluence are generally contextual ones. For example, most of the above observers conclude that contextual cognitive research must consider the influence of the changing matrix of motivation, affect, belief systems, and situation in the development of memory skills. In addition, an important focus of such research is the functional significances or adaptive value of (1) the past and (2) present memory skills (Bruce, 1985; Neisser, 1978; Wagner & Paris, 1981).

Language Acquisition and Use

For James (1890) language is a system of signs acquired by an active human organism. As is the case for thinking and remembering, language use has its origin in emotional and practical wants or concerns (Thayer, 1981). In the *Principles* (1890, vol. 2, text and note on pp. 357-358), he suggests that signs (e.g., items of speech that stand for something beyond themselves) are in some instances context dependent. Given the appropriate constitution, sign-using will develop in the child if the proper conditions are present; and furthermore signs are often associated with internal aspects of the human context (e.g., the emotions). While James addresses the problem of language only occasionally in his writings, at least one pertinent generalization may be drawn. Rather unlike some other contextualists, his version of language development (following his version of the development of mind) is primarily oriented to the individual. Social factors and external conditions, such as language community, are necessary but are not emphasized in his view of language development.

Quite the opposite obtains in the case of G. H. Mead. A more interactional, contextual, and relativistic position is adopted by Mead. The self, essentially a social structure, arises out of social experience (Mead, 1962); indeed, the self can not be complete apart from the social context. In commenting upon Mead's rejection of James' individualistic, relatively non-transactional view of the self, Miller notes that:

A self cannot, by its nature, be isolated from or exist apart from a community. Rather, the self is a *phase* of the social process, not an atomic part of a collection of individuals. (Miller, 1975, p. 70)

Mead's (1962) approach to language was complementary to his approach to the self. Briefly, his contribution may be summarized as follows. First, language is a part of social behavior (p. 13) in that it is a cooperative, interactive affair (e. g., p. 74). Second, language is of course symbolic, and as such may be seen as originating in social processes; language symbols (the functioning of which is identified with the mind) is not so much an individual phenomenon as it is a social phenomenon (p. 133). Third, language both reflects the social context in terms of its origin and its extant complexity and (in turn) contributes to the complexity of the society; language development is a continuous interaction of an active organism and a (largely social) environment in which both are changed in the process. Finally, language has a functional, instrumental value; it is in part an implement or tool for organizing experience, for continual adjustment and adaptation (Miller, 1975). Mead writes:

We want to approach language not from the standpoint of inner meanings to be expressed, but in its larger context of cooperation in the group taking place by means of signals and gestures. Meaning appears within that process. (Mead, 1962, p. 6)

As is the case for contextual thinking in general, Mead derived from Darwin *(The expression of emotions in man and animals)* (as well as from Wundt) the concept of gesture, which is basic to his view of the genesis and use of language. From Darwin, Mead took the notion of an evolutionary, biological foundation of the gesture, but criticized (as did Dewey) Darwin's subjective (i. e., gestures as outward expressions of inner psychological states) orientation (Thayer, 1981). As did Wundt, Mead proposed that the gesture reflects an intent to communicate meaning. For Darwin the gesture was primarily an individualistic self-expression; for Wundt the social context of the gesture was at least implicitly recognized; but Mead attempted to trace the "whole development of genuine communication in language from gestures" (Blau, 1952, p. 263). Social action involves gestures (Mead, 1962; Miller, 1973).

Scheffler (1974) notes that all of this results in a rather new - certainly more social - orientation to the mind-body problem. It is the social world - the context - that is given, and from interaction with it (via language) the individual mind or self is generated. Even when the social context or gesture situation is internalized it remains social. Language is the "way of arousing in the individual by his own gestures the attitudes and roles of others implicated in a common social activity" (Morris, 1962, p. xvi). Again, the organism is not at the mercy of the environment; both Dewey (1896) and Mead had already established this.

Through symbolism (or conscious gesture) the active organism could influence the environment, as well as the reverse.

Miller (1973) notes that many of the conclusions reached by Mead were also being suggested, relatively independently, and later, by Wittgenstein. While a more complete consideration of Wittgenstein's view of language use will be taken up below, it may be useful here to at least note these points of convergence, as described by Miller. To begin, Wittgenstein's early picture theory of language was rejected by Mead (and the later Wittgenstein). In addition, both the later Wittgenstein and Mead believed that:

> there can be no private language, that... the life of a word is in its use, that language is a social affair involving communication, that language is the vehicle of thought, that thoughts and ideas are not subjective... that the function of language is not simply to describe or name objects, that universality does not exist in properties particulars have in common or in identities existing in different individuals, and that the meaning of mind must be approached through behavior. (Miller, 1973, p. 67)

Other contextual views of language have been offered. There is, for example, the argument from C. S. Peirce that the human *is* a language, a "symbol, a sign, a process of knowing and communicating" (Fairbanks, 1976, p. 23). That is, the human is the practical manifestation of his/her language use. On the other hand, there is the "dialectical" approach to language of some Soviet scientists. In Luria's (1971) and Vygotsky's (1962, 1978) cultural-historical approach to psychology the roots of higher psychological functions may be found, in part, in child-adult communication and in the use of language as a tool of successful experience.

As with the contextualists, the Soviet psychologists considered practical activity as central in psychological development (Leontiev & Luria, 1968). Primary among the instruments or tools of practical activity is language or speech. Practical intelligence (or adaptive behavior) and speech development (or sign-using activity) are interwoven in this approach. Vygotsky (1962, 1978) found that children use speech, just as they might their eyes and hands, to solve difficult practical tasks. Thus, he concluded that there is a dialectical unity to the two systems (speech or language and practical activity). In the human adult this unity is the basis of the higher psychological processes. Vygotsky writes that, with regard to the child,

> the most significant moment in the course of intellectual development, which gives birth to the purely human forms of practical and abstract intelligence, occurs when speech and practical activity, two previously independent lines of development, converge. (Vygotsky, 1978, p. 24)

The first step in the child's development of consciousness is in communication, probably of a vocal nature. The human consciousness is further developed, not so much through material production, but through interpersonal contacts and continual confrontations with the prevailing culture and its artifacts (Leontiev & Luria, 1968). Thought and language reflect these relationships in such a way as to be the key to the nature of human consciousness (Vygotsky, 1929).

Thus, language is of particular interest to contextualists such as Vygotsky. It is a means of social interaction, of overall psychological development in a changing sociohistorical context, and of mastering other psychological processes. Vygotsky argues:

> The specific human capacity for language enables children to provide for auxiliary tools in the solution of difficult tasks, to overcome impulsive action, to plan a solution to a problem prior to its execution, and to master their own behavior. Signs and words serve children first and foremost as a means of social contact with other people. The cognitive and communicative functions of language then become the basis of a new and superior form of activity in children, distinguishing them from animals. (Vygotsky, 1978, pp. 28-29)

To these cultural-historical psychologists, language is a system of significance. Words are the bearers of significances, and are inseparable from them. Words may be conceived as reflecting significances, but must not be portrayed as pointing to the significances. Words are the fundamental units of consciousness (Luria, 1976), if not a veritable "microcosm of human consciousness" (Vygotsky, 1962, p. 153). The significance of a word is determined in large measure by the individual's perception of the immediate situation, of the context of its use (Luria, 1971). For both Vygotsky and Karl Bühler, the Austrian psychologist of the same period (who, as will be shown below, had an influence on the later Wittgenstein; see Innis, 1982) words serve an instrumental function. In written form a word derives its significance from the concentric contexts of phrase, sentence, paragraph, book, works of the author, and so forth (Vygotsky, 1962). As Hardy (1978) notes, this contextual portrayal of meaning is closely related to the work of the Wurtzburg School of Psychology. Of course, in its theme it is also related to the contextual pragmatic notion of meaning described above. For example, as Leontiev and Luria (1968, p. 347) describe the method: "To study psychological significance means to study the function of the word and its use in social intercourse." It is through social intercourse that one may interact with one's environment (recall Mead). Hence, the mastering of significances (of language in general) is necessary for individual psychological development and for successful individual social development. In addition, Vygotsky suggests that the writer's (or speaker's) purposes are also an integral part of the communicative network. To understand another's speech, it is

> not sufficient to understand his words - we must understand his thought. But even that is not enough - we must also know its motivation. (Vygotsky, 1962, p. 151)

As is the case with the contextual pragmatists, on the one hand, and the later Wittgenstein, on the other, Vygotsky was opposed to a full atomistic account of language. Rather, the task of the scientific investigation of language is to elucidate the changing structure and function of the cultural forms of language behavior. In sum, Vygotsky is concerned with the practical basis of language use; the development of practical activity is intimately interwoven with the development of language. In calling his method "instrumental" Vygotsky (1929, p. 430) describes its aim as the "discovery of the 'instrumental function' of cultural signs in behavior and its develoment." Symbolic activity is a product of the child's sociocultural development and is not a spontaneous discovery occurring between (about) ages one and two. Whereas the historically changing sociocultural environment plays a significant role in language development for Vygotsky, it plays more a facilitative, passive role in the contemporary theories of Chomsky and Piaget. As did Compayré, K. Bühler, Stern, and Köffka, Vygotsky (1929) recognized the similarity between the functional importance of a word as a sign and the functional importance of (for example) a stick as a tool.

As Innis (1982) points out, Bühler shared a number of contextual convictions with Mead, Vygotsky, and Wittgenstein. For example, both Bühler and Mead believed that there is an important semantic factor in the social life of human beings. And both Bühler and Wittgenstein attempted to develop a language theory on the basis of observable (especially social) data. Indeed, it is the concrete speech event that is the basic starting point for language analysis (Innis, 1982). Many of these positions characterize contemporary research in pragmatics (e.g., Bates, 1976) and functional analysis of language use or meaning (e.g., Whitehurst, Kedesdy, & White, 1982). In the following section, I explore some of the parallel thoughts of Wittgenstein.

Contextualism and Wittgenstein

Examples of Wittgenstein's contextual "thoughts" are both legion and ephemeral. Because he was neither a "contextualist" nor a developmental psychologist, and because he often wrote only in brief and disjunctive paragraph form, one must connect isolated statements or rely on the notes of Wittgenstein students and scholars. First, two points of divergence with contextualist thinking should be noted. Janik and Toulmin (1973) pointed out that (especially) the early Wittgensteinian approach was ahistorical, and even in the later approach, the implicit historicism was not pursued. Thus, while Wittgenstein was approaching a child psychology he was not yet entirely possessed of a genuinely developmental approach. This partial ahistoricism, of course, is contrary to both the pragmatic and the Vygotskian contextualism. Nevertheless, Bartley (1973, pp. 170–171) suggests that Wittgenstein accounts for differences (at one point in time) among kinds of sentences as at least in part a function of development or change in language-games and grammatical categories and concepts. Second, while evincing a profound interest in everyday language activity, in the concrete moment of utterances and meanings, Wittgenstein believed that philosophy itself has no impact on the real world.

> Philosophy may in no way interfere with the actual use of language; it can in the end only describe it.... It leaves everything as it is. (*PI*, 124)

Of course, some contextualists (recall Mead and Vygotsky) espouse quite a different view on the practical value of philosophy and science. In each case, the tendency of Wittgenstein's writing is at variance with the pattern of contextual emphases seen in Table 1. However, there are a number of similarities and it is to these that I now turn.

Wittgenstein's shift from the *Tractatus* to the *Philosophical investigations*, whether continuous or discontinuous, resulted in a philosophy of psychology that was considerably more contextualized. Some observers, in fact, have even explored the relationship of Wittgenstein's thought to dialecticism (e.g., Levi, 1964; Rubinstein, 1981). The first step to linguistic examination is to get a clear view of the context, situation, and language-game in which the problem occurs (Levi, 1964). Rubinstein (1981), as well, refers to Wittgenstein's many allusions to the impact of circumstances - the inseparability, or "dialectical" unity - on behavior. Others have examined critically whether this contextualized philosophy of psychology may sponsor empirical research (e.g., Rorty, 1977; Williams, 1984; see chapters 8-12 in this volume).

Wittgenstein's own comments - those that led observers to infer contextualism - may be found in numerous places. A few selected examples will suffice. Wittgenstein refers often to the situational factors that influence emotions (*PI*, 174), expectations and hopes (*PI*, 581, 585), as well as language (*Z*, 173), and memory (*RPP2*, 501). He writes, for example:

An expectation is embedded in a situation, from which it arises. (*PI*, 581)

And, with regard to language:

Only in the stream of thought and life do words have meaning. (*Z*, 173)

And, regarding memory:

But now you remember certain sensations and images and thoughts as you read, and they are such as were not irrelevant for the enjoyment, for the impression. - But I should like to say that they get their correctness only from their surroundings. (*RPP2*, 501)

The contexts invoked in understanding include time:

If you say "As I heard this word, it meant ... for me" you refer *to a point of time* and *to an employment of the word*. - The remarkable thing about it is of course the relation to the point of time. (*RPP1*, 175)

In brief, the context relevance of multiple phenomena is emphasized in Wittgenstein's later notes. In two successive paragraphs he notes the following:

Don't put the phenomenon in the wrong drawer. *There* it looks ghostly, intangible, uncanny. Looking at it rightly, we no more think of its intangibility than we do of time's intangibility when we hear: "It's time for dinner." (*RPP1*, 380)

And:

When we speak of the enigmatic smile of the Mona Lisa, that may well mean that we ask ourselves: In what situation, in what story, might one smile like that? (*RPP1*, 381)

The notion that psychological processes are "internal" is much berated, for example:

One of the most dangerous of ideas for a philosopher is, oddly enough, that we think with our heads or in our heads. (*Z*, 605)

This is followed by:

The idea of thinking as a process in the head, in a completely enclosed space, gives him something occult. (*Z*, 606)

Although his ahistoricism is problematic (Janik & Toulmin, 1973), some of Wittgenstein's views on psychological processes parallel those of the contextualists. For example, he often portrays processes in dynamic terms:

Attention is dynamic, not static – one would like to say. I begin by comparing attention to gazing but that is not what I call attention; and now I want to say that I find it is *impossible* that one should attend statically. (*Z*, 673)

Wittgenstein's intellectual relationship to the pragmatists, Karl Bühler and Frank Ramsey (who was a student of C.S. Peirce) has been noted occasionally (e.g., Ayer, 1985; Bartley, 1985; Rubenstein, 1981; Toulmin, 1972). Wittgenstein himself remarked:

So I am trying to say something that sounds like pragmatism. (*OC*, 422)

At one point, although certainly not always, he referred to philosphy in a way that may be seen as practical problem solving:

A philosophical problem has the form: "I don't know my way about." (*PI*, 123)

And, more than once, as we shall see later, he spoke of the pragmatic rules that govern language behavior and the tool-like function of some psychological processes (e.g., *RPP2*, 224). Even the language learning of children is cast in a pragmatic, functional light:

Children do not learn that books exist, that armchairs exist, etc. etc., – they learn to fetch books, sit in armchairs, etc. etc. (*OC*, 476)

Toulmin (1969, 1972; Janik & Toulmin, 1973) has elucidated the "contextualism" of Wittgenstein. The contexts of (e.g.) natural language behavior are many. There is the global context of the natural history of man (*PI*, 415), but there are other contexts as well.

For, if Wittgenstein's final philosophical position is at all sound, this means that the very language through which our enculturation is achieved is itself intelligible only to men who share enough of our own modes of life. Any particular "natural language" – he [Wittgenstein] argues – comprises a variety of "language games", whose significance is derived from the "forms of life" of the communities in which the language in question is learned, spoken, and put to practical use. (Toulmin, 1972, pp. 67–68)

Forms of life – shared forms of life – provide an important context of communication, a context that is determined by a confluence of social, cultural, historical, and psychological factors. In this way, Wittgenstein, a philosopher who was not a contextualist and not a developmental psychologist, sketched a psychology that appears to share the contextual form of life with a number of pragmatists, functional psychologists, and even dialectical psychologists. In the next subsection, some specific contextual features of his views on memory are outlined.

Final Comments on Wittgenstein and Memory

Throughout Wittgenstein's writings and notes, one may find penetrating questions posed regarding memory. For example:

Forgetting the meaning of a word – and then remembering it again. What sort of *processes* go on here? (*Z,* 668; italics added)

Italics are added to this quotation, which follows a series of paragraphs on remembering, to illustrate a contextual point. The term processes is, of course, plural. Very much like modern functionalists, Wittgenstein implies simultaneously a multidimensional and a processual view of memory: Consider also:

Is memory an experience? *What* do I experience? (*RPP1,* 119)

This is a topic to which he addresses considerable attention. The experience of memory is largely a contextual one. As Malcolm argues:

The picture of remembering, or meaning, or thinking, as being a "mental event," an "inner occurrence," "something that happens in the mind," has a hypnotic effect. It prevents a philosopher from observing the situations and activities, the contexts, to which the words "remember," "mean," "think," etc., belong and which give them all the significance they have. (Malcolm, 1977 b, p. 142)

There are numerous other ways in which Wittgenstein's view of memory harks to that of the contextualists (described earlier). For example, the diversity of remembering tasks is emphasized; that is, remembering is viewed as a word applied to many different remembering tasks in the everyday world.

This implies, as contemporary contextual memory researchers have suggested, that (1) there is good reason for skepticism regarding theories of *the* nature of remembering, and (2) empirical studies should differentiate among the multiple varieties of remembering tasks; that is, inferences regarding overall remembering skill may not be supported by data pertaining to a simple task, especially when that task is analyzed with respect to other tasks.

In addition, Wittgenstein (and commentators such as Malcolm, 1977 a, 1977 b) regarded remembering performance as being influenced by numerous "internal" and "external" circumstances (e.g., anxiety, concentration, enculturation). Many acts of remembering, expressions of remembering, gestures and other pieces at behavior are called memory because of the human contexts in which they appear. As are skills and behaviors that recur in non-remembering contexts, these acts are subject to a broad range of influences, and are dependent on settings and circumstances.

Finally, Wittgenstein raises several issues that are actively pursued in contemporary memory research. For example, as Malcolm (1977 a) suggests, some forms of memory are knowledge. Some recent efforts in metamemory research undertaken from a contextual perspective (Dixon & Hertzog, in press; Dixon & Hultsch, 1983) pursue this notion. Even such related topics as tip-of-the-tongue phenomena (when one knows that one knows a piece of information but cannot quite retrieve it) are mentioned by Wittgenstein (e.g., *RPP1,* 254). The process of trying to remember is elaborated from a Wittgensteinian point of view by Malcolm (1977b). Such issues as trying to remember, the use of memory mnemonics, and the accuracy of memory become important (especially) when memory is seen as practical or functional. This, indeed, is one premise of the Wittgensteinian analysis of memory.

Final Comments on Wittgenstein and Language

Wittgenstein's views on language have been well-documented. The purpose of this subsection is simply to point out some of the contextual and developmental features of his later perspective (see also Chapman & Dixon, this volume). Overall, the association of Wittgenstein and (say) pragmatism on this issue has been suggested in the positive (by Toulmin, 1969) and in the negative (by Chomsky, 1966). That is, Toulmin (1969, 1972) argued that Wittgenstein's approach was pragmatic, he

> focused his attention ... on *language-as-behaviour* – on the pragmatic rules that govern the uses of different expressions; on the "language-games" within which those rules are operative; and on the broader "forms of life" which ultimately give those language-games their significance. (Toulmin, 1969, p. 67)

What children learn regarding language is its functional use in specific contexts (see also Chapman & Dixon, this volume). Indeed, as Janik and Toulmin suggest:

> The expressions in our language acquire their specific *meaning* from the procedures by which we give them definite *uses* in our practical dealings with one another and with the world, not from their inner articulation alone, nor from any essentially "pictorial" character in the utterances themselves. (Janik & Toulmin, 1973, p. 223)

Whether this practical view of language is *instrumental* or not has been the subject of some debate (see, especially, Harris, 1980), and I will not reiterate here.

In sum, as read from the *Tractatus* the primary function of language was to picture the world. In the *Investigations* meaning takes on a new dimension: The meaning of a word is here relative to the context in which it is used and the purposes of the user. The meaning of language is established in the form of utterances being put to use in the world. It is through the use of utterances that language acquires meaning, not through the representativeness of the utterances. Language is a projection of the mind not a picture of reality; in this way it acts to create reality not represent it. In the *Investigations* Wittgenstein argues that language is a concrete, social activity,

> used not only as a device for constructing and talking about the world but also as a means of communication within the world. Language cannot be divorced from the wider human context in which it is located. (Phillips, 1977, p. 80)

Language is a product of activity in the world, a producer of new forms of human activity, and a creator of meaning (Phillips, 1977). Rather than searching for essences, the philosopher should examine concrete cases of language, the language of everyday should be used in the investigation (*PI,* 120). Phillips (1977, p. 89) summarizes these points thus: "the everyday language-game has an epistemological and ontological primacy." Philosophy should undertake a concern not just for arcane points of logic, but for the important questions of everyday life (Malcolm 1966).

Concluding Remarks

The purpose of this chapter was not to derive a theory of memory or language development from the works of the assorted theorists mentioned. Nor was it to derive an over-arching contextualism or even contextual concept of development. On the other hand, the purpose was not merely to note connections among the contextualists (read: pragmatists, functional psychologists), dialecticians, and Wittgenstein. Rather, my purpose was a preparatory one. First, it was to describe how several traditions of philosophy and psychology have relatively independently proposed some notably similar views regarding (1) the nature of psychological inquiry, (2) the functioning of remembering, and (3) the functioning of language. Second, it was to intimate how the common view and implied empirical approaches may yield useful directions for future theory and research. Developmental psychologists, especially, may have a new "colleague" in the thought of Ludwig Wittgenstein. His work is rich and multifarious, but it is not easy. As von Wright (1982, p. 31) put it: "Because of the depth and originality of his thinking, it is very difficult to understand Wittgenstein's ideas and even more difficult to incorporate them into one's own thinking." However, to paraphrase von Wright, his style, personality, and sheer intellectual power make him a valued ally in testing the range and possibilities of a contextual developmental psychology.

References

Angell, J. R. (1907). The province of functional psychology. *Psychological Review, 14,* 61-91.

Angell, J. R. (1908). *Psychology: An introduction to the structure and function of human consciousness* (4th ed.). New York: Henry Holt.

Ayer, A. J. (1985). *Wittgenstein.* London: Weidenfeld & Nicolson.

Baldwin, J. M. (1893). *Elements of psychology.* New York: Henry Holt.

Baldwin, J. M. (1895). *Mental development in the child and the race.* New York: Macmillan.

Baltes, P. B., Reese, H. W., & Lipsitt, L. P. (1980). Life-span developmental psychology. *Annual Review of Psychology, 31,* 65-110.

Baltes, P. B., & Reese, H. W. (1984). The life-span perspective in developmental psychology. In M. H. Bornstein & M. E. Lamb (Eds.), *Developmental psychology: An advanced textbook.* Hillsdale, NJ: Erlbaum.

Baltes, P. B., & Willis, S. L. (1979). The critical importance of appropriate methodology in the study of aging: The sample case of psychometric intelligence. In F. Hoffmeister & C. Muller (Eds.), *Brain function in old age.* Heidelberg: Springer-Verlag.

Bartlett, F. C. (1932). *Remembering: A study in experimental and social psychology.* Cambridge: Cambridge University Press.

Bartley, W. W., III. (1973). *Wittgenstein.* Philadelphia: Lippincott.

Bartley, W. W., III, (1985). *Wittgenstein* (2nd ed.). La Salle, IL: Open Court.

Bates, E. (1976). *Language and context: The acquisition of pragmatics.* New York: Academic Press.

Bawden, H. H. (1910). *The principles of pragmatism: A philosophical interpretation of experience.* Boston: Houghton-Mifflin.

Beilin, H. (1983). The new functionalism and Piaget's program. In E. K. Scholnick (Ed.), *New trends in conceptual representation.* Hillsdale, NJ: Erlbaum.

Blank, T. O. (1986). Contextual and relational perspectives on adult psychology. In R. L. Rosnow & M. Georgoudi (Eds.), *Contextualism and understanding in behavioral science.* New York: Praeger.

Blau, J. L. (1952). *Men and movements in American philosophy.* New York: Prentice-Hall.

Bronfenbrenner, U. (1977). Toward an experimental ecology of human development. *American Psychologist, 32,* 513–531.

Bruce, D. (1985). The how and why of ecological memory. *Journal of Experimental Psychology: General, 114,* 78–90.

Brunswik, E. (1952). *The conceptual framework of psychology.* Chicago: University of Chicago Press.

Chomsky, N. A. (1966). *Cartesian linguistics.* New York: Harper & Row.

Cole, M., Gay, J., Glick, J. A., & Sharp, D. W. (1971). *The cultural context of learning and thinking.* New York: Basic Books.

Coulter, J. (1983). *Rethinking cognitive theory.* London: Macmillan.

Dallenbach, K. M. (1915). The history and derivation of the word 'function' as a systematic term in psychology. *American Journal of Psychology, 26,* 473–484.

Dewey, J. (1896). The reflex arc concept in psychology. *Psychological Review, 3,* 357–370.

Dewey, J. (1908). What does pragmatism mean by practical? *The Journal of Philosophy, Psychology and Scientific Methods, 5,* 85–99.

Dewey, J. (1910). *The influence of Darwin on philosophy and other essays in contemporary thought.* New York: Henry Holt.

Dittmann-Kohli, F., & Baltes, P. B. (1985). Toward a neofunctionalist conception of adult intellectual development: Wisdom as a prototypical case of intellectual growth. In C. Alexander & E. Langer (Eds.), *Beyond formal operations: Alternative endpoints to human development.* New York: Cambridge University Press.

Dixon, R. A. (1986). Contextualism and life-span cognitive development. In R. L. Rosnow & M. Georgoudi (Eds.), *Contextualism and understanding in behavioral research.* New York: Praeger.

Dixon, R. A., & Hertzog, C. (in press). A functional approach to memory and metamemory development in adulthood. In F. E. Weinert & M. Perlmutter (Eds.), *Memory development across the life span: Universal changes and individual differences.* Hillsdale, NJ: Erlbaum.

Dixon, R. A., & Hultsch, D. F. (1983). Structure and development of metamemory in adulthood. *Journal of Gerontology, 38,* 682–688.

Dixon, R. A., & Lerner, R. M. (1984). A history of systems in developmental psychology. In M. H. Bornstein & M. E. Lamb (Eds.), *Developmental psychology: An advanced textbook.* Hillsdale, NJ: Erlbaum.

Dixon, R. A., & Lerner, R. M. (1985). Darwinism and the emergence of developmental psychology. In G. Eckhardt, W. G. Bringmann & L. Sprung (Eds.), *Contributions to a history of developmental psychology.* Berlin: Mouton.

Fairbanks, M. J. (1976). Peirce on man as a language: A textual interpretation. *Transactions of the Charles S. Peirce Society, 12,* 18–32.

Featherman, D. L. (1983). The life-span perspective in social science research. In P. B. Baltes & O. G. Brim, Jr. (Eds.), *Life-span development and behavior* (Vol. 5). New York: Academic Press.

Georgoudi, M., & Rosnow, R. L. (1985). The emergence of contextualism. *Journal of Communication, 35,* 76–88.

Ghiselin, M. (1969). *The triumph of the Darwinian method.* Berkeley: University of California Press.

Hardy, W. G. (1978). *Language, thought, and experience.* Baltimore: University Park Press.

Harris, R. (1980). *The language-makers.* Ithaca, NY: Cornell University Press.

Heidbreder, E. (1933). *Seven psychologies.* Englewood Cliffs, NJ: Prentice-Hall.

Hoffmann, R. R. (in press). Context and contextualism in the psychology of learning. *Cahiers de Psychologie Cognitive.*

Hultsch, D. F., & Pentz, C. A. (1980). Encoding, storage, and retrieval in adult memory: The role of model assumptions. In L. W. Poon, J. L. Fozard, L. S. Cermak, D. Arenberg & L. W. Thompson (Eds.), *New directions in memory and aging: Proceedings of the George A. Talland Memorial Conference.* Hillsdale, NJ: Erlbaum.

Innis, R. E. (1982). *Karl Bühler: Semantic foundations of language theory.* New York: Plenum.

James, W. (1890). *The principles of psychology* (2 vols.). New York: Dover.

James, W. (1907). The function of cognition. In W. James (Ed.), *Pragmatism and four essays from The Meaning of Truth.* New York: New American Library.

Janik, A., & Toulmin, S. (1973). *Wittgenstein's Vienna.* New York: Simon and Schuster.

Jenkins, J. J. (1974). Remember that old theory of memory? Well, forget it! *American Psychologist, 29,* 785–795.

Jenkins, J. J. (1979). Four points to remember: A tetrahedral model of memory experiments. In L. S. Cermak & F. I. M. Craik (Eds.), *Levels of processing in human memory.* Hillsdale, NJ: Erlbaum.

Kuhn, T. S. (1970). *The structure of scientific revolutions* (2nd ed.) Chicago: University of Chicago Press.

Leontiev, A. N., & Luria, A. R. (1968). The psychological ideas of L. S. Vygotsky. In B. B. Wolman (Ed.), *Historical roots of contemporary psychology.* New York: Harper & Row.

Lerner, R. M. (1984). *On the nature of human plasticity.* Cambridge: Cambridge University Press.

Lerner, R. M., Hultsch, D. F., & Dixon, R. A. (1983). Contextualism and the character of developmental psychology in the 1970s. *Annals of the New York Academy of Sciences, 412,* 101–128.

Lerner, R. M., & Lerner, J. V. (1986). Contextualism and the study of child effects in personality and social development. In R. L. Rosnow & Georgoundi (Eds.), *Contextualism and understanding in behavioral research.* New York: Praeger.

Levi, A. W. (1964). Wittgenstein as dialectician. *The Journal of Philosophy, 61,* 127–139.

Luria, A. R. (1971). Toward the problem of the historical nature of psychological processes, *International Journal of Psychology, 6,* 259–272.

Luria, A. R. (1976). *Cognitive development: Its cultural and social foundations.* Cambridge: Harvard University Press.

Malcolm, N. (1966). *Ludwig Wittgenstein: A memoir.* London: Oxford University Press.

Malcolm, N. (1977 a). *Memory and mind.* Ithaca, NY: Cornell University Press.

Malcolm, N. (1977 b). *Thought and knowledge.* Ithaca, NY: Cornell University Press.

Manicas, P. T., & Secord, P. F. (1983). Implications for psychology of the new philosophy of science. *American Psychologist, 38,* 399–413.

Mead, G. H. (1962). *Mind, self, and society.* Chicago: University of Chicago Press.

Miller, D. L. (1973). *George Herbert Mead: Self, language, and the world.* Austin: University of Texas Press.

Miller, D. L. (1975). Josiah Royce and George H. Mead on the nature of the self. *Transactions of the Charles S. Peirce Society, 11,* 67–89.

Morris, C. W. (1962). Introduction: George Herbert Mead as social psychologist and social philosopher. In G. H. Mead (Ed.), *Mind, self, and society.* Chicago: University of Chicago Press.

Morris, C. (1970). *The pragmatic movement in American philosophy.* New York: George Braziller.

Neisser, U. (1976). *Cognition and reality.* San Francisco: Freeman.

Neisser, U. (1978). Memory: what are the important questions? In M. M. Gruneberg, P. Morris, & R. H. Sykes (Eds.), *Practical aspects of memory.* New York: Academic Press.

Neisser, U. (Ed.) (1982). *Memory observed: Remembering in natural contexts.* San Francisco: Freeman.

Nilsson, L.-G. (1979). Functions of memory. In L.-G. Nilsson (Ed.), *Perspectives on memory research: Essays in honor of Uppsala's 500th anniversary.* Hillsdale, N.J.: Erlbaum.

Nilsson, L.-G. (1984). New functionalism in memory research. In K. M. J. Lagerspetz & P. Niemi (Eds.), *Psychology in the 1990's.* Amsterdam: North-Holland.

Pepper, S.C. (1970). *World hypotheses.* Berkeley: University of California Press. (Originally published, 1942).

Petrinovich, L. (1979). Probabilistic functionalism: A conception of research method. *American Psychologist, 34,* 373-390.

Phillips, D. L. (1977). *Wittgenstein and scientific knowledge.* London: Macmillan.

Reese, H. W., & Overton, W. F. (1970). Models of development and theories of development. In L. R. Goulet & P. B. Baltes (Eds.), *Life-span developmental psychology: Research and theory.* New York: Academic Press.

Riley, M. W. (Ed.). (1979). *Aging from birth to death: Interdisciplinary perspective.* Boulder, CO: Westview.

Rorty, R. (1977). Wittgensteinian philosophy and empirical psychology. *Philosophical Studies, 31,* 151-172.

Rosnow, R. L., & Georgoudi, M. (Eds.). (1986). *Contextualism and understanding in behavioral science.* New York: Praeger.

Rubinstein, D. (1981). *Marx and Wittgenstein: Social praxis and social explanation.* London: Routledge & Kegan Paul.

Sarbin, T. R. (1977). Contextualism: A world view for modern psychology. In J. K. Cole & A. W. Landfield (Eds.), *Nebraska Symposium on Motivation 1976* (Vol. 24). Lincoln: University of Nebraska Press.

Scheffler, I. (1974). *Four pragmatists.* New York: Humanities Press.

Smirnov, A. A., & Zinchenko, P. I. (1969). Problems in the psychology of memory. In M. Cole & I. Maltzman (Eds.), *A handbook of contemporary Soviet psychology.* New York: Basic Books.

Sternberg, R. J. (1983). Components of human intelligence. *Cognition,* 15, 1-48.

Thayer, H.S. (1981). *Meaning and action: A critical history of pragmatism.* Indianapolis: Hackett.

Titchener, E. B. (1898). The postulates of a structural psychology. *Philosophical Review, 7,* 449-465.

Titchener, E. B. (1899). Discussion: Structural and functional psychology. *Philosophical Review, 8,* 290-299.

Toulmin, S. (1969). Ludwig Wittgenstein. *Encounter, 32,* 59-71.

Toulmin, S. (1972). *Human understanding.* Princeton: Princeton University Press.

Toulmin, S., & Goodfield, J. (1965). *The discovery of time.* Chicago: University of Chicago Press.

von Wright, G. H. (1982). A biographical sketch. In G. H. von Wright, *Wittgenstein.* Oxford: Blackwell.

Vygotsky, L. S. (1929). The problem of the cultural development of the child. *Journal of Genetic Psychology, 36,* 415-434.

Vygotsky, L. S. (1962). *Thought and language.* Cambridge: The M. I. T. Press.

Vygotsky, L. S. (1978). *Mind in society.* Cambridge: Harvard University Press.

Wagner, D. A., & Paris, S. G. (1981). Problems and prospects in comparative studies of memory. *Human Development, 24,* 412-424.

White, S. H. (1968). The learning-maturation controversy: Hall to Hull. *Merrill-Palmer Quarterly, 14,* 187-196.

Whitehurst, G. J., Kedesdy, J., & White, T. G. (1982). A functional analysis of meaning. In S. A. Kuczaj, III (Ed.), *Language development, Vol. 1: Syntax and semantics.* Hillsdale, NJ: Erlbaum.

Wiener, P. P. (1949). *Evolution and the founders of pragmatism.* Cambridge: Harvard University Press.

Williams, M. (1984). Wittgenstein's rejection of scientific psychology. *Noûs, 18,* 90.

Willis, S. L., & Baltes, P. B. (1980). Intelligence in adulthood and aging: Contemporary issues. In L. W. Poon (Ed.), *Aging in the 1980s: Psychological issues.* Washington, DC: American Psychological Association.

Chapter 5 On Certainty and Universality in Human Development: Developmental Psychology Between Apriorism and Empiricism[1]

Jochen Brandtstädter

Searching for certainties, developmental psychology seems to have come up with uncertainties. Earlier generations of researchers still had comparatively firm beliefs about the course of human development in different phases of the life span. Seemingly universal milestones and general principles of physical and mental development were postulated, stage and phase models claiming a high degree of generality and universality were designed. The existence of universal developmental phenomena and laws was not questioned and the establishment of a strictly nomothetical developmental psychology modeled on natural science appeared to be a realistic goal worth pursuing.

Looking at developmental psychology today, not much of this nomothetical optimism seems to have survived. Patterns of development have proven highly context-specific (i.e., specific for social, cultural, and historical contexts; see, e.g., Baltes, Reese & Lipsitt, 1980). Longitudinal studies have evidenced considerable intra- and interindividual variability of developmental processes. Correspondingly, long-term predictions of development show a high degree of prognostic vagueness (see, e.g., Kohlberg, LaCrosse & Ricks, 1972; Eichorn et al., 1981). This state of findings - or rather this lack of findings that can be generalized and replicated - has inspired theoretical positions that emphasize context-specifity and plasticity of development in contrast to traditional notions of stability, invariance, and ordered change (cf. Baltes & Reese, 1984; Lerner, 1984). Development across the life span is increasingly understood as a process highly dependent on the more or less planned or accidental arrangement of life circumstances on socio-cultural and individual levels (cf. Bandura, 1982a, Brandtstädter, in press). Occasionally, even principal doubts concerning the possibility of universal laws of development are raised, claiming that developmental psychology should be conceived of as a discipline in need of permanent revision (e.g., Gergen, 1980).

Probably not every researcher - and I include myself - will subscribe to the idea that developmental psychology can or even should give only ephemeral commentaries on contemporary history. Such a notion could indeed easily serve as a pretext for methodological negligence and theoretical noncommitment. Apart from this, the question has to be raised whether the arguments mentioned above provide strong enough reasons for abandoning the search for developmental universals and general laws of development. Numerous developmental

[1] Acknowledgement: The author would like to extend his appreciation to Peter Jaschner for his valuable help in translating this chapter.

phenomena and sequences in the realm of cognitive, affective, verbal, motor, and physiological development indeed do show a high degree of transcontextual stability (e.g., Kagan, 1979; Warren, 1980). And even though many stage and phase models claiming universal sequences of development did not withstand empirical test, some seem to be alive and well – take, for example, those formulated by Piaget (1932) for the development of thinking or by Kohlberg (1976) for socio-moral development.

At this juncture, the question arises whether empirical arguments at all suffice to substantiate claims of general validity and universality in the strict sense. Transcontextual comparisons and replications can always encompass only a limited range of variation and contextual conditions. Strict universality cannot be inferred from observed invariance or generality of developmental phenomena within this limited range. This, of course, is the problem of inductive generalization as classically formulated by Kant (1781/1969) in the opening pages of his *Critique of pure reason*:

> An empirical judgment never exhibits strict and absolute, but only assumed and comparative universality (by induction); therefore, the most we can say is – so far as we have hitherto observed, there is no exception to this or that rule. If, on the other hand, a judgment carries with it strict and absolute universality, that is, admits of no possible exception, it is not derived from experience, but is valid absolutely *a priori*. Empirical universality is, therefore, only an arbitrary extension of validity, from that which may be predicated of a proposition valid in most cases, to that which is asserted of a proposition which holds good in all ... When, on the contrary, strict universality characterizes a judgment, it necessarily indicates another peculiar source of knowledge, namely, a faculty of cognition *a priori*. (Kant, 1781/1969, p. 26).

The issue of strictly universal laws of development thus leads to the question of if and how theoretical propositions in developmental psychology can be supported by arguments the validity of which does not depend on experiments. In dealing with this question we have to recall the Kantian distinctions between a priori and empirical judgments or, respectively, between analytical statements (true "by virtue of meaning") and empirical statements (true "by virtue of experience"). At the same time, we have to acknowledge the inherent difficulty of these distinctions: As Wittgenstein (*OC*) and, later, Quine (1951) and Putnam (1975) have shown, it would be difficult or even questionable to draw a firm and absolute line of demarcation between analytical and empirical statements. Instead, we have to acknowledge that such a distinction depends on our state of knowledge and, thus, is open in principle to revision and change (see also Bieri, 1981). In what sense, then, can there be claims of universality and generality that go beyond mere empirical generalizations? In the following I will discuss this question with reference to some pertinent reflections of Wittgenstein.

Empirical Generalizations and Structural Implications

As examples, let us consider the following statements: (1) memory performance declines in old age; (2) if A is to the north of B, then B is to the south of A; (3) if an object is 25 meters long, then its length is between 20 and 30 meters; (4) a given spot cannot be red and green simultaneously; (5) in sociograms with at least one choice per member, there will always be cliques (cyclic patterns of choice); (6) wisdom presupposes experience and calmness.

Formally, all these statements are general propositions. However, they apparently differ in the degree to which their validity depends on empirical evidence. Some appear as empirical hypotheses, some as truisms or tautologies, and some may be hard to classify. But let us take a closer look at these examples.

Statement 1 ("Memory performance declines in old age") seems to qualify clearly as an empirical proposition. It belongs to the body of well-established findings in developmental psychology; we cannot see any other reasons besides empirical ones to accept it. This means that we cannot see or establish any logical or terminological connection between the concepts of age or aging and of memory performance from which this assertion could be derived a priori without further empirical investigations. In order to determine a person's age, we do not have to refer to his or her memory performance, and vice versa. In brief, memory performance is an empirical correlate, but not a criterion for a person's age. It follows that the proposed relationship between age and memory performance cannot be conceived of as a strictly universal, nomological statement. Rather, one can inquire for conditions under which the observed correlation may not hold (e.g., by designing special training or intervention programs to enhance memory performance in the elderly). To be sure, if the notion of aging were connected conceptually to deficits in cognitive performance, statement 1 might eventually lose its empirical character. (In fact, the concept of aging is colloquially associated with performance deficits.) Here, it becomes clear already that the epistemological status (empirical or analytical) of a proposition can be determined only in connection with an analysis of terminological rules and conceptual systems.

Statement 2 ("If A is to the north of B then B is to the south of A"), on the other hand, does not seem true just because no exceptions have been found so far. Apparently, it can be derived from a terminological connection between the geographic predicates "to the north of" and "to the south of" according to which "A is to the north of B" is equivalent to "B is to the south of A." If someone tried to come up with contradictory empirical examples, we would have reason to doubt the validity of his concepts or observations. These doubts are justified insofar as statement 2 can be considered a downright standard for the correct application of the geographic terms involved. (As a similar example, consider the statement "$2 \times 2 = 4$": if a computer gives us a different result we do not doubt the correctness of the statement but the operating condition of the computer - provided that we can calculate ourselves.) To be sure, certain experiences are required for the comprehension of assertions like statement 2, experiences that involve the learning and correct application of concepts and terminological rules. To this extent, the validity of a statement like 2 is relative in a certain sense – relative to a certain system of rules. However, for one who understands its meaning, statement 2 is true beyond any empirical doubt.

The situation appears to be similar for examples 3 and 4. These are statements discussed with regard to their epistemological status by Wittgenstein and the Vienna Circle. In talks with Waismann, Wittgenstein offers the following analysis of 3:

A definite description looks like this: A certain length is 25 m. And the following would be an indefinite description: A certain length is between 20 and 30 m. Now these two descriptions become *'p'* and *'q'*. Then it is determined by consideration of the syntax of the words 'length' [sic] that the first cannot possibly be true while the second is false; i.e., '$p.\sim q$' is disallowed. Let us now construct the truth-function '$p \supset q$' (or, rather, a truth-function that is *analogous* or *similar* to implication) and allow for the requirements of syntax, then a tautology will result. (Wittgenstein, in Waismann, 1979, p. 91)

This analysis can be demonstrated by means of a truth table in the following way (with p and q in the interpretation provided, cf., Waismann, 1979, p. 92).

p	q	if p, then q
t	t	t
(t	f)	(f)
f	t	t
f	f	t

According to the formal structure or "syntax" of the concept of length, the event "p and not q" – i.e., a length is 25 meters but not between 20 and 30 meters – is not admissible, so that the second row of the truth table (in brackets) can be deleted. Statement 3 thus becomes a tautology (i.e., the implication "if p, then q" is "true" for all admissible configurations of truth values for p and q).

According to Wittgenstein, statements about the mutual exclusion of colors (see statement 4 above), like statements about lengths, are part of a system: They are syntactic rules, even though this may not be so obvious in the case of the former as it is for the latter ("we do not have a yard stick for colours" – Wittgenstein, in Waismann, 1979, p. 79). To the question of Schlick, how one could know that certain rules apply and not others, Wittgenstein replies:

In this matter it is always as follows. Everything we do consists in trying to find the liberating word. In grammar you cannot discover anything. There are no surprises. When formulating a rule we always have the feeling: That is something you have known all along. We can do only one thing – clearly articulate the rule we have been applying unawares. If, then, I understand what the specification of a length means, I also know that, if a man is 1.6 m tall, he is not 2 m tall. I know that a measurement determines only *one* value on a scale and not several values. If you ask me, How do I know that? I shall simply answer, Because I understand the sense of the statement. It is impossible to understand the sense of such a statement without knowing the rule. [I may know the rule in terms of applying it without having formulated it explicitly.] If I understand the sense of a statement about colours, I also know that two colours cannot be at the same place, and so forth. (Wittgenstein, in Waismann, 1979, pp. 77–78)

For Wittgenstein, the point of these seemingly simple examples was that rules for the logical connection of statements must be complemented by "rules that originate from the inner syntax of propositions" (in Waismann, 1979, p. 80). It was essentially this insight which prompted Wittgenstein to renounce the logical atomism of his Tractatus philosophy. It also sparked his interest in "language-games," which became a central subject of his later *Philosophical investigations* (see also Kenny, 1972).

Statements of the kind considered in examples 2, 3, and 4, as distinguished from purely empirical statements, could perhaps be called "structural implications," since they can be derived from a formal or conceptual structure (see Lenk, 1975). Again, it is important to emphasize that the distinction between empirical statements and structural implications cannot be made a priori but only in connection with structural analyses. The following examples point to possible difficulties of such a distinction.

The statement in example 5 ("In sociograms with at least one choice per member, there will always be cliques") can easily be supported by empirical evidence. But, does it refer only to an empirical regularity? At first glance, this might be difficult to answer. However, some elementary graph theory shows that this assertion follows from the formal impossibility of connecting k nodes by k or more edges without creating a cyclic substructure, that is a "clique" in the sense of sociographical analysis (see Lenk, 1975). Statement 5, then, does not denote a purely empirical regularity, exceptions to which might be conceivable, but an implication resulting from the (formal) structure of sociograms. Efforts to falsify this statement by experimentation seem therefore futile. This, however, becomes evident only against the background of some formal analysis. Such an analysis may, of course, be erroneous and then be inconsistent with empirical observations; recalcitrant evidence may promote structural insights. But this should not detract from the fact that such insights transcend purely empirical generalizations. Example 5 shows as well that structural implications are by no means always self- evident truisms without any informational content. Instead, they can indeed have a certain surprise value.

What about example 6 ("Wisdom presupposes experience and calmness")? Apparently it can be read either as an empirical statement or as an explication of the concept of wisdom. Equivocal statements of this kind are common in psychology (see also Toebe, Harnatt, Schwemmer, & Werbik, 1977). What is meant by such statements may eventually become clear when one sees how they are defended against alleged counterevidence. Let us suppose statement 6 would be countered by the objection that wisdom is *not* statistically associated with variables such as calmness or experience. Someone who considers the statement a valid explication of the concept of wisdom would presumably tend to reject such evidence as faulty and advise the investigator to revise his concepts or observational methods. In contrast, someone who considers statement 6 an empirical proposition should be more prone to blame the theory instead of the evidence. We may leave open the question of which interpretation of 6 is adequate. Ultimately, the answer depends on whether it would be possible to give a reasonable explication or reconstruction of "wisdom" without reference to concepts such as experience or calmness. This need not be investigated here. However, if experience and calmness are not simple empirical correlates, but constitutive or central elements of the construct of wisdom, then statement 6 could not be considered as a conjecture open to empirical refutation in the traditional sense. Rather, it would provide a standard for gauging the conceptual validity of empirical research on wisdom. All this, however, does not preclude the possibility that empirical arguments, if strong enough, might compel us to revise our conceptual stipulations, just as they may force us to abandon any other rules.

Structural Implications in Research Programs of Developmental Psychology

From the examples considered above it is obvious that psychological research can be seriously misled by the confusion of structural implications and empirical hypotheses. In developmental psychology, structural implications also deserve special attention because they impose certain restrictions on developmental sequences. This fact has important implications for the issues of plasticity and universality in human development (see also Brandtstädter, in press). In the following, I would like to illustrate these assertions with regard to two areas of developmental resarch: (1) the development of emotions, and (2) the development of sociomoral competence.

Structure and Development of Emotions

"Why can a dog feel fear but not remorse?," Wittgenstein asks in his remarks on the philosophy of psychology (*RPP2,* 308). He continues: "Only someone who can reflect on the past can repent. But that does not mean that as a matter of empirical fact only such a one is capable of the feeling of remorse" (*RPP2,* 309). These remarks – to put it in the jargon of contemporary psychology – touch upon the problem of the relationship between cognitions and emotions. They also raise the question of how this relationship should be understood.

In pertinent theoretical formulations of psychology, emotions are described as complex processes relating cognitive elements (i.e., the individual's cognitive appraisal of a given situation) to specific behavioral tendencies and specific patterns of somatic reactions (e.g., Lazarus, Kanner, & Folkman, 1980). To be sure, specific cognitive-emotional relationships are already stipulated in everyday language. Thus, according to common understanding, pity is associated with the perception of another person in need for help; remorse implies that one assumes responsibility for negatively valued events; worry involves anticipations of a subjectively unpleasant event in connection with doubts regarding one's ability to forestall its occurrence; gratitude (towards persons) implies the attribution of a subjectively positive event to the deliberate action of another person, and so on. We implicitly use such rules or relationships when we attribute certain emotions to other people (or to ourselves) in everyday life.

Psychological research has taken up such commonsense notions. In attributional research, for example, emotions are related to subjective explanations of positive or negative events. Thus, it is postulated that feelings of gratitude result if a positive event is seen as caused by voluntary or controlled activities of other persons; that feelings of guilt or shame occur when subjectively negative events are ascribed to causes under personal control or to personal deficiencies, and so on (for more detail, see e.g., Weiner, 1982; Reisenzein, 1985). Such assumptions have been empirically tested, for example, by instructing subjects to recall a certain emotional experience and examining whether the reported qualities and circumstances of such experiences correspond to the theoretical assumptions (see e.g., Weiner, Graham, & Chandler, 1982). Similar lines of argument can also be found, for example, in more recent versions of the theory of "learned helplessness" (Abramson, Seligman, & Teasdale, 1978; Peterson & Seligman, 1984). Here, feelings of helplessness and depression are related to specific attributional or explanatory styles: If a person considers bad events as caused by internal, global, and stable factors so that occurrence or endurance of such events seems beyond personal control, then he or she is more prone to develop depressive symptoms when bad events occur. In a similar vein, transactional theories of stress and coping (see Lazarus & Launier, 1978) relate emotional aspects of the coping process to subjective appraisals of situational demands and personal potentials to meet these demands.

This is not the place for discussing these theories in greater detail. My concern here is the question of how the cognitive-emotional relationships addressed above should be interpreted with regard to the distinction between empirical relations and structural implications. Are they simply, as is suggested in most of the studies mentioned, contingent empirical or causal relations? Is it, for example, conceivable that a person would experience pity *without* perceiving someone in need for help? Or, that feelings of resignation do *not* go along with perceived helplessness, but on the contrary with high levels of perceived control? Would such strange findings suggest eventually a revision of our hypotheses, or would they rather be indicative of conceptual or methodological flaws (be it on the part of the researcher or on the part of the subject reporting in such ways on his or her emotional experience)?

The problem that lurks behind these questions is that of distinguishing between contingent correlates or antecedents of an emotion and central or constitutive elements of meaning that cannot be dismissed without the respective emotional concept losing its essence. There seem to be strong reasons to assume that the cognitive elements of emotional experiences of the above type belong to the latter category. What arguments would remain to call some emotional experience "pity," "gratitude," or "resignation," if it could not be substantiated that the person had the characteristic cognitions associated with these terms? Suppose someone would ascribe to another person some positive emotional state such as "pride," "gratitude," or "joy," but at the same time claim that these emotions followed from the perception of a subjectively *undesirable* event. This person would not (or at least not only) diverge from a theoretical prediction, but rather violate customary rules of language. He or she connects predicates that are not "co-predicable" according to linguistic rules (Keil, 1979). But how can we be sure about this argument? With Wittgenstein, we might answer briefly: by understanding the meaning of the respective emotional concepts. A more elaborate answer could be: by observing how these concepts are acquired and used in our linguistic community.

To be sure, it would easily be possible for a person, say, not to be grateful for help obtained, or not to be worried when threatened with danger. But this does not invalidate our argument. Notice that the cognitive-emotional relations described above do not refer to an external observer's point of view but to cognitions of the person involved: What appears to be a threatening situation may, for the person involved, be simply a welcome challenge; or an apparent "help" might be experienced as a bothersome restriction of independence. It is, of course, an open empirical question which concrete situations elicit joy, gratitude, or worry in an individual. But it seems not in the same way an open question which more general structural features or prototypical characteristics a situational context must have for an individual who experiences such emotions. Rather, this question is determined to a certain degree by the structure of our concepts of emotion.

These considerations have immediate implications for research on the development of emotions. First, it becomes clear that the attribution (and probably self-attribution as well) of emotions is closely connected to the development of the pertinent linguistic concepts. Accordingly, we may assume that such hypotheses derived from attribution theory – insofar as they refer to the competent use of emotional predicates – apply only to subjects who have acquired the requisite linguistic capabilities (for empirical evidence on this point, see Brandtstädter, Krampen, & Veselý, 1985). To prevent misunderstanding, it should be added that this argument, of course, does not imply that one can *have* a specific emotion only after acquiring the respective concept of emotion. Perhaps even more important is the fact already intimated above that the conceptual structure of emotional terms (or the rules of the respective language-games) also imposes restrictions on ontogenetic sequences of emotional development. If an emotion conceptually implies certain cognitions, then the respective emotion cannot be experienced until the appropriate cognitive competence has been developed. A different finding would question the validity of the observations on which it is based. Thus, for example, we may safely assume that feelings of guilt cannot be experienced until individuals are able to relate events to normative expectations, and to evaluate their own responsibility for the event. Similarly, pride will not occur in contexts of performance before the individuals are able to relate outcomes to themselves (e.g., their ability or effort); and it is hardly surprising that empirical findings conform to this expectation (see e.g., Heckhausen, 1985).

Of course, not all details of a developmental sequence can be derived by conceptual considerations. Open empirical questions include timing of a developmental sequence and the external factors that enhance or retard certain developmental achievements. Developmental research, therefore, cannot be reduced to the analysis of language-games (cf. Toulmin, 1971). But are the sequential postulates mentioned above merely empirical generalizations that are valid only because no exceptions have been found so far? It seems that we can make a stronger claim: whenever emotions like pride, shame, joy, gratitude, or pity develop, their development will (we are inclined to say "must") follow the basic sequential postulates pointed out. One might object that in different cultural or historical contexts quite different concepts of such emotions could evolve. To this objection we would answer that concepts cannot be isolated from the contexts and the language-games that constitute their meaning. Of course, we can imagine cultural or historical contexts with partly or completely different concepts of emotions. Then, however, it would be difficult if not impossible to transfer our own terminology to such alien contexts. "When language-games change, then there is a change in concepts, and with the concepts the meanings of words change" (Wittgenstein, *OC,* 65).

Structure and Development of Sociomoral Competence

Research on moral judgment is another important area of developmental psychology that can be considered in order to exemplify the problem of distinguishing between structural implications and empirical hypotheses. Above all, I am referring here to what has come to be known as the "cognitive-developmental approach" of research on moral development.

Piaget (1932) described moral development as a transition from an heteronomous and authority-oriented to an autonomous, equalitarian moral perspective. According to Piaget, this transition is characterized by a growing awareness of the conventional nature and changeability of rules, and it involves the substitution of a concept of responsibility centering on the external effects of an action by a "subjective" concept of responsibility that accounts for the actor's intentions. Kohlberg (1964, 1973, 1976) postulates similar lines of development. His stage model, however, claims to give a more differentiated picture of developmental changes in moral perspective. Kohlberg's distinctions between "pre-conventional," "conventional," and "post-conventional" levels of moral judgment are well known and need not be considered here in detail (see Kohlberg, 1964, 1973, 1976). Like Piaget, Kohlberg sees moral development as closely interrelated to cognitive development. A key concept, in this context, is the construct of social cognition. Social cognitive competence refers to the apprehension of social situations and the capability of inferring subjective orientations (intentions, beliefs etc.) that underlie or guide other people's behavior ("role taking," "perspective sharing;" for more detail, see e.g., Edelstein & Keller, 1982). The relation between social cognitive and moral development is often specified in such a way that social cognitive competence is a "necessary, but not sufficient" condition for the attainment of higher levels of moral judgment (cf. Kohlberg, 1973, 1976). Numerous studies have dealt with the empirical test of this assumption (see e.g., Selman, 1971; Selman & Damon, 1975; Kurdek, 1978).

Rather than discussing details of this research program, I would again like to scrutinize more closely the nature of the presumed relation between social cognitive competence (SC) and competence of moral judgment (MC). Clearly the assertion "SC is a necessary (but not sufficient) condition for MC" qualifies as an empirical hypothesis in the strict sense only if between concepts SC and MC there exists no logical or terminological connection that beforehand rules out the falsifying case (i.e., the occurrence of MC without SC). Would such a case (MC without SC) be just a surprising empirical finding? Or would it rather be something like a "square circle" or "married bachelor," suggesting faulty or conceptually deficient observation? To take up Wittgenstein's (in Waismann, 1979) pertinent formulations, are we dealing here with an "internal relationship" deriving from the rules of a language-game, or with an "external relationship," that is, with a purely empirical contingency? Again, these questions should be discussed in connection with conceptual considerations.

As a point of departure, we may consider the attribution of responsibility and guilt in contexts of legal and moral judgments. The competent use of moral predicates like "guilty" or "responsible" apparently presupposes certain distinctions. First, one has to distinguish actions or events that have purposefully or willingly been brought about from events outside personal control that merely have "happened" to the person (paradigm cases are involuntary motions or inadvertent effects of actions). Furthermore, the internal and external context of the behavior to be judged must be taken into account. This involves especially, consideration of the actor's reasons and motives as well as of behavioral freedoms and restrictions (with regard to external constraints, personal capacities, and so on).

As far as the first-mentioned requirement is concerned, it is not only unusual but also in violation of linguistic rules to judge a person as guilty or responsible for events outside personal control (see e.g., Riedel, 1978). Thus, a common strategy of defense or exculpation in moral or legal contexts is to give an account that excludes personal agency or control over the event in question (e.g., by offering an alibi or pointing to unfortunate circumstances; see also Bandura, 1982b; Sykes & Matza, 1957). It is no coincidence that the ontogenetic development of the concepts of guilt and responsibility also follows these rules. As mentioned above, moral judgments become increasingly sensitive to inferred intentions as the subject advances from an heteronomous to an autonomous moral perspective (see also Heider, 1958; Shaw & Sulzer, 1964; Surber, 1977; Weiner & Peter, 1973). According to my argument, however, this developmental sequence is not a natural law but essentially reflects the acquisition of linguistic rules for the use of moral predicates.

At this point one could ask further why moral concepts of guilt and responsibility are construed just like this and not differently in our linguistic community. One reason for this might be that moral evaluation is functionally related to social control of behavior. Social strategies of imputing guilt and punishment should be consistent, then, with fundamental principles of learning and behavior modification. According to such principles, inadvertent or involuntary behaviors that are beyond the individual's control can hardly be modified by reward or punishment. Here, it becomes clear that the structure and use of moral concepts reflects our notions of human behavior and human development. The implication of this, of course, is that the concepts can change just as our notions do. "It is a fact of experience that human beings alter their concepts, exchange them for others when they learn new facts; when in this way what was formerly important to them becomes unimportant, and *vice versa*" (Wittgenstein, *RPP2*, 727).

What about cases where personal control or agency cannot be excluded? For example, it would be difficult to portray a complex and well-organized behavior such as counterfeiting a banknote or committing a burglary as inadvertent behavior beyond personal control. As intimated above, moral or legal evaluation of such cases apparently requires that the relevant behavioral context be examined more closely with regard to the actor's reasons and motives, to external and internal constraints, and so on. That is, competent moral evaluation (or the competent use of moral predicates) has to account for the fact that apparently similar behaviors may have different meanings - or represent different acts - in different contexts. For example, burglary can be an act of aggression, of selfish greed, or even an act of altruism, depending on the respective orientations of the actor (cf. Rommetveit, 1980). Obviously, only a person capable of such interpretations and distinctions - that in turn presuppose certain cognitive and conceptual capacities - can make a competent moral judgment.

These brief considerations confirm the assumption that social cognitive competencies for interpreting actions, inferring action orientations, etc., are necessary (but not sufficient) prerequisites for the competent use of moral predicates and, thus, for competent moral judgment. Given the backdrop of our analysis, however, this assumption does not appear to be an hypothesis that calls for experimental test. Rather, it follows from a consideration of the structure and use of moral predicates and refers to rules of language that have to be taken into account in the construction of observational methods or instruments for evaluating the competence of moral judgment. Thus, it hardly can be refuted when adequately designed and conceptually valid indicators of moral development are used. To forestall misunderstandings, it should be added that conceptual rules and constructions are not exempted from criticism either. Empirical findings can be relevant for the criticism of norms and rules in many regards (for more detail see Brandtstädter, 1979). Moreover, a descriptive analysis of rules may be as wrong as any other empirical description. Nevertheless, rules (being not true or false, but more or less reasonable or useful) should not be identified with empirical statements, and empirical statements about rules should not be confused with causal hypotheses. Again, however, it may be difficult or even questionable to draw firm and absolute distinctions here: As Wittgenstein cautions us, it might be that "rule and empirical proposition merge into one another" (*OC*, 309).

Problems of Demarcation and Methodological Implications

The foregoing reflections should have made clear that the problem of distinguishing between empirical hypotheses and structural implications is of central methodological significance for psychological research (cf. also Brandtstädter, 1982, 1984; Lenk, 1987). The researcher should consider how his or her assumptions and findings relate to this distinction; and he or she should be careful not to confuse experimental hypotheses with conceptual premises that have to be taken necessarily into account in the design of the research procedures.

To be sure, I have repeatedly pointed to the problem of drawing a firm and absolute distinction between empirical relationships and structural implications. This problem may be illustrated by taking a closer look at the interpretation of theoretical terms. As is by now well known, theoretical terms (particularly in psychology) cannot be reduced to single operational definitions. Rather, they are "cluster concepts" (see Putnam, 1975) whose meaning can be determined - and even then not exhaustively - only by a larger system of interpretative specifications which connect the concept at hand partly with other theoretical concepts and partly with pre-theoretical terms that are closer to observation. Thus, the meaning of theoretical concepts essentially depends on their position in a more or less complex conceptual network (Wittgenstein, in this context, uses the image of a rope made up of interlocking strands none of which, however, extends along the whole rope; cf. Putnam, 1975).

Suppose now that we explicate a theoretical concept - e.g., a concept denoting a specific emotion E - through a set X of "sufficient" reduction statements and a set Y of "necessary" reduction statements. Reduction statements in X would typically refer to situational antecedents of the emotional state E, whereas Y would typically list certain behavioral consequences of E. We then find, however, that the reductive system formed by X and Y implies propositions of the following type: Whenever an individual is in an (E-inducing) situation of type S_x, he or she will show (E-induced) behavioral (expressive, physiological etc.) reactions of type R_y. Apparently, the validity of such a proposition cannot be assumed a priori, but has to be substantiated by empirical research. An interpretive system comprising necessary as well as sufficient reductive statements is therefore not a purely analytical construction. On the other hand, if one were to abandon or replace the whole system at once - or even a critical portion of it - the theoretical term in question would lose or radically change its meaning. Thus, the system as a whole cannot be regarded as purely empirical. Stegmüller (1969) has introduced the notion of *quasianalyticity* to refer to this seemingly hybrid epistemological status of reductive systems. Metaphorically speaking, one may perhaps distinguish between central (or essential) elements that are constitutive of the theoretical term in question and peripheral (or accidental) elements that may be easily discarded or replaced to adapt to new observations (one might compare this to Piaget's notion of the interplay between assimilation and accommodation in human cognition). But, again, any attempt to draw here a sharp and absolute boundary line would be to some extent arbitrary or artificial. Theoretical concepts may gradually change with new theoretical insights or research findings, and such alterations may be related to each other only loosely in Wittgenstein's sense of "family resemblance." This notwithstanding, researchers in developmental psychology dealing with concepts such as intelligence, achievement motivation, moral judgment, or altruism cannot totally ignore the language-games that at a given time constitute the core meaning of such concepts. Thus, we want and have to hold on to the conceptual stipulations that intelligence has to do with the solution of problems, that altruistic acts involve the sacrifice of some personal advantage, that achievement motivation presupposes internalization of certain performance standards or that social-cognitive competence is necessary for competent moral judgment. Such stipulations provide standards to which we have to adjust our methods of observation and measurement. They form the hard core or the basic conceptual frame of our research programs. This frame may be extended, modified or rebuilt under the weight of new findings or theoretical insights. But at any given time there are certain constraints on such alterations that derive from the requirements of successful communication. One of Wittgenstein's metaphors illuminates this point:

> It might be imagined that some propositions, of the form of empirical propositions, were hardened and functioned as channels for such empirical propositions as were not hardened but fluid; and that this relation altered with time, in that fluid propositions hardened, and hard ones became fluid. The mythology may change back into a state of flux, the river-bed of thoughts may shift. But I distinguish between the movement of the waters on the river-bed and the shift of the bed itself; though there is not a sharp division of the one from the other. (*OC*, 96–97)

Developmental psychology between apriorism and empiricism: As it is now becoming clear, this formulation, chosen to appear in the title, does not refer to a methodological alternative or choice point. Instead, the issue is to establish a position between the extremes of rigid and closed essentialism and blurring and noncommittal empiricism that accounts for the strengths and weaknesses of both sides. For a start, one would have to recognize that conceptual analysis and empirical work are not separate enterprises but that they exist in a mutual methodological relationship. As Toulmin fittingly pointed out (1971, p. 25), we should be prepared "to reanalyze our ideas and terminology in the light of new empirical discoveries, and also to restate our empirical questions in the light of better conceptual analysis." In recent developments in philosophy of science – e.g., the structuralist conception of theories (cf. Sneed, 1971; Stegmüller, 1980) – we see a promising advance toward overcoming the traditional cleavage between apriorism and empiricism. For psychology, such methodological aspects have to be worked out yet. Without efforts in that direction, psychological research will probably remain the mixture of conceptual confusion and experimental methods, as Wittgenstein characterized it, in a formulation frequently quoted but hardly ever taken seriously.

References

Abramson, L. Y., Seligman, M. E. P., & Teasdale, J. (1978). Learned helplessness in humans: Critique and reformulation. *Journal of Abnormal Psychology, 87,* 49-74.

Baltes, P. B., & Reese, H. W. (1984). The life-span perspective in developmental psychology. In M. H. Bornstein & M. E. Lamb (Eds.), *Developmental psychology: An advanced textbook.* Hillsdale, NJ: Erlbaum.

Baltes, P. B., Reese, H. W., & Lipsitt, L. P. (1980). Life-span developmental psychology. *Annual Review of Psychology, 31,* 65-110.

Bandura, A. (1982a). The psychology of chance encounters and life paths. *American Psychologist, 37,* 747-755.

Bandura, A. (1982b). The self and mechanisms of agency. In J. Suls (Ed.), *Psychological perspectives on the self.* Hillsdale, NJ: Erlbaum.

Bieri, P. (1981). Generelle Einführung. In P. Bieri (Ed.), *Analytische Philosophie des Geistes.* Königstein: Hain.

Brandtstädter, J. (1979). Zur Bedeutung der Pädagogischen Psychologie für die Planung und Kritik der Erziehungspraxis. In J. Brandtstädter, G. Reinert & K. A. Schneewind (Eds.), *Pädagogische Psychologie: Probleme und Perspektiven.* Stuttgart: Klett-Cotta.

Brandtstädter, J. (1982). Apriorische Elemente in psychologischen Forschungsprogrammen. *Zeitschrift für Sozialpsychologie, 13,* 267-277.

Brandtstädter, J. (1984). Apriorische Elemente in psychologischen Forschungsprogrammen: Weiterführende Argumente und Beispiele. *Zeitschrift für Sozialpsychologie, 15,* 151-158.

Brandtstädter, J. (in press). Kontinuität, Wandel und Kontext: Zum Problem des Spielraums menschlicher Entwicklung. In P. Bieri & B. Hrushovski (Eds.), From gene to social text: Interpretation in context in science and culture. *Poetics Today.*

Brandtstädter, J., Krampen, G., & Veselý, H. (1985). Attribution und sprachliche Kompetenz: Zur Bewährung attributionstheoretischer Annahmen bei Grundschülern mit unterschiedlichem sprachlichem Entwicklungsstand. *Sprache und Kognition, 3,* 130-138.

Eichorn, D. H., Clausen, J. A., Haan, N., Honzik, M. P., & Mussen, P. H. (Eds.) (1981). *Present and past in middle life.* New York: Academic Press.

Edelstein, W., & Keller, M. (Eds.) (1982). *Perspektivität und Interpretation. Beiträge zur Entwicklung des sozialen Verstehens.* Frankfurt a. M.: Suhrkamp.

Gergen, K. J. (1980). The emerging crisis in life-span developmental theory. In P. B. Baltes & O. G. Brim, Jr. (Eds.), *Life-span development and behavior* (Vol. 3). New York: Academic Press.

Heckhausen, H. (1985). Emotionen im Leistungshandeln aus ontogenetischer Sicht. In L. Eggers (Ed.), *Emotionalität und Motivation im Kindes- und Jugendalter.* Frankfurt a. M.: Fachbuchhandlung für Psychologie.

Heider, F. (1958). *The psychology of interpersonal relations.* New York: Wiley.

Kagan, J. (1979). Universalien menschlicher Entwicklung. In L. Montada (Ed.), *Brennpunkte der Entwicklungspsychologie.* Stuttgart: Kohlhammer.

Kant, I. (1969). *Critique of pure reason.* London: Dent. (Originally published, 1781.)

Keil, F. L. (1979). *Semantic and conceptual development: An ontological perspective.* Cambridge, MA: Harvard University Press.

Kenny, A. (1972). *Wittgenstein.* Harmondsworth: Penguin Press.

Kohlberg, L. (1964). Development of moral character and ideology. In M. L. Hoffmann & L. W. Hoffmann (Eds.), *Review of child development research* (Vol. 1). New York: Russell Sage Foundation.

Kohlberg, L. (1973). Continuities in childhood and adult moral development revisited. In P. B. Baltes & K. W. Schaie (Eds.), *Life-span developmental psychology.* New York: Academic Press.

Kohlberg, L. (1976). Moral stages and moralization. The cognitive developmental approach. In T. Lickona (Ed.), *Moral development and behavior. Theory, research and social issues.* New York: Holt, Rinehart & Winston.

Kohlberg, G. L., LaCrosse, J. & Ricks, D. (1972). The predictability of adult mental health from childhood behavior. In B. Wolman (Ed.), *Manual of child psychopathology.* New York: McGraw-Hill.

Kurdek, L. A. (1978). Perspective-taking as the cognitive basis of children's moral judgment: A review of the literature. *Merrill-Palmer Quarterly, 21,* 3-28.

Lazarus, R. S., Kanner, A. D. & Folkman, S. (1980). Emotions: A cognitive-phenomenological analysis. In R. Plutchik & H. Kellerman (Eds.), *Emotion: Theory, research, and experience.* New York: Academic Press.

Lazarus, R. S., & Launier, R. R. (1978). Stress-related transactions between person and environment. In L. A. Pervin & M. Lewis (Eds.), *Interaction between internal and external determinants of behavior.* New York: Plenum Press.

Lenk, H. (1975). Über strukturelle Implikationen. *Zeitschrift für Soziologie, 4,* 350-358.

Lenk, H. (1987). Über einige strukturinduzierte Implikationen und deren Umkehrungen in der Soziometrie und Sozialpsychologie. In J. Brandtstädter (Ed.), *Struktur und Erfahrung in der psychologischen Forschung.* Berlin: de Gruyter.

Lerner, R. M. (1984). *On the nature of human plasticity.* New York: Cambridge University Press.

Peterson, C. & Seligman, M. E. P. (1984). Causal explanations as a risk factor for depression: Theory and evidence. *Psychological Review, 91,* 347-374.

Piaget, J. (1932). *The moral judgment of the child.* New York: Harcourt & Brace.

Putnam, H. (1975). *Mind, language and reality. Philosophical Papers* (Vol. 2). Cambridge: Cambridge University Press.

Quine, W. (1951). Two dogmas of empiricism. *Philosophical Review, 55,* 20-41.

Reisenzein, R. (1985). Attributionstheoretische Beiträge zur Emotionsforschung und ihre Beziehung zu kognitiv-lerntheoretischen Formulierungen. In L. H. Eckensberger & E. Lantermann (Eds.), *Emotion und Reflexivität.* München: Urban & Schwarzenberg.

Riedel, M. (1978). Handlungstheorie als ethische Grunddisziplin. Analytische und hermeneutische Aspekte der gegenwärtigen Problemlage. In H. Lenk (Ed.), *Handlungstheorie interdisziplinär* (Vol. 2, Part 1). München: Fink.

Rommetveit, R. (1980). *On 'meanings' of acts and what is meant and made known by what is said in a pluralistic social world.* Oxford: Blackwell.

Selman, R. L. (1971). The relation of role-taking to the development of moral judgment in children. *Child Development, 42,* 79-91.

Selman, R., & Damon, W. (1975). The necessity (but insufficiency) of social perspective taking for conceptions of justice at three early levels. In J. DePalma & J. M. Foley (Eds.), *Moral development: Current theory and research.* Hillsdale, NJ: Erlbaum.

Shaw, M. W., & Sulzer, J. L. (1964). An empirical test of Heider's levels in attribution of responsibility. *Journal of Abnormal and Social Psychology, 69,* 39-46.

Sneed, J. (1971). *The logical structure of mathematical physics.* Dordrecht: Reidel.

Stegmüller, W. (1969). *Probleme und Resultate der Wissenschaftstheorie und Analytischen Philosophie* (Vol. 1). Berlin: Springer.

Stegmüller, W. (1980). *Neue Wege der Wissenschaftsphilosophie.* Berlin: Springer-Verlag.

Surber, C. F. (1977). Developmental process in social inference: Averaging of intentions and consequences in moral judgments. *Developmental Psychology, 13,* 654-665.

Sykes, G., & Matza, D. (1957). Techniques of neutralization: A theory of delinquency. *American Sociological Review, 22,* 664-670.

Toebe, P., Harnatt, J., Schwemmer, O., & Werbik, H. (1977). Beiträge der Konstruktiven Philosophie zur Klärung der begrifflichen und methodischen Grundlagen der Psychologie. In K. A. Schneewind (Ed.), *Wissenschaftstheoretische Grundlagen der Psychologie.* München: Reinhardt.

Toulmin, S. (1971). The concept of "stages" in psychological development. In T. Mischel (Ed.), *Cognitive development and epistemology.* New York: Academic Press.

Waismann, F. (1979). *Wittgenstein and the Vienna Circle.* New York: Barnes & Noble.

Warren, N. (1980). Universality and plasticity, ontogeny and phylogeny: The resonance between culture and cognitive development. In J. Sants (Ed.), *Developmental psychology and society.* London: Macmillan.

Weiner, B. (1982). An attributionally based theory of motivation and emotion: Focus, range, and issues. In N.T. Feather (Ed.), *Expectations and actions: Expectancy-value models in psychology.* Hillsdale, NJ: Erlbaum.

Weiner, B., Graham, S., & Chandler, C. (1982). Pity, anger, and guilt: An attributional analysis. *Personality and Social Psychology, 8,* 226-232.

Weiner, B. & Peter, N. U. (1973). A cognitive-developmental analysis of achievement and moral judgments. *Developmental Psychology, 9,* 290-309.

Chapter 6 Recognition in Wittgenstein and Contemporary Thought

Jeff Coulter

> For here we are often possessed by a primitive conception, viz., that we are comparing the man we see with a memory image in our mind and we find the two to agree. I. e., we are representing 'recognizing someone' as a process of identification by means of a picture (as a criminal is identified by his photo). I needn't say that in most cases in which we recognize someone no comparison between him and a mental picture takes place. We are, of course, tempted to give this description by the fact that there are memory images. Very often, for instance, such an image comes before our mind immediately *after* having recognized someone. I see him as he stood when we last saw each other ten years ago. (Wittgenstein, *BB*, 165)

What Wittgenstein here describes as a "primitive conception" is, arguably, one of the most enduring and dominant frameworks within which theorizing about recognition has been undertaken in the behavioral sciences. Here, then, as elsewhere, Wittgenstein's views are in direct conflict with cherished and powerfully entrenched preconceptions. Many adherents to the broad picture of recognition which Wittgenstein is attacking would even argue that some such version is *unavoidable*; without it, they would say, recognition becomes a mystery, beyond rational comprehension. So deep are the waters which Wittgenstein was seeking to stir up!

In what follows, I shall try to defend Wittgenstein's attempt to *dissolve* the "problem" of recognition as it has persistently hitherto been formulated within those disciplines espousing a "scientific" attitude towards it. In a sense, the term *dissolve* (which Wittgenstein often favored as a description of his procedure for dealing with certain philosophical problems) is not quite as appropriate in the present context as the term *decompose,* for one of the main results of an analysis of the complex of issues surrounding the treatment of "recognition" in human beings is the determination that it comprises many varied phenomena in their own right. However, there are several themes involved in the position advanced by Wittgenstein, through several different writings, and I shall try to sort out the major ones as we proceed.

The Concept of Recognition in Wittgenstein's Later Writings

In the *Blue and Brown Books,* Wittgenstein develops several ideas about recognition in relation to the introduction of his concept of "family resemblance." He gets us to consider a scenario in which, among other variations, someone (*B*) is asked by another (*A*) to fetch a piece of cloth of the same color as that of a sample shown to him: *B* performs this task by forming a memory image of the sample before going to look for a matching piece of cloth; *B* alternately examines the materials and recalls the image; eventually, on obtaining a match between a particular piece of cloth (the "perceptual input") and the image ("the memory trace realized as an image"), *B* stops, says "That's it," and takes it from the shelf. Commenting upon this variant of the scenario under scrutiny, Wittgenstein makes the following suggestion:

'In [this case] he had the memory image and he recognized the material he looked for by its agreement with the image.' – But had he also a picture of this agreement before him, a picture with which he could compare the agreement between the pattern and the bolt [of material] to see whether it was the right one? (Wittgenstein, *BB*, 88)

Wittgenstein here appears to be saying that "comparing" or "matching" a memory image to an observed phenomenon is an activity which requires criteria for adequacy-assessment: One must be in a position to *recognize* an agreement between the memory image and the phenomenon. Thus, in the case discussed, *B* was asked to look for the material, recognized it by employing a memory image and a matching procedure, and this achievement was ratified as such by *A*, but one cannot extrapolate from this to a position in which such a matching procedure *constitutes* recognition itself (in such instances) without involving oneself in a regress of the following sort. In order to recognize the material, *B* compared perceptual inputs (the various bolts of material) to a memory image, but this task itself required the ability to *recognize* the match when it was achieved. Does this mean that *B* had to compare the (candidate) match with another image in order to recognize it *as a match*? If not, then matching image to object is not constitutive of recognizing; at most, it is a *part* of *some* instances, and its role is that of an enabling procedure. And, of course, as Wittgenstein also argued, there are instances of recognition in which no such conscious matching procedure is involved at all. It is the tendency to extrapolate from the kind of restricted instance just outlined to the entire domain of recognition which is the target of Wittgenstein's further criticism in the *Philosophical investigations*:

It is easy to have a false picture of the processes called "recognizing"; as if recognizing always consisted in comparing two impressions with one another. It is as if I carried a picture of an object with me and used it to perform an identification of an object as the one represented by the picture. Our memory seems to us to be the agent of such a comparison, by preserving a picture of what has been seen before, or by allowing us to look into the past (as if down a spyglass). (*PI*, 604)
And it is not so much as if I were comparing the object with a picture set beside it, but as if the object *coincided* with the picture. So I see only one thing, not two. (*PI*, 605)

Wittgenstein takes up the related theme, that comparing images with objects cannot itself explain or constitute what recognition is, in his later *Remarks on the philosophy of psychology*:

As I recognize someone I say: "Now I see – the features are the same, only ..." and there follows a description of the changes that are in fact there. – Suppose I said "The face is rounder than it was" – am I to say it is some peculiarity of the optical picture, of the visual impression, that shews me this? Of course it will be said: "No, here an optical picture comes together with a memory." But how do these things come together? Isn't it *as if* two pictures were getting compared here? But there aren't two pictures being compared; and if there were, one would still have to keep on recognizing one of them as the picture of the earlier face. (*RPP1*, 1041)

To claim that recognizing someone or something is explained by comparing or matching perceptual input to memory begs the question, for how is the correct image, picture or stored representation to be recognized as such itself? And how is the achievement of a match or agreement between the input (the "optical picture") and the stored representation to be recognized? An infinite regress threatens; clearly the argument cannot be secured. Moreover, one may easily be imagined comparing two *identical* pictures of a strange, new object without in any sense being able to "recognize" the object, either in the sense of arriving at a feeling of familiarity or in the full sense of being able to tell what it is. Matching things, comparing things by feature, structure or any other concrete property could not *constitute* recognizing those things, even though for *certain* purposes performing a matching operation (as in the case of searching a series of photographs or drawings for the face of a wanted man) may *facilitate* the achievement of recognition (e.g., of the man in one's memory as indeed John Smith, one's assailant). Furthermore, if it is argued that one need not match *two* independently available pictures (e.g., the perceptual input and the memory image), but simply bring the one (the image) into line with, or in coincidence with, the other (the percept), then it has still to be made clear how such a *fusion* of stored image with present percept can even *facilitate*, let alone constitute, recognition. In such a case, designed to save the notion of a comparison operation from the obvious phenomenological fact that many cases of recognition do not feature in experience any discrete matching of *two* or more pictures, the whole point is lost: A comparison that is not available *as* a comparison to the one engaged in it can scarcely do the same work for him as a comparison that he is engaged in performing for the purpose of trying to recognize someone.

At this point, it is as well to take stock of a consideration ignored by proponents of the "primitive conception" which Wittgenstein is attacking, although this particular issue is not dealt with by Wittgenstein in the context of his remarks on memory and recognition. It is, however, familiar from his analysis of "understanding": the argument that distinguishes a *process* from an *ability*. Recognizing is *not* a process verb, despite its pseudo-continuous-tense appearance. We distinguish in language between recognizing and *trying to* recognize, where the former is an accomplishment and the latter a process whose terminus may not necessarily be recognition as such. We distinguish (again, as in the case of "understanding") between thinking that one has recognized *X* and actually recognizing *X*. Thus, although we may intelligibly be asked how we may go about trying to recognize someone or something, there is no sense to the question: How do we recognize someone or something? As Baker and Hacker (1982) put it, "Little do we pause to wonder whether there must be a 'how' for every 'do'!" (p. 230). Further, there is a temptation to confuse "recognizing" or "performing an act of recognition" with "being able to say who/what *X* is." Again, Baker and Hacker (1984) note the contextual constraints upon such a substitution when they remark:

The term 'recognize' is abused when a theorist addresses the question of how a person recognizes that a speaker who says to him 'What time is it?' has asked what time it is. I no more recognize what time it is when I look at the face of my watch or recognize my wife when I sit down to dinner with her for an evening. Confusions are further multiplied by failing to distinguish grounds (or reasons) from causes. (p. 232 n)

Here, Baker and Hacker render perspicuously a point made by Wittgenstein in the *Philosophical investigations*:

When I talk about this table, – am I *remembering* that this object is called a 'table'? (*PI,* 601)
Asked: "Did you recognize your desk when you entered your room this morning?" – I should no doubt say "certainly!" And yet it would be misleading to say that an act of recognition had taken place. (*PI,* 602)
No one will say that every time I enter my room, my long-familiar surroundings, there is enacted a recognition of all that I see and have seen hundreds of times before. (*PI,* 603)

Malcom (1977) makes a similar point when he stresses that there are no instances of *intrinsic* remembering or recognizing, that they are contextually constituted as such:

If we study the actual details of examples of memory, not viewing them through the veil of theory, not assuming that something or other *must* be the case, we shall come upon nothing whatever that has the property of being *the remembering.* What we do find is nothing other than various actions, gestures, utterances, images and thoughts, which in some contexts are 'manifestations' of remembering, but when placed in other contexts are not. (p. 48)

Further, the concept of "recognizing" ranges over a wide variety of instances, each of which is contextually constituted as recognizing, and between which there need be no property or properies common to all and only to all, such that we call them all cases of "recognizing." We simply call *diverse* things, in *diverse* contexts, cases of "recognizing." In some cases, a sudden rush of emotion accompanies seeing someone again and the perceiver blurts out his or her name. In other cases, there is no "feeling" discernibly present, and the perceiver simply is able to reply to a question correctly about the identity of what has been perceived. In still other cases, one may require photos or other props to assist one in achieving recognition. And in yet other cases one may see someone and say his name to oneself and be right about who he is, and so forth. One can go about for years claiming that, and being personally convinced that, one had recognized someone at a certain place, only to discover that one was wrong, that one was in fact nowhere near that spot on that occasion, and that therefore whilst one thought that one recognized the person, indeed one had not.

Let us, then, pull together the main strands of the Wittgensteinian argument about the nature of recognition in series of propositions:

1. Recognizing cannot *consist in* any process of matching or comparing input to stored representation. At best, this is an occasional process that may enable one to accomplish a special sort of recognition.

2. Recognizing that a match has been achieved is as much a case of recognizing as any other, and cannot be used to explain *all* cases of recognizing without circularity.

3. Recognition is not *any* sort of process at all; it is an accomplishment, akin to an ability.

4. There are conventional constraints upon the possible object-complements in various contexts for the verb "(to) recognize."

5. Being able to say what there is in an environment encountered once again is not to be confused with engaging in sequences of "acts of recognition," although in some contexts and for some purposes being able to say what there is may be taken as a (defeasible) criterion for having "recognized" it.

6. Recognizing (and recognizing *as*, a different concept) is manifested in ways between which there need be no uniquely common properties.

Now that we have surveyed the major parameters of Wittgenstein's views on the nature of recognition, let us consider some contributions from contemporary theorizing in their light. Do these recent arguments and theoretical claims require us to correct Wittgenstein's analysis or must we rather sustain that analysis and seek to correct current thinking? It is my contention that the latter is the case, and I shall try to show in some detail why I think this.

From Distinctive Features to Catalogs of Models

In a recent overview of what he terms "memory metaphors" in cognitive studies, Roediger (1980) presents the following assessment:

> The conception of the mind as a mental space in which memories are stored and then retrieved by a search process has served as a general and powerful explanation of the phenomena of human memory. There is currently no other general conception of the mind or memory that rivals this view. (p. 238)

If we transform Reodiger's reference to the "mind" and the "mental" to the "brain" and the "neural," we can readily concur. What is the basis for such a conception, one that figures largely in attempts to explain human recognition? I think that Malcolm (1977, pp. 22, 228–229) was correct in claiming that what has happened in cognitive theorizing in recent years is a transposition of Wittgenstein's "primitive conception" from the domain of the mental to the domain of the neurophysiological in speculative model construction. Whereas we often do compare things seen with images we form in order to assist ourselves in recognizing the next thing encountered as like those already encountered, we frequently do *not* do this when confronted with such a task; therefore, according to one line of argument, our comparing and matching must be in some sense undertaken *unconsciously*. This postulated unconscious process is now claimed to facilitate *any* instance of recognizing, and, as such, becomes ubiquitous and indispensable; for some versions of this conception, it is *identical with* recognizing itself. But notice that we have subtly shifted from saying that *we* "unconsciously" undertake to effect a match between input and stored representation to saying that some such process *occurs* within us – and note as well the presupposed shift back to the level of the whole, conscious person involved in the claim that *we* benefit from such an unconscious operation! More on this later.

There is another basis for the widespread use of the "unconscious-search-and-match" model for recognition competence, and this is the development of computational mechanisms designed to detect and print out characterizations of visual and/or auditory environments (e.g., "pattern-recognition" systems). Advances in the construction of such technology, and associated programming, have encouraged the notion that feature-matching operations of the sort employed by such machines might be involved, at some different level of specification, in the putative "neural basis for recognition in humans." Moreover, the automatic nature of search-and-match operations in computers has encouraged the view that postulating a similar process in humans can enable us to overcome one of the obstacles that Wittgenstein placed in the way of earlier attempts: namely, the problem of circularity involved in a subject's "recognizing" the correct stored representation and "recognizing" the accomplishment of a match. Rakover (1983, pp. 57-59) has presented one of the clearest expositions of such a "feature analysis model." He begins by proposing a simple test situation in which a subject is presented with an array of "stimuli," among which is the one to be recognized (the "target stimulus"). Then, a test stimulus is presented to the subject whereupon the task is to tell whether or not it has been seen before. If not, it is to be characterized as a "new" stimulus. That is, the subject must determine whether the "test" stimulus and the "target" stimulus are the same. An elementary program comprises the "feature analyzer." This consists of a list of a finite set of features of all stimuli involved in the situation, including the target stimulus. The product of the analysis performed by the feature analyzer is an ordered hierarchy of ones (designating that the stimulus possesses the particular feature) and zeros (designating that the stimulus does not possess the particular feature). This ordered array forms a vector, which is transferred to the "long term store" through a "feature comparator." The subject is instructed to attempt to recognize the test stimulus. Rakover (1983) continues:

> Given these instructions the retrieval mechanism starts searching in the long term store for the vector of the target stimulus. It is not a random process [nor one governed by the subject's conscious activity]. The retrieval mechanism obtains information from the feature analyzer as to where to go. That is, *the vector of the test (or present) stimulus also functions as an address* [italics added]. For example, if the test stimuli's vector is (10,110) then the retrieval mechanism starts searching in the storage which contains all the vectors beginning with one. Then it divides this substore in two and begins to look for those vectors whose second term is zero. In this substorage of the long term store, designated by the address of (10), the retrieval mechanism removes one vector at a time and inserts it into the feature comparator's past stimulus storage. (pp. 57-58)

Because the vector (the specific organization of ones and zeros) is already held by the feature-comparator in its present-stimulus storage via a command from the retrieval mechanism, the comparator can give as output "the degree of resemblance between the test of present stimulus and the target of past stimulus. A zero means a perfect similarity and a score greater than zero is a mistake" (Rakover, 1983, p. 58). The comparator's output enters the decision-maker which is programmed to print out "old stimulus" if and only if the mistake is equal to or less then some critical value, and to print out "new stimulus" if and only if the mistake is greater than the critical value and the process continued until all of the information in the long-term store had been exhausted by the retrieval mechanism. Treated as a *Gedankenexperiment* for construing human recognition, this model has the singular virtue of avoiding the infinite regress incurred by treating the search-and-match operation as a conscious process requiring what it is supposed to be explaining, namely, recognition, and it gives us a way to think of search-and-match processes as possibly "unconscious" as well as automatic, since no one proposes that a computational device need be conscious in order to accomplish such a task as the one described. The stage is set to ascribe some such model of content-addressable storage to the human central nervous system as a basis for explaining simple recognition achievements of a comparable sort. This particular system is reminiscent of a very early model for pattern recognition developed by Oliver Selfridge in the mid-fifties, called "Pandemonium." (For some discussion, see Neisser, 1967, pp. 74–79.)

One appropriate sort of response to attempts to claim explanatory power for such models or systems when considering human recognition comes from Gunderson (1971), who writes:

> Given an appropriate computer language we can, of course, define a routine which instructs the machine to compare symbols until it finds a match. But what do we gain by this? What further illumination should we expect from constructing a computer programme which in some loose sense simply duplicates [a certain form of human] behavior? It might be assumed that the 'payoff' would come *only* after the processes underlying the computer's behavior could be shown to be analogous to the process (as yet unknown) underlying the human's protocol behavior. But this is often not assumed, and there is thought to be a theoretical-explanatory payoff simply in the construction of a programme the trace of which is roughly isomorphic to a string of human protocols. (p. 329)

The properties of the computational model are derived from a mechanizable version of certain properties of one (by now very familiar) sort of human situation involving recognition – the one outlined by Wittgenstein in the cloth-recognition example as involving explicit comparing of samples to memory images. Thus, the human "protocols" (e.g., check the percept for its features and see if these match those of the image formed from the exposure to the original) which are particular to very specific sorts of cases of recognition only, and which, when they are followed, are followed consciously, are now being generalized far beyond such a restricted domain and treated as unconscious, underlying, neurally-realized processes on the analogy with the computational-artifact system. This is an extraordinary case of confusing a derivative model of a particular process with the explanation for the entire class of cases from among which the particular process was located. But more importantly, we are never informed by those who aspire to move from synechdochal simulation to comprehensive explanation of "recognition" exactly how the brain or CNS informs one *as a person* that it has effected a match and that therefore one can now claim to "recognize" the input. If the entire process is unconscious *from start to finish,* then how can I as a conscious being benefit from its having taken place within me? Why should an interior, automatic, unconscious process of matching input to stored features (supposing, for purposes of argument, that phenomena comprise determinate and determinable arrays of context-independent "features") facilitate *my* recognizing anything at all? Moreover, I could be asked to perform an explicit, public and wholly conscious task of matching some strange, new object to one of a set of objects placed in front of me, succeed in effecting a match, but still *not recognize* the object at all. One of the problems that confronts Rakover (and others) who seek to conflate *simulation* of an aspect of a phenomenon with *explanation* of it (namely Rakover, 1983, p. 58) is to ensure that what is simulated is at least genuinely *constitutive* of what is to be explained. None of which, of course, detracts in the least from the interest one may have in developing new and more powerful computational procedures for scanning and classifying things in the world.

In order to become clear about what is involved in human recognition as a *first step* toward more abstract or theoretical formulations of it, it is sometimes said that we need to work out the *criteria* pertaining to something's being a case of "recognition." This is complex because, as we have earlier seen, the concept of recognition is a "family resemblance" concept, one that ranges over many different sorts of cases. However, being a family resemblance concept does not entail that recognition has *no* criteria (cf. Canfield, 1981, pp. 136–137). It simply means that specifications of criteria for this concept cannot take the form of specifications of a closed set of necessary and sufficient conditions (or a "finite array of features" in Rakover's terms: Thus his system could not "recognize" what we would take to be "human recognition" – the phenomena are not analyzeable into a fixed set of features). Among the different sorts of "recognition" are: (1) recognizing as ratified, explicit re-identification of something/someone seen before; (2) recognizing as knowing that one has seen *X* before, although one may not know exactly what/who *X* is; and (3) recognizing as being able to classify a given instance of *Y*, never before encountered, as a token of a specific type of phenomenon. And for each type there are various possible contextual manifestations involving diverse sorts of mental and/or behavioral particulars in different combinations. No such particular (or "feature") intrinsically constitutes recognition, however. In some set of circumstances, my sudden look of astonishment on seeing someone in the middle distance can be a manifestation of my recognizing him; in some different circumstances, merely a sign of my sudden recollection of a missed appointment with him; in other circumstances, a criterion for my surprise at seeing my very familiar acquaintance at that place rather than elsewhere; in other circumstances, a bit of pretense to fool a complete stranger, and so forth. One can ramify such examples throughout a lengthy catalog of possible features conventionally tied to recognizing someone. There are no circumstance-independent criteria for such an achievement. Thus, paradoxically perhaps, recognition itself bears witness to a centrally important but oft-neglected fact in this field: *Nothing* can constitute a "feature" generative of some phenomenon's recognizability in isolation from its circumstantiality of presentation.

It has sometimes been supposed that elementary forms of "recognition" might escape this constraint, so that if one concentrates, for example, upon simple shapes in a visual field, one can avoid the problems associated with contextualization such as the mutual constitution of feature-and-context. In this light, consider Marr's (1982, pp. 295–332) construal of recognition in his celebrated study of the neurophysiology of the human visual system. Focusing primarily upon shapes of objects and animals, Marr (1982) claims that recognition involves two things:

a collection of stored 3-D model descriptions, and various indexes into the collection that allow a newly derived description to be associated with a description in the collection. We shall refer to the above collection along with its indexing as the *catalogue of 3-D models.* Although our knowlege of what information can be extracted from an image is still limited, three access paths into the catalogue appear to be particularly useful. They are the specificity index, the adjunct index, and the parent index. (p. 318)

The "specificity index" facilitates a search among hierarchically organized 3-D models of component shapes arrayed according to the precision of the information they convey:

A newly derived 3-D model may be related to a model in the catalogue by starting at the top of the hierarchy and working down the levels through models whose shape specifications are consistent with the new model's until a level of specificity is reached that corresponds to the precision of the information in the new model. (Marr, 1982, p. 320)

Once a model for shape has been selected from the stored catalogue (e.g., of an animal limb), its adjunct relations "provide access to 3-D models for its components based on their locations, orientations and relative sizes" (Marr, 1982, p. 320). It tells, *inter alia,* that two similar components lying at the front end of a quadruped model are "general limb models" and that, in the case of, for example, a horse, they are more specific horse limb models. Finally (for this domain) the parent index can provide information about what the whole shape is likely to be. Marr (1982) writes that: "For example, the catalogue's 3-D model for a horse can be indexed under each of its component 3-D models so that the 3-D model for a horse's leg provides access to the 3-D model for a horse shape" (p. 320). In summary, according to Marr:

We view recognition as a gradual process [sic] that proceeds from the general to the specific and that overlaps with, guides, and constrains the derivation of a description from the image. After a catalogued model is selected by using one of the three indexes, we want to use it to improve the analysis of the image. (p. 321)

Marr (1982) insists that "vision is the computation of a description" (p. 355), although he admits that such a characterization is a "conceptual leap I'm asking you to make" (p. 351). Elsewhere (p. 326) he asserts that "it is clear in principle that the brain must construct three-dimensional representations of objects and the space they occupy," adding further on that there are "processes that … create and maintain the representations, and eventually read them" (p. 330).

I cannot here engage the many issues raised by models of vision that invoke a conception of an "internal representation" which must in some sense be "read," although it is perhaps pertinent to note in this connection at least one serious reservation, expressed here by Eccles (see Eccles & Popper, 1977):

we are told that the brain "sees" lines, angles, edges and simple geometrical forms and that therefore we will soon be able to explain how a whole picture is "seen" as a composite of this elemental "seeing." But this statement is misleading. *All that is known to happen in the brain is that neurones of the visual cortex are caused to fire trains of impulses in response to some specific visual input* [italics added]. (p. 225)

Although not discussing Marr's (later) work directly, Eccles here clearly states the basic observation limitations in neuroscientific theorizing and shows how much interpretive work goes into hypotheses such as those advanced by Marr for the domain of visual perception. However, our interest here does not lie in the attempt to test any such hypotheses, but rather to see to what extent they may be *intelligible.*

Marr's (1982) primary innovation in this area is to argue for a specific characterization of what he terms "a representation's primitives" (Marr, p. 304). He proposes that any perceivable object must have natural axes which form stable geometrical features. The major axis for a horse shape, say, would consist in its torso, and a set of additional, component axes (for legs, head, etc.) would together define the object's coordinate system. The idea is based upon the stick-figure representation for shapes, and it is powerfully linked in Marr's analysis to a notion of *symmetry* for the canonical axes of an object. The primary purpose of the adjunct and parent catalog indexes, then, is "to provide contextual constraints that support the derivation process, for example, by indicating where the principal axis is likely to be when such information cannot be obtained directly from the image" (Marr, 1982, p. 321).

The phenomena for which the entire apparatus of stored 3-D model is elaborated are, principally, those of shape. Marr takes to task Austin's strictures on this point. Austin had argued that there can be no rules or procedures for determining the "real shape" of his cat – in contrast to the "real shape" of a coin which might look elliptical from some points of view, but which can nonetheless be claimed to have a "real shape" in virtue of the very stable, nameable and well-defined outlines of coins in general (Austin, 1962, p. 67). For Marr, the question which Austin asks about his cat, namely, "In what posture is its *real* shape on display?" can be given an answer in terms of canonical axes. However, the actual specifications provided for such canonical axes, about which Marr (1982) asserts, "perhaps if J. L. Austin had seen such a figure, he would not have thrown up his hands in such despair at the prospect of formulating rules for representing the shape of his cat" (p. 309–310), are cylindrical sketches with marked axes for (1) a whole person, (2) an arm (left, bent at the joint downwards), (3) a forearm (in similar posture), and (4) a hand (right, nearly straight pointing to ground) (Marr, 1982, p. 306). It is difficult, to say the least, to feel confidence in Marr's opinion that such sketches embody "real shapes" such that they might meet Austin's objection, which was essentially that only human conventions and purposes expressed in a communicative form of social existence can establish for some phenomena what *real* shape they have, and that for *many* phenomena (including cats, to which one might now add Marr's other exemplars of horses, birds, ostriches, giraffes, apes and humans; see Marr, 1982, p. 319) our communicative conventions and our cultural purposes have fixed *no* rules or procedures for making determinations about real shape *independently* of a presenting context.

The debate with Austin in which Marr engages, however, is a distraction and in some ways obscures the fundamental issue which is *not* one of determining *real* shapes in some putatively context-independent fashion, but of determining *same* objects within constantly changing perceptual environments. This is very misleadingly referred to by Marr (1982) as a problem of "recognition" (but "seeing" is *not* "recognizing"), and the resultant confusion thereby generated is multiplied by his use of the phrase "derivation of a description from the image" (p. 321) in this connection. In *some* cases, a criterion for having recognized something is the ability to give ("derive") a correct description of it in a language, but *this* sense of deriving a description is not intended by Marr's usage. For him, the "description" derived seems to amount to the actually witnessed scene, and the "image" from which it is derived is the supposedly "internal" construction of the scene produced by the brain as a result of much processing of the initial arrays of "image intensity values as detected by the photoreceptors in the retina" (Marr, 1982, p. 31). A critical phase of such "processing" involves the "associating" of a newly perceived scene with an "appropriate stored description" such as a component from the catalog of 3-D "models."

I shall begin by claiming, then, that Marr does not have any theory of *recognition* at all, despite the terms in which he discusses the perception of shapes of things. Indeed, *recognizing* something by or from its shape is a very specific sort of achievement, and trying to recognize something by or from its shape a very specific sort of activity, *neither of which accompany nor constitute the bulk of perception per se.* Furthermore, any such instance of recognizing something by or from its shape is governed by contextually circumscribed criteria available as matters of public, social convention. At this juncture, it will be said, what is at issue is not the predication of the achievement of recognizing something by its shape to human beings but the predication of that to their visual cortex. But here we are cut adrift from the language-games within which the predicate actually could function at all. The operations of the visual cortex, as Eccles reminds us, consist of neuronal firings and a variety of other observable phenomena (available either directly or through instrumentation systems), none of which could possibly satisfy the criteria for ascribing the complex predicate: "recognizing something from its shape" (to which, one might add: "deriving a description," "computing a description," "constructing a three-dimensional representation of an object," "reading off a description from an image," "associating a description with a model," and so forth).

Marr's very inital theoretical decision to conceive of perception in terms of the vocabulary of information-processing, computation and representation culminates in a conflation of important conceptual distinctions. There is also a persistent tendency in his analysis to describe a process in the nervous system mathematically, and then to write as if the nervous system itself carried out the mathematical computation that described the process. (This is a similar proclivity to the Chomskian manoeuvre, much admired by Marr, which treats the rules postulated by the linguist to *describe* syntactical relationships as rules used by the brain to *produce* such relationships.)

Is there, then, no solution to the "problem" of how we discern "sameness" in "differences" at the perceptual level? This "problem" arises in the following way. As children we are, for example, shown pictures of horses, or actual horses grazing in fields, and instructed to say: "horse." When we have mastered many further language-games involving the use of the concept of "horse," we may be said to "possess the concept of 'horse.'" But how do we learn to *generalize* from the particular samples of horses to which we are "exposed" during our training so that we come to be able to identify some subsequent object with very different markings, in a very different posture in a very different environment as a "horse"? How can we tell? We must, it seems to many, carry around with us a very abstract or elemental inner model of a horse and/or of horse-parts which we can (unconsciously, cerebrally) match or associate with each successive "exposure" to a horse in order to be able to – well, what? See the horse? See the animal *as* a horse? See *that* the creature *is* a horse? Marr (1982) tends to collapse these quite different aspects of perception just as he in many passages conflates seeing with recognizing, and the process of trying to recognize with the achievement of recognition. These are not insignificant or pedantic discriminations: his failure to unpack them renders a proper interpretation and assessment of his general theoretical approach highly problematic on many levels. Nonetheless, the basic parameters of his problem are familiar enough. They constitute the "stimulus-generalization problem" for visual perception. Is the "problem" itself coherent?

I want to propose that this "problem" is an artifact of a particular way of thinking of the nature of visual "input" which conflates its description according to the relatively content-less vocabulary of physics and sensory physiology with its description according to the experiential vocabulary of ordinary language. If one initially construes the nature of visually perceivable objects to consist in arrays of image intensity values detected by the retinal receptors, then one can no longer connect back to the language-game(s) of describing person-level perceptual experiences of the world without positing a massively extensive *reconstruction* process whose end-product will appear to hang in cerebral space without eyes to see it! However, if one initially construes the nature of visually perceivable objects according to vernacular specifications (e.g., "horse"), then one can claim that, whilst all sorts of physical and physiological processes *mediate* the perception of it, it is all along a horse that one can see. (I leave aside here the further issue of opaque/transparent contexts of attribution, but see Coulter, 1983, Chapter 6). What it is that one can see is not up to one to say in a sovereign fashion; if I fail to see the horse you and everyone else sees (say, I see it *as* a centaur), then still this does not detract from the fact that *a horse is there to be seen.* The core issue, then, is the characterization of the "input." If the "input" is construed in the vocabulary of physics (e.g., as constellations of photons striking photoreceptors), then the neurophysiological substrata will be interpreted as engaged in *reconstruction*; if the "input" is given an inter-subjectively reliable, vernacular characterization (e.g., as "a horse"), then the neurophysiological substrata will be interpreted as engaged in *mediation.* My point then, is this: You can only have a "stimulus-generalization problem" where you construe the perceptual object *as* a "stimulus," that is, in some content-neutral fashion, assigning to the cortex the entire job of "putting in the content" on each next occasion of perception. If the content is there already, *in* the phenomena being seen, so to speak, then the cortex has no need to reconstruct it, only to mediate between it and the perceiver *qua* person. One can, moreover, be said to have seen a horse without having known that, or recognized that, it was a horse one has seen. These *further* aspects of perception (knowing that, recognizing that, *X* is what one is seeing; seeing *X as Y*; seeing *that* X is X, etc.) clearly involve *concept* possession; that is, the capacity to *say* (correctly) what it is one has seen (Wittgenstein, *PI,* 193-208). And mastery of a concept is criterially grounded in the capacity to say certain things and do certain things in certain sorts of circumstances. Nowhere in standard perceptual-psychological and neurophysiological accounts of perception is the concept-ladenness of various of its forms clearly articulated; the tendency is to treat concept-ladenness (when it is mentioned as an issue at all) as a mysterious sort of layering-over of a raw or brute physically described "input" by a mysterious "inner" process of "interpretation." But nothing of this sort is necessary: The concept-ladenness of my perception of a horse is purely a matter of my seeing what for everyone is there to be seen, namely, a horse, and being able to say that this is what I have indeed seen. If I am asked to give reasons for my saying of what I have seen that it is a horse, I can adduce the *conventional criteria* pertinent to my angle of vision and the disposition of the animal itself. It does not have to be claimed that my brain unconsciously deploys these criteria prior to *my* deploying them in describing the object of my looking. For, as we noted earlier in connection with a similar conception: What good would it do for me as a person to have *unconsciously* done what I must still consciously do to justify my perceptual claim?

If we now return to the way in which we set up the "problem" of "stimulus-generalization" earlier, we can perhaps begin to see how it can be dissolved. First, refuse to accept the characterization of what is perceived *exclusively* in terms of a descriptive apparatus unique to the practices of sensory neurophysiology. Second, refuse to treat the possession of perceptual concepts (or concepts of things that are visibly available) as a matter of acquiring a *generalization* for a range of instances subsumable under those concepts (e.g., an abstracted model or essence of "horseness" or "horse-limb-ness" or "general limbness," etc.), but rather as a matter of having developed the capacity to articulate and deploy conventional criteria *in giving descriptions* of what is seen. Third, refuse to characterize one's acquisition of the concepts of visible phenomena purely in terms of passive "exposure" to instances of them, but rather in terms of a wide variety of forms of training, correction, explicit instruction, explanation, drill, involvement in object-relative practices (e.g., pointing to, fetching, carrying, avoiding, etc.) and object-relative language-games.

In the course of a brief consideration of Gibsonian versions of perception,

Fodor (1975, p. 49 n) argues that construing "inputs" as full-fledged "perceptibles" (e. g., treating the perceptual object for an organism as a *bottle*) leads to trivialization. He writes:

> Thus, the answer to 'How do we perceive bottles?' would go: 'It is necessary and sufficient for the perception of a bottle that one detect the presence of the stimulus invariant *bottle*.' The trouble with this answer (which, by the way, has a curiously Rylean sound to my ears) is, of course, that the problem of how one detects the relevant stimulus invariant is the *same* problem as how one perceives a bottle, so no ground has been gained overall. (Fodor, 1975, p. 49 n)

Even if we allow for a moment the notion that a construction such as, "How do we perceive bottles?" makes sense (Baker and Hacker remind us as discussed earlier that not every "do" can have a corresponding "how"), in what sense is seeing bottles equivalent to detecting a "relevant stimulus invariant"? Fodor (1975) himself, in discussing the Gibsonian concept of a stimulus-invariant, remarked that it is an exceptionally strong empirical claim to posit a set of *physical* properties "such that the detection of those properties is plausibly identified with the perception of a thing of that type ... My impression of the literature is that ... perception cannot, in general, be thought of as the categorization of *physical* invariants, however, abstractly such invariants may be described" (p. 48 n). Wittgenstein's lengthy and well known arguments about family resemblances and descriptive categories could be included as part of this "literature." Why, then, does Fodor construe the question: "How do we perceive bottles?" in terms of a framework he has just (one page earlier) sought to discredit? Perhaps the issue is just muddled. However, Fodor claims:

> What this shows, I think, is not that the psychological problem of perception is a muddle, but that *stating* the problem requires choosing (and motivating) a proprietary vocabulary for the representation of inputs. I have argued that the vocabulary of values of physical parameters *is* appropriate on the plausible assumption that sensory transducers detect values of physical parameters and that all perceptual knowledge is mediated by the activity of sensory transducers. (p. 49 n)

Now Fodor (1975) is being a little coy in proposing that the known functions of sensory transducers are merely "plausible assumptions," but even granting these so-called "assumptions" we are not led as inexorably to embracing his "proprietary vocabulary" as might be supposed. There is no argument to connect his reminding us of the functions of sensory transducers to the postulation of a descriptive level for characterizing perceptual "inputs." If anything, the arguments he has just adduced to counter the Gibsonian "physical-stimulus-invariant" story could be invoked *against* such a move. Furthermore, one could argue, contrary to Fodor, that whilst the *physiological* picture of underlying retinal and neural processes give us information about the *mediating* functions of our sensory apparatus, only at the *experiential* level does the vocabulary of *perception* come into play; the physiological operations enable us to have experiences in which concepts such as "bottle" (and never concepts such as "patterns of light energy") have their appropriate place. The "problem of perception," as Fodor appears to see, is really an artifact of a selection (a *choice*) of a way of stating it which involves deleting the experiential level of description at the very outset in favor of a content-less form of input representation. This would do very well if one was purely concerned with the analysis of the physiological apparatus which *subserves* perception, but it creates all sorts of difficulties when it is appealed to as a basis for conjuring up a "psychological" problem about perception. But we have yet to locate the basis for any such "problem"! After all, the construction: "How do we perceive *bottles*?" *is* a muddle! Perhaps it could be read as an abbreviated form of a sentence such as: "How do we perceive bottles in such poor illumination?" or: "How do we perceive *bottles* amongst all that other debris?" or: "How do we perceive bottles - I mean, what *are* they?" (said by a peculiarly malsocialized language-user!), and so forth. On the other hand, it might be taken to mean: "What do we *do* in order to perceive bottles?" in which case it is transparently confused: We do not *do* anything *generic,* although we may do various things in various contexts *in order to get ourselves into a position to be able to see* the row of bottles we are being asked to look at. Finally, of course, the question may be read as a misleading form of this one: "How do our sensory systems enable us to see bottles (among the other things they enable us to see)?" For *this* formulation of the question, detailed descriptions of the physiological functions of our retinas, neural pathways, lateral geniculate bodies, striate cortices, and so forth, given in the vocabulary of *physical* description, will be asked for. There is here no room for, and no need for, any reference to "bottles" per se, because whilst one begins with bottles and ends with bottles, sensory neurophysiology of perception need concern itself *only* with the *mediating* middle of the story, one that can be told about incoming wave-lengths of light striking photoreceptor transducers such that X, Y and Z occur with the result that *N* neurons fire such that a (bottle, tree, cat) is seen. The filling-in of the details is the task of the sensory neurophysiologist. Why introduce a reference to "psychology" or "cognition" here?

The introduction of "cognitive" terms into what is otherwise a distinct and coherent issue for sensory neurophysiology is predicated upon a conceptual mistake. As Wittgenstein said: "In philosophy one is in constant danger of producing a myth of symbolism, or a myth of mental processes. Instead of simply saying what anyone knows and must admit" (*Z,* 211). For it is being assumed that in order to be able to say that it is a *bottle* (or some other vernacularly identifiable object) that one has seen (i. e., in order to be credited with *knowing what it is one has seen*), one must somehow have performed a complex inferential operation (or "computation") on what is really, fundamentally or essentially *only* an array of light energies or pattern of sensory stimulation. Fodor (1975) writes:

> Perception must involve hypothesis formation and confirmation because the organism must somehow manage to infer the appropriate task-relevant description of the environment *from* its physical description together with whatever background information about the structure of the environment it has available. (p. 50)

This is utterly confused; *seeing* a bottle is not identical to *having a description* of it, although if I *know that* it is a bottle that I can see in front of me, then I may well be able to give you a description, even if all I come up with is, "That's a bottle." But then if I give such a description (either to you, or to myself in silent soliloquy) I am not making any inference from a description of the object couched in the "proprietary" vocabulary of sensory neurophysiology! I do not have to know a single term from that relatively esoteric and relatively recent branch of human endeavor to be able to see (and to know that what I see are) bottles. What my nervous system does, however, which enables *me* to see the bottle may be described using the language of sensory neurophysiology which I may not know anything about; but it should not be assumed that it is my nervous system which somehow uses this language to make inferences on my behalf, either! Marr (1982) makes similar projection errors in assigning the mathematical formalisms in terms of which he describes the operations of parts of the visual system to the parts themselves as if they were computing the functions which describe their operation.

One of the several roots of these contemporay versions of what Ryle once called "the intellectualist legend" in theories of perception and recognition deserves special attention, and it will comprise my closing theme. It is, essentially, the propensity to conflate etiology with rational grounds. Whatever account may be forthcoming from neurophysiology of the structures and processes located in the human visual system subserving our perception of phenomena, there is a basic *logical* difference between any such physiological explanation of an enabling system and the kind of criteria one may conventionally invoke in explaining the *ground* for one's perceptual claims. Thus, whatever neuronal processes subserve my seeing the horse, I may be called upon to adduce my grounds for such a perceptual claim in some circumstances. I may then say such things as: The animal had the usual long, narrow head, but a very wide mouth full of teeth; it had a thick, curly mane, and four spindly legs holding up a torso; it had no spots, and I wasn't confusing it with a leopard, and so forth. Let us suppose that this account is not defeated by contextual particulars brought to bear by others of which I was unaware either when I saw the animal or when I gave my description to justify my perceptual claim: Thus, my account stands as a justification for my claim of correctness. I actually saw the horse, and did not just think that I had. Now, in contrast, suppose that I instead adduced a description of neural processes in physiological terms. Two points emerge immediately. First, my description is useless as a warrant for my particular claim because it begins with image-intensity values specified in physical terms and ends with patterns of neuronal firings in the occipital lobe specified in physical terms. Although such processes are essential for the perceptual experience of the animal to have occurred, they nowhere *mention* the animal, nor do they *fail to* mention it. Second, the exact same physiological description of the neural processes facilitating my perception would be compatible with my having seen, *not* a horse, but what turned out to have been an extraordinarily life-like, full-scale, animated model of one.

When some theorists argue for a constitutive role for "cognitive" processes in perception, I believe that they are trying to build in, so to speak, the criterially conventional grounds for a claim for correctness into their otherwise physiological account. Thus, we read that our "knowledge store" is brought to bear (somehow) on the incoming pattern of sensory stimulation; "computations" are undertaken in the cortex which result in the production of "descriptions" of the percept; "hypotheses" about the percept are entertained, checked with the "memory" or aligned against the stored "rules" and either confirmed or disconfirmed (all unconsciously, cerebrally), and so forth. But this neo-Helmholtzian apparatus is idle; the brain does not need to justify itself to itself, and, since all of these inner descriptions, inferences and confirmed hypotheses are not discursively made available to the perceiver *qua* person (indeed, he typically does not even think of the name of the creature when he espies it), they could hardly play any role in providing him with the elements of the account he may produce in defense of his perceptual claim. (For some examples of neo-Helmholtzian claims in the psychology of perception, see *inter alia,* Fodor, 1975; Gregory, 1972, and Turvey, 1974).

Concluding Remarks

Wittgenstein's great contribution to late twentieth-century thought includes, beyond his deep insights into the relationship between language and human activities, a sustained onslaught against some of the most compelling presuppositions of modern psychological theory. Among his targets were the doctrine that understanding the meaning of an utterance is a mental process accompanying the hearing of it, the doctrine that the concepts in our mental vocabulary function as labels for essentially private phenomena, and the doctrine that recognition is a constitutive feature of the perception of a meaningful environment and that its explanation requires reference to internal processes of comparing and matching akin to those employed in some instances of public, "external" recognition.

In this essay, I have tried to outline the distinctive logical grammar of "recognition" insofar as it bears upon themes in contemporary theorizing about it. Then I sought to subject three significant contributions to the topic available in the literature of the behavioral sciences to a conceptual examination in the light of some of Wittgenstein's logical strictures. Contrary to recurrent claims to be found in contemporary psychology of a cognitivist variety, namely, that Wittgenstein is now a defunct figure on the intellectual landscape, I have sought to show how powerfully he still speaks to us, and how urgently we must listen to what he had to say.

References

Austin, J. L. (1962). *Sense and Sensibilia.* Oxford: Clarendon Press.

Baker, G. P., & Hacker, P. M. S. (1982). The grammar of psychology: Wittgenstein's *Bemerkungen über die Philosophie der Psychologie. Language and Communication, 2,* 227-244.

Baker, G. P., & Hacker, P. M. S. (1984). *Language, sense and nonsense.* Oxford: Basil Blackwell.

Canfield, J. V. (1981). *Wittgenstein: Language and world.* Amherst: University of Massachusetts Press.

Coulter, J. (1983). *Rethinking cognitive theory.* London: Macmillan.

Eccles, J. C., & Popper, K. R. (1977). *The self and its brain.* New York: Springer-Verlag.

Fodor, J. A. (1975). *The language of thought.* New York: Crowell.

Gregory, R. L. (1972, June 23). Seeing as thinking: An active theory of perception. *London Times Literary Supplement,* pp. 707-708.

Gunderson, K. (1971). Philosophy and computer simulation. In O. P. Wood & G. Pitcher (Eds.), *Ryle.* London: Macmillan.

Malcolm, N. (1977). *Memory and mind.* Ithaca: Cornell University Press.

Marr, D. (1982). *Vision: A computational investigation into the human representation and processing of visual information.* San Francisco: Freeman.

Neisser, U. (1967). *Cognitive psychology.* Englewood Cliffs, NJ: Prentice-Hall.

Rakover, S. S. (1983). In defense of memory viewed as stored mental representation. *Behaviorism, 11,* 53-62.

Roediger, H. (1980). Memory metaphors in cognitive psychology. *Memory and Cognition, 8,* 231-246.

Turvey, M. T. (1974). Constructive theory, perceptual systems and tacit knowledge. In W. B. Weimer & D. S. Palermo (Eds.), *Cognition and the symbolic processes.* Hillsdale, NJ: Erlbaum.

Chapter 7 Inner Processes and Outward Criteria: Wittgenstein's Importance for Psychology

Michael Chapman

Ludwig Wittgenstein is indisputably one of the most important and influential philosophers of the 20th century. Generally known as a philosopher of language, he is remembered among other things for his dictum that the meaning of a word is to be sought in its use, for his argument against the possibility of a private language, and for his ideas on family-resemblance concepts. His contributions to the philosophy of psychology have also been widely recognized, although not, for the most part, among psychologists. Aside from references to family resemblances in research on concept formation (Rosch, 1978, this volume), and some comparisons with behaviorism (Day, 1969; Costell, 1980), the relevance of Wittgenstein's work for psychology as a science has gone largely unnoticed within the profession. The publication of his *Remarks on the philosophy of psychology* in 1980, however, has made this aspect of his thinking more accessible (Baker & Hacker, 1982).

The following essay is divided into two parts. The first is an attempt to present in a succinct form certain aspects of Wittgenstein's philosophy that are particularly relevant for scientific psychology, including the nature and validity of introspective evidence, the relation between mental states and observable behavior, and the use of psychological terms in scientific explanation and ordinary language.[1] The second part is devoted to the relevance of the later philosophy for some current issues in developmental psychology, illustrated in terms of a particular example: the problem of "response criteria" used in assessing children's cognitive development. This controversy is viewed as an example of the "conceptual confusions" that Wittgenstein described in psychology (*PI,* p. 232 e). In operationalizing psychological terms, psychologists often change the context in which those terms were originally employed. The fact that the same words are used obscures the fact that they take on different meanings in different contexts. The conceptual confusions of psychology thus constitute a special case of the capacity of language to "bewitch" our thinking (*PI,* 109). Far from undermining the possibility of scientific psychology as such, Wittgenstein's philosophy provides a method by which issues which are properly empirical or theoretical can be distinguished from issues of *meaning* (cf. Brandtstädter, this volume).

---

[1] For simplicity, this paper is limited to a discussion of the "later" Wittgenstein as represented in the *Philosophical investigations* and other late works. Readers interested in Wittgenstein's philosophical development are referred to Kenny (1973), Pears (1971), Wuchterl & Hübner (1979), or Bartley (1977).

Introspection and the Private Language

Wittgenstein's argument against the possibility of a private language is a good place to begin a discussion of his relevance to psychology, because this argument is at the same time an argument against certain uses of introspection as a method. In this context, a "private language" does not refer merely to a system of signs which one has never bothered to communicate to someone else. What Wittgenstein denies is the possibility of a language that is *necessarily* incapable of being communicated to another person. The reason for this is relatively straightforward. In a language that is necessarily private in this sense, there would be no means of determining from one case to another whether or not the rules of the language were being followed correctly.

> Let us imagine the following case. I want to keep a diary about the recurrence of a certain sensation. To this end I associate it with the sign "S" and write this sign in a calendar for every day on which I have the sensation. – I will remark first of all that a definition of the sign cannot be formulated. – But still I can give myself a kind of ostensive definition. – How? Can I point to the sensation? Not in the ordinary sense. But I speak, or write the sign down, and at the same time I concentrate my attention on the sensation – and so, as it were, point to it inwardly. – But what is this ceremony for? for that is all it seems to be! A definition surely serves to establish the meaning of a sign. – Well, that is done precisely by the concentrating of my attention; for in this way I impress on myself the connexion between the sign and the sensation. – But "I impress it on myself" can only mean: this process brings it about that I remember the connexion *right* in the future. But in the present case I have no criterion of correctness. One would like to say: whatever is going to seem right to me is right. And that only means that here we can't talk about 'right'. (*PI,* 258)

A language involves a system of rules or conventions for the employment of certain signs. Any criterion for following a rule correctly must be based on the possibility of agreement between individuals. But this is precisely what is ruled out by the hypothesis of a private language. This is not to say that individuals cannot make up and/or carry out rules in private, only that the rules must in every case be at least potentially communicable. Otherwise the individuals involved would have no independent means of checking to see whether or not they had followed the rule correctly (see Russell, this volume).

The rejection of the possibility of a private language has important implications for the use of introspection as a method in psychology. Consider first the case of sensation. Wittgenstein does not deny that sensations are private in the sense that each person experiences his or her own sensations and no one else's. Thus, I experience a sensation of a particular quality when I look at a "red" object, and so do you. I do not experience your sensations, nor you mine. The temptation is to identify the private sensation as the criterion which justifies the use of the word which names that sensation. According to this assumption, I know I am using the word "red" correctly by recognizing that the sensation I am now experiencing is the same as that which I have on previous occasions called "red." If this were the only criterion for the correct employment of the sensation-words, individuals could not communicate with each other about their sensations at all for the very reason that sensations are private. I would be sure only when I was using the word "red" correctly, never when you were! The fact that we do communicate with each other about our sensations indicates that something else is in play. The important thing according to Wittgenstein, is that we can agree among ourselves which objects are "red," which are "green," and so forth. We can agree when "red" or other sensation-words are used appropriately, even though we have no way of knowing whether or not our respective sensations are of the "same" or different qualities. This is the insight behind Wittgenstein's famous "beetle-box" example.

Now someone tells me that *he* knows what pain is only from his own case! – Suppose everyone had a box with something in it: we call it a "beetle". No one can look into anyone else's box, and everyone says he knows what a beetle is only by looking at *his* beetle. – Here it would be quite possible for everyone to have something different in his box. One might even imagine such a thing constantly changing. – But suppose the word "beetle" had a use in these people's language? – If so it would not be used as the name of a thing. The thing in the box has no place in the language-game at all; not even as a *something*: for the box might even be empty. – No, one can 'divide through' by the thing in the box; it cancels out, whatever it is. (*PI*, 293)

The criteria for the correct use of sensation-words must be publically available, otherwise we could never agree when we were using them correctly and communication on such matters would be impossible.

But if the significance of sensation-words is based on public agreement, the same is true of psychological words such as "thinking," "feeling," "intending," "believing," and so on. The significance of these terms is not known to us only from our own subjective experience, rather we come to know them by learning the appropriate contexts in which they are used. In Wittgenstein's words, "An 'inner process' stands in need of outward criteria" (*PI*, 580). These public *criteria* are the characteristic circumstances, behavior, or expressive reactions which by convention justify the use of terms denoting particular subjective states or processes. If these "external" tokens of "internal" processes did not exist, we could never have learned how to use the respective psychological words in the first place. In the case of "being in pain," for example, it is through the observation of pain-behavior in ourselves and others that we learn to use the word "pain" correctly.

How does a human being learn the meaning of the names of sensations? – Of the word "pain" for example. Here is one possibility: words are connected with the primitive, the natural, expressions of the sensation and used in their place. A child has hurt himself and he cries; and then adults talk to him and teach him exclamations and, later, sentences. They teach the child new pain-behavior. (*PI*, 244)

This example illustrates an important method of identifying the criteria of a given expression: The criteria are those publically observable circumstances which might be used in teaching the correct use of the expression to a child or someone else learning our language. Thus, different types of pain-behavior would be criteria for the use of the word "pain," since these same forms of pain-behavior would be used if one wanted to teach a child the meaning (i.e., the proper use) of the word "pain." The case is similar for many other psychological expressions.

In order to avoid possible misunderstandings, it is worth mentioning that the use of behavioral expressions of pain (or of any other subjective state) as criteria for mental states does not imply that we can speak of those states as existing only when the corresponding behavioral expressions are present. The mental state does not "reduce" to the behavioral expression; the state can occur without the behavior, and vice versa. For example, individuals can feel pain without showing it, or they can show pain-behavior without actually feeling it. In other words, the language-game involving "pain" allows for the possibility of inhibited expression as well as for dissimulation.[2] Mental states do not reduce to their behavioral expressions because those states can have alternative criteria in addition to their natural expressions. Once we are confident that persons have learned what "pain" is, we accept their avowals of pain (their statements that they are in pain) as alternative criteria. Since these avowals can function as criteria only once the concept of pain has been mastered, they are of no use in teaching someone the concept. Natural expressions are in this sense "primary." It is to the natural expressions of pain that we would return if doubts arose whether or not persons who stated they were in pain really understood the concept of pain.

Wittgenstein's concept of criteria also serves to identify important differences between ordinary language and formal discourse. Formal concepts are generally defined in terms of certain common characteristics which constitute the necessary and sufficient conditions for identifying exemplars of that concept. In contrast, the terms of ordinary language may possess several criteria, any of which may justify a particular usage (Wellman, 1962/1981). Thus, there may be no one characteristic common to all applications of a given expression. Wittgenstein argues, for example, that there is no single property or set of properties common to all games by virtue of which they can be called games. Since we have multiple criteria for deciding what is and is not a "game," different games share different overlapping similarities among themselves. Wittgenstein calls these overlapping similarities "family resemblances" (*PI,* 65ff.). The idea that all exemplars of a natural concept *must* have something in common, according to Wittgenstein, is the source of much confusion.

In contrast to the common defining characteristics of formal concepts, the criteria of many natural language usages are neither necessary nor sufficient in themselves for justifying the use of the corresponding expressions. A given criterion is not necessary for a given usage, because there might be alternative criteria as well. But neither is a given criterion sufficient in itself for justifying the expression, since it provides justification only under certain *normal conditions* (when the criterion is not specifically countermanded by additional, conventionally-determined countermanding conditions). Pain-behavior justifies the expression

[2] Wittgenstein uses the term "language-game" *(Sprachspiel)* to refer to the conventions governing certain linguistic usages together with the actions into which they are "woven" (*PI,* 7ff.; see Brose, this volume; also Bloor, 1983; Brose, 1985; Kenny, 1973).

"pain," for example, only under the normal conditions that the individual in question is not dissimilating (where "dissimilation" also has certain criteria – *RPP2,* 718). But *the possibility* that others can hide their feelings from us does not mean that the feelings of others are *necessarily* hidden from public view. The *possibility* of doubt does not yet provide the *grounds* for doubting (Baker & Hacker, 1985). When the criteria for a given mental state are present and there is no reason to believe that the person is dissimulating, "You can be as *certain* of someone else's sensation as of *any* fact" (*RPP2,* 566).

The idea that discourse regarding mental states and processes is only intelligible insofar as public criteria for those mental states exist has important implications for psychology. It suggests, first of all, that the *meaning* of terms referring to such "inner states" is not to be grasped by "looking within."

> Here we have a case of introspection, not unlike that from which William James got the idea that the 'self' consisted mainly of 'peculiar motions in the head and between the head and throat'. And James' introspection shewed, not the meaning of the word "self" (so far as it means something like "person", "human being", "he himself", "I myself"), nor any analysis of such a thing, but the state of a philosopher's attention when he says the word "self" to himself and tries to analyse its meaning. (And a good deal could be learned from this.) (*PI,* 413)

According to Wittgenstein, the way to find out the meaning of psychological expressions is not to look inside the self, but to look at the function that the respective words and concepts play in our language. This is because the meaning of such expressions is determined by the ways in which they are typically used, not by the particular subjective impressions that we happen to have in those situations.

Wittgenstein's remarks suggest that there is a fundamental confusion associated with the classical use of introspection as a method for gaining knowledge about inner states and processes. This use of introspection depends on the notion that we can inspect these states and processes much as we would inspect a physical object. But according to Wittgenstein: "One can't look at the impression, that is why it is not an object. (Grammatically.) For one doesn't look at the object to alter it" (*RPP1,* 1085). Looking at a physical object does not change the object, but in reflecting upon a subjective impression we cannot be sure that a new state of mind is not created in the very process of reflection. As Wittgenstein's comment on William James suggests, introspection leads primarily to the experience of introspecting and not to the pure experience of the "thing" introspected.

Another difference between introspecting and observing a physical object is that, in the former case, one cannot check one's observations. One may certainly introspect a second time, but in this case there is no way of checking that one's memory is correct. Checking one memory impression with another, according to Wittgenstein, is like buying two copies of the morning paper to assure onself that what it contained was really true (*PI,* 265). In order to rid oneself of this confusion, Wittgenstein prescribes the following:

> Always get rid of the idea of the private object in this way: assume that it constantly changes, but that you do not notice the change because your memory constantly deceives you. (*PI,* p. 207 e)

It is important to realize, however, that it is only a particular use of introspection that Wittgenstein objects to here: as a method for obtaining knowledge about the nature of internal states. As opposed to this "methodological" introspection, there is another sense in which it does serve a useful purpose.

> Does it make sense to ask "How do you know that you believe?" – and is the answer: "I know it by introspection"?
> In *some* cases it will be possible to say some such thing, in most not.
> It makes sense to ask: "Do I really love her, or am I only pretending to myself?" and the process of introspection is the calling up of memories; of imagined possible situations, and of the feelings that one would have if .... (*PI,* 587)

Among psychological verbs, Wittgenstein distinguishes between "states of consciousness" and "dispositions," and the relation to introspection is different in each case. *States of consciousness* are characterized by real duration, can be interrupted through a shift of attention, and typically include sensation, affects and emotions (*RPP2,* 45, 63, 148). Usually, we do not say that we know our present state of consciousness through introspection. We do not need to *introspect* in order to know that we are in pain; we simply *feel* it. Introspecting on our present state of consciousness can mean that we focus our attention on that state rather than on something else, but we cannot learn more about what pain *is* by focusing our attention upon it; at most, we can feel it more intensely.

In contrast, *dispositions* are not characterized by continous duration, are not interrupted by a shift of attention or a break in consciousness, and typically include believing, understanding, knowing, intending, among others (*RPP2,* 45). One might say, for example, "I intended to call you all day," without thereby implying that one thought of nothing else the whole day long. As with states of consciousness, we do not usually come to know our dispositions through introspection. More often, we merely *avow* them, as in: "I believe you." Or, "I intend to call as soon as I get home." As indicated in the passage cited above, however, there is a sense in which we can doubt our beliefs, intentions, or other dispositions, and in this sense, we can come to know what we really believe, intend, and so forth, through introspection.

In summary, Wittgenstein distinguishes between introspective and other types of self-reports. We may *express* our feelings or *avow* certain dispositions without necessarily introspecting upon them. On the other hand, we can introspect by focusing our attention more intensely upon our feelings or by ruminating on our dispositions. Both of these usages are consistent with the ordinary uses of "introspection." What Wittgenstein denies is that the *meaning* of psychological terms can be known through introspection, since their meaning is based on public criteria.

Knowing One's Mind (and Those of Others)

As this brief summary suggests, Wittgenstein's critique of introspectionism is much different from that of classical behaviorism and leads to fundamentally different conclusions. Watson (1913/1965) rejected introspection as a method because its results could not be publically verified. Discrepant results could always be explained in terms of the subjects' faulty observations. "If you can't observe 3–9 states of clearness in attention, your introspection is poor. If, on the other hand, a feeling seems reasonably clear, your introspection is again faulty" (Watson, 1913/1965, p.511). Because of their presumed inaccessibility to anyone but the subject, mental processes were rejected as objects of scientific research.

Wittgenstein takes a different tack. Introspection is rejected as a privileged method for knowing about subjective processes not because knowledge of these processes is accessible only to the subject, but because it is no more accessible to the subject than to anyone else! – Thus Wittgenstein's seemingly paradoxical statement, "I can know what someone else is thinking, not what I am thinking" (*PI,* p.222e). This remark is primarily concerned with the grammar of the word "knowing" as applied to psychological processes, but it also touches upon the behaviorist argument concerning their "accessibility." One wants to say that mental states and processes *as subjective experiences* are restricted to the individual subject, although *knowledge* about those states or processes are not.

As with other psychological verbs, there exist certain generally accepted criteria for the correct use of the word "knowing." Such criteria typically include, for example, being an eye witness to an event or hearing about it from a reliable source. If the criteria are satisfied, we suspend whatever doubts we might have had about the matter and assume that we know what is the case. If we find out later that we were mistaken in this assumption, this does not mean that we were not justified *at the time* in assuming that we knew. But in cases in which there was no possibility of any doubt to begin with, Wittgenstein suggests that the use of "knowing" is misplaced. In such cases, the criterion for "knowing" cannot be met because there are no possible doubts to be eliminated. In such cases, Wittgenstein argues, it would literally make no sense to say "I don't know"; therefore it equally makes no sense to say "I know" (*OC,* 58). Now subjective experience would seem to be one of those cases in which the very possibility of doubt is excluded from the beginning, and this means, following the argument, that the ordinary use of "knowing" is also excluded.

In what sense are my sensations *private*? – Well, only I can know whether I am really in pain; another person can only surmise it. – In one way this is wrong, and in another nonsense. If we are using the word "to know" as it is normally used (and how else are we to use it?), then other people very often know when I am in pain. – Yes but all the same not with the certainty with which I know it myself! – It can't be said of me at all (except perhaps as a joke) that I *know* I am in pain. What is it supposed to mean – except perhaps that I *am* in pain?
Other people cannot be said to learn of my sensations *only* from my behaviour, – for *I* cannot be said to learn of them. *I have* them.

The truth is: it makes sense to say about other people that they doubt whether I am in pain; but not to say it of myself. (*PI*, 246).

It is because the *possibility* of doubt exists that other people can be said to know that I am in pain; it is because no possibility of doubt exists in my own case that I cannot be said (in the ordinary sense) to "know" that I am in pain.

In the case of feelings and emotions, the criteria for knowing what the person is experiencing include the expressive reactions associated with the feelings in question.

"We *see* emotion." – As opposed to what? – We do not see facial contortions and make inferences from them (like a doctor framing a diagnosis) to joy, grief, boredom. We describe a face immediately as sad, radiant, bored, even when we are unable to give any other description of the features. – Grief, one would like to say, is personified in the face.
This belongs to the concept of emotion. (*Z*, 225)
"Consciousness is as clear in his face and behaviour, as in myself." (*Z*, 221)

As described above, one of the major criteria for many mental states and dispositions consists in the individual's avowals. This points out another reason why the verb "to know" is not strictly applicable to these terms in the first person. How can I check on what I am thinking or intending if the criteria for checking consist in my own statements of my thoughts or intentions? Again, this is like Wittgenstein's example of buying two copies of a newspaper in order to make sure that what it says is correct (*PI*, 265). My utterances are available to other persons, however, as criteria for what I am thinking and intending. This is the sense of Wittgenstein's statement, "I can know what someone else is thinking, not what I am thinking" (cited above). Another passage from the *Philosophical investigations* makes it clear that the same principle holds true for intending as well (*PI*, pp. 223 e-224 e).

To be sure, our knowledge about the internal states of others may turn out to be mistaken. There is a potential for uncertainty involved, especially in cases in which the other persons do not express their thoughts or feelings in any way (*RPP2*, 563) or in cases of dissimilation (*RPP2*, 588 ff.). In view of the possibility of error, one would like to say something like: "We can never be sure that we *really* know what other persons are thinking or feeling; we only *think* we can know." But the possibility of error is not limited to the case of subjective experience. It applies to knowing in general. All we can do is satisfy the criteria for knowing at a given time. In principle, we are no worse off in our knowledge of other persons' experience than in our knowledge of anything else (*RPP2*, 566; cf. *PI*, p. 224 e). Moreover, it is only because uncertainty is possible that certainty (or knowing) is also possible.

"But you can't recognize pain with *certainty* just from externals." – The *only* way of recognizing it is by externals, and the uncertainty is constitutional. It is not a shortcoming.
It resides in our concept that this uncertainty exists, in our instrument. Whether this concept is practical or impractical is really not the question. (*RPP2*, 657)

Both introspectionism and behaviorism in their classical forms share the fundamental assumption that mental processes are directly accessible only to the subject, but they draw diametrically opposed conclusions from it. By undermining this basic assumption, Wittgenstein challenges both points of view. Introspection does not put the subject directly in touch with the meanings of psychological terms, since those meanings are publically shared. But the behaviorist requirement that subjective experience be ruled out of consideration because of its presumed inaccessibility is unnecessary. To the extent that subjective experience can intelligibly be spoken about, there must exist conventional criteria for identifying them, and they are therefore as "accessible" to the psychologist as to the subject or anyone else.

Criteria, Symptoms, and Operational Definitions

According to Wittgenstein, the conceptual confusions of psychology are not to be explained by the fact that psychology is a "young science" (*PI,* p. 232e). It is misleading to draw a parallel between psychology and physics in its early stages, because the relation between scientists and their subject matter is somewhat different in each case. "Seeing, hearing, feeling, willing, are not the subject of psychology *in the same sense* as that in which the movements of bodies, the phenomena of electricity, etc., are the subject of physics" (*PI,* 571). Whereas the physicist observes the phenomena in question directly or their effects, the psychologist observes the "external reactions" of the subject. But as we have just seen, Wittgenstein does not draw the conclusion common to the classical forms of both introspectionism and behaviorism that mental states are "accessible" only to the subject. The question is, what does his approach imply for psychology as a science?

To begin with, Wittgenstein denies that psychological verbs such as seeing, believing, thinking, and willing represent *phenomena* at all (*Z,* 471; *PI,* 176). He recognizes, however, that there are phenomena *of* seeing, believing, thinking, willing, and so on, and that these are the observables of psychology (*Z,* 471). These phenomena might include expressive reactions, typical behaviors, concommitant physiological processes, or other observable events. This raises the further question as to how the subjective states (seeing, believing, thinking, etc.) which form the ostensible subject matter of psychology are related to the phenomena actually observed by psychologists (the phenomena *of* seeing, believing, thinking, etc.).

For Wittgenstein, there are at least two sorts of relations that can exist between the states denoted by psychological terms and their respective phenomena. First, the phenomena may serve as *criteria* for the state denoted by a particular psychological term in the manner described above. This does not imply that the mental state is simply identified *with* its criterial phenomena, for as we have seen, the state and its criterial phenomena can occur independently of each other. Rather, the mental state can be identified as such *by* its criterial phenomena under normal conditions.

A second way in which psychological phenomena can be related to mental states is as *symptoms* of those states. In Wittgenstein's terminology, "symptoms" refer to phenomena which typically co-occur with a given state, but do not serve as the normal criteria for it. In his prototypical example, a falling barometer is a "symptom" of rain, since it typically accompanies rain but is not used as a criterion for it (i.e., the meaning of the term "rain" is not normally taught to someone by pointing to a falling barometer) (*PI*, 354). In psychology, the physiological concommitants of psychological states and processes constitute an example of "symptoms" in this sense. Certain emotions, for example, may typically be accompanied by patterns of neural innervation, but such patterns generally do not constitute criteria for those emotions, since those patterns of innervation ordinarily play no role in teaching someone the corresponding terms in our language.

Given this distinction between the criteria and symptoms of psychological states, it becomes possible to identify some of the conceptual confusions that Wittgenstein attributed to psychology. One common source of confusion (by no means limited to psychology) occurs as a result of the fact that our use of language can change without our noticing it. Particularly in science, what was previously only a symptom of a given state or process can come to be used as a new criterion. This is frequently what occurs in the formulation of "operational definitions." This need not in itself be a source of confusion, but it becomes a confusion if we are not aware of the subtle change of usage which occurs. The original concept with its usual criterion has been replaced with a hypothetical construct defined by certain necessary and sufficient conditions. Frequently, we do not notice the shift in meaning and usage that has occurred, because the same term is used to denote both the original state and the construct which has come to replace it.

> Nothing is commoner than for the meaning of an expression to oscillate, for a phenomenon to be regarded sometimes as a symptom, sometimes as a criterion, of a state of affairs. And mostly in such a case the shift of meaning is not noted. In science it is usual to make phenomena that allow of exact measurement into defining criteria for an expression; and then one is inclined to think that now the proper meaning has been *found.* Innumerable confusions have arisen in this way. (*Z*, 438)

Indeed, the adoption of operational definitions almost inevitably results in such a shift of meaning, since it substitutes necessary and sufficient conditions for the multiple criteria which characterize ordinary usages.

Consider the case of dreaming, a much-debated example. In the *Philosophical investigations,* Wittgenstein argues that the criterion for "dreaming" is the dream report (*PI,* p. 184e). Children or other persons learning our language learn what dreaming is by reference to someone (themselves or others) reporting experiences they had during sleep. This being the case, it would ordinarily make no sense to wonder if persons reporting a dream upon awakening had "really" dreamed or had been deceived by a disturbance of memory. Whatever the origins of their experience, we are justified in calling it a "dream" in the ordinary sense – for it is precisely in terms of the dream report that "dreaming" is (ordinarily) identified as such.

Now there may be other phenomena associated with "dreaming" besides the criterial dream report. People who toss or talk in their sleep may frequently report upon awakening that they had dreamt, or certain neurological states may be identified which frequently coincide with reports of dreaming. If these associated phenomena coincide with the usual criterion frequently enough, they may be considered as "symptoms" of dreaming in Wittgenstein's terminology. It may even be the case, especially in the absence of the usual criterion, that one or another of these symptomatic phenomena come to be used as a new criterion. Thus, persons who talk in their sleep or who display the symptomatic neurological state but who do not report a dream upon awakening might under some circumstances be suspected of having dreamt and subsequently forgotten their dream. One's certainty that this is the case might even be increased if the phenomenon symptomatic of "dreaming" were followed by another phenomenon (e.g., another neurological state) symptomatic of "forgetting." This need not be a cause of conceptual confusion as long as it is realized that what had formerly been only a symptom has come to be used as an alternative criterion.[3]

Confusion may arise, however if, for some reason we believe that the new criterion is inherently superior to the old one. In psychology, for example, it might be argued that neurological measurements constitute a better "index" of dream-

---

[3] Chihara and Fodor (1965/1981) argue that it is unclear how to characterize the relation between a physiological index of dreaming and "dreaming" as a mental state in Wittgenstein's terminology. Since the meaning of "dreaming" does not seem to be altered through the use of a physiological index, the latter would not seem to have replaced dream reports as the criterion for "dreaming." But the neurological index would not appear to be merely a symptom of "dreaming," either, since symptoms are merely observed concommitants and the correlation between the neurological index and "dreaming" might possibly have been predicted in advance from our knowledge of the relation between certain types of mental states and neurological phenomena. These considerations lead Chihara and Fodor to propose that what is learned in learning about mental states are not criterial connections mapping individual terms onto characteristic patterns of behavior, but a complex conceptual system which interrelates a variety of mental states and to which we can appeal in attempting to explain someone's behavior.

According to the present interpretation, this is an oversimplification of Wittgenstein's views, and the following account is advanced instead. The neurological index indeed begins as a symptom of "dreaming," but this does not mean it could not have been predicted in advance. (The prototypical symptomatic relation between "rain" and the behavior of the barometer might also have been predicted, given a sufficient knowledge of physics.) To the extent that the neurological index is used to identify the occurrence of a dream, it comes to be employed as an alternative criterion. This need not alter the meaning of "dreaming" as long as the dream report remains the primary criterion (i.e., it is given precedence in cases of doubt). But if the neurological index comes to be *preferred* to the dream report as a criterion for "dreaming," then the meaning of the term has indeed been subtly modified. The secondary sense of the word has now become its primary sense. Further, Wittgenstein's distinction between criteria and symptoms does not rule out the possibility of complex conceptual connections among psychological concepts. The systematic interrelatedness of language-games becomes especially clear in his last book, *On Certainty.*

This account differs from that of Malcolm (1959) precisely in the provision for alternative criteria. In the present view, the assertion that a person is dreaming on the basis of muttering or other behavior during sleep is an example of using what was originally only a *symptom* as an alternative *criterion.* For Malcolm, however: "When we say that someone is dreaming on the basis of his behaviour in sleep, our words do not fall definitely into either alternative, and indeed have no clear sense" (1959, p.62).

ing than ordinary dream reports, and this for the very reason that the neurological correlate can indicate the presence of a dream even when the subject, having forgotten it, is unable to report it! The problem is, a shift in meaning occurs to the extent that the original criterion comes to be replaced by a new one. We may think we have found a more "sensitive" index of dreaming, when in fact we have introduced a new convention. "Dreaming" as identified primarily by neurological indices is by that very fact used in a somewhat *different sense* than "dreaming" as identified by the dream report. These usages may overlap to the extent that the two criteria are empirically correlated, but under some circumstances a person might be said to have "dreamt" in one sense (as determined by neurological indices) but not in the other (as determined by the dream report). "Conceptual confusion" arises if we are not aware of the new usage we have introduced – if, in continuing to use the same terms (e.g., "dreaming"), we remain unaware that the ground of meaning has shifted beneath our feet.

As Bloor (1983) has recently pointed out, much of the debate surrounding Wittgenstein's alleged "anti-cognitivism" has in fact revolved around this issue of alternative criteria. Thus, his "anti- cognitivist" interpreters have argued that many of the terms used in cognitive psychology are nonsense, because their use is no longer justified by the ordinary criteria (e.g., Malcolm, 1959). In reply, cognitive psychologists have defended the validity of their operationalizations (e.g., Chihara & Fodor, 1965/1981). According to the present interpretation, the use of the operational definitions for "mental" states and processes does not necessarily result in nonsense. This becomes a cause of conceptual confusion only to the extent that the resulting shift of meaning goes unnoticed. As Wittgenstein acknowledged in the above passage on symptoms and criteria, our language undergoes constant change. He once compared a language to an old city which is constantly being renovated and extended (*PI,* 18). According to this metaphor, the customary and sometimes irregular usages of natural language are like the winding streets and mixed architecture of the old city center, whereas the precise terminology of science and mathematics is like the more regular streets and buildings in a modern suburb. Introducing a new operational definition of an ordinary psychological term is in this view something like renovating a section of downtown in the suburban style.

But the terms of ordinary language cannot be arbitrarily changed. Wittgenstein recognized that words may have primary and secondary senses, the primary sense being the ordinary one and the secondary sense being a metaphorical usage (*LW,* 797f.). In these terms, the secondary sense is clearly dependent on the first. In the same way, many of the operational terms introduced by scientific psychology remain dependent on their original usages in natural language. Thus, "dreaming," "imagining," "intending," and so on, may come to be used in new senses when they are operationalized in psychology, but they inevitably retain many of the connotations they have in ordinary language.[4] This may be experi-

[4] One of the best examples of this in the history of psychology is the debate regarding the operational definition of "intelligence" in psychometric research (Thorndike et al., 1921). According to

enced as a nuisance by some psychologists seeking precision in their terminology. Indeed, Skinner's (1976) radical behaviorism may be viewed in part as an attempt to purify the language of psychology in order to remove the "unscientific" connotations of psychological terms in natural language. But it may be doubted whether such a purification of psychological discourse is really possible, if psychology is to retain any relevance at all to everyday life. This was one of Chomsky's (1959) criticisms of Skinner's position: that in attempting to apply the findings of research in operant learning to everyday problems, Skinner is forced to translate the purified terms of behaviorism back into the "imprecise" usages of natural language which he had sought to avoid. Wittgenstein reminds us that the imprecision of natural language is not a shortcoming. It may even be regarded as essential for its purposes (*PI,* 71 ff.). Insofar as the constructs of psychologists are related to the rest of life, their special language remains a neighborhood within a vast metropolis.

The questions that psychologists are called upon to answer, for example, may well be formulated in the terms of ordinary language. But in preparing to answer these questions, the terms in which the question is posed may be "operationalized" in such a way as to make it possible to apply certain methods. As we have seen, this can result in a subtle shift of meaning. In this way, it can occur that the question is asked in the context of one language-game, but answered in another. The question may have to do with "dreaming" (or some other ordinary language term) and the answer may be framed in terms of rapid eye movements (or some other observable phenomena). This is something like responding to a queen's pawn opening with a pair of aces. In Wittgenstein's telling phrase, "problem and method pass one another by" (*PI,* p. 232 e).

According to Wittgenstein, it is this unacknowledged redefinition of mental states and processes in order to make them more amenable to particular methods that results in the controveries regarding their nature.

How does the philosophical problem about mental processes and states and about behaviourism arise? – The first step is the one that altogether escapes notice. We talk of processes and states and leave their nature undecided. Sometime perhaps we shall know more about them – we think. But that is just what commits us to a particular way of looking at the matter. For we have a definite concept of what it means to learn to know a process better. (The decisive movement in the conjuring trick has been made, and it was the very one that we thought quite inno-

---

the present interpretation, the difficulties associated with operationalizing this term stem from the fact that "intelligence" is a family-resemblance concept in ordinary language. This means that *any* attempt to operationalize the concept in terms of necessary and sufficient conditions will be unsatisfying to our intuitions, because such an operational definition can at best capture only one of the many cases subsumed by this concept. Boring's (1923) suggestion, to define "intelligence" as "what the tests measure," is an attempt to overcome this difficulty by explicitly abandoning the attempt to measure intelligence as ordinarily understood (i. e., covering all cases subsumed by the ordinary concept). But even this pure operationalization remains dependent on ordinary language for its primary meaning. It only makes sense to call "what the tests measure" by the name of "intelligence" if this operationalization in fact overlaps with the ordinary uses of this word. It would make no sense whatever, for example, to include running speed among measures of "intelligence," however operationalized, because in this case there is no overlap at all with ordinary usage.

cent.) - And now the analogy which was to make us understand our thoughts falls to pieces. So we have to deny the yet uncomprehended process in the yet unexplored medium. And now it looks as if we had denied mental processes. And naturally we don't want to deny them. (*PI*, 308)

As psychologists, we indeed have "a definite concept of what it means to learn to know a process better." According to the functionalist (or "neofunctionalist") perspective which has influenced the thinking of most contemporary psychologists to a greater or lesser extent (cf. Beilin, 1983), "to know a process better" is to specify its causal or functional antecedents. But when applied to the relation between mental states and their associated behaviors, this explanatory scheme can be a source of confusion. To begin with, it might be supposed that the mental states are the causes of the respective behaviors (mentalism). Introspection is then understood as a privileged method by which we can learn about the causes of our own behavior (introspectionism). But if the mental state is a causal antecedent of the behavior, then it is ispo facto regarded as conceptually and ontologically independent from the behavior. In seeking to explain mental states and processes in a particular way, we have already committed ourselves to a certain way of looking at things. This conceptualization now runs into problems, for if the mental state is really distinct from all observable behavior (including verbal reports), then it is essentially hidden from public view. This raises doubts that the mental state as such is an appropriate object of scientific psychology (behaviorism). Against this, evidence of consistency between introspective reports and certain "objective" measures of cognitive processes is hailed as demonstrating that the scientific study of mental states understood in this way is indeed possible (the new cognitivism). But problems remain: The fact that introspective verbal reports do not always coincide with objective indicators of the causes of behavior leads to skepticism about our awareness of our own mental states (Nisbett & Wilson, 1977). Our mental experience is now viewed, not only as being inaccessible to others, but also as inaccessible to ourselves!

The drift of Wittgenstein's various remarks on many of these matters was summarized above. If mental states were really hidden from view, we couldn't even speak about them intelligibly. We would never know when we were speaking about *the same thing*. The fact that we can and do speak about mental states intelligibly indicates that these states, as identified by their respective criteria, are there for all to see. The relation between the state and the behavioral or other phenomena which serve as their criteria is conceptual rather than causal or functional.

In terms of Wittgenstein's own example: If the subjective sensation of pain is strictly a *cause* of writhing, then the pain itself must be distinct from the behavior which results from it. But all we see is the behavior. We are thereby committed to viewing the pain as essentially hidden from view. In fact, writhing with evident cause is one of the criteria for "pain." If we wanted to teach someone who was learning our language the use of the word "pain," we might point to a person writhing on the floor and say, "This person is in pain," or even, "This is 'pain'." Chances are we wouldn't say, "This person is writhing on the floor because of something that is hidden from us, and that thing we call 'pain'." In Wittgenstein's words: "If I see someone writhing in pain with evident cause I do not think: all the same, his feelings are hidden from me" (*PI*, p. 223 e). There is a sense in which we actually *see* the pain expressed in a person's behavior – just as we can see the emotion expressed in a person's face (*RPP2*, 570).

This is not to say that psychology cannot also be concerned with causal or functional relations – only that it is inappropriate to conceive of the relation between a mental state as ordinarily understood and its behavioral expression in these terms. By thinking of the relation between behavior and mental states in terms of a causal or functional explanatory scheme, we modify the meanings of our terms accordingly. The decisive step in the "conjuring trick" has been taken. But to the extent that we remain unaware of what we have done, we ourselves are the ones who are fooled by it! A "mental state" conceived of as a cause or functional antecedent of certain accompanying phenomena is something somewhat different than a "mental state" as identified by its criterial phenomena. At one extreme, purely artificial terms may result which no longer pretend to have any relation to natural language usages – as when physicists speak of the "charm," "color," and "spin" of subatomic particles. In psychology, however, the differences between the natural and technical uses of psychological terms is not so great as to be obvious. This is a major source of the "conceptual confusion" in psychology that Wittgenstein described.

The Problem of "Response Criteria" in Developmental Psychology

In the preceding sections, the relevance of Wittgenstein's philosophy for some problems in psychology has been summarized in a general way. But it might still be asked how this way of thinking can be applied in specific cases. The remainder of this chapter is an attempt to answer this question. Wittgenstein's method is applied to some central issues in the study of children's cognitive development.

The problem is the following: In Piaget's vast research program on the development of children's logical, mathematical and physical reasoning, it was found that "concrete operational" thinking generally did not appear before the age of about seven to eight years (Inhelder & Piaget, 1955/1958, 1959/1969; Piaget & Inhelder, 1941/1974; Piaget & Szeminkska, 1941/1964). With respect to certain difficult areas of content (e.g., weight and volume), the classifications, seriations, and conservations characterizing concrete operations might develop somewhat later (Piaget & Inhelder, 1941/1974), but it was rare that he found them in children much younger than seven years. During the 1970's, however, Piaget came under increasing criticism for "underestimating" children's abilities. Many research studies appeared to demonstrate that children below the age of seven could solve typical concrete operational tasks under certain facilitating conditions (see review by Gelman & Bargaillon, 1983). For example, five-year-olds were found capable of solving a transitive reasoning task if they were trained on the premises of the argument (Bryant & Trabasso, 1971), and even three- to four-year-olds were able to recreate the perspective of another person on a miniature landscape if they were allowed to indicate the other's perspective by rotating the display appropriately (Borke, 1975).

Such findings were interpreted in terms of what came to be known as the *competence-performance distinction.* According to this view, children's observable performance on any cognitive task has two necessary components: an underlying competence and one or more "performance factors" which translate that competence into the required behaviors. Since both competence and performance factors are necessary for success, failure may be due to the absence of either one of them. Generally, competence is equated with a basic understanding of the problem and "performance factors" with memory or verbal skills which can affect the difficulty of the task in ways which are not directly relevant to the competence being assessed. The prototypical example given by Brainerd (1978) is a verbal arithmetic test given to a group of English-speaking students in Russian: Even if the students in question are fully competent in arithmetic, they will fail the test if they lack the performance factor of mastery in the Russian language.

In these terms, it has been argued that Piaget underestimated children's competencies because his clinical assessment methods rely too heavily on certain verbal, memory, or other performance factors unrelated to the logical competencies presumably tapped by the tasks in question. Younger children tend to fail these tasks, not because they are intrinsically incapable of the logical operations required, but because they lack the additional performance factors required by the method of assessment. In Bryant and Trabasso's (1971) study of transitive reasoning, for example, it was argued that young children fail traditional transitive reasoning tasks, not because they lack transitivity, but because their memory skills are deficient: They tend to forget the premises of the argument before they are able to draw the conclusion. The results of their study seemed to confirm this interpretation: Young children given compensatory training on the premises of transitivity problems were indeed found to solve those problems at an earlier age than they would otherwise be expected to do.

One of the most significant applications of the competence-performance distinction with respect to the issues raised in this chapter is the issue of "response criteria" in assessing children's understanding. In Piaget's classical method, children are typically asked to explain their judgments in solving particular logical problems. Both judgments and explanations are used as criteria for correctness. Many of Piaget's critics, however, have argued that requiring children to explain their judgments unduly taxes their verbal skills. Giving an explanation involves certain performance factors unrelated to the competence being assessed. For this reason, it has been argued that children's judgments alone provide a more valid index of their competencies than judgments plus explanations, and many studies have accordingly used judgments alone as criteria for success.

In an influential paper, Brainerd (1973) sought to justify this practice in terms of Piaget's own theory. More accurately, the judgments only criterion was justified in terms of Flavell's (1963) interpretation of Piaget's views on the relation between language and thought. According to Flavell, Piaget's view of this relation can be summarized in the formula, "language behavior is here treated as a dependent variable with cognition as the independent variable" (Flavell, 1963, p. 271). For Brainerd, this implied that explanations in Piagetian-type tasks are sufficient but not necessary for the presence of the underlying competence. In other words, the explanations depend on language skills unrelated to the logical competence meant to be assessed. Thus, the requirement that children should explain their judgment guarantees that children's competencies will be underestimated, since there are very likely to be some children who possess the competence in question but lack whatever performance skills are necessary to give a satisfactory explanation.

It was realized early on that the use of different response criteria (judgments alone vs. judgments plus explanations) would lead to differing results, but the significance of this fact was interpreted in different ways. Gruen (1966) expressed doubts that investigators using different response criteria were even studying the same phenomena. "Transitivity" as assessed by judgments alone could be a qualitively different phenomenon than "transitivity" as assessed by judgments plus explanations. Other interpreters, of whom Brainerd (e.g., 1977) is one of the most articulate exponents, have approached the problem through the use of a measurement model. According to this view, it is assumed (1) that investigators using different response criteria are indeed studying the same competence, (2) that children may be described as either possessing or not possessing this competence, and (3) that different results are obtained using different response criteria because these criteria are associated with different rates of *measurement error*. The requirement that children should explain their judgments has a built-in source of *false negative* error, since there are likely to be children who possess the competence in question but who lack the verbal or other performance skills to explain their answers. In contrast, the judgments-only criterion may be characterized by a certain *false positive* error, since some children may give a correct answer by chance, or for some other reason unrelated to the competence being assessed. In an elaborate mathematical proof, Brainerd (1977) argues that the overall amount of error is likely to be less with the more liberal (judgments only) as opposed to the more conservative (judgments plus explanations) criterion.

This conclusion follows inevitably from the assumptions shared by the measurement model and the competence-performance distinction. But Wittgenstein reminds us that, in the very attempt to apply this model, we may be committing ourselves to a particular way of looking at things. As with any mathematical model, applying the measurement model involves a provisional acceptance of its assumptions. The results obtained are conditional upon our acceptance. In effect, we ask ourselves, "How would things look, if we look at them in this particular way"? As long as we remember the provisionality of our assumptions and the conditionality of our results, there is no problem. But insofar as we are committed to a particular mode of explanation, we may feel that the assumptions of our model are inevitably forced upon us by necessity, that there is literally no alternative. Wittgenstein's analysis of psychological concepts in ordinary language suggests that the assumptions of the measurement model are not necessarily made in ordinary usage. Not only is there an alternative way of looking at things, but the alternative is closer to our primary, or original understanding of psychological concepts.

In the next section, Wittgenstein's method is applied to the problem of "response criteria" in research on cognitive development. First, the uses of "understanding" in ordinary language will be reviewed. Then we shall consider what is involved in applying a measurement model to this concept.

Understanding a Concept and the Concept of Understanding

As described in earlier sections of this chapter, one of Wittgenstein's major concerns in his later work was to elucidate the concepts of "knowing" and "understanding" in terms of the criteria by which they may be attributed to individuals. In this respect, Wittgenstein's thinking is directly relevant to the problem of "response criteria" as reviewed in the preceding section. For this problem also involves attributions of conceptual understanding: When are psychologists justified in attributing to children knowledge and understanding of particular concepts?

The problem of "response criteria" follows from the fact that there are multiple ordinary-language criteria for "understanding a concept." Correctly using the word which denotes the concept, being able to explain it to another person, or applying it in concrete or hypothetical situations are all likely to serve as alternative criteria for understanding. But it would appear that these alternative criteria do not necessarily hang together in the process of *acquiring* competence in language use. As we have just seen, children have been found to be capable of answering certain questions regarding concrete applications of certain concepts before they are able to explain them adequately. In other cases, children are found to be able to explain a certain concept before they can use the technical term for it (as when Inhelder and Piaget's [1955/1958] subjects in the balance task explain the physical concept of "work" before they have actually learned the word). The question is how to interpret such findings? How do we decide what is the "correct" criterion for understanding a concept under conditions in which the usual multiple criteria no longer hang together?

The problem arises because we seek to define our concepts in a precise manner, that is, in terms of necessary and sufficient conditions. The multiple ordinary-language criteria for "knowing" or "understanding" thus come to be used as "response criteria": the necessary and sufficient conditions which permit one to *infer* the existence of "knowing" or "understanding". Then, if these multiple (response) criteria no longer coincide, the very concept of understanding appears to dissolve into a *family of related concepts.* "Understanding" comes to be used in different *senses,* defined in terms of the different response criteria.

Thus, "understanding" a concept defined in terms of using the corresponding word correctly no longer coincides with "understanding" that concept defined in terms of an appropriate explanation, and so on. The fact that different psychologists using different response criteria find children to understand "transitivity" and "conservation" at different ages raises the question whether they are even talking about the same thing (cf. Gruen, 1966). "Understanding transitivity" *defined as* a correct judgment in a transitivity task would appear to develop earlier than "understanding transitivity" defined as a correct explanation of a transitivity judgment. The question then becomes one of determining which definition is the more appropriate (and upon what grounds this decision is to be made). The problem might be solved through a new convention, an arbitrary consensus that under conditions when the usual criteria no longer coincide, a particular sense of "transitivity" will be acknowledged as the conventionally correct one. But this solution presupposes that the problem is recognized as a matter of convention. Psychologists have tended to approach the question differently.

The use of a measurement model, for example, appears to resolve the problem of multiple response criteria in a rigorous manner. According to the model, each different response criterion constitutes a separate indicator of the same underlying concept. Since each indicator is associated with certain false positive and false negative error rates, no single one of them need be considered the "true" indicator of the concept in question. The measurement model, however, raises questions of its own. How do we know that different response criteria for "transitivity" or "conservation" in fact measure the *same* underlying construct and not a family of related, but distinguishable concepts? How do we even decide this question? The usual psychometric method of establishing construct validity, looking to see to what extent different indicators of the "same" underlying construct actually correlate with each other, is of no use in the present case, for our problem arises from a situation in which different response criteria do not in fact correlate with each other. The question is how to interpret the fact that some children can satisfy one criterion for understanding a particular concept but not another.

To answer this question, we must consider the basic assumptions of the measurement model. Far from assuming that there is only one valid index of understanding, the measurement model assumes instead that each different "response criterion" is a fallible estimate of the child's "true" understanding. It is assumed, moreover, that the "true" understanding of a given concept is acquired once and for all at a single point in time, that at any given moment a child can be characterized as either possessing or not possessing the concept. If this were not the case, one could not meaningfully speak of false negative and false positive measurement error. According to this view, acquiring the understanding of a concept is like receiving a diploma; it marks a one-time transition from one status to another. This way of looking at things seems so natural, it is hard to see that we have any choice in the matter. It appears to be forced upon us for lack of any reasonable alternative.

Wittgenstein might say at this point that the measurement model is a "picture" which has captured our attention and forced us into looking at the problem in a certain way. One alternative model is the following: Instead of viewing the attainment of a concept as occurring all at once, it is seen as occurring in degrees. Coming to understand a concept is seen to be less like receiving a diploma than like entering a fraternal order characterized by degrees of membership. The child is viewed as passing through various *grades of understanding* on the way to becoming a full member of the linguistic community. The various criteria for understanding with their differing levels of difficulty are the conventional markers by which the community recognizes these progressive degrees of membership in their company. Instead of viewing different criteria for understanding as estimates of a hypothetical "true" understanding, they are thought of as *constitutive* criteria for each degree of membership in the community of understanding. The construct of "true" understanding, which can only be estimated and not directly observed, is replaced by a sequence of degrees of understanding, each directly *constituted* by its respective criterion. One of these degrees may even be conventionally considered by the community as constituting "full" membership in its body.

Given this choice of perspectives, how do we choose between them? One answer is that the choice is arbitrary. We choose a perspective in order to see how things look from that perspective. What we see is conditional upon our choice. Confusion crises only if we *forget that we have chosen* and the perspective adopted is taken to be necessary and absolute. But even though our choice of perspectives may be arbitrary in this sense, it may also have certain practical consequences which we do well to consider. One perspective may be more useful for our purposes, may involve fewer conceptual difficulties, may be more "sensible" linguistically than another.

The choice between the measurement and membership models, for example, has immediate consequences for the issue of "response criteria" in research on cognitive development. The use of the judgments-only criterion by Piaget's critics is based on its presumed closeness to a hypothetical "true" score. As we have seen, the application of the measurement model has resulted in favoring more "liberal" over more "conservative" criteria because of the former's presumedly lower rates of measurement error. The adoption of the judgments-plus-explanations criterion is favored by Piagetians, however, because it is understood as a conventional marker of concrete-operational understanding. In this perspective, the judgments-plus-explanations criterion is not an *estimate* of full membership, rather it *constitutes* full membership in a certain community of understanding. From the perspective of the measurement model, the latter criterion appears to underestimate children's "true" understanding. From the perspective of the membership model on the other hand, the choice of ever more liberal criteria as better estimates of a hypothetical "true" understanding means only that researchers' attention is focused on ever more partial degrees of understanding. What has usually been missed in this discussion is the fact that the two parties are (so to speak) no longer speaking the same language. Although many of the same terms are employed, they are employed in different ways. The disputants appear to differ in their description of the facts when in fact they differ in the conventions they have adopted.

This brings us back to the competence-performance distinction, for it is this distinction, when combined with the measurement model, that leads to the preference for more "liberal" response criteria. "Conservative" response criteria are suspected of resulting in high false negative measurement error, because they are believed to confound children's "true" understanding (competence) with one or more performance factors. Note that the distinction between competence and performance makes sense only if the two are conceptually distinct – if the "performance factors" considered in the particular case are not part of the concept of the competence being assessed. In Brainerd's (1978) prototypical example, this requirement is clearly fulfilled. Competence in the Russian language is conceptually distinct from competence in mathematics; the latter can be assessed independently of the former (in a language that the individual understands). It may be doubted, however, that this requirement of conceptual independence is met in every case in which the competence-performance distinction has been applied in practice.

Consider the argument that children can fail transitive reasoning tasks, not because they lack the capacity for transitive reasoning, but because their memory skills are insufficient to retain the premises of the arguments (Bryant & Trabasso, 1971). Here it might be argued that remembering the premises is *implied* in "transitive reasoning" as ordinarily understood (cf. Russell, this volume). If "transitive reasoning" is the drawing of a conclusion (e.g., "A is longer than C"), given certain premises ("A is longer than B" and "B is longer than C"), then memory for the premises in some sense would seem to be presupposed in our very concept of transitivity. This does not prevent researchers from finding that children's "transitivity" performance is statistically unrelated to memory for premises (Brainerd & Kingma, 1984), but it may be doubted that the competency assessed in such studies can be called "transitive reasoning" in any meaningful sense.[5]

---

[5] Several studies have demonstrated empirically that some attempts to reduce the performance demands of concrete operational tasks have indeed made it possible for children to solve them with qualitatively different means. With respect to transitivity, for example, Chapman and Lindenberger (1986) compared two previously-used versions of transitivity of length and weight tasks to children aged 6–9. In the standard Piagetian version, comparison objects were presented only two at a time (A compared to B, and B to C), so that a solution could be obtained only through *operational composition of relations* ("A is longer than C, because A is longer than B and B is longer than A"). In a modified version, all objects were visible during questioning, arranged in order from left to right, but too far apart for differences in length to be perceived. This allowed children to infer length *as a function* of spatial orientation ("A is longer than C, because A is to the right of C"). In short, the two tasks did not measure the same thing, even if they both have been generally called measures of "transitivity." In fact, only the standard version can said to assess the understanding of transitivity, since the latter is *defined* in terms of the composition of relations. Note that one could not distinguish between the two competencies assessed by these two tasks with a judgments-only criterion, for the judgments are the same in either case ("A is longer than B"). It was the explanations given by children in this study that distinguished their different methods of reasoning.

The argument becomes even more acute in the issue of judgments only versus judgments-plus-explanations. It is one thing to argue that there are certain language skills (e.g., understanding a foreign language) which are conceptually unrelated to the logical or mathematical competencies of interest, but it is something else to assume that language *itself* is only an inessential "performance factor" with respect to such competencies. In some cases, explanations may be presupposed in our concept of the competency to be assessed. In such cases, it makes no sense to assume that this competency can be assessed just as well (or better!) without explanations.

Consider the case of arithmetic. It is part of our ordinary concept of competence in arithmetical computation that the individuals in question can not only obtain correct answers to arithmetic problems, but also explain how they do it. This is indicated by the fact that in unusual cases (e.g., calculating prodigies) in which these two criteria no longer coincide (correct answers are obtained, but no explanation can be given how they were obtained), we are apt to doubt whether the competency that is so demonstrated is the *same* as that exhibited in the normal case. The calculating prodigy who obtains correct answers without being able to explain how certainly demonstrates a mastery of arithmetic in some sense, but is it the same intellectual competence that the rest of us demonstrate when we compute a sum or a product in a way that we can also explain? (See Baker & Hacker, 1985, on the internal relation between explanations and applications in "following a rule.")

One is inclined to say that in some cases explanations may be conceptually presupposed in the competency under consideration, in other cases not. It depends on how we understand the competency in each case. It could be argued, for example, that explanations are conceptually presupposed in the competencies of interest to Piagetians. This would seem to be implied, for example, in the argument that it is not merely a correct answer that is sufficient to identify concrete operational competence, but a demonstration of the understanding that the answer is also *necessary*.[6] Since the present essay is an interpretation of Wittgenstein and not of Piaget, this question will not be pursued (see Chapman, in press). Instead, we shall limit ourselves to the following observation: To the extent that explanations (or any other cognitive skill) are conceptually presupposed by the competency of interest, they cannot meaningfully be designated as "performance factors" which could possibly be eliminated from our "response criterion." If they were eliminated, we would no longer be assessing the "same" competency. By changing our operational definition, we would have changed

[6] According to my understanding of Piaget, Brainerd (1973) is simply mistaken when he writes that the comprehension of necessity is not an essential part of concrete operational understanding in Piaget's theory. It is in large part the feeling of necessity proper to operational thinking that Piaget seeks to explain with his theory of structures. (See "The problem of the necessity proper to the logical structures" in Piaget, 1968, pp. 120 ff.) Since it is hard to imagine how children's understanding of necessity could be determined without reference to their verbal explanations, it is difficult to see how one can argue that these explanations are not essential for assessing competence in concrete operations as defined by Piaget.

the meanings of our terms. And if we continue to believe we are talking about the same things, our thinking would be characterized by "conceptual confusion."

Applying Wittgenstein's method of criteria to the competence-performance distinction leads to the following conclusion: From being necessarily hidden behind observable performances, a person's competence is understood to be *manifest* in the performance (or average performance) exhibited under certain conventionally-determined standard assessment conditions. It is still meaningful according to this view to distinguish between competence and performance under conditions of assessment which impose difficulties above and beyond those inherent in the standard conditions. In Brainerd's example, the arithmetic performance of English-speaking students tested in Russian does not provide an accurate indicator of their competence in arithmetic, because "competence" means the performance that they would show under the standard conditions of assessment in their own language. It makes no sense, however, to assert that individuals' performance under the *standard* conditions "underestimates" their "true" competence, for how is this "true" competence to be determined? If one changes the standard assessment conditions, one alters by that very fact the competence being assessed. This is something like arguing that standard track conditions underestimate runners' "true" competence, since they show lower running times when the "extraneous" effects of air resistence are removed by a strong tail wind. This line of reasoning suggests that controversies in developmental psychology regarding the "true" ages at which children develop certain competencies may have less to do with empirical *facts* than with different *conventions* governing the definition and assessment of the competencies involved.

Conclusion: Implications of a Wittgensteinian Psychology

The foregoing discussion of the implications of Wittgenstein's philosophy for psychology was limited to a few illustrative examples. No doubt many others could be found. Buss' (1978) discussion of the confusion between causes and reasons in attributional theory and research provides an additional example. According to the present interpretation, Wittgenstein's importance for psychology consists in the fact that he calls our attention to ways in which psychological concepts are actually employed in our discourse with each other. This radical reflection on the uses of language can help to identify confusions which arise when actual differences in usage are obscured by a presumption of shared meaning. The point is not simply that we should "define our terms," but that we must reflect upon the ways in which the grammar of psychological terms may mislead us (see Coulter, this volume, on "recognition").

Without wishing to reduce Wittgenstein's message for psychology to the dimensions of a formula, the epistenological implications of his philosophy of language can be summarized by saying that our knowledge is limited by our understanding: We cannot claim to know any more than we can clearly understand. By providing a method for identifying the sources of our "conceptual confusions," Wittgenstein promises to help us understand one another better and thereby to remove certain conceptual limitations on our collective claims to knowledge.

References

Baker, G.P., & Hacker, P.M.S. (1982). The grammar of psychology: Wittgenstein's *Bemerkungen über die Philosophie der Psychologie. Language & Communication, 2,* 227-244.

Baker, G.P. , & Hacker, P.M.S. (1985). *Scepticism, rules and Language.* Oxford: Blackwell.

Bartley, W.W., III. (1977). *Wittgenstein.* London: Quartet Books.

Beilin, H.(1983). The new functionalism and the Piagetian program. In E.K. Scholnick (Ed.), *New trends in conceptual representation.* Hillsdale, NJ: Erlbaum.

Bloor, D.(1983). *Wittgenstein: A social theory of knowledge.* London: Macmillan.

Boring, E.G. (1923). Intelligence as the tests test it. *New Republic, 35,* 35-37.

Borke, H.(1975). Piaget's mountains revisited: Changes in the egocentric landscape. *Developmental Psychology, 11,* 240-243.

Brainerd, C.J. (1973). Judgments and explanations as criteria for the presence of cognitive structure. *Psychological Bulletin, 79,* 172-179.

Brainerd, C.J. (1977). Response criteria in concept development research. *Child Development, 48,* 360-366.

Brainerd, C.J. (1978). *Piaget's theory of intelligence.* Englewood Cliffs, NJ: Prentice-Hall.

Brainerd, C.J., & Kingma, J.(1984). Do children have to remember to reason? A fuzzy-trace theory of transitivity development. *Developmental Review, 4,* 311-377.

Brose, K.(1985). *Sprachspiel und Kindersprache.* Frankfurt a.M.: Campus.

Bryant, P., & Trabasso, T.(1971). Transitive inferences and memory in young children. *Nature, 323,* 456-458.

Buss, A.R. (1978). Causes and reasons in attribution theory: A conceptual critique. *Journal of Personality and Social Psychology, 11,* 1311-1321.

Chapman, M.(in press). *Constructive evolution: Origins and development of Piaget's thought.* Cambridge: Cambridge University Press.

Chapman, P., & Lindenberger, U.(1986). *Functions, operations, and decalage in the development of transitivty.* Manuscript submitted for publication.

Chihara, C.S., & Fodor, J.A. (1981). Operationalism and ordinary language: A critique of Wittgenstein. In H.Morick (Ed.), *Wittgenstein and the problem of other minds.* New Jersey: Humanities Press. (Originally published, 1965)

Chomsky, N.(1959). Review of Skinner's "Verbal Behavior." *Language, 35,* 26-58.

Costell, A.(1980). The limits of language: Wittgenstein's later philosophy and Skinner's radical behaviorism. *Behaviorism, 8,* 123-131.

Day, W.F. (1969). On certain similarities between the *Philosophical investigations* of Ludwig Wittgenstein and the operationism of B.F. Skinner. *Journal of the Experimental Analysis of Behavior, 12,* 489-506.

Flavell, J.H. (1963). *The developmental psychology of Jean Piaget.* Princeton, NJ: Van Nostrand.

Gelman, R., & Baillargeon, R.(1983). A review of some Piagetian concepts. In P.H. Mussen (Ed.), *Handbook of child psychology, Vol. 3: Cognitive Development.* New York: Wiley.

Gruen, G.E. (1966). Note on conservation: Methodological and definitional considerations. *Child Development, 37,* 977-983.

Inhelder, B., & Piaget, J.(1958). *The growth of logical thinking from childhood to adolescence.* New York: Basic Books. (Originally published, 1954)

Inhelder, B., & Piaget, J.(1969). *The early growth of logic in the child.* New York: Norton. (Originally published, 1959)

Kenny, A. (1972). *Wittgenstein.* London: Penguin.
Malcolm, N. (1958). *Dreaming.* London: Routledge & Kegan Paul.
Nisbett, R. E., & Wilson, T. D. (1977). Telling more than we can know: Verbal reports on mental processes. *Psychological Review, 84,* 231-259.
Pears, D. (1971). *Wittgenstein.* London: Fontana/Collins.
Piaget, J. (1968). *Six psychological studies.* New York: Vintage. (Originally published, 1964)
Piaget, J., & Szeminska, A. (1980). *La genèse du nombre chez enfant.* Neuchâtel: Delachaux et Niestlé. (Originally published, 1941)
Piaget, J., & Inhelder, B. (1974). *The child's construction of quantities.* London: Routledge & Kegan Paul. (Originally published, 1941)
Rosch, E. (1978). Principles of categorization. In E. Rosch & B. B. Lloyd (Eds.), *Cognition and categorization.* Hillsdale, NJ: Erlbaum.
Skinner, B. F. (1976). *About behaviorism.* New York: Vintage.
Thorndike, E. L., Terman. L. M., Freeman, F. N., Colrin, S. S., Pinter, R., Ruml, B., & Pressey, S. L. (1921). Intelligence and its measurement: A Symposium. *Journal of Educational Psychology, 12,* 123-147.
Watson, J. B. (1965). Psychology as the behaviorist views it. In R. J. Herrnstein & E. G. Boring (Eds.), *A source book in the history of psychology.* Cambridge, MA: Harvard University Press. (Originally published, 1913)
Wellman, C. (1981). Wittgenstein's conception of a criterion. In H. Morick (Ed.), *Wittgenstein and the problem of other minds.* New Jersey: Humanities Press. (Originally published, 1962)
Wuchterl, K., & Hübner, A. (1979). *Ludwig Wittgenstein.* Reinbek bei Hamburg: *Rowohlt.*

Chapter 8 Wittgenstein's "Forms of Life": A Cultural Template for Psychology

Joseph Margolis

The whole of psychology is in search of an orientation. Developmental psychology can hardly be the least of its sub-disciplines in this respect.

It is, of course, not altogether clear what conceptual boundaries should be imposed on the legitimate issues of developmental psychology. At one extreme, for instance, Marxist and Hegelian speculations about the historical conditions of human consciousness seem not altogether ineligible - quite convincingly so, if one considers only the promise and obvious power of the line of investigation favored by Vygotsky (1978) and Luria (1976) and its increasing attraction for Western psychologists and theorists otherwise hard put to formulate a resourceful account of the dynamics of social history within the context of which, individual development may be effectively located. At the other extreme, it is impossible, at the present stage at which psychology and the so-called cognitive and informational sciences are conventionally taken to be interconnected, to disallow questions of the machine simulation of human intelligence to count as professionally pertinent regarding the study of individual development (see Boden, 1977). And within the implied span marked by these two extremes, the more biologically centered quarrels about the nature of developmental processes cannot be more instructively focused than it is in the well-known debate between Jean Piaget and Noam Chomsky (see Piattelli-Palmarini, 1980) - which obliges us to weigh the competing claims of versions of nativism and of interactional models, both, of course, peculiarly slimly occupied with the structure and structuring functions of living societies. Nor, within those same limits, can the bare complexity of the diachronic processes of societal history (pertinent to our issue) be more clearly glimpsed than in texts largely ignored in standard discussions of developmental psychology - for instance, in Bourdieu (1977; see Bourdieu & Passeron, 1977), in Gadamer (1975), in Habermas (1979), and in Bakhtin (1981).

It is in some such prepared setting that one asks what the bearing of Ludwig Wittgenstein's work may be on the direction of developmental psychology. Obviously, despite the profound sense in which Wittgenstein was (perhaps best viewed as) a speculative mind centered on the puzzles of developmental psychology, even his most pertinent reflections cannot be easily incorporated within the usual canonical literature. Both Wittgenstein's style of comment and his well-known double messages about philosophical or conceptual theorizing tend to block any ready reference to his views, at the level of first-order empirical psychology (see Williams, 1985). Nevertheless, within a framework of the large sort just sketched, it seems entirely natural to pose the question.

Indeed, once it is so posed, the general shape of the answer - at least a viable and pertinent answer – stares one in the face. Put somewhat indirectly, for the sake of tact and the advantages of strategy, what Wittgenstein contributes most is a sense of the proper *balance* and *gauge* of work most central to the field. These are terms of art, of course, designed to postpone confrontation until certain preparations are in place. The point to be pressed is simply that Wittgenstein himself failed to develop even very promisingly what is most promising in his own conception of the conditions of human development; that what *is* promising about it may be forcefully recommended to the profession; and that that cannot be effectively pursued without going beyond the usual boundaries of the discipline, to just the sort of text already mentioned: that is, to texts not usually consulted, texts that link developmental psychology to the whole array of human science, social science and cultural criticism, texts preeminently "Wittgensteinian" in the minimal sense here intended. So placed, or preplaced, the required argument is entirely straightforward. However that may be, we must concede that its theme is, on its face, somewhat removed from first-order developmental studies, much more concerned with promoting a conceptual orientation within which to pursue such studies. The developmental psychologist will wonder about its full pertinence and benefit.

The terms "balance" and "gauge" may be taken, respectively, as epithets signifying the horizontal and vertical dimensions of an ideally organized developmental psychology: Whereas "balance" signifies the proper placement of our discipline within the range of overlapping issues shared by the biological and social sciences, "gauge" signifies the proper model of the dynamics of – the forces and conditions affecting – the relevant processes of development. The charm and power of Wittgenstein's contribution, then, lies with the intuitively convincing simplicity with which he managed to articulate the most difficult issues regarding both dimensions – through his inimitable conceptual vignettes – so as to suggest how, favorably, to resolve theoretical questions affecting all forms of rational inquiry and what, dialectically, must be assigned the central role in any of the best alternative explanatory accounts likely to be relevantly formed and ebated.

Forms of Life

It will come as no surprise to those familiar with Wittgenstein that the dual benefit may be traced to the notion of "a form of life" *(Lebensform).* One commentator, Finch (1977), usefully observes that the expression occurs only five times in the *Philosophical investigations* (it does occur elsewhere), and that Wittgenstein makes no attempt to define it (Finch, 1977, p. 89).[1] It is certainly one of the master concepts of Wittgenstein's entire "later" philosophy, possibly the most strate-

[1] Finch rightly criticizes one of the few earlier, quite uninstructive, analyses of Wittgenstein's notion in Hunter (1968).

gic – and it is the one most intimately connected with the issue of developmental psychology. But although he correctly objects to construing the expression as making merely "factual or quasi-factual" distinctions as opposed to "grammatical or semantic" ones (the easy linkage of "grammatical" and "semantic" is itself an unintended warning that something is wrong), Finch takes it that those interested in the social sciences will probably understand that:

> *forms of life* are roughly what they call 'social facts' or 'institutional facts'; only for Wittgenstein they are not 'facts,' but units of meaningful action which are carried out together by members of a social group and which have a common meaning for the members of the group ... [that is, not really as] *facts*, but rather as *forms* which means possibilities of meaning, analogous to language-games, but in the area of human social actions. Forms of life [then] are established *patterns of action* shared in by members of a group. (Finch, 1977, p. 90)

Insofar as this is nearly right, it hardly says more than Wittgenstein himself makes mention of; but insofar as it is wrong, it is quite disappointingly misleading – precisely because it fails to feature what is so remarkable about Wittgenstein's much-admired theme. Roughly, what Finch does not altogether fail to note, what nearly everyone who reads Wittgenstein can hardly miss, is part of the essential clue about what we've dubbed the "balance" of the account: *the proper placement of developmental psychology within the context of societal life*. That is surely part of the obvious thrust of Wittgenstein's notion. But Finch gets the "gauge" wrong, *the point and nature of the descriptive and explanatory model of human behavior construed generically in developmental terms*. One senses this for instance in the choice of such terms as "units of meaningful action," "common meaning," "established patterns of action," and the like. These are the terms of *system* – in that sense of "system" that may be said to be shared by the *Tractatus*, the structuralists, the Chomskians, formal logicians, the positivists, and those favorably disposed to the progressive simulation of human behavior by finite machine programs construed as exhibiting artificial intelligence. By "system," we may understand any domain construed as: (1) determinately structured; (2) deterministic; (3) homonomic with respect to a match between descriptive and explanatory vocabularies; (4) closed with respect to finitely many universal explanatory principles, laws, rules or the like; (5) totalized with respect to all possible phenomena pertinent to that domain and to its explanatory concern; (6) ideally capable of being thus characerized synchronically. The two principal (quite dissimilar) models of systems developed in our own time are those of the unity of science program (which favors physicalist reduction) and of (chiefly French) structuralism (which favors "unconscious," formal, generative syntaxes or related schemata). Wittgenstein was certainly utterly opposed to conceptions of these sorts insofar as he invoked the notion of forms of life. To grasp the linkage between the two issues (balance and gauge) is the essential key to the *Philosophical investigations* and to its promised contribution (together with the rest of Wittgenstein's "later" philosophy) to the theory of developmental psychology.

The correction of Finch's suggestions is not here intended in a merely exegetical sense: It is meant rather to assist us to recover the peculiar power and distinction of Wittgenstein's quite original notion, while at the same time it prepares us for recognizing the need to flesh out that notion in ways Wittgenstein never really pursued – and may well not actually have ever considered. First of all, forms of life are *not* analogues of language-games in the context of action; for as Wittgenstein pointedly remarks: "Disputes do not break out (among mathematicians, say) over the question whether a rule has been obeyed or not. . . . That is part of the framework on which the working of our language is based (for example, in giving descriptions)" (*PI,* 240). It's not that "human agreement decides" what is true and false: What humans say may be true and false. They agree "in the *language* they use. That is not agreement in opinions but in form of life" (*PI,* 241). Language-games are really *based* on our forms of life (forms of life are that through which a particular language "works" *[wirkt]*).[2]

It is easy to understand the confusion, but it is important to correct the error. Wittgenstein says, quite remarkably: "You must bear in mind that the language-game is so to say something unpredictable. I mean: it is not based on grounds. . . . It is there – like our life" (*OC,* 559). Wittgenstein's uniquely powerful point moving throught these various passages is that, though we may formulate what we take to be the "rules" of mathematical or linguistic practice – or their counterparts in social behavior of other sorts – the would-be rules themselves are, rather, based on our forms of life (to which in a sense we "agree"), where agreement itself cannot be captured by further rules, cannot be independently determined with certainty or on epistemic first grounds or the like, and nevertheless "work." Furthermore, the linkage is such that our behavior thus groomed remains "unpredictable" – in the sense that both it *and* the putative rules by which it functions are grounded in the very same way and for the very same reason: in the sense that the extension of such behavior *is also* the extension of the "rules," that there is no rule for continuing or changing the rules, that behavior is never really determined by the rules to which (in some regard) they do conform or may be said to conform. "Language-games" is an expression Wittgenstein characteristically uses when he refers to a restricted practice parasitic on richer natural language practices or abstracted from such richer practices; it is linked, therefore, with the equally abstracted notion of a formal rule. "Forms of life" designate the *ultimately unsystematizable* complex of actual societal life on which any *provisionally formulable regularities or rules* of behavior are *based.*

So, one essential theme in Wittgenstein's notion of a form of life is that *it is not a system of any sort.* This is what is missing in Finch's account, and what separates Wittgenstein's fundamental theme from those for example of nativists like Chomsky or structuralists like Saussure and Lévi-Strauss (see Chomsky, 1980; Lévi-Strauss, 1963). Wittgensteinian "forms of life," then, enable and oblige us to focus on the actual careers of aggregated human agents within their divergent social milieux – without presuming that their development is explicable solely in biological terms or in interactional terms grounded in ways that preclude reference to their having internalized their own contingent cultures. The Wittgen-

[2] Cf. Finch (1977, Chapter 6), which is incompatible with his present thesis (and closer to Wittgenstein's sense).

steinian model eliminates neither biological constraints or determinants nor individual human agents as actual, effective entities – within the descriptive and explanatory scope of the human sciences. The Wittgensteinian perspective permits us to address developmental questions: (1) without invoking systems; (2) without grounding human practices in foundationalist terms; and (3) without ignoring the essential symbiosis between the individual and the societal at the level of human psychology.

It is true that Wittgenstein occasionally invokes the notion of a "system," as when, in *On certainty,* he remarks that our beliefs and our knowledge form "a whole system of propositions," "an enormous system" (*OC,* 141, 410). But in speaking thus, he never construes a system in the sense given by (1)–(6), above. He means rather to emphasize the distinctive features of how we acquire the beliefs and practices of an actual, viable society, in a way that precludes the need for any privileged certainty about single propositions or foundational rules for reliably fixing, proposition by proposition, what we may rightly claim to know. By "system," Wittgenstein means that what we learn in growing up is the presence of an *interconnected* network of beliefs or propositions, the largely tacit, implicit, entailed, linked, and mutual relatedness of which precludes any reliance, claim by claim, on foundational propositions and bypasses the need for any such reliance within the stable practices of our society. It is not closure, therefore, that Wittgenstein intends but the idea of the habituated reliability or palpable presence of a complex world that, however open-ended in the extension of its practices, "dawns" on those it grooms from childhood as a "system" that "holds fast" because of what we sense (and need only sense) "lies around" our every particular, explicit belief (*OC,* 141, 144). Wittgenstein's use of the term, then, actually supports the thesis that forms of life are cognitively and practically effective despite the fact that they do not form or are not known to form any system in the sense defined above.

Rules, on Wittgenstein's view, are, relative to actual societal life, neither empirically nor conceptually prior to, nor separable from, nor metalinguistically fixed with respect to, the practices of such life. They are invariably no more than abstractions and projections (in would-be universalized form) from merely finite manifestations of our forms of life reflexively reviewed. This is surely part of the meaning of that famous paragraph – possibly one of the most profound in Wittgenstein: "If language is to be a means of communication there must be agreement not only in definitions but also (queer as this may sound) in judgments. This seems to abolish logic, but does not do so. . . . what we call 'measuring' is partly determined by a certain constancy in results of measurement" (*PI,* 242). On any reasonable reading, one sees that Wittgenstein *must* have intended (could not possibly otherwise have explained) that the relevant forms of agreement are more tacit than explicit *and* involve both the different forms of life of historically contingent societies and the generic societal dispositions of the entire species, humankind. Differences between species affect the possibilities of grasping or entering into the practices (or language-games) of particular societies within this or that species: thus, "If a lion could talk, we could not understand him" (*PI,* p.223 e) (whether Wittgenstein is right or wrong in this regard). Similarly, Wittgenstein remarks, in the same general passage, that "one human being can be a complete enigma to another," even whole *human* societies whose language we may even have mastered. In this sense the relative constancy of "agreement" is not an outcome of inquiry, it is the precondition of any consensus regarding its outcome; also, it is not determinate but only the generic precondition that we must assume obtains if any effective social action, social communication, science or the like also obtains.

In fixing the sense of Wittgenstein's notion of forms of life, we shall not yet have fixed the "gauge" of his model – but we shall be well on our way. What we may conclude, fairly broadly, are at least the following: (1) "forms of life" is to be construed as the most fundamental, most comprehensive category bearing on the description and explanation of human life – possibly of other species if capable of language or language-like behavior; (2) it makes no sense to talk of possible or imagined forms of life, unless parasitically, since the primary function of that notion concerns the description and explanation of actual life; (3) forms of life are essentially assigned actual human societies (or their surrogates if there are any), both in the sense of plural, historically contingent communities within the species and in the sense (presumably projected by comparing communities) of the common, species-wide "society" of man (that is, the capacity of the species to understand alien cultures); (4) forms of life designate the entire complex of the behavior and activity of viable human societies (and of whatever regarding thinking, desire, intention and the like is involved in such behavior and activity); (5) "agreement" regarding forms of life signifies the tacit (essentially biological or praxical) conditions obtaining within human societies, with regard to which individual members are "naturally" groomed from infancy to adult competence (that is, merely in growing up in a society of apt practitioners of given forms of life); (6) forms of life are not systems in any sense, that is, closed domains of activity actually subject to formulable, finite sets of rules that govern, influence, generate, or in any fundamental sense explain the behavior or regularities of behavior of the aggregated members of a given society; (7) the sense in which rules, practices, and "agreement" regarding rules and practices are "grounded" in forms of life is not cognitively definable or confirmable, but signifies roughly the actual viability and survival of a human society insofar as such survival depends upon (is mediated by) such effective "agreement"; (8) rules and practices of actual societies are, therefore, conceptually symbiotic, not hierarchically linked, and not universalizable in any transhistorical way; (9) individual behavior is intelligible only within the framework of particular forms of life, though the variations of socially interpreted (such) behavior may support the projection of alternative would-be rules and may, as socially tolerated improvisations, lead, over time, to significantly distinct alternative rule-like projections; (10) "changes" in social rules (actually, changes in our projections of what, relative to finite specimens of behavior, we formulate as the rules such behavior fits) are as much a part of our forms of life as patterns of behavior that seem not to require altering our sense of such prevailing rules; (11) forms of life, therefore, never enter in any distributed or determinate description or explanation of human behavior, but signify rather the distinctive nature of the description and explanation of human behavior itself; (12) our cognitive reflection on the properties and regularities of whatever falls within the scope of our form of life is itself part of that form of life and subject, therefore, to the same contingencies as the phenomena thus examined; and (13) there is no escape or exit from our form of life, just as there is no escape or exit from our natural languages; to be human is to share a form of life, in the sense of sharing a natural language and whatever that entails and makes possible.

Armed with this schematized account, we may now consider what the "gauge" is of Wittgenstein's model – and what its distinctive promise is for developmental psychology. Once again, the principal clue is quite simple and straightforward: Wittgenstein never, except accidentally, addresses (in speaking of forms of life) any particular empirical hypothesis about developmental processes; he offers instead the largest conceptual template (in his own view) for any and all empirically promising developmental theories and hypotheses. In effect, his model rules out – for cause – potentially competing ways of construing developmental psychology. Thus, even if it were true (as many have wrongly supposed) that Wittgenstein was a behaviorist, his "behaviorist" hypotheses (such as they are) may well be defeated without at all affecting his larger conception; also, such hypotheses would themselves have to be suitably reconciled (in terms of coherence) with that very conception. The doctrine of the forms of life is itself "empirical" in that large sense in which it is to be dialectically fitted to the widest range of pertinent data – against competitors – that we can claim to address; but it is not empirical in the narrower sense that it never takes the form of a determinate, middle-sized theory. It is, rather, the generic template for an indefinitely extendable set of middle-sized theories of one sort rather than of another. The question it addresses, we must remember, concerns what kind of a model it would be best to favor if we are to point developmental psychology in the most fruitful direction we can imagine. The issue, therefore, concerns that vexed no-man's land between "empirical" philosophy and empirical science. And, although Wittgenstein eschews philosophy, there can be little doubt that he practices it in the sense in which he draws attention to what he himself takes to be most compelling about his proposed template.

"Bottom-up" Theories and Structuralism

The power of Wittgenstein's model – what we are considering as its "gauge" – is best seen by placing it ("vertically," so to say) between two alternative extremes that are very well represented in contemporary theorizing both with regard to the human sciences in general and with regard to the particular question of individual psychological development. There are theories, for instance, that construe whatever would be normally designated as distinctly human as describable and explicable in terms of sub-human, ultimately *physicalist* or *"Leibnizian"* processes. The bare physicalists, that is, those who believe that psychological discourse can be reduced (in alternative ways) to an idiom minimally or most economically adequate for description and explanation within physics, count among their number such figures as Rudolf Carnap, J. J. C. Smart, Wilfrid Sellars, D. M. Armstrong, J. B. Watson, B. F. Skinner, C. L. Hull, and more recently Paul Feyerabend, Donald Davidson, Mario Bunge, Daniel Dennett, Paul Churchland, and Stephen Stich (see Margolis, 1984a). The "Leibnizians" (as we may call them) also seek to reduce the characteristic processes of individual psychology to more fundamental sub-psychological powers but to powers that are, either provisionally or for theoretically principled reasons, inherently complicated in informational respects that cannot be reduced physicalistically. The relationship between what we are calling Leibnizian systems and physicalistic systems is, of course, critical to current disputes about the relationship between genetics and physics – and the jury is still out on the verdict. But it is primarily in the context of linguistic and fully cognitive behavior that the reduction of the Leibnizian alternative is most ardently contested. Hence, the contemporary Leibnizians include such figures as Chomsky, Jean Piaget, Jerry Fodor, Fred Dretske; and, conceding the relatively primitive state of any current empirical management of versions of mind/body and informational/physical identity theories, we may note that the classification of such figures as Herbert Simon, R. J. Nelson, Hilary Putnam, as physicalists or Leibnizians, cannot rightly be resolved in terms of mere avowals or with complete assurance (see Margolis, 1985). In fact, some among those rightly classified as physicalists may actually waver in the Leibnizian direction every bit as much as some, classified as Leibnizians, waver in the opposition direction.

Also, theorists tempted by the Leibnizian option may well fail to develop a full Leibnizian account of persons, or may not be interested in developing one. This is obviously true, for instance, of both Piaget and Chomsky – both strongly motivated in terms of genetic considerations (in quite different ways) as well as in terms of developmental structures that are meant to accommodate the psychological. In this sense, there is, quite simply, something seriously missing in the developmental accounts of both Piaget and Chomsky, that their own doctrines of development essentially require (see Chomsky, 1980 and Piaget, 1970, 1971). Put most directly, we cannot be quite sure of their full theory of persons *vis-à-vis* physicalist and Leibnizian strategies. Dretske's theory, by contrast, is clearly Leibnizian but not pursued along developmental lines (see Dretske, 1981). In a certain sense, something similar is true of Freud, obviously also focused on developmental psychology in his most mature work, if viewed in terms of the orientation of the *Project for a scientific psychology* – which he never quite gave up or suitably revised and which provides the essential clue to Freud's original physicalism (Freud, 1966). It is an irony, therefore, that these three basically reductive options bearing on developmental psychology are defective in just the way they are.

The physicalists and Leibnizians constitute the two principal sorts of "bottom-up" reductionists, in the fairly strict sense that they construe human persons as *composed* - in any of various possible ways congruent with versions of the so-called unity of science program (see Causey, 1977) - of whatever elements, atoms, monads or the like are postulated as the fundamenta of the natural world; or else (if they are "eliminationists" or eliminative materialists) they construe discourse about human persons as artifactual distortions of or rhetorical figures or reflexively introduced conveniences superimposed on whatever of such a compositional sort would be adequate for the description and explanation of human phenomena. This is surely the common conviction among Feigl, Sellars, Skinner, Feyerabend, Davidson, Fodor, Dennett, Churchland, and Stich. But the demonstration is notoriously missing; and *all* known attempts to provide a detailed proof are clearly blackmail arguments of one kind or another. Apart from the variable objective of reconciling the science of psychology - including developmental psychology - with some more-or-less canonical form of the unity of science program, physicalists and Leibnizians may be distinguished in at least two critical respects. First, they fail to address any of the characteristic conceptual puzzles about the relationship between societal categories and categories restricted to the description of individual persons (or, more loosely, to the description of whatever involves individual agency in a narrow sense). Second, they fail to address any of the characteristic conceptual puzzles regarding the seemingly *sui generis* nature of human language - which is only or primarily assignable to *societal* life and which is the precondition and paradigmatic manifestation of human culture. Without a favorable resolution of these two clusters of questions, it's quite hopeless to expect to confirm any version of the unity program or to succeed in any physicalist or Leibnizian reduction.

The Leibnizian model is further at risk because, on any reasonable view, *if* its fundamenta are not merely heuristically intended, then it seems either impossible or peculiarly difficult (in a way no one has yet accounted for) to construe the informational or "coded" or teleological or functional or semiotic dimension of such fundamenta in other than specifically *propositional* terms; and to construe its fundamenta propositionally (e.g., as that a normal zygote will develop by stages, within a normal environment, into a normal human adult) appears to make the Leibnizian idiom itself an artifact of a peculiarly parasitic or dependent sort: subordinate to the very level of human speech and activity that, in principle, it means to reduce (or eliminate). To appreciate the paradox is to see at a glance the potential advantage of Wittgenstein's forms of life. It is not amiss to remind ourselves again that, in the *Project,* Freud was fully as radical and consistent a physicalist as any more recent writer one could name and that he never managed to come to grips with the theoretical underpinnings of the metapsychology which he found himself obliged (by his own clinical material) to favor. Of course he realized this metapsychology threatened to obscure or block altogether the transparent sense in which he adhered, in a Helmholtzian spirit, to something like the unity model. From this point of view, such Freudian developmental theorists as Erikson (1950) and Rieff (1961) rather naively ignore the central question Freud himself rather discontentedly postponed. The suspicion the

Leibnizian alternative fosters is simply that the would-be information governing development is nothing but an obscure version of the old teleological idiom. That it is not such would require a clear account showing both how it manages not to collapse into the physicalist alternative *and* how it is not merely to be construed as an anthropomorphized reading of physical nature itself.

We cannot do full justice here to the complexities these alternatives introduce affecting developmental issues. But it may help to note the following: Fodor, as a Leibnizian of a strongly nativist cast, impoverishes the developmental question by enriching the nativist resources with which that question must deal – without attention to supporting empirical evidence (see Fodor, 1981). Dennett, as a physicalist masquerading as a non-reductive, "top-down" theorist bypassing the Leibnizian, makes use of societal distinctions only heuristically, that is, only in order to be sure to build into his ulterior physicalist reduction of the (provisionally) "homuncular," a causal network putatively adequate for "whatever" may be salient at the "molar level" (see Dennett, 1978 a). Dennett, therefore, has no interest in the "developmental" as such. By contrast, the Wittgensteinian opposes both physicalist and Leibnizian reduction, insisting (for cause) on the ineliminability of human "forms of life" – inherently symbiotic as between the individual and the societal, featuring both the individual nature of human *agency* and the duality of the psychological and societal aspects *of* such agency. The Wittgensteinian model preserves these themes without (it must be admitted) contributing directly to the empirical study of actual developmental processes. It does, however, provide a natural schema for collecting the empirical studies of such theorists as Bruner, Piaget, Bronfenbrenner, Vygotsky, and Luria. It provides such a schema but, fairly viewed, it cannot be said to do more. For Wittgenstein's actual reflections never really come to grips with the actual dynamics of historical societies as such or with the historical structure of actual societies. To press the point, however, is just to indicate the promise of integrating Wittgensteinian "forms of life" and empirical studies in developmental psychology (as well as in the social sciences). In fact, the "developmental" is, here, both a metonym and an exemplar of the concerns of all the human sciences.

At the other extreme of our continuum regarding gauge, one must mention such seemingly unlikely figures as the analytic structuralists (for instance, the theorists of language – Ferdinand de Saussure and Louis Hjelmslev – and the anthropologist, Claude Lévi-Strauss), structuralist Marxists like Louis Althusser, structuralists *manqués* (or antistructuralists) like Michel Foucault, and what may be called "informal" structuralists or structuralist-inspired investigators like the historians of the *Annales* movement (Fernand Braudel, for instance) (see Margolis, 1984 c). It is important to bear in mind that theorists like Chomsky and Piaget, who are distinctly concerned with what may fairly be called developmental psychology, *cannot* be classified as structuralists (Chomsky has resisted the appelation and Piaget has skewed it for his own uses); for both are Leibnizian reductionists (insofar as they are explicit) – although of opposed sorts. The structuralists – and, perhaps similarly, certain extreme (but doubtless wrongheaded) partisans of Hegelian and Marxist persuasion – tend to agree at least on construing human individuals as the heuristically identified epiphenomenal intersection of processes belonging to the totalized *system* of the "human" world. In Saussure (1966), this takes the extraordinarily paradoxical form of denying that there can be a science of actual human speech, of language in actual use *(parole).* Among the *Annalistes,* in following as they do the forces shaping the destiny of entire civilizations, one need almost never, except perhaps in catering for the intuitions of mere human readers, attend to the apparent interventions of particular human agents as such – in formulating the narrative structures of history (see Braudel, 1980). In this sense, the structuralists really preclude developmental psychology, even though many of them are profoundly preoccupied with aspects of developmental influences. In fact, it is a further irony that the structuralists' emphasis on the systematic or internally coherent structures of very large societal orders – particularly historical structures (whether affirmed or denied, as in Lévi-Strauss, Althusser, Foucault, historicists of the Hegelian sort, *Annalistes*) – bears in a most important way (often ignored among developmental psychologists themselves) on the theory of development, in spite of the fact that their theoretical framework is unfavorably disposed to the latter's specific problems. For the developmental psychologist means to center his or her attention on selected features of the careers of individual human persons, and the structuralists (as opposed to the physicalists, for instance) disallow the scientific study of such agents (without necessarily denying the existence or the occurrence of phenomena involving them).

By and large, the structuralists attempt to bring into accord – with something like the unity of science program – the recalcitrant materials of the human and social sciences. They do this primarily by making a myth or fiction of the life of human individuals. They take the phenomena of *societal life* as an imperfect manifestation (seen through the recording distortions of individual investigators wedded to the categories of their own individual lives) of an *ideal system,* either closed in terms of finite formational and transformational processes or teleologically closed in the limit of historical change (eternally, for instance, as in Augustinian or Hegelian terms – though of course Augustine himself is hardly a structuralist in the sense intended). The upshot is that, in expunging human beings, except in heuristic or epiphenomenal ways, structuralists effectively dismiss the very point of developmental psychology. This is why Saussure ignores the acquisition of language; why Althusser treats the members of the proletariat and bourgeoisie as merely embodying the significant phases of evolving human societies; why Lévi-Strauss (1962) opposes (against Sartre, for instance) human histories of the allegedly question-begging, anthropomorphizing form we all know and spontaneously favor; why Foucault (1980) regards the human being as a quite contingent artifact of subterranean powers that, as humans, we cannot possibly fathom or be responsible for. The trouble with all these theories – call them *structuralist,* to collect a useful contrast with what we have termed the *reductionist* alternative – is that they fail to explain the very conditions under which the presupposed system invoked is validly invoked, is empirically confirmable in any sense, is the proper instrument of a human science. They regard whatever is or functions as a human perspective as a distinct impoverishment, distortion, falsification of an idealized order (whether idealist or materialist seems not to matter), although the specification of *that* would-be order – whether a formulable, finite system (as Lévi-Strauss) or an open-ended but explicitly or cryptically teleologized process (as in Hegelian or Althusserian accounts) – is itself, and cannot possibly fail to be, the work of responsible human investigators.

The reductionists, then, do not actually need to eliminate developmental psychology – witness Freud, Piaget, Chomsky, Skinner. But they cannot succeed in their project *vis-à-vis* developmental psychology if they cannot overcome the puzzles of sociality and language already noted. The structuralists do really eliminate developmental psychology, except perhaps as a kind of fiction or heuristic convenience – witness Saussure, Lévi-Strauss, the *Annalistes*. But they cannot explain how they make sense of their own undertakings as scientists; and because of that, they cannot convincingly eliminate developmental psychology. The reductionists impoverish the entire dimension of social existence – witness the classic dispute between Piaget and Vygotsky (that is, the dispute regarding the question whether human existence and development are inherently *social or societal* [as Vygotsky insisted], or whether much of what is distinctive of human development is biologically *innate* [as Chomsky later insisted], or *interactional* though not particularly or initially social [as Piaget assumed]). The structuralists make an utter mystery of the reality of social processes and of the interconnection between the individual and the social. Language *(langue)*, for instance as in Saussure, has *some* relationship with actual human speech *(parole)*; but we cannot say what it is or how the connection is articulated in actual practice. By and large, the same can be said of the work of Lévi-Strauss, Althusser, Foucault, and *Annalistes* – although, mysteriously, the *system* that actual human life seems to "invoke" or "remind" one of has its own apparently coherent structure. Furthermore, despite what they do claim (insofar as they manage to be explicit on the question), the structuralists are up to their ears in explaining distinctly human life and human development. Ultimately (on the structuralists' own account), we are more interested in the "adequacy" of the totalized system than in its descriptive and explanatory role within the episodic inquiries of actual human agents. If we see matters this way, we see quite precisely the sense in which Wittgenstein's forms of life constitute a middle or moderate position between that of the reductionists and the structuralists. To press the point is to oblige ourselves to come to terms with the challenge of the unity of science program and to explain the viability at least of the Wittgensteinian option.

"Top-down" Theories and the Wittgenstein Template

Recall that we are not viewing Wittgenstein's notion of forms of life as a specific empirical hypothesis regarding the psychological development of human beings – in any sense at all, for instance, in which it might be compared with the views of Freud, Skinner, Piaget, Vygotsky, Chomsky, Bruner or others. No, we are construing it rather as a generic template of a distinct sort that serves to orient all such competing developmental theories within the conceptual space it provides – or, dialectically, the space it opposes to that of other such templates (the reductionists' and the structuralists' in particular) with which it cannot be reconciled. We have already taken note of internal oddities or insufficiencies within reductionism and structuralism. The reductionists, as we observed, characteristically fail to address the seemingly *sui generis* nature of language and the seeming irreducibility of sociality to the terms of individual psychology; and the structuralists ignore the entire question of the relationship of the "totalized" systems of language and social existence they posit to the empirical reality of actual, contingent, diachronically varying human communities – whose linguistic and social behavior is, in some unexplained way, conceptually, causally, and developmentally linked to those same putative systems. Furthermore, both reductionists and structuralists characteristically ignore the complications imposed by admitting that their own work is the work of distinctly human investigators.

What we must now consider are the specific advantages of the Wittgensteinian strategy beyond merely overcoming weaknesses of these internal sorts – which of course is not at all to suggest that such weaknesses are negligible in any way. Furthermore, in pursuing the matter, we must take care to concede the limitations in Wittgenstein's own use of his notion, and in so doing, to draw attention to its further potential fruitfulness and the implications of going beyond Wittgenstein in this regard.

No one, of course, who considers the question of psychological development can fail to posit the careers of human persons from infancy to maturity and the phases through which such development passes, in both a biologically and a culturally centered sense, within the context of particular human societies. This can be said just as well of Skinner and Hull and Freud and Chomsky and Piaget (and even, grudgingly, of Althusser and Lévi-Strauss) as it can of Vygotsky and Luria and Bruner and Bronfenbrenner and Bourdieu. But there is an essential difference. On the argument already sketched, the former theorize in ways that make an (as yet) unresolved or unresolvable puzzle of psychological development itself; and the latter are, in a sense generously focused on what we have already drawn out as Wittgenstein's theme regarding forms of life, broadly Wittgensteinian (and more) in their orientation. Insofar as they are "Wittgensteinian," there is no comparable bafflement in their orientation, regardless of any doubts we may have about their respective theories.

There is, therefore, a conceptual weakness involved, for example, in comparing Quine's *The roots of reference* (1973) with, say, Bruner's *Child's talk* (1983); or Bruner's book with Piaget's *The language of thought of the child* (1926). The weakness is this: The comparison of apparent developmental sequences is *not* sufficiently grounded, in Quine and Piaget, with regard to their respective theories of the relationship between the human person and the physical or biological order that, respectively, Quine and Piaget insist on – when discussing the more global features of their systematic views. The result is that there is a peculiarly disengaged sense in which, say, Bruner (1983) is prepared to agree in this or that detail with Quine and Piaget; or in which Chomsky (1972, 1980) opposes details in Quine's or Putnam's views. We simply don't know what we should make of the notion of a "person" or a "human society" or "natural language" or "human thought and activity" in theorists of the first sort, to be sure that comparisons of detail between theorists of the two sorts make coherent sense in terms of the relatively developed interpretation of these notions among thinkers of the second sort.

The latter do not agree among themselves of course. But their differences are, largely, the differences among competing empirical theories of developmental psychology formulated within what we are here calling Wittgenstein's conceptual space – the space of forms of life. When, therefore, Bronfenbrenner (1979) introduces the notion of an "ecology" of human development, we must seize the central point: that it is a human, a societal, ecology that he has in mind – not merely a generic, environmental, or biological setting but one that is cultural, diachronically or historically shifting, distinctly institutional in nature. There is a world of difference between Bronfenbrenner's use of "ecology" and, say Gibson's (1979) notion of "ecological optics" – which has, really, no cultural or historical or societal structure as such, even though "social" factors may affect perception within particular ecological niches. (In fact, in Gibson there are, once again reductively, no persons or perceptual agents to acknowledge, in discoursing about perception.) Again, when Bronfenbrenner (1979) favorably airs Luria's empirical studies (1976, 1982) of Asian Soviet communities offered in the spirit of a Marxist analysis of psychological development, we readily see that the convergence between their respective views lies as much in the congruity of their notions of the conceptual space within which their differences may be compared as it does in the narrow agreement of their actual views within that space.

This is the reason we are singling out Wittgenstein's conception of forms of life – and resisting more detailed questions about developmental sequences themselves. Thus construed, we are not emphasizing differences of what might be called first-order empirical doctrine. Let us say that George Herbert Mead, John Dewey, Vygotsky, Luria, Bourdieu, Bruner, Bronfenbrenner may all reasonably be said to converge on the master themes of that abstracted notion of life we have already summarized. One could add to the list indefinitely many others – notably, among Continental philosophers, Gadamer, Habermas, Ricoeur, and, among English-language philosophers, Peters, Hamlyn, Harré, Winch, and Taylor: all focused to one degree or another on the problems of developmental psychology. But the master theme remains: (1) that human persons are, relevantly, neither reducible in sub-personal terms (whether in the physicalist or Leibnizian sense) nor adequately characterized as mere nodes of the primary intersecting forces of the real structures of suprapersonal systems: and (2) that, although only human agents are actual effective agents (which is not to deny non-agentive causal forces in social contexts), human agency is essentially socialized or societal, in the sense in which language, human institutions, historical styles and the like are assignable only to entire societies, social ensembles (that are never, for conceptual reasons, actual *agents*). This is the double force of Wittgenstein's "gauge" of developmental psychology: Language, say, is irreducibly societal, but only individual human persons speak; and we know of no convincing way to account for phenomena at that level of manifestation – in either the *"bottom-up"* manner of the reductionists *or* the manner of the structuralists, who effectively "raise" the level of relevant reference and then inexplicitly "reduce" (in quite a different sense, i.e., epiphenomenally or heuristically) the individual to the fundamenta of the altered world. In this sense, the Wittgensteinian "gauge" is the gauge of what may be termed *"top-down"* strategies of analysis: factorial rather than compositional, *not* symmetrical with bottom-up strategies,[3] committed to the full reality of the human, and committed as well to the conceptual symbiosis (and mutual irreducibility) of the societal and the psychological (see Margolis, 1984b, in press-b).

Wittgenstein's notion offers an ingenious economy here – both with regard to his own orientation and with regard to assessing his contribution to the issue of psychological development. First of all, *our* sharing certain forms of life makes it possible to interpret and comprehend the forms of life of other human communities. This draws attention to the biological, species-wide similiarities on which all cultural divergences depend; the inescapable cultural skewing of all such interpretation and comprehension; *and* the possibility of being *culturally* baffled, despite whatever may be the pertinently common biology of the species. (This is the point of Wittgestein's remark [*PI*, p. 223 e] about entering a "strange country with entirely strange traditions.") Second, sharing a form of life essentially entails, and is paradigmatically manifested in, sharing a natural language. Hence, to the extent that we attribute forms of life to animals – or patterns of social existence that favorably resemble human forms of life – we anthropomorphize them; and we are conceptually bound to do so if we suppose we can "understand" them at all. (This is the point of Wittgenstein's remark about our not being able to understand a lion who could speak.) Third, insofar as we understand ourselves – that is, each one himself and his fellows – our ability presupposes and manifests our sharing a form of life; so there is an effective consensual tolerance of behavior and activity that is *not* capable, in principle, of being or needing to be independently fixed in cognitive terms, but itself insures the "general" effectiveness of any and every cognitive activity. (This is the point of Wittgenstein's famous remark [*PI*, p. 226 e], "What has to be accepted, the given, is – so one could say – forms of *life*.")

Now, Wittgenstein does not adequately explore these issues in terms of the details of psychology or the social sciences. They are all open to some adjustment and challenge. And they require an account of issues that Wittgenstein hardly broaches at all. For example, there is good reason to think that chimpanzees have an incipient capacity for self-reference, are capable of lying, are capable of interpreting photographs, and are capable of being trained to communicate by using rudimentary parts of human language (see Premack & Premack,

[3] On a quite different use of the "top-down"/"bottom-up" idiom, see Dennett (1978b).

1983). Again, it is obvious that human infants normally and skillfully learn natural languages, from an initial condition in which they apparently lack language. Without directly opposing or adopting Chomsky's thesis, we must admit that the achievement raises questions about sublinguistic proto-cultural aptitudes. And again, as Bruner (1983, Chapter 2) has insisted, the "achievement" of language itself argues social and communicative aptitudes of an innate sort among human infants, that cannot be explained merely as an artifact or entailment of that achievement.

The concept of a form of life, then, is a very high-order concept, fitted, in an empirical sense, to the widest range of human behavior and pertinently analogous behavior among the higher animals. Adjustments in first-order developmental psychology are bound to require adjustments from time to time in the template function of the very notion of a form of life; and particular adjustments are bound to affect our tolerance of what will count as empirically disciplined comparisons. So the rejection, on Wittgenstein's part, of all forms of cognitive certainty (foundationalism, in the jargon) does not yet bear on the empirical adjustability of the concept of forms of life. Wittgenstein, however, did not pursue the matter beyond the initial orientation we have already sketched. He may, for example, be quite mistaken about the point regarding lions, should it turn out that alien, extraterrestrial species prove to be accessible to human understanding and communication.

Beyond this caveat and beyond the consequences of sheer inquiry in developmental psychology – most notably, as in the close study of the acquisition of a human language – there are at least three foci of investigation that Wittgenstein "implicitly" makes provision for but does not satisfactorily himself pursue. They are absolutely essential to the issue at hand. They are these: (1) the import of the historicized variability of human societies – both synchronically divergent and diachronically changing – on infra-societal understanding, communicative interpretation, and psychological development (entailing such understanding and capacity for such interpretation); (2) the analysis of the difference between and the relationship between predicates designating individual psychological attributes and predicates designating attributes of societies considered as ensembles not obviously reducible to mere aggregates (for example, as in speaking of languages, institutions, traditions and the like); and (3) the analysis of the notion of a human culture itself (qualified by the sharing of forms of life) in contrast with the notion of physical nature *and* of sub-cultural animal sociality.

It cannot be said that Wittgenstein does not address these matters at all (see Wittgenstein, *CV, RPP1, RPP2*). But it is notable that he lacks a developed interest in history – in the dual sense critical to contemporary theory: the detailed study of the import of diachronically changing practice on individual lives and on the social functioning of individual lives thus affected, as well as and the hermeneutic significance of the very historicity of human existence (for example, at least in terms of the themes that have become so prominent in all the human studies since the appearance of the work of such figures as Heidegger, Gadamer, and Foucault).

Similarly, Wittgenstein does not seriously address what, since Popper's (1961) important (though, frankly, relatively primitive) reflections has come to be called the problem of methodological individualism. Popper's thesis, which is "Wittgensteinian" in the sense already provided, holds at once that only individual human beings are actual agents in social contexts, but nevertheless that social institutions and traditions cannot be described in terms restricted to the predicates of individual agency. This may well be the most strategic theme of Wittgenstein's (and of course Popper's) bearing on the study of human psychological development. It is just the point that is missed by the reductionists and structuralists, as earlier described. The fact remains that, at the present time, we lack a ramified account of the puzzle of methodological individualism - in anything like a Wittgensteinian "gauge." Finally, in the same spirit, we are just on the point in recent years of effectively examining the concept of a human culture in terms that bear directly on the prospect that the human studies (including developmental psychology) could even count as human sciences - in a sense that avoids the reductive tendencies we have already sketched. In general, we lack what may be called an ontology of persons, societies, cultures, languages, histories, actions congruent with whatever may be the defensible sense in which the challenge of the unity of science thesis may be effectively met (see Margolis, 1978, 1980, in press-a).

We cannot of course attempt here a full resolution of the ontological and methodological puzzles of what may be taken to count as a rigorous inquiry into the phenomena of human culture. But there are a number of minimal clues, which we have not yet pressed, that are decisive for assessing the standing of developmental psychology and allied disciplines - and that are peculiarly favorable to Wittgenstein's notion of forms of life. First of all, a theory of psychological development will attempt to abstract the relatively universal, biological processes of development from the more variable, contingently local, possibly even idiosyncratic, processes of a culturally determinate sort. Against, say, Chomsky, Piaget, Erikson, Kohlberg, and similar theorists, there can be no antecedent reason against disbelieving either that there is a universal (species-wide) developmental sequence of a biological, sub-cultural sort, or that whatever are the most general features of such development are more instructive or more influential than culturally variable factors with respect to the acquisition of a natural language, moral grooming, intellectual growth or the like.

The cultural is not opposed to the biological, here. It is always incarnate in the biological, very much in the same sense in which the various "conventions" of pictorial representation must be alternative ways of training biological aptitudes of visual perception. Furthermore, there is in principle (once one rejects the so-called cognitive transparency of nature, the theme of the correpondence theory of truth and knowledge) no way of *independently* comparing the biological and the cultural; on the contrary, biological regularities are themselves abstracted from a culturally skewed inquiry that is itself historically distinctive. It is a feature and advantage of the Wittgensteinian template that it strongly accommodates both of these aspects of pertinent inquiry. In fact, if we historicize the study of psychological development in a radical way (as well we may, possibly along such lines as are favored by Vygotsky and Luria or Foucault or Bourdieu or perhaps Feyerabend), then those who favor biological universals of development will be thought to hold a distinctly implausible thesis. Wittgenstein makes room for both a relatively conservative account of development as well as for a radical account. But of course, since he fails to develop his own views of history, he also fails to give us much of a sense of how to proceed. The very notion of "forms of life," however, confirms Wittgenstein's emphasis on the incarnation of the cultural *in* the biological *and* economically confirms his emphasis on the conceptual indissolubility of what *we* take nature to be and what *nature* is independent of such accounts. In this sense, the replacement of the correspondence thesis of the *Tractatus* by the image of forms of life in the *Investigations* effectively focuses the problematic nature of biological universals themselves and that of the relationship between the biological and cultural dimensions of psychological development.

Wittgensteinian forms of life also make it quite impossible to escape the sense in which languages, rules, practices, institutions and the like can only be attributed to entire societies - never to mere aggregations of individuals - even though it is the case that only individual persons actually speak or act in culturally relevant ways. The Wittgensteinian template, therefore, obliges us to grasp the importance of viewing psychological development in terms of acquiring certain cultural aptitudes interpreted as would-be institutional regularities or rule-like uniformities - which (notably in Bourdieu, but also in Luria and Bruner, and even in Skinner for that matter) accommodate a consensual tolerance for and expectation of individual improvisation, deviance, variability, and diachronic shifts in orientation and manner of social performance. Such regularities (contrary to the views, for instance, of Piaget, Lévi-Strauss, Althusser, and Chomsky) are never construed as logically or compositionally more fundamental than, or as fixed or independently normative with respect to, the actual contingent behavior they are made to fit. For example, a "Chomskian" speaker does not really *learn* his or her native language: His or her genetic grammatical endowment (perhaps coordinated with other modular linguistic and nonlinguistic endowments) "interact" with "environmental" factors to yield, at the surface of apparent human performance, a natural language (see Chomsky, 1980, 1982). Development, for Chomsky, is modelled on the growth and development of organ systems. By contrast, it only seems as if, for Dennett (1978), a molar human agent actually learns: What happens is that a "society" of homunculi process seeming molar inputs in accord with *their* programs. Molar development is, then, nothing but an impressionistic picture of a deterministic physicalism itself provisionally characterized in homuncular terms.

In the same sense, when Wittgensteinian forms of life are linked to the preceding theme, the Wittgensteinian template makes quite clear the effective conditions under which relatively alien cultures may be examined - say, with respect to comparative developmental patterns. For the intelligibility of an alien culture is partly dependent on common biological aptitudes on which diverging cultural patterns themselves depend, and partly dependent – through that mediation and the incarnate potential of any particular culture – on an inquirer's capacity to grasp the idiosyncrasy of another culture's form of life.[4]

There cannot be a bifurcation between "our" culture and "their" culture – as, one may argue, theorists like Winch and Garfinkel either say or very strongly suggest: For one thing, the problems of inter-cultural understanding and interpretation are very much like those of infra-cultural understanding and interpretation; for another, the very demarcation of distinct cultures is posited within the space of effective communication and depends on aptitudes spontaneously developed through species-wide dispositions and the improvisational capacities of every culture. (Here, one may think of the provisional sense in which we demarcate distinct languages, the ubiquity of bilingual competence among all known societies, and the capacity to learn any other language through the resources of one's own.) Third, drawing on Gadamer's (1975) helpful thesis of the "fusing of horizons," which accords very well with Wittgenstein's notion of forms of life, what ("methodologically") are the features of a society studied are, effectively, a function, at least in part and ineliminably, of the tacit orientation of the society that studies it. In this sense, the Wittgensteinian template has decisively strong advantages – when compared with those of reductionists and structuralists – not only of a descriptive and explanatory sort but also of a general methodological sort.

One final methodological observation may be helpful here. The physical sciences, particularly wherever they favor the unity of science model, are strongly disposed to a "bottom-up" or compositional strategy of explanation. The usual challenge to the scientific pretensions of the human and social sciences (hence, of developmental psychology in accord with a Wittgensteinian template) is that those would-be disciplines fail to preserve the required bottom-up strategy. And this is certainly true. On the other hand, the Wittgensteinian effectively opposes the reducibility of the human, the cultural, and the linguistic. Hence, insofar as he or she remains loyal to this theme (let us suppose, for very good reasons), a crucial discontinuity in all bottom-up strategies is affirmed. Nevertheless, he or she need not oppose the general thesis that, *somehow,* human language and culture must have emerged from sub-cultural sources. How can these two themes be reconciled?

The answer is quite straightforward and focuses very neatly the fundamental differences between the physical and the cultural sciences. In just the sense in which Piaget cannot question the infant gradually acquiring human languages and culture but must speculatively reconstruct his genetic epistemology – though always in a empirically responsible way – the "Wittgensteinian" developmentalist (or other cultural scientist) must reconstruct whatever of the precultural and

[4] This bears for instance on the vexed disputes regarding Winch's (1958) often misread but also somewhat ill-formed conception of a Wittgensteinian social science, as well as on disputes regarding the claims of ethnomethodology. See for instance MacIntyre (1971), Jarvie (1970), Garfinkel (1967), and Mayrl (1973).

subcultural most plausibly contributes to a particular culturally significant achievement *already conceded to be in place*. In that sense, explanation in the human sciences is always controlled by "top-down" considerations. But more significantly, the very phenomena to be explained are identified only at the emergent level at which they are (and only are) significant and actual. Hence, the explanation of psychological developmental is itself, in a profound respect deeper than any in which the same may be said of physics, *an artifact of the emergent culture it would explain*. The study of psychological development is first of all - and paradigmatically - reflexive, in a societal sense. This is not true of physics, even though every science is of course a cultural artifact. The peculiarity of the human sciences is just what must (and can) be reconciled with an enlarged conception of science, if we are ever to admit studies of the sort already identified; and it is only within the space of the Wittgensteinian template, as opposed to that of the reductionist and the structuralist, that it can be so reconciled at all. The reductionist denies the fundamental contrast (here sketched) between the natural and the human or cultural sciences (see Chomsky, 1980, Chapter 1, and Hockney, 1975), the structuralist never explains at all the relationship between the two, or the bare sense in which the societal systems he or she examines are even actual or ideal or are related (in any formulable way) to the usual forms of life manifest and reflexively recognized, in every known human society, *in* the actual lives of human individuals who share societal practices.

Short of a demonstration of some fatal incoherence affecting the Wittgensteinian template itself, or short of a demonstration of how, in a ramified way, any competing template (probably of either of the two sorts identified) could really replace the Wittgensteinian, there seems to be no serious alternative to proceeding with the study of psychological development along "Wittgensteinian" lines.

References

Bakhtin, M. (1981). *The dialogic imagination*. Austin: University of Texas Press.

Boden, M. (1977). *Artificial intelligence and natural man*. New York: Basic Books.

Bourdieu, P. (1977). *Outline of a theory of practice*. Cambridge: Cambridge University Press.

Bourdieu, P., & Passeron, J.-C. (1977). *Reproduction in education, society and culture*. London: Sage Publications.

Braudel, F. (1980). *On history*. Chicago: University of Chicago Press.

Bronfenbrenner, U. (1979). *The ecology of human development*. Cambridge, MA: Harvard University Press.

Bruner, J. (1983). *Child's talk*. New York: Norton.

Causey, R. L. (1977). *Unity of science*. Dordrecht, Holland: Reidel.

Chomsky, N. (1972). Linguistics and philosophy. In *Language and mind* (enlarged ed.), New York: Harcort Brace Jovanovich.

Chomsky, N. (1980). *Rules and representation*. New York: Columbia University Press.

Chomsky, N. (1982). *Lectures on government and binding*. Dordrecht, Holland: Foris.

Dennett, D. C. (1978 a). *Brainstorms*. Montgomery, VT: Bradford Books.

Dennett, D. C. (1978 b). Artificial intelligence as philosophy and as psychology. In *Brainstorms*. Montgomery, VT: Bradford Books.

Dretske, F.I. (1981). *Knowledge and the flow of information.* Chicago: University of Chicago Press.

Erikson, E.H. (1950). *Childhood and society.* New York: Norton.

Finch, H.L. (1977). *Wittgenstein – the later philosophy.* Atlantic Highlands, NJ: Humanities Press.

Fodor, J.A. (1981). *Representations.* Cambridge, MA: The M.I.T. Press.

Foucault, M. (1980). *Power/knowledge.* New York: Pantheon.

Freud, S. (1966). Project for a scientific psychology. In J. Strachey et al. (Eds.), *The standard edition of the complete psychological works of Sigmund Freud* (Vol. 1, 1886–1899). London: Hogarth Press and the Institute of Psycho-analysis.

Gadamer, H.-G. (1975). *Truth and method.* New York: Seabury.

Garfinkel, H. (1967). *Studies in ethnomethodology.* Englewood Cliffs, NJ: Prentice-Hall.

Gibson, J.J. (1979). *The ecological approach to visual perception.* Boston: Houghton Mifflin.

Habermas, J. (1979). *Communication and the evolution of society.* Boston: Beacon Press.

Hockney, D. (1975). The bifurcation of scientific theories and indeterminancy of translation. *Philosophy of Science, 42,* 411–427.

Hunter, J.F.M. (1968). Wittgenstein's *Philosophical investigations. American Philosophical Quarterly, 5,* 233–243.

Jarvie, I.C. (1970). Understanding and explanation in sociology and social anthropology. In R. Borger & F. Cioffi (Eds.), *Explanation in the behavioral sciences.* Cambridge: Cambridge University Press.

Lévi-Strauss, C. (1962). *The savage mind.* Chicago: University of Chicago Press.

Lévi-Strauss, C. (1963). *Structural anthropology.* New York: Basic Books.

Luria, A.R. (1976). *Cognitive development; its cultural and social foundations.* Cambridge, MA: Harvard University Press.

Luria, A.R. (1982). *Language and cognition.* Washington, D.C.: Winston.

MacIntyre, A. (1971). The idea of a social science. In *Against the self-images of the age.* London: Duckworth.

Margolis, J. (1978). *Persons and minds.* Dordrecht, Holland: Reidel.

Margolis, J. (1980). *Art and philosophy.* Atlantic Highlands, NJ: Humanities Press.

Margolis, J. (1984a). *Philosophy of psychology.* Englewood Cliffs, NJ: Prentice-Hall.

Margolis, J. (1984b). *Culture and cultural entities.* Dordrecht, Holland: Reidel.

Margolis, J. (1984c). 'The savage mind totalizes.' *Man and World, 17,* 157–174.

Margolis, J. (1985). Information, artificial intelligence, and the praxical. In C. Mitcham & A. Huning (Eds.), *Research in philosophy and technology* (Vol. 8). Greenwich, CT: JAI Press.

Margolis, J. (in press-a). Emergence and the unity of science. *Philosophical Forum.*

Margolis, J. (in press-b). Psychology and its methodological options. In J. Margolis et al., (Eds.), *Psychology: Designing the discipline.* Oxford: Blackwell.

Mayrl, W.W. (1973). Ethomethodology: Sociology without society. *Catalyst, 7,* 15–28.

Piaget, J. (1926). *The language and thought of the child.* London: Routledge & Kegan Paul.

Piaget, J. (1970). *Structuralism.* New York: Basic Books.

Piaget, J. (1971). *Biology and knowledge.* Chicago: University of Chicago Press.

Piattelli-Palmarini, M. (Ed.) (1980). *Language and learning: The debate between Jean Piaget and Noam Chomsky.* Cambridge, MA: Harvard University Press.

Popper, K.R. (1961). *The poverty of historicism* (3rd ed.). London: Routledge & Kegan Paul.

Premack, D., & Premack, A.J. (1983). *The mind of an ape.* New York: Norton.

Quine, W.V. (1973). *The roots of reference.* La Salle, IL: Open Court.

Rieff, P. (1961). *Freud: The mind of the moralist.* New York: Viking.

Saussure, F. de (1966). *Course in general linguistics.* New York: McGraw-Hill.

Vygotsky, L.S. (1978). *Mind in society; the development of higher psychological processes.* Cambridge, MA: Harvard University Press.

Williams, M. (1985). Wittgenstein's rejection of scientific psychology. *Journal for the Theory of Social Behavior, 15,* 203–223.

Winch, P. (1958). *The idea of a social science and its relation to philosophy.* London: Routledge & Kegan Paul.

Chapter 9 Wittgenstein and Categorization Research in Cognitive Psychology

Eleanor Rosch

Research in psychology tends to reflect, sometimes self-consciously, prevailing philosophical viewpoints. Categorization is the area in cognitive psychology which deals with the ancient problem of universals, that is, with the fact that unique particular objects or events can be treated equivalently. Prior to the 1970s, categorization research tended to mirror the simplified worlds described in early Wittgenstein and in logical positivism. However, Wittgenstein's later philosophy has revolutionary implications for many aspects of human thought, among them issues in categorization. In this paper, I will argue that modern research in natural categories is actually derived from Wittgensteinian insights, but ambivalently so: It has tended to work with the symptoms rather than the root of his challenge.

Background

For the early Wittgenstein of the *Tractatus,* categories were the objects of reference of words. Language functioned as a picture of reality; it was made up of propositions, each word of which stood for an object. The relations among the words stood for the ways in which the objects were related. This can be seen as a linguistic version of the long-standing tradition in philosophy to treat categories as objects of knowledge. In Plato these objects were the Forms; in Aristotle, the formal causes of the categories, for example, their definitions in terms of genus and differentia. For the British empiricists who followed Aristotle in this respect (see Fodor, 1981), concepts consisted of a *connotation* (meaning, intension), which was a specification of the qualities that a thing must have to be a member of the class, and a *denotation* (extension), which was just those objects in the world which belonged to the class. Because categories were objects of names (in the special sense of the *Tractatus*) and/or objects of knowledge, they had to have certain properies. First, they had to be exact rather than vague; that is, boundaries had to be clearly defined. One cannot have vague knowledge. Second, category members had to have something in common; after all, that was the object of reference. And that which the members had in common had to be the necessary and sufficient conditions for membership in the category. Third, following from the other properties but never explicitly stated, was the assumption that all members of a category were equally good with regard to membership; either they had the necessary common features or they didn't. Thus categories were seen as a common set; all positive instances should manifest the common characteristic(s) defining membership, and negative instances should lack it.

It is somewhat paradoxical that the issue of categories did not enter into experimental psychology until the 1950s. From the 1920s American psychology had been dominated by behaviorism. The natural analog of the philosophical problem of universals in the conditioning paradigm is stimulus generalization. However, none of the behaviorists appeared to make this connection nor to speak of generalization gradients as relevant to concepts or categories (this, despite the fact that Clark Hull had performed a concept learning experiment for his doctoral research in 1920; see Brown, 1979). We might speculate that this was due not only to the mentalistic flavor of the word *concept* but also to the fact that generalization gradients violate all of the requirements for a proper category of empirical reference as laid down by logical positivism, which was the philosophical position explicitly espoused by the behaviorists (Marx, 1968). The *Tractatus* was seminal in the formation of logical positivism and the criteria for the reference of a category term in empirical discourse were just those stated above.

It was not until the publication of Bruner's *A study of thinking* (Bruner, Goodnow, & Austin, 1956) that research in categorization began to come into its own. Bruner's emphasis was on the active rather than passive aspects of learning and on the necessity of reintroducing cognitive theoretical terms such as *concept*. The main body of the book is the report of a specific program of experimentation in concept learning. It is in the design of these experiments that we can see a reflection of the prevailing philosophical assumptions about the nature of categories. Stimulus arrays typically consisted of items which represented all possible orthogonal combinations of an arbitrary set of attributes. For example, there might be forms which were squares and circles, each one of which was either red or blue and each one of which had one or two borders. The concepts which subjects learned were defined by specific attributes combined by a logical rule; for example, *red, blue and square, round or blue*. For such concepts, once the subject had learned the rule(s) defining the positive subset, boundaries of the concept could only be well-defined and any instance which fit the rule(s) was equivalent to any other. In fact, in the terms of the early Wittgenstein work, these tasks and the concepts derived from them are as close as one can imagine to simplified language-games in which reference and the mapping of simple elements onto reality has its clearest portrait. Research on this type of task burgeoned (Erickson & Jones, 1978; Neimark & Santa, 1975).

In developmental psychology, concept learning also became an area of interest. Input came from the traditions of Piaget (1972) and Vygotsky (1962) as well as from the concept identification paradigm outlined above. Much of the emphasis was on how children's concepts and learning strategies differ from the adult mode; the guiding image seemed to be one in which children's "irrational" and ill-structured concepts could be seen to develop into the clear and logical concepts of adulthood (Bruner, Olver, & Greenfield, 1966).

The later philosophy of Wittgenstein entirely reverses the position of the *Tractatus* and offers a profound criticism of virtually all previous philosophy.

His central point is that it is false (actually meaningless) to claim that language is necessarily a description of the world and that words and propositions get their meaning through the objects to which they refer. It is this image of language which has produced the false problems of philosophy - metaphysics, skepticism of all sorts, atomism, logical positivism, and so on. By dissolving the root position, the "false picture which had us in its grip," he can dissolve these problems. He has an alternative view of language: Rather than being referential, rather than giving us the "facts," language is part of our actions, part of the most basic practices which make up our physical and social "forms of life."

This view has radical implications for categories. They are no longer objects of words or knowledge but are part of our delicately shifting forms of life. Therefore, they need not meet any of the conditions for categories outlined previously.

1. They need not be precise; boundaries can be ill-defined. In Wittgenstein's words:

> Frege compares a concept to an area and says that an area with vague boundaries cannot be called an area at all. This presumably means that we cannot do anything with it. - But is it senseless to say: "Stand roughly there?" Suppose that I were standing with someone in a city square and said that. As I say it I do not draw any kind of boundary, but perhaps point with my hand - as if I were indicating a particular *spot*. And this is just how one might explain to someone what a game is. (*PI*, 71)

2. They need not have anything in common, any common defining attributes:

> Consider for example the proceedings that we call "games." I mean board-games, card-games, ball-games Olympic games, and so on. What is common to them all? - Don't say: "There *must* be something common, or they would not be called 'games'" - but *look and see* whether there is anything common to all. - For if you look at them you will not see something that is common to *all*, but similarities, relationships, and a whole series of them at that.... And the result of this examination is: we see a complicated network of similarities overlapping and criss-crossing: ...
> I can think of no better expression to characterize those similarities than "family resemblance"; for the various resemblances between members of a family: build, features, colour of eyes, gait, temperament, etc. etc. overlap and criss-cross in the same way. - And I shall say: games form a family. (*PI*, 66-67)

3. All members need not be equally good members. Wittgenstein does not explicitly discuss this issue in relation to categories but he seems aware of it:

> Someone says to me: "Show the children a game." I teach them gaming with dice, and the other says "I didn't mean that sort of game." Must the exclusion of the game with dice have come before his mind when he gave me the order? (*PI*, p. 33 e)

These are some of the implications of Wittgenstein's refutation of the object of reference view of categories. My contention in this paper is that it is these implications *only* which have received the attention of Wittgenstein-oriented categorization research in cognitive psychology. The root which produced them, Wittgenstein's challenge to the object-of- reference view of language, has tended to disappear from focus. Thus the Wittgensteinian ideas (prototypes, family resemblances) which have replaced criterial attributes of categories have tended to be reified and eventually simply substituted for criterial attributes as that to which category terms refer – by the critics, at least, if not also by the proponents of the now well-known "non-classical view" of categories. I will attempt to trace, and perhaps place in a broader context, this tendency.

The Entrance of Wittgenstein's Ideas into Categorization Research

Prototypes. By the end of the 1960s, a new cognitive psychology and new approaches to language were rapidly appearing (Kessel & Bevan, in press). Chomskian linguistics, Neisserian cognitive psychology, developmental psycholinguistics, cultural relativity, ethnoscience – there were a wealth of new ideas. Since it is my own categorization research, growing out of issues in cultural relativity, which was the most explicitly influenced by Wittgenstein, I will describe something of its origins.

In 1969, I was involved in research on color categories. Colors, which had once seemed the clearest imaginable case of linguistic relativity (Brown & Lenneberg, 1954), now appeared to have a universal aspect (Berlin & Kay, 1969). I was working on the hypothesis that for basic color terms, categories formed around physiologically salient points in the color space. These points were most easily remembered, and thus first became attached to color names. Adjacent colors became part of the category by stimulus generalization. Thus color categories universally became structured around these same salient points. Evidence from the naming, memory, and learning of colors both in the United States and for a New Guinea people, the Dani of West Irian, who lacked basic hue terms, seemed to support this story (Heider, 1971; Rosch, 1973). What had this to do with the general issue of categorization?

Colors seemed markedly unlike the kinds of categories studied in the concept attainment literature. First, they do not have definite boundaries; not only is there experimental evidence that people disagree with each other and with themselves about the category boundaries (Berlin & Kay, 1969; McCloskey & Glucksberg, 1978) but, in fact, it was this very aspect of colors that had given rise to the view of their cultural relativity. Second, there are no identical attributes in common to all members of the category; physical properties of light, such as wavelength, vary continuously. Wittgenstein comments on color: What do all blue things have in common? – Just that they are blue (*PI,* 72). Third, some members of the category (for example the central, universal, salient points) are clearly better examples of their category than others. How could we have concepts like this?

"But is it senseless to say: 'Stand roughly there'? ... point[ing] with my hand – as if I were indicating a particular *spot*" (Wittgenstein, *PI,* 71). As the result of a dispute between two neighbors in the street on which I lived as a child, it became apparent that none of our property lines were exactly known, and I remember thinking how remarkable it was that we could know that our houses were firmly in the middle of their yards without knowing where any of the yards ended. Might color categories, and other categories as well, be of this nature? I called the salient points at the centers of the color categories *prototypes* and must admit that I was ambivalent from the start about whether I thought of "prototype" simply as a placemarker indicating the center of a "Wittgensteinian" category or whether I thought of it as an actual something, for example, a mental code to which the category name might refer.

Upon returning from New Guinea, I set about operationalizing the extension of the color work to other natural categories. Did semantic categories in general, like colors, have best examples and gradients of membership? The first concern was whether subjects would agree on typicality ratings of items. The categories used were common superordinates such as "bird" and "vehicle," and their instances were the words listed as examples of the category in the Battig and Montague (1969) norms. Experimental instructions are often revealing. The subjects were being asked to rate, on a 7-point scale, the extent to which each instance "represented their idea or image of the meaning of the category term." And how were these instructions conveyed to them?

> This study has to do with what we have in mind when we use words which refer to categories. Let's take the word *red* as an example. Close your eyes and imagine a true red. Now imagine an orangish red ... imagine a purple red. Although you might still name the orange red or the purple red with the term *red,* they are not as good examples of red (as clear cases of what *red* refers to) as the clear "true" red. In short, some reds are reder than others. The same is true for other kinds of categories. Think of dogs. You all have some notion of what a "real dog" a "doggy dog" is. To me a retriever or a German shephard is a very doggy dog while a Pekinese is a less doggy dog. Notice that this kind of judgment has nothing to do with how well you like the thing; you can like a purple red better than a true red but still recognize that the color you like is not a true red. You may prefer to own a Pekinese without thinking that it is the breed that best represents what people man by dogginess. (Rosch, 1973, pp. 131-132)

(Needless to say, neither *red* nor *dog* were categories in the experiment.)

These instructions (even the phrase "what red refers to") were meant quite innocently. They were intended, and in fact accomplished, the task of communication to subjects - by whatever experiences or presuppositions or folk theories we shared - what I meant by good examples and typicality. In fact, subjects had no trouble in understanding these instructions. Typicality ratings of items were highly correlated and reliable, and were found to predict reaction times in a variety of categorization tasks (Rips, Shoben, & Smith, 1973; Rosch, 1973). Yet note what is happening: It is remarkably easy to describe - and think of - prototypes as particular "things."

In subsequent research the reification of prototypes continued - though it was never complete. The idea of cognitive representations was by then established in cognitive psychology, and it became natural to think of categories as represented by a mental code (Posner, Boies, Eichelman, & Taylor, 1969). It was an unknown code about which, with suitably ingenious experimental methods, one could make discoveries, perhaps finding answers to age old questions such as the nature of abstraction or imageless thought (Posner, 1969; Rosch, 1975a). What was the intension (meaning) of a category actually like? I conceived of this code as the "mental representation generated by hearing the category name," and by use of the technique of priming (Beller, 1971; Posner et al., 1969) in a series of experiments (Rosch 1975a, 1975b) drew the following types of conclusions: (1) that such a representation was more like good than bad examples of the category; (2) that it was in a form common to both words and pictures but somewhat closer in format to pictures; and (3) that it was manipulable through practice for semantic but not color categories. Although the representation was treated as a definite thing, no specific claims were made for its functions or for its relation to meaning. However, any proposed concrete code, as we shall presently see, makes an easy target for such claims.

Family Resemblances. Where do prototypes and typicality orderings come from? With colors the origin can be argued to be physiological. But for semantic categories? At the same time as the emergence of the concept identification paradigm there had been developing a strain of research on abstract mental representations called schemas (Bartlett, 1932). Using primarily artificial stimuli, schemas tended to be operationalized as the central tendencies, such as means and modes, of the quantifiable dimensions on which members of the category differed. Schemas could also be centers of axes in a multidimensional scaling space. And there is an extensive literature on schemas derived from gestalt configurations having no definable attributes, such as families of random dot patterns (see reviews in Posner, 1969; Mervis & Rosch, 1981; and Medin & Smith, 1984). Here is a clear convergence of schema and prototype research: One type of prototype would seem to be explainable by the organism's computation of central tendency. But what of categories that do not seem to consist of quantifiable dimensions or even gestalt configurations – as perhaps *games?*

Wittgenstein enters, at this point, as the guide to a specific research proposal. The concept of family resemblances played the role in Wittgenstein's argument of a counterexample. His "opponent" claims that categories *must* have something in common in order to be proper referents of words. Wittgenstein points out that, in fact, categories such as game do not have anything in common; all that they have is a complicated network of similarities which we may call family resemblances. Philosophically it is a relatively peripheral part of the argument – snipping at the leaves and branches of the object of reference model rather than attacking the roots as he does elsewhere. Might it, none the less, form a central part of the empirical investigation of categories? Wittgenstein (in *PI*) says of family resemblances "look and see," and Carolyn Mervis and I decided to look and see.

In order to investigate family resemblances one needs a set of categories, many instances of these categories, and a computation of the attributes of the instances. Accordingly, we had subjects list all the attributes they could think of for 20 instances of each of six superordinate categories (an example of a category is *furniture* and of an instance *chair*) and for 15 pictures of instances of each of six basic level categories (an example of a category is *chair* and of an instance a picture of a chair). Independent ratings were obtained of how good an example each instance was of its category. From the lists of attributes we then computed family resemblance scores for each item, for example, the number of attributes which each item shared with other members of its category (Rosch & Mervis, 1975).

The first part of the family resemblance claim is that all instances of categories need not have attributes in common. It was in fact the case that, for the superordinate categories of this study (as in a previous study: Rosch, Mervis, Gray, Johnson, & Boyes-Braem, 1976), few attributes were given which were true of all members of any category – for four of the six categories, there was only one such item; for two of the categories, none. Furthermore, the single attribute which did apply to all members, in three cases was true of many other items besides those within that superordinate (for example, "you eat it" for fruit). But, of course, if all you can say about a group of items is that they have no attributes in common, one might well ask, why should there be a category here at all?

The second part of the family resemblance claim is the positive one that instances do share family resemblances. We next analyzed our family resemblance measures. The results both for superordinate and basic level objects were very clear: Family resemblance scores correlated highly with ratings of typicality. The better subjects rated an item as a member of its category, the more attributes it shared with other members of that category. Furthermore, thinking that this finding could account for the persistent "illusion" that all members of a category do have attributes in common, we further analyzed the five most typical items in each category. These did, indeed, prove to have many attributes in common: For example, chair, sofa, table, dresser and desk do share a number of attributes with each other, and they do not share these with mirror, stove, clock, picture, vase, telephone or other marginal items of furniture. We reasoned that if, on hearing the category name, people tend to think of the most typical category members, then – even when not under the sway of philosophical reasoning – one would have the impression of commonality of attributes.

There is a third aspect of family resemblance that Wittgenstein does not mention in the *Philosophical investigations* but which played an important role in his rejection of the logical implications of the *Tractatus* (Waismann, 1979). Categories do not occur in isolation. Any time one places an item into one category one is simultaneously not placing it into other contrasting categories. We also had subjects list attributes of members of contrasting categories. Negative correlations were obtained between typicality ratings and an item's possession of attributes characteristic of contrasting categories.

In summary, we found that the most prototypical items in categories have most attributes in common with other members of their own category and least attributes in common with other categories. To establish this finding irrefutably we conducted two more experiments using artificial categories consisting of letter strings in which family resemblance relationships could be built in and possible confounding factors excluded. Results were the same as for the natural categories. In fact, family resemblance not only correlated with typicality ratings but also with ease of learning the item and with reaction time to identify the item after learning – the standard independent variables with which typicality ratings had correlated in other research on prototypes.

Growth of Nonclassical Categorization Research

Although the empirical evidence challenging the criterial definition view of categories has aroused wide interest, the concept of prototypes and family resemblances has seemed underspecified or in other ways inadequate to many researchers. A host of new models which specify what the prototype is and how it functions in decision procedures have been proposed and investigated. These models can be classified roughly into (1) exemplar models, in which specific exemplars are stored and membership for new instances computed by means of a similarity function, and (2) probabilistic models, in which the category is stored in terms of a core on which operate probabilistic functions for classifying new members (see Smith & Medin, 1981, for a detailed account of these models).

Noncriterial attribute accounts of categories (often called "nonclassical," whether they are prototype, exemplar, probabilistic or otherwise) have generated an enormous body of research (see Mervis & Rosch, 1981; and Medin & Smith, 1984, for reviews). On the whole, typicality (used now in a generic sense) has been found to correlate highly with verification times for category membership, order and probability of production of category exemplars, and many important variables in the learning and development of categories. It has been applied to the natural language use of words, and in linguistics, Lakoff (in press) has recently compiled an enormous body of evidence for nonclassical effects in language, which he uses as an attack on Chomskian linguistics. The nonclassical view has been incorporated into models of semantic memory and into artificial intelligence programs. In philosophy, it has become an inevitable part of the discussion of natural kind terms (see, for example, Kelley & Krueger, 1984). And it is being applied to various issues in social and clinical classification. What has all of this to do with Wittgenstein?

Prototypes, Etc. as Objects of Reference

Prototype was initially conceived as a noncommittal designation for the central regions of categories such that nonclassical category structure could be investigated empirically. The term gradually became reified as indicated. The result is that a prototype account or any other model of nonclassical category structure is expected to fulfill the very functions of the classical criterial attribute view –

namely, to be an object of reference that gives meaning to words and makes true knowledge possible. This may be most clearly seen in some of the criticisms of prototypes.

1. *Formal Semantic Conditions.* If it is the prototype (exemplars, etc.) that are to provide the meaning for words, then prototypes must fulfill the requirements of a formal semantic model; for example, account for synonymy, contradiction, and conjunctive categories. Osherson and Smith (1981) modeled prototype theory with fuzzy set logic and showed that prototypes of conjunctive categories did not follow the rule of conjunction as maximization; for example, a pet fish is neither a prototypical pet nor a prototypical fish. This was taken as a refutation of prototype theory. Hampton (1985) accepting these same requirements, argued that prototypes do account for pet fish.

2. *Context Effects.* The *meaning* of a word must not change with conditions of its *use*. One of the great virtues of the criterial attribute view is that critical attributes are just that which is unchanging over contexts. If prototypes are to fulfill this function, they must be unaffected by context. But many studies have shown changes in comprehension or memory of category terms as a function of context (Anderson & Ortony, 1975; Anderson, Pichert, Goetz, Schallert, Stevens & Trollip, 1976; Barclay, Bransford, Franks, McCarrell & Nitsch, 1974; Barsalou, in press; Potter & Faulconer). For example, typicality ratings for animals are different in the context of African than American animals. And different words will cue memory for *piano* when it occurs in the context of *playing* versus *moving* a piano. Context effects are often taken as a refutation of protoype theory.

3. *Typicality Effects Are Too Universal.* If the classical definition of a category is taken as the meaning to which the term refers and if the prototype is taken as the meaning to which a term refers, then no category can have both a classical definition and a prototype (unless it is a strange case of polysemy – because a prototype and a classical definition are not the same). Armstrong, Gleitman, and Gleitman (1983) demonstrated that all of the typicality effects associated with empirical categories such as *furniture* and *fruit* are also found for categories which are argued to have, by necessity, a criterial definition, such as *odd number*. It is only by assumptions such as we have outlined that this could possibly be taken as a refutation of prototypes.

4. *Core Concept and Processing Heuristics.* A class of models of categorization have been proposed in which the actual meaning for category terms is a classical definition onto which is added a processing heuristic or identification procedure that accounts for typicality effects (Armstrong et al., 1983; Caramazza, 1979; Glass & Holyoak, 1975; Hampton, 1979; McClosky & Glucksberg, 1979; Smith, Shoben & Rips, 1974). This is, in fact, the way in which Armstrong et al. (1983), resolve the finding that *odd number* can "have" both a classical definition and a prototype. By this masterful stroke, data are consigned to prototypes and other

nonclassical models for their explanation and criterial definitions, freed at last, can perform unhampered the philosophical function which is their heritage.

But what is wrong with meanings as objects of reference? Couldn't prototype or other such models perhaps fulfill this function for category terms in the way that classical definitions could not?

Wittgenstein's Criticisms of Objects of Reference

Suppose that prototypes are the objects to which category names refer, the objects which are their meaning. To have meaning in the reference view a word must (1) have an object for which it stands – in this case the prototype, and (2) knowing what the word stands for should be a sufficient condition for its having meaning, for understanding it. How will this work with prototypes? In the first place, if prototypes are to serve as the objects of reference, the meanings of words, they cannot simply be hypothetical constructs in the theory (or mind) of the experimenter; they must also be in the world or in the mind of the individual using the word. (The four criticisms of prototypes just enumerated would not be coherent without such an assumption.) So we may ask *where* they are.

In present cognitive science there are two basic possibilities for the location of such "entities," the external world or the cognitive representation. Since cognitive variables are usually placed in the cognitive representation let us first follow the logic of that possibility. If prototypes are in the cognitive representation, there is a sense in which they can be said to be private; my prototypical *dog* or *red* need not be identical to anyone else's and only I can know what my prototypes are like. There are two possibilities regarding this privateness: one in which the representation of the prototype is *inherently* private and the other in which both public and private criteria are applicable.

Suppose the representation to be inherently private. To set up the meaning for a category term and to remember or use the term subsequently I need simply associate (connect) the term with something in my cognitive representational system – a sensation, image, exemplar, prototype, rule, or anything else that is in it. Then I can use the term; for example, I can keep a record of the occurrence of that thing in my representational system – perhaps I could keep an actual diary (*PI,* 258). And *how* do I associate the word; how do I set up the connection? Perhaps one concentrates one's attention on the cognitive thing while writing down the word and thus impresses on oneself the connection between the word and the thing. But, Wittgenstein explains, "'I impress it on myself' can only mean: this process brings it about that I remember the connection *right* in the future" (*PI,* 258). Being inherently private, I can only use private modes of justifying that I have remembered the connection right and am using the term correctly.

Wittgenstein makes two objections to private justification. The first is that it leads to an infinite regress: "'Well I *believe* that this is the [cognitive thing] again' – perhaps you *believe* that you believe it" (*PI,* 260). The second is that it isn't justifying. Wittgenstein (*PI*, 258–267) asks us to compare: checking our memory by looking up a word in a real dictionary compared with an imagined dictionary; checking a real timetable compared to checking a remembered timetable; buying several copies of the morning paper to assure ourselves that what it said was true; the difference between the result of an experiment and the result of an imagined experiment; and the difference between what we would call justifying an imagined choice of dimensions for a bridge and imagining what is called justifying the choice of dimensions. This is summed up thus:

Why can't my right hand give my left hand money? – My right hand can put it into my left hand. My right hand can write a deed of gift and my left hand a receipt. – But the further practical consequences would not be those of a gift. When the left hand has taken the money from the right, etc., we shall ask: "Well, and what of it?" And the same could be asked if a person had given himself a private definition of a word; I mean, if he has said the word to himself and at the same time has directed his attention to a sensation. (*PI*, 268)

In the present case, one may object that one didn't mean to claim that kind of strict privacy for one's cognitive representations. But notice that in this example, we had all of the conditions necessary and sufficient for a term having meaning in the object of reference view – we had an object for which the term stands and we had knowing that the word stood for it. But without something more than this we did not have meaning.

Wittgenstein then presents a case where we *lack* the necessary and sufficient conditions for meaning under the object name view yet the word still has meaning:

"Imagine a person whose memory could not retain *what* the word 'pain' meant – so that he constantly called different things by that name – but nevertheless used the word in a way fitting in with the usual symptoms and presuppositions of pain" – in short he uses it as we all do. (*PI*, 271)

To reiterate: Given the necessary and sufficient conditions for meaning under the object of reference view, Wittgenstein has shown a case in which a word met those conditions yet we could not say it had meaning as well as a case in which it did not meet the conditions and yet did have meaning. The next move of the adherent of the object of reference view might be to remove the claim of inherent privacy and instead suppose that both public and private criteria are applicable. Wittgenstein has this to say:

Suppose everyone had a box with something in it: we call it a "beetle." No one can look into anyone else's box, and everyone says he knows what a beetle is only by looking at *his* beetle. – Here it would be quite possible for everyone to have something different in his box. One might even imagine such a thing constantly changing. – But suppose the word "beetle" had a use in these people's language? – If so it would not be used as the name of a thing. The thing in the box has no place in the language-game at all; not even as a *something*: for the box might even be empty. – No, one can 'divide through' by the thing in the box; it cancels out, whatever it is.
That is to say: if we construe the grammar of the expression of sensation on the model of 'object and designation' the object drops out of consideration as irrelevant. (*PI*, 293)

At this point, the proponent of the object of reference view might wish to abandon altogether the claim that the object of reference is in the cognitive representation, and place it instead in the world. This is not an unreasonable position; after all, we might argue, when we speak or point it is usually directed to *things* not to hypothetical cognitive representations. We point to public exemplars, signposts, rules telling us how to proceed with a category word. Wittgenstein has this to say:

> A rule stands there like a sign-post. – Does the sign-post leave no doubt open about the way I have to go? Does it shew which direction I am to take when I have passed it; whether along the road or the footpath or cross-country? But where is it said which way I am to follow it; whether in the direction of the finger or (e.g.) in the opposite one? – And if there were, not a single sign-post, but a chain of adjacent ones or of chalk marks on the ground – is there only *one* way of interpreting them? (*PI,* 85)

This argument may perhaps be seen in an even purer form when it is applied to the "certainties" of mathematics. Suppose that the mathematical Platonist is right and that we do have some kind of external "archetype" of mathematical truths – of the number series, let us say. Suppose even an extreme case in which mathematical objects can be literally perceived; they are a shadow world in which the answers are already written down faintly:

> And continuing the series just means copying them out . . . [but] this cannot explain how we know that what we are copying is the correct answer. The Platonist's problem is like that of the schoolboy who cheats. He has to know who has the right answers to copy from. (Bloor, 1983, p. 86)

Or in Wittgenstein's words, there are "an infinity of shadowy worlds . . . we don't know which of them we're talking about" (*LFM,* 145).

Wittgenstein is often taken as simply attacking privacy, that is, mentalistic interpretations of phenomena such as meaning. In fact he is equally critical of public, external objects, rules, pictures, behaviors or anything else claimed to be the object of reference or necessary meaning of language or knowledge. Simply changing the putative object of reference – whether prototypes are substituted for definitions or exemplars for prototypes or rules of probabilistic inference for exemplars – or changing the location of those objects from private to public or to some combination of both will have no effect upon the arguments.

What Might be a Wittgensteinian Investigation of Categorization?

Wittgenstein does not leave us without any account at all. Language and knowing are part of the activities, language-games, meanings in use, conventions, and forms of life of an entire people. "Only in the stream of thought and life do words have meaning" (*Z,* 173). What implications might this have for the study of categorization?

Wittgenstein left the idea of conventions and forms of life, perhaps deliberately, unspecified. Almost any proposal that one tries to derive from it seems to violate the delicate and precise balance of understanding that Wittgenstein creates. For example, from the pervasiveness of context effects one might want to claim that categories are created anew each time on the spot (Barsalou, in press); but then, as Barsalou himself points out, one must still distinguish between categories that are already part of the language like *chair* and those created by a particular novel goal like *things to carry out of the house in a fire.* One might wish to argue with Gleitman, Armstrong and Gleitman (1983) that there is no single field of categorization to be studied; but then organisms still do treat discriminably different objects and events equivalently. It might be tempting to argue that the criterial definition view of categories has no place at all in cognitive psychology if its philosophical underpinnings have been removed and that we should concentrate on the investigation of processing heuristics. But criterial definitions certainly have a place in our life and culture; indeed, we cling to them tenaciously. Wittgenstein himself acknowledges this in his remarks on the distinction between *justifications* and *symptoms* of category membership. There is even some empirical evidence about justification (Landau, 1982).

There are at least three current programs of research in categorization that have a somewhat Wittgensteinian flavor (see also Neisser, in press). Perhaps the narrowest of these is my own work on basic objects (Rosch, 1978; Rosch et al., 1976). In taxonomies of material objects there is often one level of abstraction at which we feel we have the true category, the real name of the object (*chair* as opposed to *furniture* or *kitchen chair*). The basic object hypothesis was that this level actually maps real world structure; it is the level at which attributes cluster - physical, perceptual, functional, and social. It is here that we have our most basic language-games with the everyday material world. It is at this level that similar motor movements are used when interacting with the objects in a category; this level at which objects are imaged and at which they are first categorized in perception of the environment; and this is the earliest level categorized by children and the most necessary level for vocabulary in languages. The idea of basic level applies also to social objects (Brown, 1986; Cantor & Mischel, 1979; Tversky & Hemenway, 1984). Presently, work on the development of basic level categories as a flexible negotiation between the mother, child, and environment is being carried out by Mervis (1984; also Mervis & Pani, 1980).

Most category learning occurs not in a specialized categorization language-game, but as part of the ordinary events of daily life. Interest in such events in cognitive psychology was spurred some years ago by the use in artificial intelligence of the concept of scripts (Schank & Abelson, 1977). A programmatic study of the development of scripts and children's knowledge of events is being carried out by Nelson (in press). Nelson argues that language itself can be seen as arising from participation in scripted events and that it is generalized event representations which are the building blocks of cognitive structure. Analysis of the relation of language and events at a more micro level has proved quite generative in developmental psycholinguistics (Slobin, 1981).

Being human, our language-games have a special quality - we have theories. Carey (1982) argues that what may look like a single category such as animal is actually part of an entire theory of living things; it is part of our beliefs about biology. As early as age four, children who usually say that a mechanical monkey is more similar to a person than is a worm, when told that people have a spleen inside them, readily attribute the spleen to the worm but not the monkey. This cannot be accounted for, Carey argues by reference to a simple similarity metric; it requires a knowledge of folk biology. In fact it is possible to argue, though this may be committing the opposite of one of those skeptical errors, that all categories are theories of sorts (Murphy & Medin, in press).

In conclusion, one might wish to ask - how to proceed with this research? Can we look to Wittgenstein for advice, if not on topic, at least on strategy? Perhaps not, but Wittgenstein's own tactics might be described as perpetually trying to find the correct "focus" from which to analyze a problem (as Merleau-Ponty, 1962, claims we always do in the very act of perception). If one gets "too close" to the problem, looking for what "lies hidden" beyond the uses of language, one's subject matter begins to look queer - and perhaps metaphysical. "In order to find the real artichoke, we divested it of its leaves" (*PI,* 164). If one fails to get close enough, Wittgenstein asks "Do you mean *this?*" giving a further definition, a distinction, a specific case, or constructing a language- game. For Wittgenstein the criterion for having reached the right focus point is the disappearence of the philosophical problem: "For the clarity that we are aiming at is indeed *complete* clarity. But this simply means that the philosophical problems should *completely* disappear" (*PI,* 133). For empirical issues, perhaps this means rather that the problems are brought completely into view. And that is the beginning of the investigation.

References

Anderson, R.C., & Ortony, A.(1975). On putting apples into bottles. - A problem of polysemy. *Cognitive Psychology, 7,* 167-180.

Anderson, R.C., Pichert, J.W., Goetz, E.T., Schallert, D.L., Stevens, K.V., & Trollip, S.R. (1976). Instantiation of general terms. *Journal of Verbal Learning and Verbal Behavior, 15,* 667-679.

Armstrong, S.L., Gleitman, L.R., & Gleitman, H.(1983). What some concepts might not be. *Cognition, 13,* 263-308.

Barclay, J.R., Bransford, J.D., Franks, J.J., McCarrell, N.S., & Nitsch, K.(1974). Comprehension and semantic flexibility. *Journal of Verbal Learning and Verbal Behavior, 13,* 471-481.

Barsalou, S.W. (in press). The instability of graded structure: Implications for the nature of concepts. In U. Neisser (Ed.), *Concepts reconsidered: The ecological and intellectual bases of categories.* Cambridge: Cambridge University Press.

Bartlett, F.C. (1932). *Remembering: A study in experimental and social psychology.* Cambridge: Cambridge University Press.

Battig, W.F., & Montague, W.E. (1969). Category norms for verbal items in 56 categories: A replication and extension of the Connecticut category norms. *Journal of Experimental Psychology, 80* (Monograph Supplement 3, Part 2).

Beller, H.K. (1971). Priming: Effects of advance information on matching. *Journal of Experimental Psychology, 87,* 176-182.

Berlin, B., & Kay, P.(1969). *Basic color terms: Their universality and evolution.* Berkeley: University of California Press.

Bloor, D. (1983). *Wittgenstein: A social theory of knowledge.* New York: Columbia University Press.

Brown, R. (1979). Cognitive categories. In R. A. Kasschau & C. N. Cofer (Eds.), *Psychology's second century: Enduring issues.* New York: Praeger.

Brown, R. (1986). *Social psychology: The second edition.* New York: The Free Press.

Brown, R., & Lenneberg, E. (1954). A study in language and cognition. *Journal of Abnormal and Social Psychology, 49,* 454-462.

Bruner, J. S., Goodnow, J. J., & Austin, G. A. (1956). *A study of thinking.* New York: Wiley.

Bruner, J. S., Olver, R. R., & Greenfield, P. M. (1966). *Studies in cognitive growth.* New York: Wiley.

Cantor, N., & Mischel, W. (1979). Prototypes in person perception. *Advances in Experimental Social Psychology, 12,* 3-52.

Caramazza, A. (1979). *Are concepts ill-defined or vague?* Paper presented at the Conference on Word and Concept, Stanford University, Stanford, CA.

Carey, S. (1982). Semantic development: The state of the art. In E. Wanner & L. R. Gleitman (Eds.), *Language acquisition: The state of the art.* Cambridge: Cambridge University Press.

Erickson, J. R., & Jones, M. R. (1978). Thinking. *Annual Review of Psychology, 29,* 61-90.

Fodor, J. (1981). The current status of the innateness controversy. In J. Fodor (Ed.), *Representations.* Montgomery, VT: Bradford Books.

Glass, A. L., & Holyoak, K. J. (1975). Alternative concepts of semantic memory. *Cognition, 3,* 313-339.

Gleitman, L. R., Armstrong, S. L., & Gleitman, H. (1983). On doubting the concept 'concept.' In E. K. Scholnick (Ed.), *New trends in conceptual representation: Challenges to Piaget's theory?* Hillsdale, NJ: Erlbaum.

Hampton, J. A. (1979). Polymorphous concepts in semantic memory. *Journal of Verbal Learning and Verbal Behavior, 18,* 441-461.

Hampton, J. A. (1985). *Overextension of conjunctive concepts: Evidence for a unitary model of concept typicality and class inclusion.* Unpublished manuscript.

Heider, E. R. (1972). Universals in color naming and memory. *Journal of Experimental Psychology, 93,* 10-20.

Kelley, D., & Krueger, J. (1984). The psychology of abstraction. *Journal for the Theory of Social Behavior, 14,* 43-67.

Kessel, F., & Bevan, W. (in press). In C. W. Buxton (Ed.), *Points of view in the modern history of psychology.* New York: Academic Press.

Lakoff, G. (in press). *Women, fire and dangerous things: What categories tell us about the nature of thought.* Chicago: University of Chicago Press.

Landau, B. (1982). Will the real grandmother please stand up? The psychological reality of dual meaning representations. *Journal of Psychological Research, 11,* 47-62.

Marx, M. H. (Ed.) (1968). *Theories in contemporary psychology.* New York: Macmillan.

McCloskey, M. E., & Glucksberg, S. (1978). Natural categories: Well defined or fuzzy sets? *Memory and Cognition, 6,* 642-672.

McCloskey, M. E., & Glucksberg, S. (1979). Decision processes in verifying category membership statements: Implications for models of semantic memory. *Cognitive Psychology, 11,* 1-37.

Medin, D. L., & Smith, E. E. (1984). Concepts and concept formation. *Annual Review of Psychology, 35,* 113-138.

Merleau-Ponty, M. (1962). *Phenomenology of perception.* London: Routledge & Kegan Paul.

Mervis, C. B. (1984). Early lexical development: The contributions of mother and child. In C. Sophian (Ed.), *Origins of cognitive skills.* Hillsdale, NJ: Erlbaum.

Mervis, C. B., & Pani, J. R. (1980). Acquisition of basic object categories. *Cognitive Psychology, 12,* 496-522.

Mervis, C. B., & Rosch, E. (1981). Categorization of natural objects. *Annual Review of Psychology, 32,* 89-115.

Murphy, G. L., & Medin, D. L. (in press). The role of theories in conceptual coherence. In U. Neisser (Ed.), *Concepts reconsidered: The ecological and intellectual bases of categories.* Cambridge: Cambridge University Press.

Neimark, E. D., & Santa, J. L. (1975). Thinking and concept attainment. *Annual Review of Psychology, 26,* 173-205.

Neisser, U. (in press). From direct perception to conceptual structure. In U. Neisser (Ed.), *Concepts reconsidered: The ecological and intellectual bases of categories.* Cambridge: Cambridge University Press.

Nelson, K. (in press). Social cognition in a scripts framework. In L. Ross & J. Flavell (Eds.), *The development of social cognition in children.* Hillsdale, NJ: Erlbaum.

Osherson, D., & Smith, E. E. (1981). On the adequacy of prototype theory as a theory of concepts. *Cognition, 9,* 35-58.

Piaget, J. (1972). *The principles of genetic epistemology.* New York: Basic Books.

Posner, M. I. (1969). Abstraction and the process of recognition. In G. H. Bower & J. T. Spence (Eds.), *The psychology of learning and motivation.* New York: Academic Press.

Posner, M. I., Boies, S. J., Eichelman, W. H., & Taylor, R. L. (1969). Retention of visual and name codes of single letters. *Journal of Experimental Psychology Monograph, 79* (1).

Potter, M. C., & Faulconer, B. A. (1979). Understanding noun phrases. *Journal of Verbal Learning and Verbal Behavior, 18,* 509-521.

Rips, L. J., Shoben, E. J., & Smith, E. E. (1973). Semantic distance and the verification of semantic relations. *Journal of Verbal Learning and Verbal Behavior, 12,* 1-20.

Rosch, E. (1973). On the internal structure of perceptual and semantic categories. In T. E. Moore (Ed.), *Cognitive development and the acquisition of language.* New York: Academic Press.

Rosch, E. (1975 a). Cognitive representations of semantic categories. *Journal of Experimental Psychology: General, 104,* 192-233.

Rosch, E. (1975 b). The nature of mental codes for color categories. *Journal of Experimental Psychology: Human Perception and Performance, 1,* 303-322.

Rosch, E. (1978). Principles of categorization. In E. Rosch & B. B. Lloyd (Eds.), *Cognition and Categorization.* Hillsdale, NJ: Erlbaum.

Rosch, E., & Mervis, C. B. (1975). Family resemblances: Studies in the internal structure of categories. *Cognitive Psychology, 7,* 573-605.

Rosch, E., Mervis, C. B., Gray, W. D., Johnson, D. M., & Boyes-Braem, P. (1976). Basic objects in natural categories. *Cognitive Psychology, 8,* 382-439.

Schank, R. C., & Abelson, R. P. (1977). *Scripts, plans, goals and understanding: An inquiry into human knowledge structures.* Hillsdale, NJ: Erlbaum.

Slobin, D. K. (1981). The origins of grammatical coding of events. In W. Deutsch (Ed.), *The child's construction of language.* London: Academic Press.

Smith, E. E., & Medin, D. L. (1981). *Categories and concepts.* Cambridge, MA: Harvard University Press.

Smith, E. E., Shoben, E. J., & Rips, L. J. (1974). Structure and process in semantic memory: A featural model for semantic decisions. *Psychological Review, 81,* 214-241.

Tversky, B., & Hemenway, K. (1984). Objects, parts, and categories. *Journal of Experimental Psychology: General, 113,* 169-197.

Vygotsky, L. S. (1962). *Thought and language.* New York: Wiley.

Waisman, F. (1979). *Wittgenstein and the Vienna Circle.* New York: Barnes & Noble.

Chapter 10 Wittgenstein, Psychology, and the Problem of Individuality[1]

Charlotte J. Patterson

I believe that my originality (if that is the right word) is an originality belonging to the soil rather than to the seed.... Sow a seed in my soil and it will grow differently than it would in any other soil. (Wittgenstein, *CV*, p. 36 e)

Wittgenstein's dissatisfaction with academic psychology is well known. In perhaps the most widely available statement of his discontent, Wittgenstein wrote, "The confusion and barrenness of psychology is not to be explained by calling it a 'young science'." In psychology, he added, "there are experimental methods and *conceptual confusion*. ... The existence of experimental methods makes us think we have the means of solving problems which trouble us; though problem and methods pass one another by" (*PI*, p. 232 e).

What is the nature of Wittgenstein's criticism of psychology, and what might it mean for research in developmental psychology? Building to a greater or lesser extent on the philosophical literature (e.g., Anscombe, 1957; Cavell, 1979; Hamlyn, 1978; Kenny, 1973; Pitcher, 1968; Rorty, 1979; Taylor, 1971; Toulmin, 1972; Vesey, 1974; von Wright, 1971; Winch, 1958), a growing number of psychologists have proposed answers to this question that involve shifts from realist to constructivist philosophies of science (e.g., Bruner, 1976; Gergen, 1982, 1985; Scarr, 1985) or from behavior theories to theories of action (e.g., Chapman, 1984; Harré & Secord, 1972; Patterson, 1982, 1984). Still others have focused specifically on Wittgenstein's criticisms of the idea of a private language, doctrine of family resemblances, or notion that the meaning of a word is to be found in its use, and on the implications of these for developmental research (e.g., Bruner, 1974/75; Markman, 1973; Rosch, 1978, this volume). Valuable as all of these directions would seem to be, I wish to focus attention here on another set of themes.

Although there are many different ways in which to receive Wittgenstein's critical remarks about psychology, the interpretation that I offer here centers on some of his fundamental assumptions about human life. I suggest that Wittgenstein's remarks are not only the disappointed commentary of one who, after surveying a field, concludes that intriguing phenomena have gone unstudied or that empirical data have not supported popular theories. They also express Wittgen-

[1] I wish to thank Mary D.S. Ainsworth, Jude Cassidy, Michael Chapman, Deborah A. Cohn, M. Jamie Ferreira, William P. Gardner, and Sandra Scarr for their helpful comments on earlier drafts of this manuscript. I also wish to thank Roger Kobak for directing my attention to the inspiring work of Stanley Cavell, and Cora Diamond for her gracious encouragement of my interest in Wittgenstein.

stein's belief that psychologists have generally started from inappropriate assumptions about the human situation, and hence that the questions they have posed as psychologists have been misleading or ill-conceived. When experimental methods are employed to answer such questions, "problem and methods pass one another by," and the result can be only "barrenness and confusion." What psychology needs, from this standpoint, is a reorientation, a more appropriate set of basic assumptions; and this, I will suggest, is something that Wittgenstein attempts to provide.

The kinds of assumptions that I have in mind are interpretations of the nature of social being or social reality. They are ways of describing what in human life is natural, to be taken for granted; and what is surprising, or in need of explanation. In providing these accounts, such assumptions propose the kinds of questions that might be answered by psychologies; and hence, they are the philosophical soil out of which empirical psychologies can grow.

For my purposes here, it will be useful to distinguish in a very rough way between three categories of fundamental assumptions. *Individualist* assumptions emphasize the primacy of the individual person, underlining the integrity and independence of each human life. *Collectivist* assumptions, on the other hand, emphasize the primacy of collective ways of living, underlining the interconnectedness and interdependence of social lives. *Relational* assumptions assert the fundamental reality of both persons and of the collective life. Although there have been contrasting voices (notably Vygotsky, 1962, 1978, among collectivists; and Mead, 1934, Piaget, 1965, and Sullivan, 1953, among relational theorists), there can be little doubt but that the mainstream of contemporary academic psychology in the United States has grown out of assumptions of the first type (cf. Harré, 1979, 1984; Sampson, 1983).

Wittgenstein's philosophical remarks stem from assumptions of the third type. While recognizing the relational character of human existence, and without denying the reality of either persons or of institutions, Wittgenstein's work brings the collective or collaborative aspects of our lives into the foreground. Wittgenstein's writings thus treat as misguided many of the most cherished philosophical and psychological questions from the individualist tradition, and they propose for examination questions of a very different sort. Wittgenstein's philosophical writings, in short, suggest the possibility of a different kind of psychology.

In this chapter, I will focus mainly on the collectivist emphasis of Wittgenstein's work, and will sketch some possible implications of this approach for the practice of developmental psychology. Not wishing to enter into debate here about the continuities and discontinuities of Wittgenstein's thought, I will focus entirely on material written during the last 20 years of his life – i.e., on the later Wittgenstein. Within this context, I will focus principally on the best-known work of Wittgenstein's later years, the *Philosophical investigations*. Before turning to Wittgenstein, however, I want to outline very briefly some aspects of the individualist assumptions against which he struggled.

Individualist Assumptions and Contemporary Psychology

The mainstream of contemporary academic psychology, at least as it is practiced in American universities, originated at the end of the last century from the union of German physiology on the one hand and of British empiricism on the other. It is the latter side of the lineage that is of greater interest here, for it had the distinction, as Boring (1950, p. 169) has put it, of being "most peculiarly the philosophical parent" of experimental psychology, and of its academic descendants. Because the liberal values of independence, self-reliance, and individualism are so much a part of the predominant system of values in the United States today (cf. Bellah, Madsen, Sullivan, Swidler, & Tipton, 1985), they often seem to be natural reactions rather than invented products of ideological systems. That this should be the case is a tribute to the thoroughness with which our culture has inherited the ideas of the liberal tradition handed down to us in part by the empiricists.

Individualism is a hallmark of the philosophical tradition to which the empiricists belong. As human beings, in this view, we are first and foremost to be regarded as free and independent individuals, autonomous selves, indivisible social atoms. For the empiricists, as for the liberal tradition in general, the basic unit of discourse is, and ought to be, the individual person. This general approach results in social and epistemological questions of characteristic form, and these have been enormously influential both in the history of philosophy and in that of psychology.

Although the empiricist school begins chronologically with Hobbes, and although many of its guiding ideas are still active in psychology today, its best representative for my purposes here is John Locke. It was Locke who, in the 17th century, gave classic formulation to individualist questions about knowledge that lead to skepticism. It was also Locke who formulated individualist concerns about the possibility of social life that would be answered by different conceptions of the social contract. Locke's ideas in these two domains, and their resonance in contemporary academic psychology, will be considered very briefly below.

Knowledge and Skepticism

As a student at Oxford, Locke had read Descartes, and had become interested in his philosophy (Boring, 1950). Much as he found himself in disagreement with the Cartesian doctrine of innate ideas, Locke did, however, accept the picture offered by Descartes of each human being as a solitary center of consciousness, for whom the central dilemma is the possibility of knowing the outside world. We have direct access, Locke believed, to the contents of our own consciousness. The problem, then, is to explain how we come to know anything of the world outside our own skins, especially how we come to know anything of the contents of other minds (Locke, 1690/1966). This is the problem of philosophical skepticism.

Since Locke believed that all knowledge results either from sensation or from reflection, one's knowledge of the world and of the other people in it must, he thought, arise in these ways (Locke, 1690/1966). Whether from sensation or reflection, we get ideas; simple ideas are combined into complex ones; complex ideas may themselves be recombined to form our everyday concepts of objects and of other people. In this way, Locke believed, we gradually build up knowledge of the outside world, including of course the other people who are in it. Locke's answer to skepticism was thus his belief in direct access to the contents of one's own mind together with his doctrine about the ways in which ideas are combined.

The influence of Locke and the empiricists on the selection of problems for study, particularly in the early years of psychology, is well known. It is the empiricist tradition that made sensation and perception central topics around which Wundt (1912/1973) and Helmholtz (Kahl, 1971) organized their work. The empiricist emphasis on association of ideas was taken up by Ebbinghaus (1885/1913) as the foundation for his studies of memory, and forms a portion of the conceptual background of contemporary cognitive psychology. The empiricist influence is evident today in the way that introductory psychology textbooks are most often organized – beginning with the "primary" topics of individual sensation, perception, and cognition, and concluding with the more "derivative" subjects of interpersonal attraction, language, and behavior in groups.

Empiricist influence is also apparent in the history of research in developmental psychology. Research on cognitive development in infancy and childhood can be seen as a way of responding to questions inherited from the empiricist tradition about the origins of an individual's knowledge about the world. Particularly in the study of social cognition, where research has focused heavily on the ontogenetic growth of perspective-taking skill (i.e., the ability to know what another person thinks, sees, or feels), the influence of the individualist's skepticism has been widely felt. By framing the skeptic's questions in ontogenetic terms and applying empirical methods to their solution, research on cognitive development can be seen as providing one kind of response to traditional skepticism.

Sociality and Social Contract

If the principal epistemological questions of individualist social ontologies are those of skepticism, the great social questions concern whether and how it is possible for free and independent individuals to adjust to, much less to flourish in, the context of civil society. The liberal individualist assumption that human beings are fundamentally self-sufficient entities leads on, in other words, to questions about the possibilities of communal or collective life. This group of questions I will refer to as the individualist problem of sociality. It is in answer to this individualist problem of sociality that the idea of a social contract emerged in the thought of, among others, John Locke.

Locke believed that human beings were, "by Nature, all free, equal, and independent" (1690/1965, p. 374). In what he called the state of nature, Locke thought of each individual person as an independent, essentially solitary creature. Faced, then, with the undeniable fact that human beings live in social communities of various kinds, Locke was forced to devise some kind of explanation for this phenomenon. As is well known, he went about this task by adapting the already-venerable notion of a *social contract,* the idea that the origins and legitimacy of civil society rest on the consent of its members.

It puzzled Locke, however, why a man in the state of nature, who already enjoys perfect freedom and independence, would ever consent to the constraints of collective life: "If a man in the state of nature be so free as has been said; if he be absolute lord of his own person and possessions; equal to the greatest and subject to no body, why will he part with his freedom?" (1690/1965, p. 395). Locke answered by pointing out that, subject as he is to the invasions of others, man in the state of nature is unsafe and insecure. He thus consents to unite in social life with others in order to provide for "the mutual preservation of their lives, liberties, and estates" – what Locke called "property" (1690/1965, p. 395). The promise of the social contract, as Locke envisioned it, is thus fulfilled to the extent that it guarantees each man the enjoyment of his own property.

For present purposes, Locke's answer to the individualist problem of sociality – that is his particular version of the social contract – is of much less importance than his framing of the problem itself. The problem of sociality – of how fundamentally separate individuals ever come to live together, much less to derive satisfaction from this arrangement – is one that has occupied psychologists in one form or another at least since Freud (e.g., 1930/1961). In the mainstream of research in developmental psychology, for instance, the process by which an infant becomes a full-fledged member of society is called "socialization." The traditional assumption is that we are born as individuals who have impulses, needs, and desires, at least some of which must be restrained or diverted before we will be able to live successfully in the social world. In a process thought to require considerable effort on the part of parents, children must, in this view, be "socialized" before they will be able to adjust to life in the social world.

In summary, the mainstream of academic psychology in the United States has grown in part from philosophical roots in liberal individualism, especially as this tradition was represented by the British empiricists. Since in this tradition, we are thought to have direct access to the contents of our own minds but not to those of others, a principal question is whether and how we come to know other people, and the contents of other minds. In developmental psychology, research on the development of social cognition, especially on the acquisition of perspective-taking skills, has reflected these concerns. Since in the liberal individualist tradition, each person is considered to be inherently free and independent, another crucial question concerns whether and how we as individuals can adjust to, much less find happiness within the confines of life in a social community. In developmental psychology, these concerns are strongly reflected in the tradition of research on socialization. It is against the background of these views that I want to present some of Wittgenstein's ideas and to suggest some of their possible implications for psychology.

Collectivist Emphases in Wittgenstein's Later Work

As against the individualist assumptions of traditional liberalism, Wittgenstein begins from very different assumptions, and hence comes to ask very different questions. When pushed to the furthest extremes of doubt, Descartes and Locke had believed that one's own existence as a thinking being is indubitable. For Wittgenstein, however, what is indubitable, what he called the "rock bottom" (*BB,* 24) is that we live together in particular ways which he called "forms of life." "What has to be accepted, the given, is - so one could say - *forms of life*" (*PI,* p. 226 e).

What is particularly important, Wittgenstein wrote, is not that we know ourselves or that we know the contents of our own minds, but rather that as human beings, we live in social groups, and that we take part in group activities and characteristic practices. For Wittgenstein, shared practices, actions, and interactions provide the basis upon which mental life rests. As instances of the sorts of activities that he thought of as forms of life, Wittgenstein offered very concrete examples.

> Instead of the unanalysable, specific, indefinable: the fact that we act in such-and-such ways, e.g., *punish* certain actions, *establish* the state of affairs thus and so, *give orders,* render accounts, describe colours, take an interest in others' feelings. What has to be accepted, the given - it might be said - are facts of living. (*RPP1,* 630)

Something to notice about the examples that Wittgenstein gives here is how ordinary are the activities he mentions. Giving orders, describing colors, and administering punishment are far from unusual acts. When we undertake them, we may often do so almost without thinking; they are part of our ordinary patterns of living. That it is exactly this everyday, conventional kind of activity that Wittgenstein meant to describe with the term "forms of life" is made clear elsewhere when he remarks, "here we strike rock bottom, that is we come down to conventions" (*BB,* 24). Forms of life are conventional patterns of activity, and as such, Wittgenstein believed them to be fundamental.

Prominent portions of the forms of life in which we as human beings participate are, of course, the languages that we speak. "The *speaking* of language is part of an activity, or of a form of life ..." (*PI,* 23). As Wittgenstein's examples show, the ways in which we live together are quite unimaginable outside of language. He emphasizes this idea by suggesting that:

> Commanding, questioning, recounting, chatting, are as much a part of our natural history as walking, eating, drinking, playing." (*PI,* 25)

The languages that we speak, whether simple or complex, are fundamentally to be regarded as shared activities, shared ways of doing things. As such, one can imagine simpler and more complex ways of doing the same kinds of things:

It is easy to imagine a language consisting only of orders and reports in battle. – Or a language consisting only of questions and expressions for answering yes and no. And innumerable others. – And to imagine a language means to imagine a form of life. (*PI*, 19)

Regardless of how simple or how complicated, however, all languages are based on actions:

The origin and the primitive form of the language game is a reaction; only from this can more complicated forms develop. Language – I want to say – is a refinement, 'in the beginning was the deed.' (*CV*, p. 31 e)

Forms of life such as the ways of speaking to one another that we establish among ourselves not only create the possibilities of our lives as human beings, but they also depend absolutely upon our agreement with one another in what Wittgenstein calls judgments:

If language is to be a means of communication there must be agreement not only in definitions but also (queer as this may sound) in judgments. (*PI*, 242)

The idea of agreement in judgments that Wittgenstein proposes is *not* intended to suggest debate, discussion, or persuasion. The idea, rather, is one, as Cavell has suggested, "of being in agreement throughout, being in harmony, like pitches or tones ... mutually *attuned* top to bottom" (Cavell, 1979, p. 32). We use language together as well as we do because we generally agree *without* discussion about what counts as an exemplar of a concept or of a rule, and because we generally agree *without* discussion in our judgments about whether or not a particular rule has been followed.

"How does it come about," Wittgenstein asks (*PI*, 454), for example, "that this arrow > > > - - - - - - > *points?*" It points, he replies, "only in the application that a living being makes of it." It is understood as pointing only because we all agree in seeing it that way, only because we all agree in our judgments about it. If one of us questioned the arrow's meaning, we would think this odd, but would simply explain, perhaps with an accompanying gesture, that the arrow *points* – that it directs us to look or move or search in *this* direction, not *that* one. To understand the arrow's meaning is to know what to *do* in response to it; knowing what to do is knowing the conventions of action that we all agree upon.

Similar arguments hold, Wittgenstein suggests, for our use of words. Nothing is deeper that the fact or the extent of our agreement on the use of our words. Under normal circumstances, we just do agree about what we call red or hot or summer or fast. When occasionally it happens that we do not agree (for example, in a borderline case), one person may challenge another's interpretation. To resolve this kind of dispute, we fall back on justifications. We explain, as best we can, why it seems to us as if the object in question should be described as we have described it.

In many cases, the sequence of challenge and justification leads to acceptance of a common view by both parties. It may happen, for example, that one person is acknowledged as the greater authority, or as more persuasive, or as in a better position to observe the object. The view offered by this speaker may then prevail, and be accepted by both. Conversation may then continue.

Occasionally, however, no resolution can be negotiated. The resulting situation is, Wittgenstein suggests, quite distressing. It is alarming to discover that we are no longer in our customary state of mutual attunement with one another, that we do not any longer agree in judgments, that in effect we do not any longer "speak the same language." Unless we are willing to forfeit the possibilities of community between us, our only recourse is to fall back on the "common behaviour of mankind" as a point of reference against which to interpret an unfamiliar language (*PI*, 206).

In the end, the only real justifications for my judgments are the conventions with reference to which they are made.

> How do I know that this colour is red? – It would be an answer to say: 'I have learnt English.' (*PI*, 381)

"I do it this way because I speak English" means roughly, in other words, "this is how we do it." As Wittgenstein says:

> If I have exhausted the justifications I have reached bedrock, and my spade is turned. Then I am inclined to say: 'This is simply what I do.' (*PI*, 217)

In the end, what must be accepted is that we live within and indeed draw the very possibility of our lives from our mutual attunement. Our tendency to make judgments in the same ways is what makes it possible for us to talk to one another at all.

One consequence of these views is that what we call "knowledge" (i.e., propositions that can be thought of as true) is derivative of our acceptance of the forms of life within which one can say anything at all. Outside of language there is neither truth nor falsity, because the idea of knowledge is made possible only by our acceptance of the conventions that govern our language. It is our life within the conventional frameworks provided by common languages that we speak and common activities in which we take part that provides the possibility of propositional truth or falsity.

This position is sometimes taken to be a form of relativism (i.e., that whatever is agreed upon is true), but Wittgenstein's meaning is not the relativist one:

> So you are saying that human agreement decides what is true and what is false? – It is what human beings *say* that is true and false; and they agree in the *language* they use. That is not agreement in opinions but in form of life. (*PI*, 241)

To speak our language, and hence to live this life, we have no choice but to acknowledge other people as such – i.e., as others who speak our language, who agree with our judgments, with the forms of life that underlie our languages. This is not a matter of truth or falsity, not – in other words – a matter of knowledge. It is rather an *attitude* without which we cannot live in the ordinary human ways. Wittgenstein expresses this idea as follows:

> My attitude toward him is an attitude towards a soul. I am not of the *opinion* that he has a soul. (*PI*, p. 178 e)

It is simply crucial to the framework within which we experience the world that other people have feelings, thoughts, and intentions. That the world is this way is not a proposition that we can freely accept or reject. It is not a fact that we can know or doubt, but an *attitude* that we express in our actions.

I did not get my picture of the world by satisfying myself of its correctness; nor do I believe it because I am satisfied of its correctness. No, it is the inherited background against which I distinguish between true and false. (*OC*, 94)

For Wittgenstein, our lives as human beings require that we acknowledge the humanity of others around us. The structure of our ways of living requires that we accept other people as speakers of the language, as human beings who have thoughts, expectations, hopes, and the like. If, like the Cartesian skeptic, one begins to doubt the existence of other minds, one may become the target of Wittgenstein's sarcasm:

If I do not believe in an inner state of seeing and the other says: 'I see ...', then I believe that he does not know English, or is lying. (*RPP1*, 79)

The thoroughgoing skeptic, in other words, cannot function in a human world, and hence must forego the possibilities of human community. Only a madman, somebody who was literally insane, could doubt what forms the very fabric of our daily lives.

I, L. W., believe, am sure, that my friend hasn't sawdust in his body or in his head, even though I have no direct evidence of my senses to the contrary.... To have doubts about it would seem to me madness .... (*OC*, 281)

In short, "You can be as *certain* of someone else's sensations as of *any* fact" (*RPP2*, 566).

The facts of our living are, Wittgenstein insists, *social* facts. We live within, we take our lives from, certain common activities, prominent among which is the speaking of language. Because it is only by drawing on our fundamental attunement that we are able to talk with one another at all, the speaking of language presupposes or requires that we view one another as fellow speakers. It is only because we do this as a matter of course that differences of opinion or disputes about truth can arise. It is thus only within the framework of belief that doubts can be entertained. As Wittgenstein said, "knowledge is in the end based on acknowledgement" (*OC*, 378).

The whole edifice of knowledge and of knowing is thus, in the Wittgensteinian view, based on our willingness to acknowledge one another as fellow creatures and sentient human beings, as speakers of the language. Rational inquiry, logical debate, scientific methods, and the like are all quite literally unthinkable without our willingness to acknowledge community with other "speakers of the tongue." Acknowledgement itself, and the uses of language which it makes possible, are neither reasonable nor unreasonable; they are *before* reason; their existence creates the *possibility* of reason.

You must bear in mind that the language-game is so to say something unpredictable. I mean: it is not based on grounds. It is not reasonable (or unreasonable).
It is there – like our life. (*OC*, 559)

For Wittgenstein, then, the entire project of knowing, of scientific knowledge, is a secondary sort of activity that is parasitic on the primary reality of our mutual attunement. Our primary relation to the world, in other words, is not one of knowing at all, but one of acceptance. "My *life,*" Wittgenstein said, "consists in my being content to accept many things" (*OC,* 344).

To the extent that doubt occurs, then, it can occur only *within* the context of the languages that we already speak. The "absence of doubt belongs to the essence of the language-game" (*OC,* 370). Doubt with respect to the languages that we speak does not make sense; the languages themselves can be neither "right" nor "wrong," neither "true" nor "false." They are simply *there.* When we learn to speak them, and to live within them, we simply accept the reality of their existence.

Since the individualist skeptic imagines one's primary link to the world to be that of knowledge, the skeptic's doubts about knowledge of other minds are in effect doubts about the possibility of living in a world of other people (cf. Benfey, 1984; Cavell, 1979); as such, they carry great urgency. Since Wittgenstein suggests, to the contrary, that we do not so much know as acknowledge our links with the world anyway, skeptical doubts come to seem much less urgent. If our connections to the world are of a different sort, and already secure, then why should we worry so much about knowledge?[2]

To the classic social and epistemological questions of the liberal tradition, then, Wittgenstein offers not so much answers as deflections. The traditional individualist questions about whether and how we can come to know other minds and about whether and how free, independent individuals can come to find satisfaction in a social life are, Wittgenstein teaches, misconceived. We just *do* live together in certain ways; we do not so much need to explain as to accept this fact, and to expand in whatever ways we can upon its possibilities. Whether we can know one another or not is less important than the skeptic believes because our primary relationship with the world and with one another cannot be one of knowing anyway; it must be one of acknowledgement.

What, then, are the central questions that Wittgenstein would pose? To the extent that Wittgenstein's assessment of his achievement with regard to the individualist tradition ("What we are destroying is nothing but houses of cards ..." *PI,* 118) is widely shared, it is of interest to determine what he can offer in return.

[2] This question can be read, if one desires, as a query about the extent to which knowledge or its pursuit can serve us at all – i. e., as a query about the value of scientific psychology not just as commonly conceived, but no matter how conceived. If we cease to believe in knowledge of one another as valuable in itself, in other words, we may well come to question whether it is of any value at all. A Wittgensteinian answer to this question, I think, is that if we could all live together in ways that we could wholeheartedly endorse, then there *would* be no need for the kinds of knowledge that psychologists seek. Until that time, however, – which is to say as long as we live human lives – knowledge can be useful by allowing us to see the ways in which our world is most in need of transformation, by moving us to imagine and to sustain collaborative efforts to create ways of living that we could honestly call humane. The cost of ignorance, then, is not insecurity about the existence of a world, but refusal to transform ourselves – not solipsism, but stagnation.

What kinds of psychological questions emerge from Wittgenstein's philosophical work?

Let us begin by considering a passage that occurs very early in the *Philosophical investigations:*

> ... ask yourself whether our language is complete; – whether it was so before the symbolism of chemistry and the notation of the infinitesimal calculus were incorporated into it; for these are, so to speak, suburbs of our language. (And how many houses or streets does it take before a town begins to be a town?) Our language can be seen as an ancient city: a maze of little streets and squares, of old and new houses, and of houses with additions from various periods; and this surrounded by a multitude of new boroughs with straight regular streets and uniform houses. (*PI,* 18)

One idea that the comparison of languages with cities suggests is the extent to which we must take language as given. We are born into one or another language, and into its traditions, much as we might be born into a city and its neighborhoods. We have no choice as to the district of our birth and little with regard to that of our upbringing. As the remark brings up our memories of different cities in which we have lived or that we have visited, it also reminds us of the many-faceted ways in which languages, like cities, may differ. It suggests that languages, like cities, are environments in which we live, locales that we inhabit.

What I wish to draw attention to here is the extent to which Wittgenstein's comparison of our languages with our cities can be seen as inviting the question: How shall we inhabit them? Just as we might ask questions of our relations to a city, so we might also ask them of our relations to language. In what district was I born? In what neighborhoods did I play as a child, go to school, grow up? In what areas do I feel at home, and in what parts do I feel a stranger? In what sections can I live, and which of these do I choose? By what means will I live, with whom, and in what ways participate in the common life? Do I wish to live in an old, established area, or in a newer, growing one? Shall I build, renovate, maintain, destroy, abandon? If we think of languages as places that we inhabit, we may begin to ask of ourselves: Who am I, and what am I doing here?

That Wittgenstein viewed philosophy as a process of locating or placing oneself in language, and hence in the world, seems clear.

> Working in philosophy – like work in architecture in many respects – is really more a working on oneself. On one's own interpretation. On one's way of seeing things. (And what one expects of them.) (*CV,* p. 16e)

Working in philosophy, then, is not a matter of doing anything to language, or to the world, at all. On the contrary, "philosophy simply puts everything before us" (*PI,* 126). Doing philosophy well is a matter of placing oneself properly.

This kind of problem occurs not just to the philosopher, however, but to others as well.

> Counterpoint might present an extraordinarily difficult problem for a composer; the problem namely: what attitude should *I,* given *my* propensities, adopt to counterpoint? He may have hit upon a conventionally acceptable attitude and yet still feel that it is not properly *his.* That it is not clear what counterpoint *ought* to mean to him. (I was thinking of Schubert in this connection; of his wanting to take lessons in counterpoint right at the end of his life. I think his aim

may have been not so much just learning more counterpoint as determining where he stood in relation to it.) (*CV*, p. 40e)

Here Wittgenstein seems to suggest that the composer's problem is very like that of the philosopher. By asking himself, "Where do I stand with respect to counterpoint?", the composer asks not only about the musical conventions of his time, but also about his own proper attitude toward them, his own interpretation. It is as though Wittgenstein imagines Schubert asking how he should place himself, how he should inhabit, the musical "cities" in which he found his life as a musician.

What can be said of the composer in this sense can also, of course, be said of any one of us. Whereas the traditional epistemological problems involve overcoming doubts about the world and the other people in it, the problem posed by Wittgenstein is for me to find out where I stand with regard to a world that I cannot doubt. For Wittgenstein, the problem is for me to discover what I am properly to do, "with whom I am in community, and to whom and to what I am in fact obedient" (Cavell, 1979, p. 25). Although the existence of the world and of the people in it are indubitable, my proper stance in that world and toward those people is not. The central human questions that Wittgenstein's philosophy proposes are thus questions about the nature and origins of the self.

The Problem of Individuality

Considered as a straightforward hypothesis, the idea that the self is a promising topic for psychological study is anything but new. An enormous research literature about the nature and origins of the self is already in existence (e.g., Gergen, 1984; Harter, 1983; Suls, 1982; Suls & Greenwald, 1983; Wylie, 1974, 1979). The principal emphasis of this research, however, has been on self-esteem – on the extent to which value (i.e., esteem) is attached to a known quantity (i.e., the self). On the assumption that there is a self to be known, and on the assumption that the self *is* known, psychologists have most often asked simply how the self is evaluated (Wylie, 1974, 1979).

To interpret Wittgenstein's teaching as directing our attention to questions of this sort would be, however, to overlook its significance. One may recall in this connection that Wittgenstein described his contribution as "belonging to the soil rather than to the seed" (*CV*, p. 36e). What Wittgenstein offers is not so much another hypothesis about how the self is known or valued, but another way of conceiving the social realities into which any such hypothesis would need to fit. Without producing psychological theories as such, Wittgenstein was rather involved in clearing the ground into which different hypotheses might, like seeds, be sown, and out of which more fruitful theories might grow.

Wittgenstein suggests that we should let ourselves be struck by the fact that is most taken for granted by the individualist: that we view ourselves not only as persons, but also as selves (cf. Harré, 1984). The "individuality of a human being as it is publicly identified and collectively defined" can be distinguished, as Harré (1984, p. 76) has pointed out, from "the individuality of the unitary subject of experience." In these terms (Harré, 1984), the person is the social, the objective, and the self is the psychological, the subjective aspect of individuality. In these terms, Wittgenstein invites us to inquire how it is that we view ourselves as unique selves at all.

Whereas liberal individualism had simply assumed the existence of autonomous selves, Wittgenstein suggests the need for a theory of individuality. Such a theory would attempt to explain how, in the sociality of our shared existence, we come to form ideas of ourselves as individual, autonomous, unique agents – as unified selves. The central question for psychological theory, then, would be how, against all evidence to the contrary, people come to believe in the idea of the self at all, and how it is that people come to see themselves in such terms.

This view is not, of course, unique to Wittgenstein. Just as skepticism is generic to individualist approaches, the problem of individuality is generic to those that emphasize collectivist themes. Thus, for Marxist psychologies such as the one proposed by Vygotsky (1962, 1978) as well as for ethologically oriented theories of development (Ainsworth, 1983; Bowlby, 1969, 1973), questions about the nature and origins of the self are also central. Recent work emerging from both of these traditions would seem to confirm this belief (Cassidy, 1985; Lee, Wertsch & Stone, 1983; Main, Kaplan & Cassidy, 1985; Smith, 1985). For those emphasizing collectivist themes, the existence and influence of the modern idea of self is a puzzle in need of solution.

Wittgenstein's first point about the emergence of individuality, then, is that it cannot be taken for granted. Far from being the necessary condition from which the individualist philosophers began, the experience of self as a unified, unique identity is regarded by Wittgenstein as an achievement. The construction of personality is a task that we need to undertake in part because the acknowledgement of differences and the cultivation of special skills is what makes novel contributions to the collective life possible. Because it is individuality that creates the possibilities for particularly effective participation in the group life, we need to ask how and under what conditions the creation and acknowledgement of individuality can take place.

Certainly it is clear that Wittgenstein viewed the process of coming to acknowledge individuality as difficult and uncertain. For example, he wrote:

> In former times people went into monasteries. Were they stupid or insensitive people? – Well, if people like that found they needed to take such measures to be able to go on living, the problem cannot have been an easy one! (*CV*, p. 49 e)

In the context of the sociality and interdependence of our lives, how do we come to see ourselves as unique individuals, as *selves?* The extent to which this occurs at all is by no means certain, but to the extent that it does, it is, Wittgenstein suggests, an extremely difficult process. Why should it be so difficult to think of oneself as a unique self, to acknowledge the dimensions of one's individuality?

Consider in this regard a remark that Wittgenstein once made to a friend:

> No, I don't think I would get on with Hegel. Hegel seems to me to be always wanting to say that things which look different are really the same. Whereas my interest is in showing that things which look the same are really different. I was thinking of using as a motto for my book a quotation from *King Lear:* 'I'll teach you differences.' (Wittgenstein in Rhees, 1984, p. 157)

To be able to see oneself as a unique personality, one must be willing to acknowledge differences between oneself and the others with whom one believes oneself to be in community, and this is – in Wittgenstein's view – a difficult and treacherous task. The book referred to in this remark is the masterwork of Wittgenstein's later years, the *Philosophical investigations,* and Wittgenstein's suggestion of "I'll teach you differences" as the motto for this book reveals the centrality of this thought to his teaching.

How are we to understand the difficulties involved in acknowledging difference? As social creatures embedded in conventional forms of life, Wittgenstein suggests that we expect and depend upon our attunement – which is to say our similarities – with the others around us. Because agreement in judgments is so crucial to the human community in which we find our life, any threat to it ought to be taken with utmost seriousness. If agreement between us is threatened, then so is the reality of our community, and hence so is the possibility of our lives as we had envisioned them. The risk inherent in acknowledgement of difference is thus the possibility that community between us will be lost, that our conversations with one another will be ended, that we will be condemned in this way to solitude and to silence. To say that we can be terrified by the prospect of running such risks is to say that we fear the loss of our lives, however we may conceive them.

Of course, there are differences and there are differences, just as there are lives and there are lives. If I prefer Beethoven and another person prefers Brahms, this difference is unlikely to threaten many possibilities of community between us. If my life is passionately committed to music, and another person is deaf, or cannot understand why I should care so much about mere sounds, however, then this may be quite a different matter. If they are to arouse our genuine fears, we must believe that real or imagined differences run deep, that they are central to our lives. There may be some forms of agreement in judgments without which we feel that we could not imagine our lives at all. What is central to one person's imagination of life may be peripheral to that of another, but in every person's life, some kinds of community matter more than others; and for this reason, in every person's life there is room to fear the possibility of difference, division, and loss.

If acknowledging difference is so difficult, and involves such risks, then why should we undertake it at all? For Wittgenstein, it is only through our willingness to acknowledge (i.e., our refusal to avoid) differences that our conceptions of individuality can possibly arise. And it is only through our willingness to see ourselves as embodying difference that the possibilities for creative participation in the collective life appear. When Wittgenstein suggested "I'll teach you differences" as a motto, he was offering to describe the origins of personality, of individuality; and in this manner, to explain a way of broadening the possibilities of collective life.

But how can Wittgenstein possibly make good his intention to teach us differences? If we grant both the importance and the difficulty of the endeavor, we still may want to ask what there is here that could be taught or learned, and by what means? If we undertake to answer such questions, then we commit ourselves to the process that Wittgenstein called "philosophizing."

The philosopher's search is not for knowledge, or for wisdom; what the philosopher seeks is not knowledge, but something of a different sort. "Thoughts that are at peace. That's what someone who philosophizes yearns for" (*CV,* p. 43 e). The philosopher seeks an end to philosophy, a way of being finished with philosophizing that would allow better ways of finding the possibilities of life:

> I am by no means sure that I would prefer a continuation of my work by others to a change in the way people live which would make all these questions superfluous. (*CV,* p. 61 e)

We will begin to see the end of our philosophizing when we can allow ourselves to acknowledge the broader possibilities for our living. To say that it is by no means clear by what method or methods we could achieve such an end is only to acknowledge the need for philosophy in our lives as we imagine them.

Recognizing the difficulty in but also the deep necessity for acknowledgement of differences between us, and perhaps being willing also to call the necessity as well as the difficulty philosophical, we may feel puzzled to think of ourselves as stepping off a rooftop into thin air when we ask of Wittgenstein that he explain what makes acknowledgement of difference possible. We will better understand our thoughts of thin air, however, when we receive Wittgenstein's reply, because his suggestion is that the willingness to acknowledge significant differences between us results from the exercise of a particular sort of courage; and this courage he calls *faith.* Denying neither risks nor dangers, and even in the face of our very real fears, we sometimes find it in our power to acknowledge the most difficult things in ourselves and in others; when this happens, Wittgenstein suggests, the name of our power is faith.

If acceptance of difference rests on faith, then we may well inquire what sort of faith this might be. One answer that Wittgenstein offers rests on what Cavell (1979) has called the depth of our attunement with one another. When we worry about real or suspected differences between us, and about the loss of community that their recognition might engender, we sometimes forget, Wittgenstein suggests, to take notice of the depth, extent, and unchallenged solidity of the community that would remain.

The human experience of difference is often the experience of alienation or loss of community, of feeling oneself foreign to another or to oneself, as though one is in a foreign land and cannot understand the language. What is one to do in such circumstances? "The common behavior of mankind," Wittgenstein replies, "is the system of reference by means of which we interpret an unknown language" (*PI,* 206).

The common behavior of mankind underlies such a broad range of our activities that we are able to learn new languages, find new communities, live in new ways, and all the while remain entirely - or even especially - human. No matter how we conceive ourselves or our lives, the fact that we do conceive them renders us human. No matter what we do, as long as we live, we will not fall out of this human community, this world. In this we can have faith, Wittgenstein tells us, and from this we can take courage.

Even acknowledging this underlying faith, however, many more specific obstacles to acceptance of difference can emerge. We can, for example, feel afraid to acknowledge to one another our shortcomings or our fears:

A man can bare himself before others only out of a particular kind of love.... We could also say: Hate between men comes from cutting ourselves off from each other. Because we don't want anyone else to look inside us, since it's not a pretty sight in there. (*CV,* p.46e)

If we bare ourselves before another, and in so doing, reveal our inevitable or even perhaps surprising flaws, we run the risk that the other will recoil from repulsion at our failings, withdraw from disgust at our shortcomings, disappear from our lives from distrust of our dispositions; in short, we risk rejection. To risk the loss of important connections with another, we must believe that even if this particular attempt at the realization of community should fail, there will be other opportunities, other days and moods, other people with whom we *will* connect. To acknowledge our differences fully, we must love one another; we must have faith in ourselves and in one another.

There can be little doubt but that Wittgenstein identified such faith with passion on the one hand, and with religious experience on the other. For example, he wrote, "Someone who ... penitently opens his heart to God in confession lays it open to other men too" (*CV,* p.46e). Contrasting faith with the wisdom that springs from knowledge, Wittgenstein also wrote, "Wisdom is cold and to that extent stupid. (Faith on the other hand is a passion)" (*CV,* p.56e). "'Wisdom is grey.' Life on the other hand and religion are full of colour" (*CV,* p.62e). Faith, passion, religion, and the possibilities of life in community fall on one side here; science, mistrust, skepticism, and separation fall on the other. In this framework, we can ask: Where do we fall, what is the nature of our falling, and what say do we have in the matter?

Over and over again, Wittgenstein asks how we can be "saved" - saved, that is, from silence and from separation, from loneliness and from loss. In what seems to me one of the most moving passages in all of his writings, Wittgenstein engages this question:

We are in a sort of hell where we can do nothing but dream, roofed in, as it were, and cut off from heaven. But if I am to be REALLY saved, - what I need is *certainty* - not wisdom, dreams or speculation - and this certainty is faith. And faith is faith in what is needed by my *heart,* my *soul,* not my speculative intelligence. For it is my soul with its passions, as it were with its flesh and blood, that has to be saved, not my abstract mind. (*CV,* p.33e)

It is difficult to read this passage without reflecting on some aspects of what is known or surmised about Wittgenstein's own life. As one who was fascinated by Christianity and its promise of redemption, Wittgenstein nevertheless seems to have considered himself a Jew. As one who appears to have been tormented by his physical passions (see, for example, Bartley, 1985), he nevertheless seems rarely if ever to have tolerated discussion of physical love, even with otherwise close friends; and indeed appears throughout most of his years to have sought an ascetic and largely celibate life (Bartley, 1985; Rhees, 1984). Of course, another meaning of passion available in the Christian tradition is that of suffering – as in the passion of Christ – and in this sense Wittgenstein's experience of passion appears by all accounts to have been very great.

"A confession," Wittgenstein wrote, "has to be part of your new life" (*CV*, p. 18 e). Coming back to the same thought 15 years later, he wrote:

> I believe that one of the things Christianity says is that sound doctrines are all useless. That you have to change your *life*. (Or the *direction* of your life.) (*CV*, p. 53 e)

Perhaps it is not too much to suggest that it was Wittgenstein's refusal to make full confession – the failures of his faith – that made it so difficult for him to change his life by creating broader grounds for community in the flesh, that kept him at the disembodied business of philosophy so long. If that is so, then it may also be that the products of his passion can turn others toward one another, toward redemption. And if *that* is so, what more worthy contribution to the collective life could the creation that was one man's individuality have made?

As psychologists, then, the central questions bequeathed to us by Wittgenstein concern the creation of individuality, and hence of the possibilities of communities that are at once both transformed and transforming. "That man will be revolutionary," Wittgenstein wrote, "who can revolutionize himself" (*CV*, p. 45 e). That this should require faith or involve passion is far less surprising than the extent of our ignorance about the conditions under which it is possible for us to be passionate, or to believe. When we have finally counted the costs of refusing to know, perhaps then we will be ready to acknowledge the dimensions of the task before us.

Summary

I have suggested that one source of Wittgenstein's dissatisfaction with academic psychology is the individualist tradition out of which it has grown. Liberal individualism suggests a variety of psychological questions that are viewed by Wittgenstein as misconceived; the application of empirical methods to solution of these problems cannot but result for Wittgenstein in a situation in which "problem and methods pass one another by." Wittgenstein did not, in my view, propose new psychological theories as such, nor did he attempt to do so. The problems that were of interest to him, Wittgenstein said, "are solved, not by giving new information, but by arranging what we have always known" (*PI*, 109). After rearranging what we have always known, however, new questions – like the one I have called the "problem of individuality" – may come into view. Wittgenstein's principal legacy to psychologists is thus not a way of answering long-standing questions; rather, it is a set of methods for breaking the hold that these questions, though misconceived, have had on us; and it is a glimpse of new questions that, if acknowledged, might also be pursued.

References

Ainsworth, M.D.S. (1983). Attachment. In J.McV. Hunt & N. Endler (Eds.), *Personality and the behavior disorders* (2nd ed.). New York: Wiley.

Anscombe, G.E.M. (1957). *Intention*. Oxford: Blackwell.

Bartley, W.W., III. (1985). *Wittgenstein* (2nd ed.). LaSalle, IL: Open Court.

Bellah, R.N., Madsen, R., Sullivan, W.M., Swidler, A., & Tipton, S.M. (1985). *Habits of the heart: Individualism and commitment in American life*. Berkeley, CA: University of California Press.

Benfey, C.E.G. (1984). *Emily Dickinson and the problem of others*. Amherst, MA: University of Massachusetts Press.

Boring, E.G. (1950). *A history of experimental psychology* (2nd ed.). New York: Appleton-Century-Crofts, Inc.

Bowlby, J. (1969). *Attachment and loss, Vol. 1: Attachment*. New York: Basic Books.

Bowlby, J. (1973). *Attachment and loss, Vol. 2: Separation, anxiety, and anger*. New York: Basic Books.

Bruner, J.S. (1974/75). From communication to language: A psychological perspective. *Cognition, 3,* 255–287.

Bruner, J.S. (1976). Psychology and the image of man. Herbert Spencer Lecture delivered at Oxford University, 1976. Reprinted in the *Times Literary Supplement,* Dec. 17, 1976.

Cassidy, J. (1985). *The relationship between self-esteem and quality of attachment*. Unpublished dissertation, University of Virginia.

Cavell, S. (1979). *The claim of reason: Wittgenstein, skepticism, morality, and tragedy*. New York: Oxford University Press.

Chapman, M. (Ed.) (1984). Intentional action as a paradigm for developmental psychology: A symposium. *Human Development, 27,* 113–144.

Ebbinghaus, H. (1913). *Memory*. New York: Teacher's College, Columbia University Press. (originally published, 1885).

Freud, S. (1961). *Civilization and its discontents*. New York: Norton. (originally published, 1930).

Gergen, K.J. (1982). *Toward transformation in social knowledge*. New York: Springer-Verlag.

Gergen, K.J. (1984). Theory of the self: Impasse and evolution. In L. Berkowitz (Ed.), *Advances in experimental social psychology* (Vol. 17). New York: Academic Press.

Gergen, K.J. (1985). The social constructionist movement in modern psychology. *American Psychologist, 40,* 266–275.

Hamlyn, D.W. (1978). *Experience and the growth of understanding*. London: Routledge & Kegan Paul.

Harré, R. (1979). *Social being*. Oxford: Blackwell.

Harré, R. (1984). *Personal being*. Cambridge, MA: Harvard University Press.

Harré, R., & Secord, P.F. (1972). *The explanation of social behaviour*. Oxford: Blackwell.

Harter, S. (1983). Developmental perspectives on the self system. In P. Mussen (Ed.), *Carmichael's manual of child psychology* (Vol. 4). New York: Wiley.

Kahl, R. (Ed.) (1971). *Selected writings of Hermann von Helmholtz*. Middletown, CT: Wesleyan University Press.

Kenny, A. (1973). *Wittgenstein.* Cambridge, MA: Harvard University Press.
Lee, B., Wertsch, J.V., & Stone, A. (1983). Towards a Vygotskian theory of the self. In B. Lee & G.G. Noam (Eds.), *Developmental approaches to the self.* New York: Plenum.
Locke, J. (1965). *Two treatises of government.* New York: Mentor. (originally published, 1690).
Locke, J. (1966). *An essay concerning human understanding.* New York: Mentor. (originally published, 1690).
Main, M., Kaplan, N., & Cassidy, J. (1985). Security in infancy, childhood, and adulthood: A move to the level of representation. In I. Bretherton & E. Waters (Eds.), *Growing points in attachment theory and research, Monographs of the society for research in child development, 50,* (1-2), serial no. 209.
Markman, E. (1973). The facilitation of part-whole comparisons by use of the collective noun "family." *Child Development, 44,* 837-840.
Mead, G.H. (1934). *Mind, self, and society from the standpoint of a social behaviorist.* Chicago, IL: University of Chicago Press.
Patterson, C.J. (1982). Self-control and self-regulation in childhood. In T. Field, A. Huston, et al. (Eds.), *Review of human development.* New York: Wiley.
Patterson, C.J. (1984). Development of prosocial and aggressive behavior. In M.H. Bornstein & M.E. Lamb (Eds.), *Developmental psychology: An advanced textbook.* Hillsdale, NJ: Erlbaum.
Piaget, J. (1965). *The moral judgment of the child.* New York: The Free Press.
Pitcher, G. (Ed.) (1968). *Wittgenstein.* Notre Dame, IN: University of Notre Dame Press.
Rhees, R. (1984). *Recollections of Wittgenstein.* Oxford: Oxford University Press.
Rorty, R. (1979). *Philosophy and the mirror of nature.* Princeton, NJ: Princeton University Press.
Rosch, E. (1978). Principles of categorization. In E. Rosch & B. B. Lloyd (Eds.), *Cognition and categorization.* Hillsdale, NJ: Erlbaum.
Sampson, E.E. (1983). *Justice and the critique of pure psychology.* New York: Plenum.
Scarr, S. (1985). Constructing psychology: Making facts and fables for our time. *American Psychologist, 40,* 499-512.
Smith, R.J. (1985). Propositions for a Marxist theory of personality. *Human Development, 28,* 10-24.
Sullivan, H.S. (1953). *The interpersonal theory of psychiatry.* New York: Norton.
Suls, J. (Ed.) (1982). *Psychological perspectives on the self* (Vol. 1). Hillsdale, NJ: Erlbaum.
Suls, J., & Greenwald, A.G. (1983). *Psychological perspectives on the self* (Vol. 2). Hillsdale, NJ: Erlbaum.
Taylor, C. (1971). Interpretation and the sciences of man. *Review of Metaphysics, 12,* 3-52.
Toulmin, S. (1972). *Human understanding* (Vol. 1). Princeton, NJ: Princeton University Press.
Vesey, G. (Ed.) (1974). *Understanding Wittgenstein.* Ithaca, NY: Cornell University Press.
von Wright, G.H. (1971). *Explanation and understanding.* Ithaca, NY: Cornell University Press.
Vygotsky, L.S. (1962). *Thought and language.* Cambridge, MA: The M.I.T. Press.
Vygotsky, L.S. (1978). *Mind in society: The development of higher psychological processes.* Cambridge, MA: Harvard University Press.
Winch, P. (1958). *The idea of a social science.* London: Routledge & Kegan Paul.
Wundt, W. (1973). *An introduction to psychology* (2nd ed.). New York: Arno Press. (originally published, 1912).
Wylie, R.C. (1974). *The self-concept* (Vol. 1). Lincoln, NE: University of Nebraska Press.
Wylie, R.C. (1979). *The self-concept* (Vol. 2). Lincoln, NE: University of Nebraska Press.

Chapter 11 Socializing the Theory of Intellectual Development[1]

Daniel Bullock

Man ... manifestly owes this immense superiority to his intellectual faculties, to his social habits, which lead him to aid and defend his fellows, and to his corporeal structure.... Through his powers of intellect, articulate language has been evolved; and on this his wonderful advancement has mainly depended. (Darwin, *The Descent of Man and Selection in Relation to Sex,* 1871/1981, pp. 46-47)

Does a child learn only to talk, or also to think? Does it learn the sense of multiplication *before* – or *after* it learns multiplication? (Wittgenstein, *Z,* 324)

Darwin's remarks on the descent of man mark off a domain of inquiry that has remained a troubled focus of developmental studies. Though human history appears somehow discontinous from prior natural history, our sense of theoretical order creates a need to comprehend it as another chapter of natural history. The difficulty has been to find a way to so comprehend it that does not reduce the themes of our chapter of natural history to those used in prior chapters. There is to be something genuinely new in our chapter, just as there was something genuinely new in each prior chapter of the natural history.

But what is that new thing? Darwin points to articulate language, and suggests that a conspiracy of intellectual powers, social habits, and bodily form enabled the evolution of language. However, Darwin appears to treat language as a fixed phenotype. He says that it *has been evolved,* as if its development were complete. Though Darwin probably didn't think of language this way, many others observers have, and do. One who did not, and for very Darwinian reasons, was Ludwig Wittgenstein.

Wittgenstein was one of the most tenacious and clear-headed thinkers of the twentieth century, and his later work contains many ideas of great potential importance to developmental psychology. However, because of his academic classification as a philosopher, and because of the difficulties associated with reading his work, few psychologists have more than a passing familiarity with Wittgenstein's intellectual legacy. Among those who do have a passing familiarity, moreover, misunderstandings abound. Some developmentalists have cited Wittgenstein as if he would answer the questions posed in his *Zettel* (quoted

[1] I would like to thank Rick Canfield, Michael Chapman, Jeff Coulter, and Ennio Mingolla for helpful comments on an earlier draft of this chapter. Part of the chapter's preparation was supported by NSF grant IST-8417756 to Stephen Grossberg and the Center for Adaptive Systems at Boston University. This chapter presents my portrait of the cognitive developmental landscape as a reworking and detailing of sketches found in the late folios of Wittgenstein. The chapter is dedicated to four social-cognitive theorists to whom I am equally indebted: J. M. Baldwin, L. S. Vygotsky, Donald Campbell, and Albert Bandura.

above) as follows: that a child learns "only to talk" and that the sense of multiplication is learned before multiplication. In fact, the Platonist (and contra-Darwinian) bases for such answers were intricately analyzed and firmly rejected by Wittgenstein. Other commentators have read passages like the following and concluded that Wittgenstein was a behaviorist:

> One of the most dangerous of ideas for a philosopher is, oddly enough, that we think with our heads or in our heads. The idea of thinking as a process in the head, in a completely enclosed space, gives him something occult. (*Z*, 605–606)

Here readers are likely to overlook the subtleties of the statement (signaled by the "oddly enough" and by the "in a *completely* enclosed space"), and those who are anti-behaviorist may abandon their study of Wittgenstein prematurely. In fact, a deeper grasp of Wittgenstein's work eliminates any tendency to give this and similar remarks a behaviorist reading. What Wittgenstein abhorred were occult, i.e., non-naturalistic, descriptions of mental phenomena. Though this abhorrence is shared by behaviorists, it is also shared by cognitive scientists. Thus it cannot be taken as an indicator of behaviorist sympathies.

Although several developmental researchers (e.g., Rosch, 1978; Bruner, 1975, 1983) have achieved a deeper grasp, and have explored the research implications of isolated Wittgensteinian themes, many of the critical elements of his naturalistic view of human mental life remain to be assimilated by developmentalists. In this chapter, I hope to further the assimilation of Wittgensteinian thinking by showing how a group of his recurring themes can help clarify issues in the domain of intellectual development. Because he avoided overt systematization in his later work, it would be a partial distortion (and an exegetical headache) to try to reconstruct Wittgenstein's "theory of development." Instead, I will try to celebrate Wittgenstein's continuing relevance for developmental psychology by sketching, with the aid of the kinds of intellectual tools Wittgenstein worked so hard to refine, a new picture of intellectual development. This strategy will be in line with the recent work of Bloor (1983), and with the pedagogical hope expressed by Wittgenstein in the preface to his *Philosophical investigations:* "I should not like my writing to spare other people the trouble of thinking. But, if possible, to stimulate someone to thoughts of his own." The constructive tack taken here should also help put to rest the mistaken but widely shared impression that Wittgenstein's relevance for psychology is primarily critical.

To what kinds of questions can Wittgenstein's legacy help us construct better answers? Many of the questions that drove Wittgenstein's work are still critical in cognitive science and developmental studies. Such questions as: What are the outlines of a non-question-begging explanation of human intelligence? What are the recurring weaknesses in past and current attempts to provide such explanations? Why is it that, having given an account of humans internal representational capacity, we would still lack an understanding of what separates human intelligence and intellectual development from that observed in our nearest animal cousins, or in the electronic progeny we have produced to date? And finally, how can intelligence be treated as an evolving product of natural history? This chapter is a sustained argument to the effect that Wittgenstein's emphasis on social-interactive "forms of life" can be taken as the starting point for a new type of answer to such questions. The answer I propose is meant to exemplify a new kind of systematic research on the diversity of roles played by modes of interaction, both social and asocial, symbolic and nonsymbolic, in cognitive development.

A final word of introduction concerns the social aspect of Wittgenstein's thinking. The idea of human sociality as an important factor in mental development emerged as a focal (if often implicit) theme only in Wittgenstein's later work, which was undertaken after he had spent several years as a teacher. It seems likely that reflection on his experiences with child nurturance was part of what led Wittgenstein to the interlocking set of formulations that mark his mature work. His famous naturalistic turn, for example, was not just a turn away from his logicist beginnings. It was also a turn towards an appreciation of cognitive nurturance achieved through apprenticeships in cultural practices - especially practices that depend on symbol deployment, which he referred to as "language-games." Unfortunately, the importance of nurturant social interactions, in contrast to other types, has been overlooked in otherwise excellent discussions of Wittgenstein's "social theory of knowledge" (e.g., Bloor, 1983). A principal goal of this chapter is to illustrate some consequences of correcting this oversight. The aggregate effect of the correction is a strengthening and completion of the naturalistic turn initiated by Wittgenstein. What began as a naturalist philosopher's critique of the confusions of past thinkers will have become, once again, an invitation to new kinds of empirical and theoretical research.

Wittgenstein's Legacy

The treatment of all these phenomena of mental life is not of importance to me because I am keen on completeness. Rather because each one casts light on the correct treatment of *all*. (Wittgenstein, *Z*, 465)

Whenever I try to pick out anything by itself, I find it hitched to everything else in the universe. (attributed to John Muir)

A brief treatment of Wittgenstein's legacy will set the stage for the major argument of the chapter. That legacy can be divided into two parts for present purposes: a set of *prescriptions* and a set of *constructions*.

Prescriptions

Implicit throughout Wittgenstein's later work is the message that one must adopt the attitudes characteristic of a good naturalist and ecologist. In particular, the student of mental phenomena is enjoined to scan widely and to *respect* the diversity that such scanning inevitably turns up. Such respect, it should be noted, was legitimized in the biological sciences by one of the great insights of Darwinian thought: Diversity and variability are essential aliments of evolutionary processes, and must not be denied their fundamental role in a bootless effort to discover the "true" essences of natural kinds. A related message is that conceptual analyses are often starved when the analyst arbitrarily restricts his or her diet of examples. Thus, for example, analyses of language prior to Wittgenstein typically focused exclusively on one variety of language use: propositions. Wittgenstein was instrumental both in showing a tremendous diversity in language forms and functions (thus stimulating, along with J. L. Austin, modern speech-act analyses), and in showing that any generalizations about language that were based solely on a study of propositions were bound to misrepresent linguistic, and thus mental, reality.

Two ways that an exclusive focus on propositional forms (and on associated issues of inference and representation) misrepresents mental reality are by desocializing it and by masking its dependencies and connections with other aspects of the natural world. As Bruner (1983) has recently emphasized in his Wittgenstein-inspired treatment of language development, propositional form originates as a more powerful means to the already established goal of managing others attentional states; that is, propositional language is rooted in (but is of course not reducible to) a phylogenetically and developmentally prior matrix of social interactions. To neglect this matrix – as is common among those who focus solely on the representational character of propositional language – is to begin to distort our view of mental life.

To combat such distortions, Wittgenstein, like the great naturalist John Muir, constantly brings our attention back to the humble supportive matrix without which even the loftiest processes of mental life would have no purchase. His description of the plight of the linguistic formalist is one of the most striking in the entire *Investigations:* "[In trying for a purely formal analysis of actual language] we have got onto slippery ice where there is no friction and so in a sense the conditions are ideal, but also, just because of that, we are unable to walk. We want to walk: so we need *friction*. Back to the rough ground!" (*PI,* 107). Like perceptual psychologist James Gibson, Wittgenstein was acutely aware of the problems arising from "air theories" of mental phenomena. If this chapter succeeds, we will see part of what it will mean to construct an alternative type of theory, a genuine "ground theory" of mental development (see Bullock, 1981; Gibson, 1966).

Besides prescribing ecological methods, Wittgenstein constantly warned against allowing one's intelligence to be bewitched by means of language. The two types of bewitchment he focused on can be encapsulated with two observations: (1) words mask diversity, and (2) misleading descriptions lead to false puzzles. To explore the first point, he showed how words like "game," "language," and "tool" mask tremendous diversity – often so much that what we learn about one exemplar of a category (e.g., propositions) tells us very little about another exemplar of the category (e.g., requests). This line of thinking led to his famous suggestion that natural categories are based on context- and purpose-dependent judgments of featural overlap (family resemblance categories, Rosch, 1978; see also Adams and Bullock, 1986) rather than on logical rules such as set union or set intersection. However, the observation can also serve as a tool for promoting theoretical advance: When we use a word like "intelligence," what diversity are we masking, and what can be learned by resisting the word's masking effect (by studying the diversity)?

To explore the second point (regarding misleading descriptions and false puzzles), he followed a path very similar to that followed by Gibson in his early discussions of the "problem of space perception." When we describe the child's problem as one of learning to perceive space, our grammar invites us to think of space as if it were an object, and as if the child, in learning to perceive space, were learning to perceive another kind of object. By transforming the description – how does the child pick up information specifying the layout of surfaces – Gibson avoids the need to solve a number of false puzzles generated by the traditional formulation of the problem. Similarly, Wittgenstein shows that many false puzzles cloud our understanding of mental terms like "meaning" and "understanding." To make progress, it is necessary to abandon the misleading formulations of the problems of meaning and understanding that have been uncritically accepted from prior generations of philosophers. (Both these cases are treated below.)

Constructions

Although Wittgenstein considered himself to be primarily a conceptual therapist – a curer of misunderstandings – he in fact constructed the kernel of a new theory. Kuhn's (1970) work suggests that some such constructive work is always necessary in practice. To successfully displace a well-entrenched vision of reality, it is necessary to offer an alternative vision. Conceptual therapy, like any other therapy, is never neutral. Either the would-be therapist offers a substitute mode of living or thinking, or the attempted therapy fails: The man on the flying trapeze lets go of the first trapeze only if a second is swinging within reach. Thus, in addition to his methodological and critical offerings, Wittgenstein was required in practice to lay the foundations for what may be called an ecological theory of meaning.

Wittgenstein's first move in the game of constructing a theory of meaning was to ask about the criteria governing our everyday use of the word "meaning." His second move was to examine existing (primarily philosophical) theories of meaning. And his third move was to note how the theories fell short – typically far short – of capturing the richness implied by our everyday concept. Although he claimed only to be explicating our everyday concept, doing so required him to begin the dual processes of mechanistic specification and of locating the variegated phenomena lumped under the word "meaning" within a wider range of natural phenomena – and these steps constitute critical first components of any adequate theory of meaning. They have played a critical role in subsequent conceptual analyses of linguistic meaning (cf. Bennett, 1976); Harrison, 1973; Millikan, 1984), and they are fundamental for the only approach likely to appeal to those psycholinguists for whom evolutionary explanations are paradigmatic (cf. Bullock, 1983; Lieberman, 1984; Premack, 1972).

Among the philosophical theories that Wittgenstein found wanting, two of the most important were that the meaning of a word is (1) the thing for which it stands (or an image of the thing for which it stands), or (2) a mental activity that accompanies the word as it is spoken. The first proposal was and is common within species of associationist theory, and the second was and is common among rationalist critiques of associationist theory. Wittgenstein decisively rejected both accounts, on grounds that to establish a table of correspondences between sound-shapes (words) and things (or pictures of things, or mental acts) is only a preliminary to meaning. To fix the representational status of items in the table, they must be put to use in a particular way. Note that a simliar (but less comprehensive) point was recently made by Anderson (1976) when he argued that a cognitive model that presents only a format for internal representations, without also specifying the procedures that will make use of the representations, is really only a preliminary to a cognitive model. Without the procedural specification, items appearing in the representational format only have representational status by courtesy, as it were. A related point can be made about the products of automatic theorem-proving programs written by artificial intelligence researchers. Until the programs become capable of *using* the results of their derivations to order some performance with respect to the referents of the presumptive internal representations, the latter are just that: presumptive,[2] rather than "live" representations. Wittgenstein encapsulated this insight with remarks like the following:

To imagine a language means to imagine a form of life. (*PI*, 19)
For a *large* class of cases – though not for all – in which we employ the word "meaning" it can be defined thus: the meaning of a word is its use in the language. (*PI*, 43)
Hence it would be stupid to call meaning a 'mental activity,' because that would encourage a false picture of the function of the word. (*Z*, 20)
Only in the stream of thought and life do words have meaning. (*Z*, 173)

This notable insight was only the starting point for Wittgenstein's ecological theory of meaning. When one begins to explore its corollaries, it becomes clear that the same presumptive representational format can be given different representational statuses by merely changing the configuration of procedures that make use of that format (though, to be sure, formats and uses typically coevolve and exemplify both a function-selects-form and a form-constrains-function principle). Such interpretational variability is most striking when a natural (but conventionalized) class of events or objects – such as the ways the entrails may spill

[2] My use of the word "presumptive" is borrowed from embryology, where, for example, a mass of undifferentiated cells that will eventually become neural tissue – after a suitable history of interactions – is often referred to as "presumptive neural tissue." Any precursor, with the potential of serving as a structural basis for some function G – once appropriately modified by its history and while embedded within the proper context – can be called a presumptive (structural basis for) function G. The phrase "presumptive representation" is short for "presumptive structural basis for representation."

out of a sacrificial animal – is used to augur different futures in different primitive cultures. Here, the same representational format has different predictive representational statuses (one concerns weather, the other herd movements, for example) as a function of culture-specific uses. Such cases are paradigmatic of Symbolism. For an example of interpretational variability closer to home, compare the way numbers spilling from statistics mills are variously used to predict economic trends by those from different econometric subcultures.

As might be expected, Wittgenstein's emphasis on meaning as culture-specific use has led many to think of Wittgenstein as a conventionalist and relativist. Indeed, this is one of the major themes of Bloor's (1983) excellent treatment of Wittgenstein's mature work, a theme ably captured in Bloor's title, *Wittgenstein: A social theory of knowledge.* Such a reading of Wittgenstein is certainly appropriate. In fact, his work presents one of the most secure bases for getting clearer on claims regarding the objectivity or relativity of knowledge. However, it is also important to recognize the incompleteness, and the potentially misleading nature, of this way of reading Wittgenstein. The phrase "relativity of knowledge" hides a diversity of quite distinct positions. Wittgenstein himself signaled the need for caution regarding his intentions in the following passage, where he poses to himself the "relativity of truth" question:

> "So you are saying that human agreement decides what is true and what is false?" – It is what human beings *say* that is true or false; and they agree in the *language* they use. That is not agreement in opinions but in form of life. (*PI,* 241)

This passage illustrates two critical points. First, it shows, as prior quotations also documented, that Wittgenstein uses the word "language" in a much different – and much more enlightened – way than is typical in contemporary discussions of, say, child language development. For him, to imagine a language truly is to imagine an entire form of life: the set of representational (and instrumental) devices and the mode of their deployment in everyday activities. Second, the passage shows that in a sense all knowledge is relative, but also that objectivity is not in direct competition with relativity. The relativity that Wittgenstein acknowledges as ineliminable is one of finitude, of necessary selection. The symbol-enriched form of life lived by any social group forces encounters with a finite number of aspects of the natural and artificial world, never with all possible aspects.

It is also clear from this and other passages that there are two types of departure from objectivity. One type comprises lies and everyday mistakes, both of which are made within the horizons established by a language-game or form of life. The second type is an ill-adapted language-game, e.g., the one once played by chemists who postulated the existence of phlogiston. Some who give Wittgenstein a conventionalist reading take him to suggest that every language-game has equal claim to our loyalties. But this is a mistaken interpretation of Wittgenstein's intent. Recall that he was passionately involved in a battle against the bewitchment of our intelligence by means of language, and that his method was to expose and abandon the ill-adapted, free-sliding language-games played by prior philosophers (including the younger Wittgenstein). To be sure, Wittgenstein argued for the general thesis that one language-game cannot typically be reduced to others (Danford, 1978), and that language should not be seen as striving toward some single, ideal, form. But such a non-reductionist argument cannot be taken to warrant an equal-merit stance toward different language-games, and Wittgenstein himself did not take it to warrant such a stance. To counter another widespread misinterpretation, it must be added that his anti-reductionism should also not be taken to imply opposition to mechanistic explanations of human action. Nothing about a mechanistic explanation requires that it be reductionist, in the relevant sense.

These remarks about Wittgenstein's purported conventionalism raise the topic that will be central in the remainder of the chapter. Bloor's title invites us to think of Wittgenstein's ecological theory of meaning under the rubric of a social theory of knowledge, and throughout his treatment he has an eye on the sociological strain in Wittgenstein's thinking. In later chapters of his book, for example, he shows how to use Wittgenstein's insights as a stepping stone for systematic treatment of how knowledge may be relative to one's social status, or to the nature of social stratification in one's society. Though Bloor's is certainly a valid (and for me an exciting) approach, Wittgenstein did not extend his own ideas in this way, and it is only one plan according to which a house built on Wittgensteinian foundations might be constructed. Another plan, which I pursue in this chapter, is suggested by asking whether Wittgenstein also laid foundations for *a social theory of intelligence.*

What is the difference between a social theory of knowledge and a social theory of intelligence? The former suggests a concern with developmental products (knowledge structures) and with how such products are relative to social status. It also typically leads to increased skepticism (and often cynicism) regarding knowledge claims. The latter, on the other hand, suggests a need to reform standard accounts of intelligence, a need to socialize them, as it were. It focuses on the question of how we may be more intelligent (or at least differently intelligent than we might otherwise be) because of our sociality. It is not, by itself, an invitation to skepticism regarding knowledge claims.

In my own judgment, pursuit of a social theory of intelligence is more in tune with the spirit of Wittgenstein's later work than pursuit of a social theory of knowledge. Wittgenstein's rejection of the facile skepticism of prior philosophers, as well as his caveats regarding reading him as a simple conventionalist (see quote above), suggest that he would have resisted aspects of what has come to be known as the sociology of knowledge. However, I stress this point not in an attempt to invalidate Bloor's extension (which avoids too-facile skepticism), but to undercut those who have seen too much of the conventionalist in Wittgenstein himself. Consider the following passage from Millikan (1984):

> Descartes and then Locke, it is said, opened an era in which philosophers sought vainly to reach the world through a veil of ideas.... They placed themselves behind this veil by beginning with a vision or theory of mind as a realm in which ideas lived but which was outside the world these philosophers wished to reach with their ideas – the world, at least, of nature. Today, influ-

enced ... by Wittgenstein and Quine, there is a new school of philosophers who live behind a veil of "theories," entangled in "language games" or in the "logical order." They too have placed themselves behind a veil by beginning with a certain vision or theory, this time a theory about language ... floating loose from the rest of the world. (p. 332)

The phrase "influenced by Wittgenstein" leaves it unclear whether Millikan thinks that Wittgenstein was himself an early member of this new school of philosophers, or whether his ideas regarding language-games have been misappropriated by this new school. My own view has already been hinted at above in several places. Like Millikan, Wittgenstein had an abhorrence of "air theories" of our mental life, and he invented the concept of a language-game to show how our representations are parts of, and are articulated with other parts of, the world. This is made clear in the following sketch for a primitive language-game, which shows (again) that for Wittgenstein a language-game was a hybrid phenomenon consisting of representational and non-representational parts, as well as socially shared habits for relating such parts to one another and to some ongoing activity:

I shall call the whole, consisting of language and the actions into which it is woven, the "language-game."
A gives an order like: "d – slab – there." At the same time he shews the assistant a colour sample, and when he says "there" he points to a place on the building site. From the stock of slabs B takes one for each letter of the alphabet up to "d," of the same colour as the sample, and brings them to the place indicated by A....
What about the colour samples that A shews to B: are they part of the *language?*... It is most natural, and causes least confusion, to reckon the samples among the instruments of the language. (*PI*, 7, 8, 16)

Far from cutting language loose from the remainder of the world, the language-game fixes the representational status of presumptive symbols by anchoring them within a matrix of actual activities and objects. Note that, unlike a formalist such as Chomsky, Wittgenstein reckons the humble color samples among the instruments of the language. This serves a dual function: It secures due status for the matrix factors without which presumptive representational forms would remain presumptive, and it shows that the representational forms are themselves objects in the world. This maneuver closes off many of the confusions that have beset the Platonic and Cartesian tradition, and which continue to beset modern writers like Chomsky and Fodor.

To these remarks it could be replied that even in this example, the knower remains behind the veil of the human's conceptualization of color space, which is known to be "inadequate" by comparison with the physicist's theory- and instrument-based description of light and surface reflectivities. However, for Wittgenstein, the skeptical conclusions invited by such a reply are to be blocked by recalling the fact (noted above) that representations function within – and should be judged adequate or inadequate within – some particular behavioral cycle. For the purposes of mounting a given enterprise in the world, a representation may capture the relevant aspects of the world, yet may also prove inadequately predictive for some new class of purposes, such as those of the research physicist. Indeed, *purpose-specificity is the normative condition of a representation.* Thus, for example, the color of an apple as we perceive it truly predicts (under normal conditions) its edibility. As a Gibsonian would say, we see that the apple affords eating. It is an illicit maneuver to use the physicist's criteria for what counts as a veridical representation of light or surface reflectivity (which criteria are determined by the physicist's purposes) to judge the adequacy of representations evolved to serve a different purpose, e.g., that of deciding whether an apple or fig is worth the climb by noting its color.

Moreover, the same conclusions hold even if the representation yielded by the assessment is mediated by cultural-specific modes of probing and measuring the social environment, e.g., when an adult checks (for the purpose of predicting future social interchanges) an infant's level of *irritability* by subjecting it to a standard range of perturbations, then comparing its reactions to some norm. To become skeptical of claims to knowledge in all such cases, in Wittgenstein's analysis, is to illicitly presuppose the existence of some representational format that would prove equally good for all purposes. Note that this is just the sort of representational omniscience imputed by Descartes (who inaugurated the modern era of skeptical philosophy) to the mind of his god.

Thus to acknowledge the purpose-relativity of our procedures for constructing representations, as Wittgenstein certainly did, is not to warrant a free-floating skepticism about knowledge claims. Indeed, such skepticism results from a failure to appreciate what representations normatively *are* within a naturalistic framework (see also Millikan, 1984), and frequently involves implicit appeal to the supernatural. (Recall Wittgenstein's reference to the occult in the passage cited in the second paragraph of the chapter.) This is an important conclusion, because otherwise the case made below for a social theory of intelligence – which is based on observations about culturally-transmitted, and often culture-specific, modes of probing and measuring the environment – would be on shakier ground. As will be seen, the normative purpose-relativity of representations can actually be used to combat another type of skepticism that has dogged developmental psychology since Descartes' time: namely, skepticism regarding experience-based growth in the power of the child's representational system. In particular, Fodor's (1975) nativistic critique of Piaget's belief in interaction-based growth in cognitive powers cannot be maintained once the issues are clarified with the aid of a social theory of intellectual development constructed on Wittgensteinian foundations.

A Social Theory of Intellectual Development

Earlier it was noted that our intelligence is often bewitched by the tendency of words to hide diversity. This Wittgensteinian principle can be used as a lens to promote a clearer understanding of intelligence itself. In answering the question of what intelligence is, most theorists have been biased by certain dominant images, such as the image we have of ourselves as big-brained creatures. Indeed, this image has led to what Gould (1980) has referred to as a 'brain-centered' view of human evolution. Thus, to explain human intelligence, most theorists point their finger at our big brain, and begin to talk about the information processing it subserves. And to explain human evolution, most theorists focus on the somatic problem of encephalization, of growing a bigger, more elaborate, brain. Throughout, intelligence is thought of as something that is localizable within the skull. Is there reason to try to break free of this dominant image?

When we begin to vary our diet of examples of human intelligence in action, as Wittgenstein would have recommended, we find that intelligence is not something localizable within a single skull, and that such a brain-centered view of intelligence is actually *more* distortive of the reality of human-class intelligence than of the kind of intelligence observed in other species. Human intellectual potential is unique for the extent to which it requires social embeddedness in order to be realized according to the normative developmental pattern. This point will become much clearer as the argument proceeds, but a quick sketch will help set the stage. The brain truly is a device with prodigious potential, but it remains a mere lump of protoplasm unless it's involved in the kinds of interactive behavioral cycles that, as we've seen, allow its internal states to actualize their potential representational statuses. In no terrene species other than humans has the content and structure of the requisite interactive behavioral cycles - which as much as anything else *constitute* our actual intelligence - become so dependent on social processes, which cannot, in principle, be localized within a single skull. Therefore, it is more ecologically valid, when thinking of our (human) kind of intelligence, to think of it as a socially-distributed phenomenon. Though this may initially seem an almost mystical or occult proposal itself, it ultimately has the effect of removing many of the false mysteries attached to the idea that "thinking is a process in a completely enclosed space."

A Socializing Syllogism

These remarks suggest that a first step toward a more ecologically valid theory of intelligence is to rigorously establish sociality's constitutive role in intelligence, or at least in the kind of intelligence humans exhibit. To that end, consider the following argument:

1. Intelligence can be defined as "the power of an adaptive engine to use its neuro-muscular resources as a means to maintain an adaptive fit with a dynamic environment."
2. Because environments are unpredictably dynamic, even the more intelligent creatures (e.g., those which have significant internal-simulation capacities) are constantly drifting away from adaptedness at some rate.
3. In environments that change quickly, there is selection pressure for adaptations that promote rapid convergence toward new states of adaptedness. Such adaptations might be called "second-order adaptations."
4. Because these second-order adaptations contribute to the power of the adaptive engine, they too, if achieved by promoting adaptive use of neuro-muscular resources, are constituents of intelligence.

5. Species can be located within a convergence-rate hierarchy (Bullock, 1983, 1984; Fischer & Bullock, 1984) on the basis of the speed with which average members move toward new states of (neuro-muscularly based) adaptedness after environmental changes. By 1 through 4, this convergence-rate hierarchy is also a hierarchy of levels of intelligence.
6. Examination of the convergence-rate hierarchy within our lineage shows that social relationships and modes of social interaction play an integral role in determining species' relative positions within the hierarchy.
7. Therefore, sociality must be considered to be an important constituent of human intelligence. Moreover, it should be examined as possibly a necessary constituent of human-level intelligence in general.

This argument places the problem of intelligence in a naturalistic context, and defines intelligence in terms of both a functional and a structural criterion. The functional criterion involves the idea of improvements in rate of achieving new adaptations. The structural criterion insists that such rate gains be achieved via increased power to adaptively utilize one's neuro-muscular resources. (This would rule out our counting as intelligence-based the strategy of having larger litters of individuals with less learning potential - a strategy actually "chosen" by many extant biological lineages; see Eisenberg, 1981.) By focusing on rate, and correlatively on the idea of second-order adaptations, the argument emphasizes some of the same features of the everyday concept of intelligence that Dennett (1975) claims have been brought into sharper focus within the field of artificial intelligence research. In particular, it emphasizes the idea that intelligence essentially involves more than having a grab-bag of stock solutions to adaptive problems ("first-order adaptations"). It also involves more or less sophisticated provisions for adding to one's stock of solutions in an open-ended way ("second-order adaptations").

A major point of the argument is that the constituents of human-class intelligence appear to be quite heterogeneous. *Any* adaptation that promotes rapid convergence toward new states of adaptedness gets counted among the constituents of intelligence. If a new neural circuit that allows better pattern registration or less biased learning emerges (Grossberg, 1982), that counts as a constituent of intelligence. On the other hand, if a new tendency to attend to others' performances, which allows rudimentary imitation, emerges, that also counts as a constituent of intelligence, as does the culturally-transmitted practice of recoding continuous quantities with the aid of standard measures and the modern number system. Allowing such heterogeneity within the category of constituents of intelligence amounts to treating *intelligence* as a family resemblance category (Rosch, 1978; Wittgenstein, *PI*). At the very least, this Wittgensteinian tactic allows an escape from the brain-centered view of the development of human intelligence. In practice, it should also open the way to a much more adequate view, by reducing the power of the term "intelligence" to mask whatever diversity is to be found among its natural constituents. The next step is to begin to build up an inventory of the latter (Bullock, 1984), a task to which I now turn.

Modes of Interaction and Intelligence

Among the most important constituents of intelligence, because of their central role in generating new adaptations, are the *modes of interaction* available to a species (or community) member. A concern with such interactive modes carries us towards a more socialized description of human intelligence even as it carries us away from the brain-centered description, because there is a cline (Givon, 1979) from relatively asocial modes to modes that are either pragmatically or logically dependent on social relations (for discussions of this distinction, see Feldman & Toulmin, 1976; Haroutunian, 1983).

Consider first some relatively asocial modes. Many students of infancy have been duly fascinated by the infant's interactive repertoire, which includes capacities for spontaneous visual search and scanning (Haith, 1980), for tactile exploration, for orienting to sounds, and for the famous circular reactions that were studied by Piaget (1962). Such modes, though they have an organization of their own that is no doubt rooted in brain organization, *require* external aliments if they are to perform their normative developmental functions, which include, among others, the generation of new, adapted, representations. Scanning builds up representations of particular forms. Circular reactions allow the discovery of particular transformative relations. Such interactive modes are essential for the realization of cognitive potential. Though any single interactive mode might arguably be eliminated without causing irremediable cognitive deficits, some substitute mode will have to be found if remediation is actually to occur (see Kaufmann, 1980, Chapter 3). To get a clear view of the developmental role of such modes is to recognize that cognitive potential has characteristically co-evolved with mechanisms for its realization (Bullock, 1983), just as plants that use pollen transfer for propagation have coevolved with the insects that serve as one mechanism for the realization of their reproductive potential. In the case of cognition, this coevolution has been such that *actual* intelligence (like actual reproductive power) is as much a matter of realization mechanisms (interactive modes) as it is a matter of structural potentials (having a suitably plastic brain).

When we ask what modes of (cognitive-development-promoting) interaction individuate our lineage, and ultimately our species and particular communities, we find a rich array of social-relations-based modes of interaction. Any mode of interaction can be said to be based on social relations if it is either pragmatically or constitutively (and thus logically) dependent on social relations for its normal expression or development.

Examples of such modes can be taken from the convergence rate hierarchy shown in Table 1. This is the hierarchy alluded to under point 5 in the syllogism presented earlier. At each level of the hierarchy, something new is added to the species repertoire, and this new thing enables faster convergence toward new adaptations, as schematized in Figure 1. Thus these new things count as constituents of intelligence. Consider first level 5, which is distinguished by the emergence of exploratory play in our lineage's modal repertoire. Exploratory play may seem to be just as asocial an interactive mode as the infant's visual scanning.

Table 1. A hierarchy of factors affecting convergence rate

1. Natural Selection (NS).
2. NS + Reflex Conditioning (RC).
3. NS + RC + Conditionable Goal Directed Activity (CGDA).
4. NS + RC + CGDA + Affective Bonding/Communication (ABC).
5. NS + RC + CGDA + ABC + Exploratory Play (EP).
6. NS + RC + CGDA + ABC + EP + Constructive Imitation (CI).
7. NS + RC + CGDA + ABC + EP + CI + Purposive Teaching (PT).
8. NS + RC + CGDA + ABC + EP + CI + PT + Presyntactic Symbolic Communication (PSC).
9. NS + RC + CGDA + ABC + EP + CI + PT + PSC + Syntactic Symbolic Communication (SSC).
10. NS + RC + CGDA + ABC + EP + CI + PT + PSC + SSC + Writing (W).
11. NS + RC + CGDA + ABC + EP + CI + PT + PSC + SSC + W + Advanced Literacy (AL).

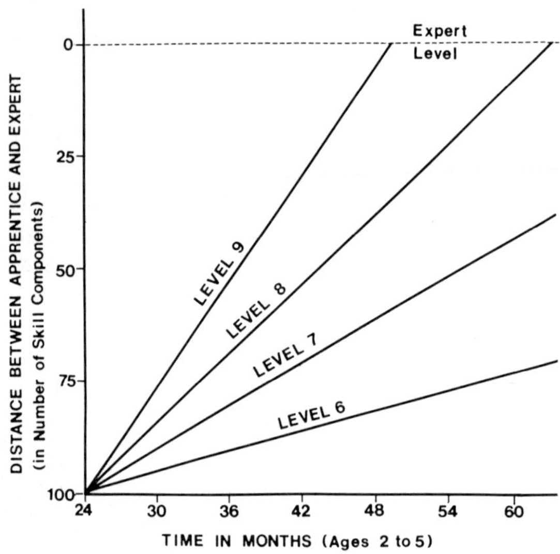

Figure 1. A highly schematic illustration of convergence rates at four levels of the convergence-rate hierarchy (adapted from Bullock, 1983).

Should it, nonetheless, be counted among the social-relations-based modes that promote cognitive development? Because few would deny that it is a development-promoting mode of interaction, let's examine its dependency on social relations. In fact, its placement after social attachment in the hierarchy is based on the hypothesis that exploratory play is a relatively fragile mode that achieves its normal expression only when the individual is in a state of felt security, which serves to buffer the individual against the fears generated by novelties encountered in the course of play. Such felt security, in turn, depends on the quality of the social relationships between the would-be explorer and others in the social group. If this hypothesis is correct, as abundant evidence seems to indicate, then exploratory play – though it appears on the surface as a relatively asocial mode – is in fact pragmatically dependent on social relations.

Level 6 of the hierarchy marks the emergence of constructive imitation, a mode of interaction that is more than merely pragmatically dependent on social relations because it is a socially-constituted phenomenon. Constructive imitation occurs when an individual, in order to recreate some performance observed in another, must learn a new way to use his or her neuro-muscular resources. Thus constructive imitation is, by definition, both developmentally progressive and an inherently social phenomenon. Equally important for my argument is the fact that constructive imitation has an enormous impact on convergence rate (Bandura, 1971), and thus serves as a fundamentally important constituent of intelligence, in two ways. First, it affords observers rapid convergence toward particular adaptive solutions that have been discovered by some other member of the group. Second, it allows rapid convergence toward new modes of interaction discovered by others, and these modes have the potential, in turn, to generate further adaptive solutions. I can, with effort, come to imitate your intricate technique of chipping sharp flakes from stone for immediate use as scrapers. But I can also imitate your technique of probing the universe for its secrets, e.g., your way of playing with a large sample of different types of stone and different percussive methods.

Once constructive imitation entered the species repertoire as a dominant mode of interaction, our type of intelligence had passed a threshold to become normatively a socially distributed phenomenon. That is, once the pattern of intellectual development comes to depend on frequent operation in the imitative mode, it follows that much of an individual's achieved adaptive power is an inheritance from others' problem-solving efforts. In such a species, the individual's actual power to arrive at new adaptive solutions is a joint function of imitative propensity and mnemonic or inventive efforts by members (including self) of the social network. Thus the individual's adaptive power is best measured by looking jointly at the individual's imitative propensity and at the groups within which the individual interacts and freely shares information. This measure of adaptive power will be different for different individuals because of differences in imitative propensity and in group memberships. Because the power so measured is socially-distributed, and is just what we have called intelligence, it follows that we should consider intelligence to be normatively socially-distributed in any species where imitation has become a dominant mode.

This point – which requires ignoring the skin as a critical boundary in discussions of the referent of "intelligence" – is made even stronger by noting that even *more* of the imitative mode is socially-distributed than we typically realize, because it has been complemented by further social developments (see also Kaye, 1982). To see how, ask how often an imitator's success depends on a helping hand from the model. Level 7 in the hierarchy marks the emergence of purposive teaching, which amounts in most contexts to aiding the would-be imitator's attempts to construct a skill (or other cognitive structure) which matches that of some model. Perhaps the simplest way to teach is to take the time to repeat an act so as to create for the imitator a prolonged opportunity to function in the imitative mode. Here we see again the pattern seen in the case of exploratory play: Social relations support operation within modes of interaction that would not otherwise exist, or would not otherwise exist in the same form, or be manifested with the same frequency.

Note, however, that the pattern has also been transformed in a rather remarkable way once imitation is combined with purposive teaching. In the case of exploratory play, to a first approximation, the social other acts as a mere affect modulator, and one could imagine getting the same effect with, say, a drug of some sort. With level 7, the intelligence of the other comes into play, and this leads to a kind of adaptive co-development (see Fischer & Bullock, 1984) that, although without a precise analogue elsewhere in nature, is reminiscent of co-development among the various part-circuits of suitably plastic macro-circuits located within individual brains. For this reason, I've proposed (Bullock, 1983, 1984) that the innovation at level 7 can be fruitfully thought of as the "closing" of a single *modeling circuit* that happens to have its parts distributed in different individuals. The innovation at level 7 thus amounts to completion of an integrated, but complex, phenotype - a phenotype that is, in our case, species-characteristic.

Of course, intermeshing achieved by activation of complimentary circuits in different individuals has precedent in the domain of reproductive behavior and in the domain of emotional communication. However, the modeling circuit is special because the intermeshing it achieves is more dynamic and open-ended: Any performance exhibited by the other can come to serve as a "topic" for the imitative "conversations" made possible by the level 7 mode. I would like to claim that this socially-distributed circuit should have a status in our theories of intelligence equal to the circuit that enables visual scanning, or the circuits that (according to the best available theory) exist within the brain to ensure such fundamental intellectual powers as the ability to learn new things without overwriting what was learned in the past (see Grossberg, 1982). Whereas the former circuit builds new representational codes (as we've seen), and whereas the latter circuit stabilizes extant codes against erosive influences, the modeling circuit serves both functions.

In addition, it can be argued that the modeling circuit solves a unique and fundamental problem associated with intellectual plasticity. Allowing one's development to be fundamentally open-ended requires relaxing the sure hand of instinctive guidance (Stenhouse, 1974). Such relaxation, if not undertaken in concert with compensating provisions, could be disastrous, because the individual could be left without any established procedures for coping with the tasks of life. The level 7 mode (which, as Table 1 indicates, incorporates many prior modes) can be considered nature's exquisite mosaic solution to this problem. With its assembly, nature had effectively pieced together a way to make development both closely regulated and essentially open-ended. The evolving adult, as nurturant teacher, came to assume more and more of the burden of ensuring that the child's development would follow an adaptive trajectory, thus allowing the success of children who, because of correspondingly weaker control by instinct, were at greater and greater freedom to extend the frontiers of cultural practice.

Because our cognitive development is so critically dependent on functioning within the mode enabled by the modeling circuit, our intelligence is socially-distributed in a much more pervasive sense than that of a species classifiable at any prior level of the convergence rate hierarchy. Level 7 is truly a watershed in the evolution of intelligence. Yet, the emergence of the modeling circuit is hardly the last chapter in the story of interactive modes as constituents of intelligence. The next section returns to Wittgenstein's concept of language-games, which are further interactive modes distinguished by their use of arbitrary symbol systems.

Before that return, however, it will be useful to deal with a potential objection to the foregoing steps toward specification of a social theory of intelligence. Some readers may be tempted to balk, in particular, at my treatment of the level 7 mode as a complex phenotype. It may seem a violation of some well-established paradigm to treat between-brain circuits on the same footing as within-brain circuits. However, to treat the modeling circuit differently solely because it is socially-distributed – to think it somehow less legitimate a constituent of intelligence, or less genuine a phenotype, for *this reason* – is to surrender to the prejudice that the skin-boundary should be the final arbiter in judgments of what intelligence is, and of what phenotypes are. Such surrender is a mistake, for two related reasons. Note that the reference case here (what's supposedly being violated) is the brain itself considered as the seat of intelligence. Yet the brain itself is unique precisely for the extent to which – unlike other organs such as the liver or pancreas – it depends on interactions with structuring influences from beyond the skin to realize the purposes for which it evolved. The brain has made a career of ignoring the skin's claim to be a boundary! Moreover, if we look at how relatively asocial interactive modes are actually enabled by neural circuits, then we find an anticipation of the distributed solution. For example, the macro-circuit that enables infant scanning actually has critical sub-circuits scattered over at least a dozen spatially segregated neural regions (Grossberg & Kuperstein, 1986). In short, the only paradigm that the socially-distributed modeling circuit violates turns out to be a false image of how the real brain actually accomplishes intelligent functions. In fact, it is entirely "in character" for the brain eventually to emerge as something that develops normally only when embedded within a social network of a specially evolved type, namely one in which imitation is complemented by purposive teaching on the part of nurturant others.

A similar reply can be made to the objection that something logically dependent on the participation of two individuals cannot be called a phenotype without violating standard biological practice. In fact, both logic and current practice recommend using the word in such contexts (Dawkins, 1982). If beavers' dams, bower birds' bowers, and mating rituals are all proper phenotypes (and they are), then so is the imitation/teaching mode and the (distributed) macro-circuit that makes it possible in any particular social unit.

Human-class Intelligence Constituted by Language-games

An intention is embedded in its situation, in human customs and institutions. If the technique of the game of chess did not exist, I could not intend to play a game of chess. In so far as I do intend the construction of a sentence in advance, that is made possible by the fact that I can speak the language in question. (Wittgenstein, *PI,* 337)

In this section, we will build rapidly toward an understanding of how the developments noted in the last section potentiated the emergence of human-class intelligence. We will also expose the nature of the mistakes made by such writers as Fodor and Chomsky who, unlike Wittgenstein, have tried to treat language as a fixed phenotype. The entire exercise will reinforce the theme that our kind of intellectual development is remarkable for being closely regulated yet also essentially open-ended, a pattern that would seem impossible to achieve in a less fundamentally social species.

It is critical to begin by defining *language-game* in such a way as to ensure appropriate generality. In particular, a definition is needed that allows the inclusion of mathematics, because, as we will see, mathematics provides an especially clear instance of how language-games play a constitutive role in human-class intelligence. The following passage indicates that this is in keeping with Wittgenstein's own views:

Do not be troubled by the fact that languages (2) and (8) consist only of orders. If you want to say that this shews them to be incomplete, ask yourself whether our language is complete; – whether it was so before the symbolism of chemistry and the notation of the infinitesimal calculus were incorporated in it; for these are, so to speak, suburbs of our language. (*PI,* 18)

As with the earlier definition of intelligence, I will specify the concept of a language-game via both a functional and a structural criterion. By way of introduction, consider the following characterization given in a recent paper by Alison Adams and myself:

Though initially odd-sounding, "language-games" is quite an apt term for the various language-informed activity modes elaborated through cultural evolution. When the *games* component of "language-games" is stressed, we are reminded that there is great diversity across exemplars of language (e.g., naming, counting, greeting) just as there is diversity within the class of games (e.g., games of skill, games of chance, card games, ball games, etc.). We are also reminded that linguistic devices are of vital importance in the performance of certain *activities;* they are not merely representational devices (Austin, 1962; Searle, 1969). Finally, we are reminded that linguistic phenomena, like the events that may be observed on a game field, are simultaneously constrained by physical law, biological functionality, and social convention. When the *language* component of "language-games" is stressed, we are reminded that whatever activity mode we are discussing owes part of its form to the participation of linguistic structures. Thus "language-game" is shorthand for *an organized, culturally transmitted mode of activity, performance of which depends on, and provides the rationale for, some particular linguistic device.*
There is somthing quite special about this definition of "language-game." The particular mode of activity (e.g., quantificational activity involving the range of terms "all," "some," and "none"; or rhetorical activity involving terms like "equality for all" and "enemy of the people") both depends on, and provides the rationale for, the linguistic device. Neither the mature form of the mode of activity, as such, nor the linguistic device, as such, is prior to the other. In prac-

tice they must emerge together. This point has far-reaching consequences for the theory of semantic development. It implies, as Wittgenstein was quick to note, that without the mode of activity, the linguistic device lacks meaning. If so, then semantic development is fundamentally a matter of mastering modes of activity that depend on the organized deployment of linguistic devices. Learning a word, for example, is a matter of learning a module of cultural practice. From this, Wittgenstein derived the famous dictum that "meaning is use," that is, the meaning of a linguistic device is determined by its normative role in environmentally adapted human action (Adams & Bullock, 1986, pp. 159–160).

The historical record shows that the critical new idea here is extremely difficult to grasp, so it will be well to approach it from several distinct directions. From the perspective of the developmentalist, the core idea is that constructing a new mode of activity frequently involves, as a constitutive process, learning both a new symbol system and a method of deploying it. Here it is easy to go wrong by misconstruing what is happening: One is tempted to think that the mode of activity already exists in its mature form, and that the symbol system is added on at the last moment for the purposes of interpersonal communication. This construal is one traditional pole of the ancient debate about the relations between language and thought: Language is misconstrued as the mere outward garb of thought, which is presumed capable of taking the same form without the participation of language.

This misconstrual can best be blocked by studying examples where a more primitive mode of thought is displaced by another mode that clearly depends on mastery of a new language-game. As such an example, consider the case of a painter who faces the general problem of making a living and the immediate problem of painting a ballroom floor that is made from an unfamiliar material. The general problem of making a living places a premium on completing the ballroom in an efficient manner – one not wasteful of time and other resources. Assume that the painter mixes his own paint and that it is wasteful both to mix too much paint, and to stop in the middle of painting in order to mix more.

The efficiency (read "adaptive power") of the painter's solution will depend on the nature of his representation of the problem. Consider first a relatively primitive representation. The painter looks over the ballroom and remembers a similar job done last year. But that room is remembered as being smaller than the present one. So the painter resolves to mix more paint than he remembers having mixed for the former job. He does so, but something goes awry, and he mixes either too much paint (and incurs the cost associated with wasting materials) or too little (and thus incurs the costs associated with having to stop and mix new materials).

Now consider a relatively sophisticated solution, based on a qualitatively different representation of the problem. Along perpendicular walls of the room, the painter lays out rows of unit squares. He then counts the rows to derive a length and a width, and multiplies the two numbers to derive the area. Next he mixes a small, standard amount (say a half liter) of paint and tests to see how many unit squares worth of floor it will cover (this is necessary because different kinds of flooring are more or less absorbent, etc.). To be quite precise, he assesses his test-plot coverage in terms of fractional parts of unit squares. He then divides the quantity of unit-squares covered into the total area, thus deriving the number of standard paint quantities he needs to mix. He mixes two percent more than necessary to allow for undetected variations in absorbency (sampling error), in anticipation of modest needs for retouching, and to err on the side of avoiding remixing costs.

Although there is much in common between the two painters – both exhibit a kind of practical reasoning, for example – their modes of interaction are quite different. In particular, the second painter's mode is built up from a number of prior innovations that have become the common social inheritance of members of our culture. Area, for example, is no longer treated solely as an enclosure bigger or smaller than some remembered enclosures. Instead, it is treated *in the terms* made available by mastery of the representational paradigm: Area is now something constructed by multiplying unit squares. Moreover, though the painter may not understand why, his possession of this concept of area amounts to being more intelligent, in just the sense discussed throughout this paper. For this class of problems, the culturally transmitted representational paradigm allows rapid development of responses that are closer to what an expert on this ballroom and this type of floor would do without need for calculation (see Figure 1).

Note that this eminently Wittgensteinian example of thought constituted by a new language-game is also just the sort of example that Piaget held to be paradigmatic of cognitive development: a highly fallible strategy based on perceptual-mnemonic estimation is replaced by a much less fallible strategy based on explicit quantitative calculation. Yet, from all I have said, Wittgenstein appears to be diametrically opposed to the view, commonly attributed to Piaget, that thought always develops first, and is only later mapped by language for the purposes of communication. How, without contradiction, can both theorists be equally happy with his example?

The apparent paradox can be eliminated by taking account of two factors. The first has already been remarked numerous times. For Wittgenstein, language was much more than words and concatenations of words. In fact, he used "language" as a synonym for the open-ended collection of socially-learned games we play with representational paradigms, whether the latter be image-based, word-based, or formula-based. To imagine a language, for him, was to imagine a form of life. Thus merely to learn to distinguish and concatenate sound-shapes (presumptive words) by rote would not count as learning a new module of the language for Wittgenstein. In short, rote speech, which Piaget dismissed as mere language learning, Wittgenstein would count, at best, as only a preliminary to language learning. If the second painter had merely learned his multiplication table, without learning any application of it, he would not be credited with learning the language-game by Wittgenstein. Piaget would say that he had learned some language, but without understanding. Thus to locate Wittgenstein and Piaget at different poles of the language and thought debate is to overlook Wittgenstein's more enlightened use of the term "language."

Although noting this basic difference in how Piaget and Wittgenstein use the phrase "language learning" closes much of the gap that initially appeared to separate them, it does not close the gap completely. In particular, Wittgenstein remains distinct from Piaget for his greater sensitivity to the *symmetry* of consequences produced by dissociating thought from language or language from thought. Piaget felt a need to decide in favor of either language's or thought's claim to developmental priority. And, after noting the dissociability of genuine understanding from mere speech, he decided in favor of thought's claim to priority. However, as indicated in the quote from Adams and Bullock (1986), Wittgenstein saw that claiming priority for either party in the traditional dispute was a mistake. Parallelling the observation that one can have rote speech in the absence of genuine understanding is the equally valid observation that one cannot have genuine understanding in the absence of *some speech-based or other representational paradigm*. For when we analyze particular cases, we find that to dissociate or subtract out the representational devices is also to destroy thought. One is left with mere occult wisps, not with the *understanding* one is mistakenly led to expect by thinking of understanding as if it were some independently existing accompaniment of the words (or other representational paradigm). As in the parable of the two painters, any advance to a new mode of adapted thought involves mastering both a representational paradigm and a method for deploying it. There is no learning the method of deployment (no understanding or thought) without *some* representational format to deploy! In short, once one uses the word "language" in Wittgenstein's sense, the very disjunction of language and thought as distinct sets becomes problematic. At best, one can maintain that language is a subset of thought: language comprises that subset of representational paradigms that are socially shared and socially transmitted.

One of the problems with Piaget's relative insensitivity to this issue is that it invites (but does not logically require – see Flanagan, 1984; and Haroutunian, 1983) the sort of skeptical views regarding cognitive development that Fodor (1975) recently tried to defend. If one does not explicitly acknowledge the dependency of new modes of thought on the invention and social transmission of new representational paradigms, then one may drift, by default, toward explaining all of cognitive development as a matter of realizing the potential of some pre-existing representational paradigm (or a small number of successively maturing representational paradigms). This creates fertile ground for Fodorian claims that there are no genuine learning-based increases in the power of the developing child's conceptual system, because all *candidate* increases may be treated either as maturational (genuine, but not learning-based) or as mere alternative realizations of potentials already present in some general, preformed or "matured," representational paradigm. Though perhaps learning-based, such alternative realizations would not count as true increases in the system's representational powers.

Wittgensteinians are in a much better position than Piagetians to resist such skepticism about learning as an engine of genuine expansions of our conceptual horizons. The key to such resistance lies in the distinction already elaborated between a presumptive symbol system and a true linguistic device: The former is a mere set of discriminable tokens taken together with any static and dynamic relational rules defined over the tokens. A linguistic device, on the contrary, is a symbol system as deployed (in one of the myriad ways it might be deployed) for the structuring of a particular mode of activity.

In the following passage, Wittgenstein exemplifies the typical case in which children learn a new way of thinking by learning how a symbol system may be deployed in actual life, a learning process which transforms the presumptive representational paradigm into a genuine linguistic device:

Does a child learn only to talk, or also to think? Does it learn the sense of multiplication *before* – or *after* it learns multiplication? (*Z*, 324)

As noted earlier, Wittgenstein answered the first question with "yes," the second with "after." If either after or during, then one kind of cognitive development involves the senseless learning of how to play a symbolic game with a set of discriminable tokens according to arbitrary rules, followed by learning to map some of the regularities found in that symbolic microcosm onto some particulars of experience, which leads simultaneously to a restructured understanding of those particulars and a "conferral of sense" on the heretofore senseless symbol game.

In this paradigm of cognitive development, the first episode involves learning what may be called a *raw pattern* defined over presumptive symbols. The second episode involves learning how to apply this pattern to structure interactions with some other aspect of the world, and, as an intrinsic consequence, learning a sense for the presumptive symbol system. In this scheme, the adaptive learning cycle is divided into two parts governed by different principles, just as the great cycle of adaption by variation and natural selection is divided into two such parts. It is this insight that is glaringly absent from Fodor's (1975) treatment of concept development, and from many other treatments within the conceptualist (as opposed to the symbolist) tradition (see Kaufmann, 1980). Moreover, it is just this insight that the phrase *language-game,* properly understood, helps us remember. For it reminds us of a characteristic human capacity: the ability to playfully work out (and, later, socially transmit) arbitrary games played with symbols and standard samples – in the painter's case, a game involving unit squares and number construction played according to the rules of arithmetic. Here the working out is playful in the sense that it need not be constrained at every moment by an extrinsic concern for representational adequacy. Yet such activity is constantly generating presumptive representational paradigms that have the potential of informing (literally, giving form to) new, serious, modes of interaction. So understood, the concept of a language-game becomes a major tool in the battle against conceptual preformism.

Because Fodor lacks Wittgenstein's insight, he finds it natural to presuppose that the learner must know how a presumptive representational paradigm will be applied *before* it has been learned as a raw pattern, and before any attempt to discover how it might prove relevant to some reference domain. This peculiar presupposition is tied up with his initial decision to restrict "learning" to cover only the process of judging whether a particular representation validly applies, in what must then be a *prespecified* way, to a domain of reference. Note that this reduces all learning to the case of testing the validity of a belief, which, as we saw earlier, always happens within the horizons established by the language-game. Left out of Fodor's picture is the kind of nonexplicit learning (and training in the use of a paradigm) that serves to establish the language-game itself. It is Fodor's Procrustean definition of learning that leads him to the mistaken conclusion that nothing in cognitive development genuinely counts as a learned increase in the representational power of the child's conceptual system.

From the Wittgensteinian perspective, Fodor effectively lops off all of part 1, and fundamentally distorts part 2, of the learning cycle that produces our cognitive development. The need to resist such Procrustean efforts is one point over which Wittgensteinian and Piagetian cognitive-developmentalists ally themselves with both the poets and the mathematicians in a two-millenia war against the formalist school of nativist psycholinguists. To deny the first part of the learning cycle is to ignore the sort of esthetically guided symbolic play that is constantly extending the representational powers of pure mathematics and literature. Moreover, to distort the second part of the cycle, by assuming that the *way* a new symbol system is to be mapped onto other aspects of the world is predetermined, is to deny the creative aspect of comprehending a new metaphor (see Lakoff & Johnson, 1980) or of discovering a genuinely novel way to make "real world use" of what was theretofore a pure mathematical construction. In each of the latter cases, a mapping often doesn't exist until the presumptive representational paradigm and the potential reference domain rub up against each other. Hence the resulting mapping (which Wittgenstein called a "method of projection") may be literally unprecedented in its nature. Thus, for example, the nature of the method of projection worked out between Riemannian geometry and the basic properties of the physical universe was something genuinely new on the cognitive landscape. The concept of a two-phase learning cycle helps us see the working out of this mapping as a major *event* in the natural history of human cognition.

Regarding such events, preformists like Chomsky and Fodor recommend a fundamental misconstrual based on another - widely validated yet locally inapplicable - paradigm of our experience. To draw once again on Wittgenstein:

> It is difficult for us to shake off this comparison: a man makes his appearance - an event makes its appearance. As if an event even now stood in readiness before the door of reality and were then to make its appearance in reality - like coming into a room. (*Z*, 59)

Ironically enough, the contrast between Wittgenstein and the preformists can be characterized in terms of two types of generativity (one of the watchwords of Chomskian grammar and cognitive theory). Wittgenstein, Piaget, and others have recognized, as a fundamental type of cognitive developmental phenomenon, the kinds of generativity that result from playing with changes in both the axiom set of a symbol system and in methods of projection. Chomsky and

Fodor, to the contrary, have limited themselves, in effect, to the type of generativity that results from tracing the implications of a fixed set of axioms applied in a predetermined way (see also Bullock, 1981).

When one has mastered the perspective presented above, it becomes easy to see a second point at which Fodor's argument – that there is an innate language of thought which bounds our cognitive development – has gone wrong. It *is* the case, as Fodor argues, that in order to learn the normative sub-activities involved with a new representational paradigm (such as the sub-activities of choosing equal unit squares, of laying unit squares end-to-end without gap, and of counting unit squares) one often uses already-available perceptual descriptors. However, none of these sub-activities, taken alone, amounts to the new representational paradigm. The latter depends on patterned deployment of the sub-activities. Neither this patterned deployment, nor any conceptualization enabled by it, can be adequately captured (without behavioristic distortion) in terms of pre-existing descriptors. This second way of summarizing what goes wrong in Fodor's treatment shows that his argument conforms to the preformist norm by being implicitly reductionist: In effect, his argument presupposes that what is true of the part (the sub-activity) is also true of the pattern into which the part is woven.

To salvage *any* of his argument, Fodor would have to shift ground and argue that there are constraints on human pattern learning itself, i.e., constraints on what can be learned as a presumptive representational paradigm. While this might prove a fruitful tack, it would no longer amount to arguing that there is an innately bounded *language* of thought. As we have seen, the raw pattern, by itself, is not yet a genuine linguistic (representational) device. It is only a preliminary. Thus there is no way for Fodor to salvage his preformist claim that intellectual development cannot involve genuine learning-based increases in the representational power of our conceptual systems. Quite the contrary. As Wittgenstein implicitly argued, our relatively arbitrary pattern-learning and pattern-application-learning abilities preclude the possibility of treating language as a fixed phenotype.

A final possibility worth noting is that the power of the two-part learning cycle to generate radical conceptual innovations may depend on (and thus may help explain the rapid evolution of) one of the most conspicuous design features of human language: its non-iconicity. As Wittgenstein himself noted:

> It is very difficult to describe paths of thought where there are already many lines of thought laid down, – your own or other people's – and not to get into one of the grooves. It is difficult to deviate from an old line of thought *just a little*. (*Z*, 349)

If this is true for non-iconic symbolic thought – where the non-iconicity helps free one from the "drag" of perceptually salient relations and thus promotes play in the space of possible relations – it would appear to be all the more true of thought based entirely on an iconic code. With respect to the latter, Fodor's view is more apt, because the relations among code elements are constrained from the start by one's immediate recognition of how presumptive representations are 'supposed' to project onto a particular reference domain. Here, to paraphrase Wittgenstein, the grooves are both many and deep. Perhaps developmental psychology would have much to gain from a systematic study of the innovation-rate-limiting properties of alternative coding strategies (see also Goody, 1977; Halford, 1982; Kaufmann, 1980; Lieberman, 1984; Premack, 1972).

In summary, this and the prior section have gone some distance toward showing that culturally transmitted language-games play a constitutive role in human-class intelligence. Much of what is recognizable as human intellectual history has been made by the coalescence of new language-games that have enabled the rapid generation of whole families of conceptual innovations, which in turn have multiplied the speed with which we could solve many classes of problems. Our linguistic culture can be likened to a giant glass ball, filled with representational paradigms and modes of interaction produced by many generations, and kept aloft by the efforts of variously motivated hands. The game played with this ball involves using, adding to, and subtracting from its contents, as well as passing it safely into the hands of the next generation. The modeling circuit ensures the safe transfer. Anyone lacking either the social-interactive competence needed to learn the subset of language-games played by a particular community of problem-solvers, or lacking sufficient opportunities to learn them at the knee of some community member, will lack the *actual intelligence* needed to participate fully in the community's life - whatever the person's hypothetical intellectual potential may have been. Moreover, contrary to the claims of Fodor, new language-games do not merely fill out a space already delineated by some pre-existing language of thought. They are the instruments by which we break beyond the current limits of language and thought.

This is not, of course, to say that there are *no* limits on human cognition. My arguments against Fodor's thesis are not pertinent to many other proposals regarding constraints on human cognition. In particular, nothing I have said contradicts the thesis of various neo-Piagetians (Case, 1980; Fischer, 1980; Fischer & Bullock, 1981; Halford, 1982) that there might be an upper bound on the complexity of human thought. Nor have I argued against the thesis that our cognitive growth is biased by predispositions, some of which are open to being either confirmed, or "over-written," by experience (e.g., Bates & MacWhinney, 1982; Bickerton, 1981). Both of these latter ideas appear to have considerable merit, and complement the ideas presented in this chapter. Moreover, it should be clear that no theory of language-games as constituents of intelligence will be complete until we know something of the determinants of selective transmission of language-games: The modeling circuit is actually an adaptive filter rather than a passive conduit. Finally, a balanced view will have to address the topics recently discussed by Spiro (1984), who reminds us once again of the extra-representational aspects of language- games, and of the need to study the dynamics of group commitment to, and rejection of, competing language-games.

Conclusion: Six Syndromes with Brief Therapy

To develop the arguments and conclusions sketched above, it was necessary to overcome several related habits of thinking that work to obscure our view of the developmental landscape. It may be useful to gather into one list some of these conceptual syndromes, and to prescribe a brief "therapy" for each. Along the way, the major themes of the chapter will be revisited.

Table 2 lists six syndromes. Paired with each is one or more phrases meant to recall conceptual alternatives which, once assimilated, tend to loosen the syndrome's hold on our thinking. The first syndrome is *essentialism,* the presumption that all the natural phenomena named by a given term must share a single set of distinctive features, which define the "true" nature of the class of phenomena. Biologists overcame this syndrome by learning to think in terms of evolving populations rather than in terms of perfect members of eternal species. Wittgenstein overcame it by learning to think of categories by analogy with families, whose members, though distinguishable from members of other families on the basis of features, nevertheless fail to exhibit any universally shared set of such distinctive features. Note that without the essentialist presumption, it is very hard to continue to believe that a single representational paradigm – the one that captures the referent's essence? – might be equally good for all purposes. Thus a rejection of essentialism is bound up with the insight that it is the normative condition of a representation that it be purpose-specific. Naturally enough, the prescription listed in Table 2 is to recall the facts about biological populations, overlapping family resemblances, and the purpose-relativity of representational paradigms.

A second pervasive syndrome is *preformism.* Preformism is a species of pseudo-explanation best understood by reference to the paradigm for genuine developmental explanations, which, following Piagetian and embryological precedent, may be called the epigenetic paradigm. The latter involves explaining

Table 2. Prescriptions for six conceptual syndromes

Syndrome	Prescription
Essentialism	Population thinking Family resemblances Purpose-relativity of representations
Preformism	Epigenesis "Snow mounds"
Downward projection	Deductive vs. empirical solutions Hierarchical dependencies among language-games
False disjunction	Alternative set relations
Social atomism	Cognitive-social co-evolution
Encapsulation	Mosaic evolution Convergence-rate explanations

how new order emerges in nature as a result of interactions among pre-existing factors which, although also exhibiting an order, are notably *different* in form than that which emerges. A preformist "explanation" deviates from the epigenetic paradigm in one critical way: It implicitly or explicitly gives the pre-existing factors the same structure as the emergent order. Thus it really makes no progress in understanding how new structure emerges in nature, at least not beyond noting that some "new" structures arise by the reproduction of prior structure. Fodor and Chomsky are both preformists in the sense that both effectively reduce all the later structure seen in mature individuals to structures present at birth. This raises an important distinction for developmental psychology: The distinction between nativists and preformists. Nativism, considered as the expectation that there must be tremendously rich structure present at birth, is a positive force in developmental psychology. However, nativism coupled with preformism, the view that all subsequent structures were effectively included in the innately given set, is a disaster for developmental psychology (as for science in general).

The remedy for preformism is to focus on the need to explain the emergence of *new* structures. In embryology, epigenesis displaced preformism long ago, hence the first entry under prescriptions in Table 2. The second entry, "snow mounds," alludes to the following classroom-tested example. Imagine that you come upon a rectangular path freshly cleared of snow (see Figure 2). In the middle of the path is a flower bed now completely covered with snow. At each end of the bed is a mound - an elevated region - of snow. How did the snow mounds emerge? The preformist would be happy to conclude his search by finding that an oddly shaped cloud (rectangular, with thickenings at both ends) had actually dropped the snow in the pattern found, or that the person shoveling the snow had purposely built up the mounds (thus matching some pre-existing image that instantiates the same form). The epigeneticist would be profoundly unhappy with either account. He or she would try to explain the *origin* of the structure, not just its replication. In this case (for this is a true story) the epigeneticist would find that there were several pre-existing factors which together conspired to create the snow mounds, but that none of these factors had the same structure as the final pattern of snow. A right-handed shoveler working anti-clockwise around any path with a similar geometry will always generate more snow for the bed at its ends than at its middle, hence will always generate snow mounds. Yet

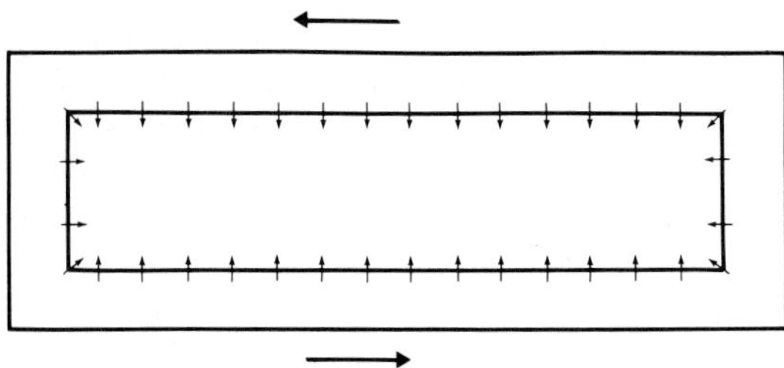

Figure 2. Snow mounds: How an initial geometry and an oriented process can conspire to generate a new structure

neither the right-handedness, nor the geometry of the path and bed, nor the anticlockwise motion have the snow-mound structure in them: the double-mound pattern is a genuine emergent.

The third syndrome, *downward projection,* is closely related to preformism. It involves seeing more in an early developing structure than is really there. Much of Piaget's special genius lay in his ability to overcome this tendency. This is clearest in his many experiments showing that the same solutions generated deductively by older children can only be generated by empirical assessments in younger children. Thus one cure for this syndrome is a familiarity with Piaget's experiments on deductive versus empirical solutions. However, note that Piaget himself showed a residual tendency toward downward projection through his pervasive logicism, and when he argued that advances in language are always mere reflections of prior advances in thought.

A closely related therapy for downward projection is the study of Wittgenstein's treatment of hierachical dependencies among language-games, exemplified by the following passage:

> When he first learns the names of colors – what is taught him? Well, he learns e.g., to call out "red" on seeing something red.... Why doesn't one teach a child the language-game "It looks red to me" from the first? Because it is not yet able to understand the rather fine distinction between seeming and being?
> The red visual impression is a new *concept.* The language-game that we teach him then is: "It looks to me ..., it looks to you ..." In the first language-game a person does not appear as perceiving subject. (*Z,* 421–424)

And, one might add, necessarily so. Today, the field is undergoing an epidemic of downward projection, as researchers stumble over each other to project ever more mature competencies into the heads of ever younger babes. What they overlook, as noted by Adams & Bullock (1986, p. 162), is that "sameness of meaning amounts to sameness of language-game and nothing less." Thus, this is another area where Wittgenstein's work has much to offer us (see also Chapman, this volume).

The fourth syndrome is *false disjunction.* To ask whether language follows thought, or thought language, is to presuppose that language and thought are disjoint sets. If this presupposition is incorrect – as I've argued – then the very disjunction "language first or thought first" is false and can only lead to a muddle. Another false disjunction popular among developmentalists is that of nature versus nurture. The persistence of this opposition retards refinement of developmental theory because, as Dennett (1975) has pointed out, nothing of theoretical significance is likely to hinge on whether research shows that a particular ability is present entirely "by nature" or "by nature with help from nurture." Thus most of the energy spent on this issue is at the expense of the advance of developmental theory. One way to see beyond the opposition is to note that *a type of nurture can be a product of nature,* a point exemplified by the convergence rate hierarchy proposed earlier. Among our most important *natural* abilities is the (distributed) ability to "close the modeling circuit," yet the latter's reason for being is the provision of *cognitive nurturance.* Thus it is incorrect to maintain that a given explanatory factor must fall under the heading of nature, or nurture, but not both. The reason why the language-thought and the nature-nurture oppositions do not work in practice is that what we really have are set-subset relations: a very substantial subset of what we call thought depends on mastery of language-games; a very substantial subset of what we are "by nature" was selected to establish our unprecedented style of nurture. To escape the syndrome of false-disjunction, one must entertain other possibilities for relations between classes. We must, in Wittgenstein's terms, search for an apt logical grammar.

The fifth syndrome is *social atomism*. This is the tendency to succumb to the ideology of individualism, and hence to underestimate just how much of the normative human developmental trajectory owes its present shape to the evolutionary and ontogenetic scaffolding provided by social interactions, especially nurturant social interactions. Put another way, it is the habit of proceeding as if the kind of development we exhibit could have evolved in an asocial species. Among the remedies that can be brought to bear against this syndrome is one of the basic points already made with the aid of the convergence rate hierarchy: Our cognitive potential has co-evolved with socially distributed mechanisms for its realization. Since those realization mechanisms have now been so distributed for many millions of years, much of our hypertrophied neo-cortex may have to be credited, as it were, to our social nature (Bullock, 1983; see also Humphrey, 1984).

One research implication of such a co-evolutionary view is that the depth of the social contribution to the shape of our development can only begin to be measured by such things as social isolation studies. Although such studies typically find strong evidence of social determination of developmental outcomes, the status of such studies as an acid test for social theories of intelligence is in need of clarification. In particular, a negative finding – that certain abilities now develop in relative autonomy from social interaction – unfortunately does not preclude that they may once have depended on ontogenetic social scaffolding; nor does it preclude that their evolution depended on socially generated selection pressures. For example, Goldin-Meadow and Feldman (1977) argued that deaf children could "acquire sign language without exposure to a model." The first problem with their case is that even if we accept the claim that the children in the study were not exposed to any adult gesturing, it must be noted that the children were exposed to each other, hence *had each other as models*. This is an extremely important point for an epigeneticist, but one likely to be overlooked by preformists. The second problem is that the study unfortunately says nothing about the role of social interactions in determining the normative shape of intellectual development, because it doesn't rule out the possibility (virtual certainty?) that some genetic assimilation of originally social-interaction-dependent abilities has occurred since the first appearance of language on the human scene. This is an example of an issue that doesn't arise until one begins to work out the details of a social theory of intellectual development, with development interpreted to encompass both ontogenetic and phylogenetic time scales and processes.

The final syndrome I have called *encapsulation* (but see Bloor's, 1983, related treatment of "condensation"). This is the tendency to treat a property of some distributed system as if it were entirely attributable to (encapsulated within) some subset of the system. This syndrome underlies popular misconstruals of remarks like: "The gene for property A is on chromosome N"; or "Language is localized in the left hemisphere." In this paper, I have exposed two examples of encapsulation. In the case of representation, I have shown that representational status, far from being located in a form, depends jointly on formats and procedures for using them within human activities. In my more general consideration of intelligence, I emphasized that our kind of intelligence is an essentially *mosaic* phenomenon: It depends on a conspiracy (a "breathing together") of many factors of diverse type. In particular, it depends on both social and asocial modes of interaction (and their aliments) as much as on plastic brain structures; without the former, the latter would never be able to achieve their representational statuses.

A first prescription for avoiding encapsulation, then, is to study how evolution has repeatedly groped its way to mosaic (structurally distributed) solutions to adaptive problems. A second prescription is to study why mosaic solutions are the norm. Simon (1969) has argued that they are normative because they can be expected to take less time to evolve than non-mosaic solutions. If so, then what is essentially a convergence-rate argument helps explain the mosaic character of human-class intelligence - which I have schematized as itself a level within a convergence-rate hierarchy. Such a recursion of explanatory principles increases my confidence that a few of the ideas presented in this chapter might serve as foundation stones for a principled treatment of human intelligence as a natural phenomenon (see also Bonner, 1980). If so, much of the credit must go to Wittgenstein who, in his greatest work, was himself careful to temper his claims to originality - as befits anyone contributing to the foundations for a theory of intellectual achievement as a socially distributed phenomenon.

References

Adams, A. K., & Bullock, D. (1986). Apprenticeship in word-use: Social convergence processes in learning categorically related nouns. In S. A. Kuczaj & M. D. Barrett (Eds.), *The development of word meaning*. New York: Springer-Verlag.

Anderson, J. R. (1976). *Language, memory, and thought*. Hillsdale, NJ: Erlbaum.

Austin, J. L. (1962). *How to do things with words*. Cambridge, MA: Harvard University Press.

Bandura, A. (1971). Analysis of modeling processes. In A. Bandura (Ed.), *Psychological modeling: Conflicting theories*. Chicago: Atherton.

Bates, E., & MacWhinney, B. (1982). Functionalist approaches to grammar. In E. Wanner & L. Gleitman (Eds.), *Language acquisition: The state of the art*. New York: Cambridge University Press.

Bennett, J. (1976). *Linguistic behaviour*. London: Cambridge University Press.

Bickerton, D. (1981). *Roots of language*. Ann Arbor: Karoma Publishers.

Bloor, D. (1983). *Wittgenstein: A social theory of knowledge*. New York: Columbia University Press.

Bonner, J.T. (1980). *The evolution of culture in animals*. Princeton: Princeton University Press.

Bruner, J.S. (1975). From communication to language - a psychological perspective. *Cognition, 3,* 255-287.

Bruner, J.S. (1983). *Child's talk*. New York: Norton.

Bullock, D. (1981). On the current and potential scope of generative theories of cognitive development. In K.W. Fischer (Ed.), *Cognitive Development*. San Francisco: Jossey-Bass.

Bullock, D. (1983). Seeking relations between cognitive and social-interactive transitions. In K.W. Fischer (Ed.), *Levels and transitions in children's development*. San Francisco: Jossey-Bass.

Bullock, D. (1984). *Attentional dynamics and pattern completion processes as organizers of parent-child interaction*. Paper presented at the Biennial Meeting of the Southwestern Society for Research in Human Development, Denver, Colorado, USA.

Case, R. (1980). The underlying mechanism of intellectual development. In J.R. Kirby & J.B. Biggs (Eds.), *Cognition, development, instructiôn*. New York: Academic Press.

Danford, J.W. (1978). *Wittgenstein and political philosophy*. Chicago: University of Chicago Press.

Darwin, C. (1981). *The descent of man and selection in relation to sex*. Princeton: Princeton University Press. (Originally published, 1871).

Dawkins, R. (1982). *The extended phenotype*. San Francisco: Freeman.

Dennett, D.C. (1975). Why the law of effect will not go away. *Journal for the Theory of Social Behaviour, 5,* 169-187.

Eisenberg, J.F. (1981). *The mammalian radiations*. Chicago: University of Chicago Press.

Feldman, C.F., & Toulmin, S. (1976). Logic and the theory of mind. In J. K. Cole & W.J. Arnold (Eds.), *Nebraska Symposium on Motivation* (Vol. 23). Lincoln: University of Nebraska Press.

Fischer, K.W. (1980). A theory of cognitive development: The control and construction of hierarchies of skills. *Psychological Review, 87,* 477-531.

Fischer, K.W., & Bullock, D. (1981). Patterns of data: Sequence, synchrony, and constraint in cognitive development. In K.W. Fischer (Ed.), *Cognitive Development*. San Francisco: Jossey-Bass.

Fischer, K.W., & Bullock, D. (1984). Cognitive development in school-age children: Conclusions and new directions. In W.A. Collins (Ed.), *Development during middle childhood*. Washington, D.C.: National Academy Press.

Flanagan, O.J. (1984). *The science of mind*. Cambridge, MA: The M.I.T. Press.

Fodor, J.A. (1975). *The language of thought*. New York: Crowell Co.

Gibson, J.J. (1966). *The senses considered as perceptual systems*. Boston: Houghtin-Mifflin.

Givon, T. (1979). *On understanding grammar*. New York: Academic Press.

Goldin-Meadow, S., & Feldman, H. (1977). The development of language-like communication without a language model. *Science, 197,* 401-403.

Goody, J. (1977). *The domestication of the savage mind*. New York: Cambridge University Press.

Gould, S.J. (1980). Our greatest evolutionary step. In *The panda's thumb*. New York: Norton.

Grossberg, S. (1982). *Studies of mind and brain*. Boston: Reidel.

Grossberg, S., & Kuperstein, M. (1986). *Neural dynamics of adaptive sensory-motor control: Ballistic eye-movements*. Amsterdam: North-Holland.

Haith, M.M. (1980). *Rules that babies look by*. Hillsdale, NJ: Erlbaum.

Halford, G.S. (1982). *The development of thought*. Hillsdale, NJ: Erlbaum.

Haroutunian, S. (1983). *Equilibrium in the balance*. New York: Springer-Verlag.

Harrison, B. (1973). *Meaning and structure*. New York: Random House.

Humphrey, N. (1984). *Consciousness regained*. Oxford: Oxford University Press.

Kaufmann, G. (1980). *Imagery, language, and cognition*. Oslo: Universitetsforlaget.

Kaye, K. (1982). *The mental and social life of babies*. Chicago: University of Chicago Press.

Kuhn, T.S. (1970). *The structure of scientific revolutions*. Chicago: University of Chicago Press.

Lakoff, G., & Johnson, M. (1980). *Metaphors we live by*. Chicago: University of Chicago Press.

Lieberman, P. (1984). *The biology and evolution of language*. Cambridge, MA: Harvard University Press.

Millikan, R. G. (1984). *Language, thought, and other biological categories*. Cambridge, MA: The M. I. T. Press.
Piaget, J. (1962). *Play, dreams, and imitation in childhood*. New York: Norton.
Premack, D. (1972). Concordant preferences as a precondition for affective but not symbolic communication (or how to do experimental anthropology). *Cognition, 1*, 251-264.
Rosch, E. (1978). Principles of categorization. In E. Rosch & B. B. Lloyd (Eds.), *Cognition and categorization*. Hillsdale, NJ: Erlbaum.
Searle, J. (1969). *Speech acts*. London: Cambridge University Press.
Simon, H. A. (1969). *The sciences of the artificial*. Cambridge, MA: The M. I. T. Press.
Spiro, M. E. (1984). Some reflections on cultural determinism and relativism with special reference to emotion and reason. In R. A. Shweder & R. A. LeVine (Eds.), *Culture theory*. New York: Cambridge University Press.
Stenhouse, D. (1974). *The evolution of intelligence*. New York: Barnes & Noble.

Chapter 12 Grammar, Psychology and Moral Rights

Rom Harré

The intimate relationship Wittgenstein discerned between language and thought encourages one to adopt the methodological maxim, "If one wants to understand thought, first analyze the linguistic practices through which that kind of thought (or feeling) is realized." But this maxim will not do without qualification. Two ambiguities need to be resolved. What sort of analysis of linguistic practice is likely to be illuminating? Is it just a study of grammar? And is this the only public and collective phenomenon we need to study to understand some such psychological matter as the emotions or human rationality? I believe we should distinguish between a purely grammatical investigation and one devoted to revealing the "logical syntax" of a linguistic practice. Any student of human life must also take into account the local moral order, the system of rights, obligations and duties obtaining in a society, together with the criteria by which people and their activities are valued.

Logical Syntax Versus Grammar

A grammatical study of a segment of language must take practice as it finds it. Whatever may be our theory about pronominal reference, be it anaphoria or deixis, we need to include among well-formed sentences such oddities as "There we are"! and a gem from Peter Muhlhausler, "Toilet rolls: that's me." Grammar must somehow account for them and, post Chomsky, it had better not be too promiscuous in throwing in enthymematic forms, base structures and the like. But we are under no such constraints in portraying the logical syntax of pronominal forms, and other person-referring devices. We can draw on hypotheses about what a language and its extensions *must* be capable of achieving, and then look at linguistic practices in that light. Of course working from role to use to structure does throw light onto purely grammatical issues. Muhlhausler and I (Muhlhausler & Harré, in press; see also Muhlhausler, 1986) have recently been using a kind of dialectic between grammar and logical syntax to explore the question of whether the behavior of pronouns in English can be accounted for by anaphoria (standing for nouns) or whether their indexical properties are such that they are an autonomous deictic system. We have come to favor the latter. For the psychologist grammar must, I believe, be treated as an indicator of logical syntax, but the streamlined forms revealed by the latter need not be qualified too heavily by the myriad uses to which items from particular lexical categories are put.

What is a "Form of Life"?

Wittgenstein's social world is plainly hierarchical. While a myriad of language-games stand alongside one another as daily practices resembling one another in a variety of ways, they cluster into forms of life. Of all the grand concepts of Wittgenstein's thought, "form of life" was the least well developed. A form of life is something like that which anthropologists call a culture. It involves material practices (for instance the block-slab game must be embedded in a form of life in which people build houses rather than hunt for warm, dry caves). And material practices of that sort are related to and necessitate many other practices, such as drawing plans, mixing cement and getting planning permission from the local authority. A form of life also involves a moral order and, in the kind of cultures we frequent, there may be a multiplicity of interacting, overlapping and complementary moral orders (cf. Gilligan's [1982] *In a separate voice,* which suggests that the moral orders within which men and women live in the same society are quite radically different). Language-games must realize and facilitate both aspects of a form of life. Marx's idea that we should pay attention to the way forces of production can shape social relations among the producers has to be taken seriously, at the same time as one must insist on the relative autonomy of the historically situated moral orders which also bear upon how people live. I owe to Tony Holiday the idea that language is among the forces of production, and that it may be that in some deep way the core language-games without which no culture could survive, such as truth telling (sometimes), can be used to reveal features that must *somehow* be realized in every moral order. Nevertheless, after the hectic universalism of the Chomsky era it is perhaps time to emphasize the variety of moral orders and the cultural distinctiveness of many language-games. For instance a case can be made for the thesis that while Japanese arguably has lots of pronouns for the first person it achieves reference to second and third persons by other means.

The Social Constructionist Point of View

Social constructionism is the doctrine that by and large the form and to a lesser extent the content of human minds derives from the social worlds those people inhabit. Prominent among the social practices that shape minds is conversation. To put the point dramatically but a little too strongly, "the mind of an individual just is that part of the conversation that he or she has managed to keep private." But this doctrine needs to be fleshed out as a theory of developmental psychology. In particular the processes by which the practices of a community become the forms of a mind need to be limned in. What is going on in Vygotsky's "zone of proximal development"? Social constructionism is certainly set against Piagetian orthodoxy, that we are by nature set to mature in a certain way, stage by inexorable stage, as the appropriate experiences occur, forcing us to advance via assimilation and accommodation. Furthermore the evidence against Kohlberg's generalization of the same idea to moral development is now overwhelming (cf. Kitwood, 1980; Davies, 1982, etc.).

In what follows I will be suggesting a hypothesis about the psychological process involved in development that has the merits of testability, simplicity and plausibility, and you cannot ask for more than that!

Psychological Symbiosis

Any investigation of cognitive development must take into account that human beings treat each other as persons within a moral order, for instance, as responsible actors. The processes by which merely animate beings become self-conscious agents must be looked for in social episodes in which certain kinds of language-games are played, engendering talk with appropriate cognitive properties, for instance self-expression of feelings and intentions. All this is to be found in the phenomenon of psychological symbiosis. The idea of psychological symbiosis was first voiced by Spitz (1965) in his *The first year of life,* but has been developed by others, particularly by Shotter and Newson (1974) in the study of the kind of talk in which mothers imbed their infant offspring. Psychological symbiosis is a permanent interactive relation between two persons, in the course of which one supplements the psychological and moral attributes of the other as they are displayed in social performances. By this means the other is made to appear as a complete and competent social and psychological being. The general definition of psychological symbiosis does not specify the relationship between the two persons who form a symbiotic dyad. There are many possibilities. For example, there are cases of considerable practical importance where, though the supplementations are mutual, the power relations in the dyad are asymmetrical. But with respect to its external relations a symbiotic dyad is to be conceived as a single social being. There is plenty of evidence from the work of Richards (1974) that the dyad as a social being may interact socially with one of its own constituent persons, who displays individually proper attributes and powers. The same principle applies to the interaction between infants (and indeed older children) and others. If the senior member of the symbiotic dyad is present the interaction takes place between the *supplemented* junior member and the third person.

The relevant characteristics of mother-talk have been noticed by psychologists other than Richards and Shotter and Newson, but not correctly described. Snow is reported in Bruner and Garton (1978) as saying, "Mothers constantly talked about the child's wishes, needs and intentions" (p. 76). The use of "about" in this sentence misconstrues the relationship as it is seen from the standpoint of psychological symbiosis. In psychological symbiosis mothers do not talk *about* the child's wishes and emotions; they *supply* the child with wishes, needs, intentions, wants and the like, and interact with the child as if it had them. Psychological symbiosis is a supplementation by one person of another person's public display in order to satisfy the criteria of personhood with respect to psychological competencies and attributes in day-to-day use in a particular society in this or that specific social milieu. A mother may undertake to supplement her daughter's psychology differently in a medical consultation from the way she does it for a visiting relative. The idea of psychological symbiosis can be extended beyond the context for which it was originally introduced, namely for the ways mothers publicly supplement the psychology of their children. I shall use the term for every case in which a group of people complete though public symbiotic activity, particularly in talking for each other, inadequate social and psychological beings. There may be several persons involved in the supplementation process.

Why do these practices exist? I believe the answer can be found by reference to the requirements of moral orders, as they are defined and sustained in particular collectives. A moral order includes a collectively maintained system of public criteria for holding persons in respect or contempt and rituals for ratification of judgments in accordance with these criteria. The moral value of persons and their actions are publicly displayed by such a system. It is realized in practices such as being deferential to someone or censuring someone, by trials, by punishments, by insults, by apologies and so on. Psychological supplementation of another may be required if a display of personal incompetence or deficit is routinely taken as a reason for unfavorable moral assessment. Goffman (in "On facework") adds the thought that support of this sort may be forthcoming, not so much on behalf of the moral standing of the one who is supplemented as in defense of the reputations of those with whom he or she is seen to be consorting.

The term psychological symbiosis has also been used by Mahler (1975) in her book *The psychological birth of a human infant*. For her the term refers to an emotional dependence of the infant on its caretakers somewhat similar to the emotional bonds of attachment and loss so vividly described by Bowlby (1969). Psychological symbiosis in my sense has nothing much to do with emotional ties, though as a cognitive process it is important in processes such as those by which mere feeling is publicly and collectively defined as emotion. It is an act of psychological symbiosis to define someone else's display of feeling as anger, hunger, frustration, misery, and so forth. The definienda, of course, are the referents of concepts of a very high order of sophistication and are properly applied only in the dyad or other group created by the symbiotic relationship.

The crucial person-engendering language-games involving the indexical and referential features of the uses of pronouns, and all sorts of other devices by which concept pairs like "self and other," "agent and patient," complementary points of view, continuity and discontinuity of experience, and so forth, are shared with an infant, take place in conditions of psychological symbiosis. One who is always presented as a person, by taking over the conventions through which this social act is achieved, becomes organized as a self. That is the main empirical hypothesis which I believe to be a consequence of the considerations so far advanced, and in the testing of which the limits of the conceptual system from which it springs can be discovered. Profound consequences follow for developmental cognitive psychology from admitting the existence and central place of psychological symbiosis.

Infant psychological symbiosis provides us with forms of thought, our basic psychology; the social representations embedded in the collective conversations of our culture provide the rest.

Introducing the notion of psychological symbiosis I defined the relationship in terms of supplementation of the psychology of one animate being by another. Typically, mother-talk has the effect of presenting an infant to herself and to others as psychologically mature within the local cultural conventions for being a person. I noticed that a case can be made for applying the notion generally, even to the relationships of small groups of adults, but I treated the changes that take place in the mother-infant dyads, by which the locus of psychological work shifts from mother to infant, wholly in terms of changing capacity. The infant can do more, so it does more.

This is insufficient to account for the way symbiotic dyads behave in real life. Some years ago I was studying the way small children assign meanings to times and places in the Skovangsveg Bornhaven in Aarhus, Denmark. By chance, I noticed something odd about the behavior of parent-infant pairs. At the end of the day a parent, sometimes the mother, sometimes the father, would call to collect their child. In leaving, farewells were exchanged with the kindergarten director. When the child was collected by its mother the director bade farewell to the dyad by speaking only to the mother, but when the father appeared, both infant and parent were addressed. This suggested that symbiotic dyads have an internal social structure. One way of describing that structure would be in terms of differential distributions of rights to conduct this or that part of a performance. With the father, a child has separate social rights from when it is in symbiosis with its mother; social rights recognized both by the father and by the kindergarten director. Do we find similar distribution of rights for the display of cognitive competence? Davies (1982) has shown that there are different rights of display for competence in moral reasoning. Since cognitive skill is part of the criteria that determines standing in our social world, it is clear why there are differential rights of display.

If my intuition that psychological symbiosis is a ubiquitous phenomenon is correct, psychological development theory must take on a very different color from the one to which we have been accustomed. Not only do the capacities of members change, but so too can their rights. What someone does on an occasion will have to be analyzed in two-dimensional space, with one axis representing personal capacity, and the other socially recognized rights (see Figure 1).

Empirically observed "development" is the "resultant" of two radically different growth processes; there may be a stable system of rights embodied in the discipline of the dyad and changing capacities. More often these may be stable capacities and changing rights. But it seems reasonable to suppose that in most cases capacities and rights to display those capacities are both changing. I have gradually become convinced that the way the language-games of psychological symbiosis change is, after the first two or three years of life, more a matter of right than of competence. Davies (1981) described an interesting case where children control an adult by exploiting the ambiguity in this distinction. They show a teacher that they can use adult reasoning, applying a moral principle universally,

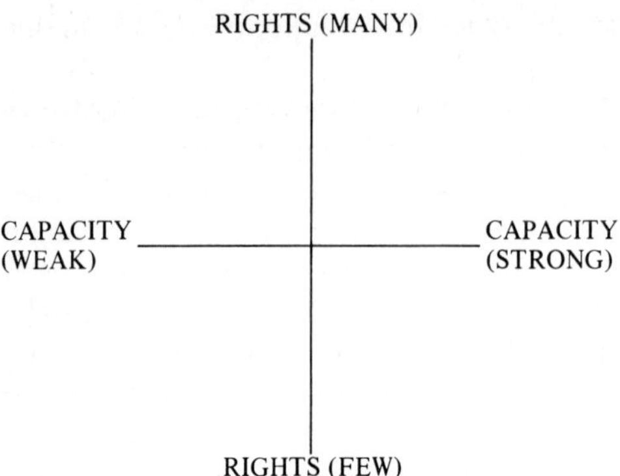

Figure 1. Two-dimensional space: personal capacity and socially recognized rights

but when they are trapped into engaging in debate on this level they leave him mouthing and gesticulating by reminding him that they are only little kids, with whom it is improper to engage in such an argument. This move is made possible just by the ambiguity in the fact that children do not use adult moral reasoning techniques, at least in conversation with adults. Is it because they lack the capacity so to do or is it because they are tacitly, or sometimes explicitly, denied the right to do so ("Don't give me any of your lip," for instance)? The evidence points to the latter. Psychological interest should then shift from a Kohlbergian emphasis on a (mythical) ladder of capacities, to a study of the moral orders within which children and the relevant adults conduct their conversations.

The dual nature of psychological symbiosis should be taken into account by developmentalists in search of the origins of personal being. Moral development research has of necessity to be conducted by creating a public discourse (in Kohlberg's case in the form of work with printed documents), to which an individual taken to be typical of, say, an age group makes a contribution abstracted from the moral order within which he or she usually engages in dialogue or monologue about moral issues. The research presumes that there is no problem in deducing an attribute of an individual person from an attribute of a public discourse to which he or she contributes. The ambiguity of this technique is something like this: There is a difference between the explanation of the production of a saying for which an individual can or could formulate a practical syllogism and the explanation of the production of a saying when the speaker feels that what others have said provides for and often requires that speech act. The train of reasons are what the others say. In strong symbiotic dyads there might even be promptings ("What do you think?"). In the second case the train of reasons is public-collective, and there is no need for any one person to recognize it as having a logical structure, provided that each contribution is seen as right or wrong, proper or improper, according to social conventions expressed by the local arbiters of propriety. The very same saying might be said in the one case as in the other, but the cognitive capacities involved could be radically different, depending on the social relationships of those present. Socially dependent capacities would only show up by their extinction when an individual is isolated. But equally, if the individual is isolated, what he or she can then do by way of generating practical syllogisms does not show what they can be called upon to do in the course of everyday life. But their moral practice may (and usually does) depend on the latter.

We must also take into account the recent discoveries in developmental psychology which have shown us reciprocal influences between the members of a symbiotic dyad. The behavior of infants calls forth a certain repertoire of speech acts available to mother, ensuring the suitability of her supplementations. This sets out the agenda, as it were, for the psychology created by supplementation. In so far as these early forms of infant behavior are biological, seeking a food source, for example, they are universal and so set boundaries to a supplementation process.

In the linguistic aspects of psychological symbiosis, the infant's initial contribution is necessarily zero. The question can be raised as to whether there are any intentional movements intelligible to the mother before they are made intelligible by her speech contributions. One could also ask whether there are any structurings of conscious or other mental fields before the acquisitions of the speech forms which are the vehicles of the local self-theory by which a person organizes his or her experience. I believe that the evidence is far from clear. Perhaps all mind organization comes from the learning of theories in language-games (see Bruner's [1977] "peek-a-boo"); but again this is a matter for empirical research.

The weight of the argument lies against the idea that somehow actions arise spontaneously, naturally and individually, and that they are then encoded in speech or some other semiotic form such as gesture. An infant first acquires the capacity to imitate speech acts: for example, in displays of intentions the possibility for which has been created by the mother issuing speech acts on the child's behalf. Since the mother creates the initial intentions and emotions of the infant and acts towards *them,* her actions *must* be coordinate with the infant's actions or emotions. A course of action can be biologically inappropriate but initially it

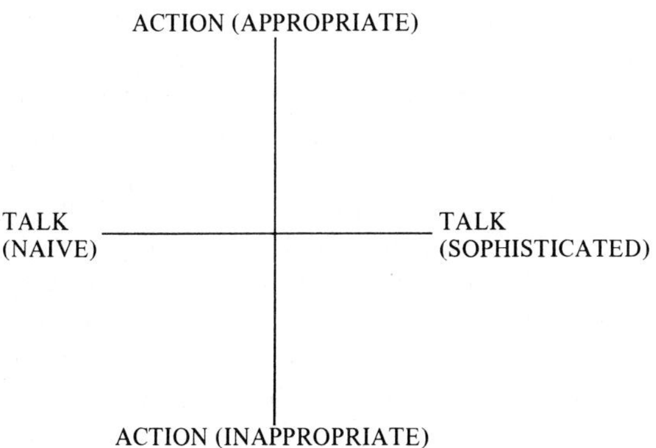

Figure 2. Two dimensions of mother-infant interactions: biological appropriateness and level of psychological sophistication

cannot be psychologically inappropriate. Mother-infant interactions must be graphed on to space defined by two axes: biological appropriateness on one and level of psychological sophistication implicit in talk on another (see Figure 2).

The Imitation Hypothesis

The Piagetian scheme had the great merit of a clearly defined if complex hypothesis about the *process* of development. Social constructionism owes developmental psychology some surrogate. The language-games of psychological symbiosis are played out within different and changing systems of rights, obligations and duties, the state of which, at any moment masquerades as level of development. But *something* is changing. By what process is an infant passing from a condition in which its conversational contributions are of such a general kind that the senior members of its symbiotic dyads can make almost what they will of them, to the highly specific contributions of a two-year-old in which the main structures of mind are readily discerned? I believe we can manage with something quite simple, set within a framework of theory borrowed from biology.

Proteins of enormous structural complexity are produced in the body by a process which is in essence very simple. The structures of sections of DNA are mapped onto sections of messenger RNA by a simple process of imitation. When the string of amino acids reaches a certain aggregate size, without any pre-existing structural template, it folds into a quite definite form, a form which is latent in the fragments, but not represented therein. Suppose the same general idea were applied to the development of mind. Psychological symbiosis provides the infant with lots of instances of high-grade psychological activity, deixis, emotional displays and so on to begin with; more elaborate but related linguistic acts a little later. Suppose only that an infant imitates bits and pieces of this activity, *in no particular order,* just as they come. At a certain measure of aggregation, and when enough is enough we can leave to empirical research to reveal, a structure appears. There need be no structural template, "Psychological folding" might be guessed at as a process that has much in common, formally speaking, with chemical folding. The bits and pieces start to go together, and like the constituent amino acids of proteins, this process goes on pulling the whole thing into shape. There is no pre-existent Piagetian schedule through which we all go as each trigger is pulled. Rather when the right bits are there, by imitation alone, folding occurs.

Now we can say what is likely to be found in Vygotsky's "zone of proximal development." It is bound to be different from culture to culture, and from person to person, if the above theory is right. Only at the very last moment, before "folding" occurs, must there be a certain gross totality of bits. But how and when they are imitated, during what pre-organized phase, will not necessarily display any generality at all. So any efforts to try to find an orderly structure in the "zones of proximal development" of human individuals is likely to be a waste of time. Generalities of structure will no doubt manifest themselves in the conversations of families and in the families of cultures, but no one individual need pick up the fragments he or she needs in the same order.

An Example: Ascriptive Practices and the Organization of a Self

In one way or another the writings of Wittgenstein *(PI)* and Vygotsky (1962) all suggest that the way the mentation of persons is organized is the result of imposition of a structure that stems ultimately from language. For example conceptions of self are not a native endowment but a product of social forces mediated by favored grammatical models for self-ascription and self-exhortation. I want to sketch one of the ways in which social forces could be responsible for the genesis of selves. In essence this is through apprentice persons acquiring the linguistic resources for acts of self-description.

Imagine an infant in a social world. Among the linguistic features of that social world are grammatical models for the performance of certain kinds of speech acts appropriate to the realization of certain intentions. There is also a moral order with rituals that mark the evaluation of one's actions and person according to the criteria of the day. Even one's feelings come up for moral evaluation and causal interpretation. In addition, that social world is full of stories, exemplary anecdotes that reveal the forms of proper and improper social encounters. Each of these features that mark particular social worlds has a part to play in creating an order in a manifold of otherwise inchoate thoughts and feelings.

The concept of "self-consciousness" shares the ambiguity of the word "self" itself. In the sense in which self-consciousness is a painful awareness that one is being scrutinized by others, "self" seems to mean roughly "person." It is a public being who comes under public gaze. But when one speaks of self-consciousness as that which differentiates humans from other primates, who no doubt are conscious of much that goes on around them, we have another sense of "self" in mind. To be self-conscious in this latter sense is to know that one's mental states are one's own. And to know that, one must have a concept of the self of which those states are attributes. Yet it is the concept of self-consciousness as consciousness of self philosophers have so pointedly criticized. That which has mental states cannot itself appear as a mental state. The view I wish to advocate is that to be self-conscious in this sense is to have an ability, the ability to play a certain language-game, that of self-ascription, a language-game partly defined by the use of certain grammatical forms.

We owe to Wittgenstein *(PI)* the observation that first-person statements in which a mental state term is predicated of "I" behave very differently from third-person statements predicating the very same mental state term of "He" or "She." To take his famous example, to say "I am in pain," is not to make an empirical statement about myself on the basis of some private feeling. The statement is itself part of the expression of pain. It is an avowal not an assertion. If I say it when I am not in pain this is a misleading avowal not a false description. It is more like uttering an insincere promise than it is like telling a lie.

But when I say that someone else is in pain or joyful or thoughtful, and so on, I am ascribing a state, condition, ability, and so on, to them on the basis of criteria. Wittgenstein makes use of a distinction between "criteria" and "symptoms" to differentiate those conditions which, when satisfied, necessitate the ascription of the state from those which merely give good reasons for the ascription. In some psychological contexts this is an important distinction but it need not detain us in this discussion.

What does this tell us about the point of using the first person, say in English the pronoun "I"? To understand its use in avowals one can compare its behavior with that of the expressions "here" and "now," the indexicals of place and time. In a statement like "put it here now"! the time and place of the utterance of the sentence give specific sense to the indexicals. These expressions index a speech with its own location by virtue of our knowledge of its time and place of utterance. In a similar way "I" and other pronouns are indexicals, fixing the content by our knowledge of who is speaking or of whom something is being spoken. A sentence containing an indexical includes more information than the corresponding sentence with a proper name (or in the case of space and time indexicals, geographical references). Compare the information in "Rom Harré wants you to sign this" and "I want you to sign this." In the second case you know which person wants your signature, namely the speaker. But in the first case you know only that somebody wants your signature, and unless you can acquire the extra information that Rom Harré is the speaker you know less in the first case than the second. Indexicals show how a speech act is related to some location in a spatio-temporal grid of some sort. "Here" and "now" index speech acts to locations in the grid of space-time, the location and time of the act of speaking. I and other pronouns index speech acts to the speaker in the array of all speakers.

Using the theory of indexicals we can give a more detailed account of first-person avowals. The speech act, "I can see a tarantula in the wash basin," is not an ascription of a state of seeing to some mysterious inner being, myself. It is an avowal of information, knowledge, or belief, indexed to me. It shows how the world looks from where I am standing and who is taking responsibility for introducing this bit of information into the conversation. The statement asserts that the speaker is aware of a tarantula, not that a state of awareness is or pertains to him or her. Only a cognitive psychologist would be interested in the unattended information processing that preceded the avowal.

If self-consciousness is the capacity to ascribe states to myself as mine then we would expect there to be more complex grammatical forms available by means of which more complex thought forms could be managed. An example of such a form might be, "I think I can see a tarantula." Typically, such complex sentence forms take epistemic verbs in the first clause, such as "think," "know," "believe," and so on. They serve to express an assessment of the epistemic quality of the avowal made by the use of the embedded clause, in which typically perception verbs and verbs of action appear: "I know that I hid the film in the hollow doorknob." The whole complex sentence is used to make avowals, to express my attitude to the embedded avowal. The pronoun "I" that appears in the first place is an indexical expression for persons and refers only to the public speaker; it indexes the epistemic attitude as his or hers. But now the speaker is commenting on the quality of a speech act, namely that expressed by the embedded clause.

Such a speech act stands to the speaker who produces the whole utterance in just the same relation as he or she would stand to the speech act of another person. It is as if it were in the third person. But under that condition it has the force of an ascription and so can be considered for its truth value. But to whom or what is the relevant mental state, process and so on, ascribed? It is at this point, I believe, that the concept of "inner self" gets a purchase. We seem to need it to make this kind of discourse intelligible, since it is this "self" that records, so to speak, the characteristic unity of each person's mind. Conversations could be conducted and avowals exchanged without there being any more to the background cognition than physiological processing. As a matter of fact we experience our thoughts, feelings, recollections, intentions, and so on, as belonging in one ordered system. To ascribe a mental state and so forth to myself is to locate it in that unified and ordered system. But our grammar demands that there be a subject for any ascription, and the self is that subject.

What sort of concept is the self? In the natural sciences there is a class of concepts that seem to perform very much the same role as the self performs in common-sense psychology. These are the theoretical concepts that obey the general grammatical rules of empirical concepts in that they behave like referring expressions, but whose referents are for some reason problematic. Such terms unify scientific discourses by serving as the grammatical subject for ascriptions, allowing us to express the clustering of properties and dispositions into systems. The content of these terms is often created by analogies with the content of terms that do have empirical referents. The logical grammar of the term "self" is something like that of "electron" and not like that of "horse." To understand such terms fully we must find the source of the analogy by which they get their meaning. I propose that the public concept of person is the source of meaning, through analogy, for culturally receptive concepts of self.

Considered from this point of view, to be a self is not to be a certain kind of being but to be in possession of a certain kind of theory. One uses the theory to organize one's own knowledge and experience of one's own states in the way that one uses the physical theories of which one is in command to organize one's knowledge and experience in the physical world. Just as the concepts of a physical theory are drawn from analogies with source concepts, so are the concepts of self drawn from analogies with person concepts. The explanation of why selves are unified follows as a trivial consequence of this proposal. Since persons are embodied in such a way that each person has one and only one spatially and temporally continuous body, all analogies of the person concept must preserve the same unity. This should be so regardless of cultural setting.

Is "the self" then just a grammatical feature of how people converse? The intellectual ancestor of the psychological theory I have been sketching is Immanuel Kant's doctrine of synthesis. Kant believed that minds were created out of undifferentiated fluxes of thoughts and feelings by the imposition of order. Order was created by synthesizing the flux into structures in accordance with certain categories. "The transcendental unity of apperception," that is, our conception of ourselves as unified conscious beings, was a product of the structuring or synthesizing activity which at the same time as it brought order into our sensory experiences created a unified structure of mind; the self was not an object but a concept. Nevertheless the intimate relationship between the possession and use of that concept and the ordered mentation we call mind allows us to explore selfhood through studies of the kinds of structures which that mentation exhibits. We should not mistake this for an empirical study of self. The empirical study of self is to be made in the public-collective world of conversational conventions and moral orders.

References

Bowlby, J. (1969). *Attachment and loss.* London: Hogarth Press.

Bruner, J. S. (1977). Early rule structure. In R. Harré (Ed.), *Life sentences.* Chichester: Wylie.

Bruner, J. S., & Garton, A. (1978). *Human growth and development.* Oxford: Clarendon Press.

Davies, B. (1981). An analysis of primary school children's accounts of classroom interactions. *British Journal of the Sociology of Education, 1,* 27–43.

Davies, B. (1982). *Life in the classroom and playground.* London: Routledge & Kegan Paul.

Gilligan, C. (1982). *In a separate voice.* Cambridge, MA: Harvard University Press.

Kitwood, T. (1980). *Disclosures to a stranger.* London: Routledge & Kegan Paul.

Mahler, M., Pine, F., & Bergman, A. (1975). *The psychological birth of the human infant.* London: Hutchinson.

Muhlhausler, P. (1986). *Pidgin and creole.* Oxford: Blackwell.

Muhlhausler, P., & Harré, R. (in press). *Pronouns and selves.* Oxford: Blackwell.

Richards, M. P. M., (Ed.) (1974). *A child's entry into a social world.* Cambridge: Cambridge University Press.

Shotter, J., & Newson, J. (1974). How babies communicate. *New Society, 29,* 345–347.

Spitz, R. A. (1965). *The first year of life.* New York: International University Press.

Vygotsky, L. S. (1962). *Thought and language.* Cambridge, MA: The M.I.T. Press.

Author Index

Subject Index